MORE Taste of Home

TEST KITCHEN
FAVORITES

• RDA ENTHUSIAST BRANDS, LLC • MILWAUKEE, WI

© 2021 RDA Enthusiast Brands, LLC.
1610 N. 2nd St., Suite 102, Milwaukee WI 53212-3906
...ghts reserved. Taste of Home is a registered trademark of RDA Enthusiast Brands, LLC.
Visit us at *tasteofhome.com* for other Taste of Home books and products.

International Standard Book Number:
978-1-62145-760-2
International Standard Serial Number:
2690-3792
Component Number:
119700112H

Executive Editor: Mark Hagen
Senior Art Director: Raeann Thompson
Designer: Arielle Anttonen
Deputy Editor, Copy Desk: Dulcie Shoener
Contributing Copy Editor: Deb Warlaumont Mulvey

Cover Photography: *Taste of Home* Photo Studio

Pictured on front cover:
Herb-Brined Cornish Game Hens, p. 18
Hearty Penne Beef, p. 138
Over-the-Top Cherry Jam, p.184
Honey Buffalo Meatball Sliders, p. 31
Mom's Best Pumpkin Cheesecake, p. 21

Pictured on title page:
Chai Cupcakes, p. 225

Pictured on back cover:
Slow-Cooker Spaghetti & Meatballs, p. 147
Challah, p. 73
Apple Pie Ricotta Waffles, p. 48
Sunny Citrus Cheesecake, p. 245

Printed in USA

1 3 5 7 9 10 8 6 4 2

More ways to connect with us

MORE
Taste of Home
TEST KITCHEN
FAVORITES

TASTE OF HOME BOOKS • RDA ENTHUSIAST BRANDS, LLC • MILWAUKEE, WI

Taste of Home

© 2021 RDA Enthusiast Brands, LLC.
1610 N. 2nd St., Suite 102, Milwaukee WI 53212-3906
...ghts reserved. Taste of Home is a registered trademark of RDA Enthusiast Brands, LLC.
Visit us at *tasteofhome.com* for other Taste of Home books and products.

International Standard Book Number:
978-1-62145-760-2
International Standard Serial Number:
2690-3792
Component Number:
119700112H

Executive Editor: Mark Hagen
Senior Art Director: Raeann Thompson
Designer: Arielle Anttonen
Deputy Editor, Copy Desk: Dulcie Shoener
Contributing Copy Editor: Deb Warlaumont Mulvey

Cover Photography: *Taste of Home* Photo Studio

Pictured on front cover:
Herb-Brined Cornish Game Hens, p. 18
Hearty Penne Beef, p. 138
Over-the-Top Cherry Jam, p.184
Honey Buffalo Meatball Sliders, p. 31
Mom's Best Pumpkin Cheesecake, p. 21

Pictured on title page:
Chai Cupcakes, p. 225

Pictured on back cover:
Slow-Cooker Spaghetti & Meatballs, p. 147
Challah, p. 73
Apple Pie Ricotta Waffles, p. 48
Sunny Citrus Cheesecake, p. 245

Printed in USA

1 3 5 7 9 10 8 6 4 2

More ways to connect with us: Facebook Twitter Instagram Pinterest

Our Kitchen Is Your Kitchen

DISHING WITH

Sarah Farmer
Taste of Home
Executive Culinary Director

Welcome to the *Taste of Home* Test Kitchen—a spot I adore with all my heart. Why don't you help yourself to a cup of coffee, pull up a chair and join me for bit?

You see, for the past several years I've made this Test Kitchen my home away from home, and I wouldn't change a minute of it. Every day I get to do what I love best...testing and tasting recipes sent by home cooks from coast to coast. I also get to work with an amazing staff of smart, creative experts. Each day we chop, stir and cook up dishes in this kitchen, all while enjoying laughs, friendship and an incredible passion for food.

At *Taste of Home*, we try every recipe we publish in our magazines and cookbooks and on our website, *tasteofhome.com*. And that's what makes this kitchen yours as much as mine. By sharing their recipes, our readers have a welcome presence in this Test Kitchen each day.

From Paulette Balda's recipe for Grandma's Chicken & Dumpling Soup (page 98) to Josephine Triton's Heavenly Cheese Danish (page 66), it's reader recipes that are the hallmark of *Taste of Home*. The spirit in which these dishes are shared keeps us happily cooking and creating.

Savory appetizers, weeknight entrees, holiday classics and memorable desserts...our staff members test all sorts of recipes and gladly sample all the dishes we work on. And, trust me, we sample a lot of foods. After all, we test about 3,000 dishes a year!

Having access to so many mouthwatering specialties, I'm always copying recipes to bring home to prepare for my family—and the rest of the staff happily does the same. That's why we asked which of the dishes they've taste tested were the ones they liked best. We collected 367 of their all-time favorite *Taste of Home* recipes for this new cookbook.

We even included some recipes our Test Kitchen pros developed on their own, as well as creations we worked on as a team—like Slow-Cooked Mexican Meat Loaf on page 127.

I hope you enjoy them, along with all the Test Kitchen classics you will find here. Our kitchen is your kitchen, and at *Taste of Home*, we wouldn't have it any other way.

Happy cooking,

Sarah Farmer

Top Test Kitchen Tips for Today's Home Cooks

Not only do the pros at the *Taste of Home* Test Kitchen love sharing recipes, they like to share their cooking tips, tricks and hints as well. We've collected a few of their tried-and-true practices for kitchen success. Keep these ideas in mind whenever you're cooking up something special.

Read the recipe first.
It might sound basic, but always read the recipe in its entirety before you start cooking. No one wants surprises midway through a recipe.

Prep all ingredients.
You'll save time and stay more organized as you move through a recipe if you take the time to properly clean, cut, measure and weigh ingredients before you even start cooking.

Let it sit.
When a recipe suggests letting something sit for a bit, be sure to do just that. For instance, when instructions say to let cookie dough chill in the fridge before moving on to the next step, it's because our Test Kitchen staff found that the dough is easier to handle, and/or bakes up better, when it's chilled.

Trust your intuition.
Every oven heats differently and can have hot and cold spots. In addition to keeping an eye on the cook/bake time, rely on your senses to inform you when food looks as if it's done. This is why so many *Taste of Home* recipes give both a visual doneness description and cook time—for example, "Bake until lightly browned, 7-9 minutes."

Check the nutrition information.
Before you prepare a recipe, be sure the dish's nutritional stats fits with everyone's eating goals. Even if something is described as "light," it may still offer more sodium or sugar than some at your table can handle. Review the recipe and plan accordingly so everyone can enjoy the meal.

Review directions for new devices.
Whether you recently purchased an all-in-one cooker, an air fryer or an electric pressure cooker, read the manufacturer's directions. Reviewing the device's best practices means you'll avoid any guesswork while getting to know your new kitchen helper.

Be honest about timelines.
All *Taste of Home* recipes include useful prep and cook timelines formulated by our Test Kitchen staff, but be honest with yourself about how long a recipe might take you personally. If you've never baked a loaf of yeast bread, for instance, a busy weeknight may not be the best time to give it a try. Always consider the amount of time you have in the kitchen and plan accordingly.

Know when to take license.
Substituting ingredients to suit your taste or adding an extra dash of this or that is a fairly safe practice. But tweaking ingredients when baking, where precision is critical, can be troublesome. Also, remember that some recipes with cultural significance shouldn't be changed if they're to remain authentic. The recipe reflects the authors' intentions, and it carries the essence of what the cook wanted you to experience.

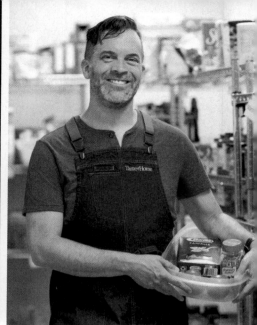

CONTENTS

FAVORITE...

JIMMY'S BANG BANG
CHICKEN SLIDERS, PAGE 15

Staff Recipes

Our Test Kitchen pros love creating and perfecting new dishes, and they're sharing some of their specialties here. Try one and discover a new family favorite today!

CLASSIC AU JUS

When roasting prime rib, don't throw out those leftover juices after you remove the roast from the pan! Those drippings are the key to making this flavorful juice to serve with tender slices of beef.
—Rashanda Cobbins, Food Editor

- -

Prep: 15 min. • **Cook:** 20 min.
Makes: 1¼ cups

¾	cup meat drippings
1	cup chopped carrot
1	cup chopped celery
1	cup chopped onion
½	cup dry red wine
2½	cups beef stock
½	tsp. salt
¼	tsp. coarsely ground pepper

1. In a roasting pan, heat meat drippings over medium-high heat. Add carrot, celery and onion; cook and stir until vegetables are lightly browned and tender, 3-5 minutes, scraping brown bits from bottom of roasting pan. Add wine; simmer until reduced slightly, 3-5 minutes.
2. Add beef stock; simmer until mixture is reduced by about half and slightly thickened, 8-12 minutes. Strain through a fine sieve. Season with salt and pepper. Serve with prime rib or other cooked beef.
2 Tbsp.: 154 cal., 15g fat (6g sat. fat), 15mg chol., 275mg sod., 2g carb. (1g sugars, 0 fiber), 1g pro.

PEANUT BUTTER COOKIE IN A MUG

This peanut butter treat is just perfect when you have a sweet tooth but don't want to make an entire batch of cookies. So quick and easy!
—Rashanda Cobbins, Food Editor

- -

Prep: 10 min. • **Cook:** 2 min.
Makes: 1 serving

1	Tbsp. butter, softened
3	Tbsp. creamy peanut butter
3	Tbsp. sugar
1	large egg yolk
¼	cup all-purpose flour
3	Tbsp. 2% milk
⅛	tsp. vanilla extract
1	Tbsp. chopped unsalted peanuts

1. Spray 12-oz. mug with cooking spray. Add the butter; microwave on high until melted, about 10 seconds. Stir in the peanut butter and sugar until combined. Add egg yolk; stir in flour. Add milk and vanilla extract. Top with chopped peanuts.
2. Microwave on high until set, 1-1½ minutes. Serve immediately.
1 serving: 782 cal., 46g fat (15g sat. fat), 219mg chol., 327mg sod., 77g carb. (46g sugars, 4g fiber), 20g pro.

CLASSIC
AU JUS

SLOPPY JOE SLIDER BAKE
—Rashanda Cobbins, Food Editor

Prep: 20 min. • **Bake:** 15 min.
Makes: 1 dozen

- 1 pkg. (18 oz.) Hawaiian sweet rolls
- 12 slices cheddar cheese
- 1½ lbs. lean ground beef (90% lean)
- ½ cup chopped onion
- 1 can (15½ oz.) sloppy joe sauce
- 1 Tbsp. packed brown sugar
- 1 Tbsp. soy sauce
- ¾ tsp. pepper

GLAZE
- ¼ cup butter, melted
- 1 Tbsp. packed brown sugar
- 1 Tbsp. Dijon mustard
- 1 tsp. soy sauce
- ½ tsp. garlic powder
- 1 tsp. sesame seeds
- 1 tsp. black sesame seeds
- 1 tsp. dried minced onion
  Dill pickle slices, optional

1. Preheat oven to 350°. Without separating rolls, cut rolls in half horizontally; arrange bottom halves in a greased 13x9-in. baking pan. Top with half of cheese slices; set aside.
2. In a large skillet, cook the beef and onion over medium heat until beef is no longer pink and onion is tender, breaking up beef into crumbles, 6-8 minutes; drain. Stir in the sloppy joe sauce, brown sugar, soy sauce and pepper. Cook and stir until combined, 1-2 minutes. Spoon beef mixture evenly over rolls; top with remaining cheese. Replace top halves of rolls.
3. For glaze, stir together butter, brown sugar, mustard, soy sauce and garlic powder. Brush over rolls; sprinkle with sesame seeds and minced onion. Bake, uncovered, until the tops are golden and cheese is melted, 15-20 minutes. If desired, top sandwiches with dill pickle slices.
Freeze option: Cover and freeze unbaked sandwiches; prepare and freeze glaze. To use, partially thaw in the refrigerator overnight. Remove 30 minutes before baking. Preheat oven to 350°. Pour glaze over buns and sprinkle with seeds and minced onion. Bake sandwiches as directed, increasing time by 10-15 minutes, until cheese is melted and a thermometer inserted in center reads 165°.
1 slider: 392 cal., 19g fat (10g sat. fat), 91mg chol., 668mg sod., 32g carb. (15g sugars, 2g fiber), 23g pro.

DISHING WITH

Rashanda Cobbins
Food Editor

Ground beef is turned up a notch in these party sliders that are sure to please your crowd. I love how easy they are!

SLOPPY JOE
SLIDER BAKE

QUICK ROASTED RED PEPPER SPREAD

This red pepper spread is easy to make and can be used in many ways! The spread is amazing on top of grilled meats, mixed into a hearty stew or a soup for extra flavor, stirred into cream for a rich pasta or dipping sauce, combined with mayonnaise as a sandwich condiment, or served alongside crab cakes. By freezing it in small portions, I can remove exactly the amount needed for each use.

—Josh Rink, Food Stylist

- -

Takes: 10 min. • **Makes:** 8 servings (1 cup)

- 1 jar (12 oz.) roasted sweet red peppers, drained
- 1 Tbsp. fresh rosemary leaves
- 2 garlic cloves, minced
- 2 tsp. grated lemon zest
- ½ tsp. kosher salt

Place all ingredients in the bowl of a food processor fitted with the blade attachment; process until smooth, scraping down sides of bowl as needed. Red pepper spread can be refrigerated up to 2 weeks or frozen up to 3 months.

2 Tbsp.: 16 cal., 0 fat (0 sat. fat), 0 chol., 276mg sod., 2g carb. (1g sugars, 0 fiber), 0 pro.

BEEF STEW SKILLET PIE

BEEF STEW SKILLET PIE

Puff pastry makes a pretty topping for this homey skillet potpie.
—Josh Rink, Food Stylist

- -

Prep: 1½ hours • **Bake:** 30 min. + standing
Makes: 6 servings

- 6 Tbsp. all-purpose flour, divided
- 1½ tsp. salt
- ½ tsp. pepper
- 1 lb. boneless beef round steak, cut into 1-in. pieces
- 2 Tbsp. canola oil
- 1 large onion, chopped
- 2 garlic cloves, minced
- ¼ cup dry red wine
- 2 cups beef broth, divided
- 1 Tbsp. tomato paste
- ½ tsp. Italian seasoning
- ½ tsp. dried basil
- 1 bay leaf
- 2 medium potatoes, cubed
- 3 large carrots, peeled and sliced
- 1 sheet frozen puff pastry, thawed
- ½ cup frozen peas
- 2 Tbsp. minced fresh parsley
- 1 large egg, beaten

1. In a large resealable container, combine 3 Tbsp. flour, salt and pepper. Add the beef in batches; shake to coat. Invert a 10-in. cast-iron or other ovenproof skillet onto parchment; trace circle around pan ¼ in. larger than rim. Cut out circle and set aside. In same skillet, saute beef in canola oil until browned. Add onion and garlic; cook and stir until onion is tender. Add wine, stirring to loosen browned bits.

2. Combine 1½ cups broth, tomato paste, Italian seasoning and basil; stir into skillet. Add bay leaf. Bring to a boil. Reduce heat; cover and simmer until the meat is tender, about 45 minutes. Add the potatoes and carrots; cook until the vegetables are tender, 20-25 minutes longer.

3. Meanwhile, roll out puff pastry to fit skillet, using parchment circle as a guide; carefully cut venting slits in pastry. Keep chilled until ready to use.

4. Combine the remaining flour and broth until smooth; gradually stir into skillet. Bring to a boil; cook and stir for until thickened and bubbly, about 2 minutes. Discard bay leaf. Stir in the peas and parsley.

5. Brush beaten egg around edge of the skillet to help pastry adhere; carefully place pastry over filling. Using a fork, press pastry firmly onto rim of pan; brush with egg. Bake pie at 425° until pastry is dark golden brown, 30-35 minutes. Let stand for 10 minutes before serving.

1 serving: 473 cal., 19g fat (4g sat. fat), 73mg chol., 1088mg sod., 49g carb. (4g sugars, 6g fiber), 25g pro.

JOSH'S MARBLED RYE BREAD

—Josh Rink, Food Stylist

Prep: 50 min. + rising • **Bake:** 45 min. + cooling • **Makes:** 1 loaf (16 pieces)

- 5 cups bread flour, divided
- 2 cups plus 1 Tbsp. rye flour, divided
- ½ cup potato flour
- ⅓ cup nonfat dry milk powder
- 2 Tbsp. sugar
- 2 Tbsp. caraway seeds
- 3 tsp. instant or quick-rise yeast
- 2½ tsp. onion powder
- 2 tsp. salt
- 2¾ cups warm water (110° to 115°)
- ¼ cup vegetable oil
- 2 Tbsp. dark baking cocoa
- 1 large egg, lightly beaten with 1 Tbsp. water

1. In a large bowl, whisk together 4 cups bread flour, 2 cups rye flour, potato flour, milk powder, sugar, caraway seeds, yeast, onion powder and salt. In another bowl, whisk together warm water and oil; pour over flour mixture and stir until combined. Dough will be sticky. Turn dough onto a lightly floured surface; with floured hands, knead dough, incorporating remaining 1 cup bread flour as needed until dough becomes smooth and elastic, 8-10 minutes. Divide dough in half. Mix dark cocoa powder with remaining 1 Tbsp. rye flour; knead cocoa mixture into 1 portion of dough until fully incorporated.

2. Lightly coat 2 large bowls with oil. Place 1 portion of dough into each bowl and turn to coat. Cover and allow dough to rise until doubled in size, 1-1½ hours. Working with 1 portion of dough at a time, turn onto lightly floured surface; roll each into a 14x12-in. rectangle. Place dough with cocoa on top of remaining dough; starting with a long side, roll jelly-roll style to form a spiral, pinching seam together to seal. Place seam side down in a greased 13x4-in. Pullman loaf pan, tucking each end under to form smooth loaf. Loosely cover and allow to rise until doubled in size, 1-1½ hours; dough should rise about ½ to ¾ in. above edge of loaf pan.

3. Brush loaf with egg wash; using a sharp knife, cut 3-4 deep diagonal slashes on top of loaf. Cover with nonstick foil and place in preheated 400° oven; bake 15 minutes. Reduce the heat to 375°; bake 20 minutes. Remove foil. Bake until loaf is deep golden brown and reaches an internal temperature of 200° when measured with an instant-read thermometer, about 10 minutes longer. Remove from oven; cool for 10 minutes. Remove from pan. Cool completely on a wire rack.

1 piece: 273 cal., 5g fat (1g sat. fat), 12mg chol., 312mg sod., 49g carb. (3g sugars, 4g fiber), 8g pro.

DISHING WITH

Josh Rink
Food Stylist

This impressive marble rye bread may look like it would be difficult to make, but it's actually quite easy! The flavors of the bread are mild yet satisfying. I enjoy eating it with just a simple spread of butter or on a hearty sandwich loaded with my favorite fixings.

JOSH'S MARBLED
RYE BREAD

SKILLET CHOCOLATE CHUNK WALNUT BLONDIES

Put these beauties out at a potluck and you'll find only crumbs on your platter when it's time to head home. Everyone will ask who made those scrumptious blondies, so be sure to bring copies of the recipe!
—Peggy Woodward, Senior Food Editor

Prep: 15 min. • **Bake:** 30 min.
Makes: 3 blondies (8 servings each)

- 1 cup butter, melted
- 2 cups packed brown sugar
- 2 tsp. vanilla extract
- 2 large eggs, room temperature
- 2 cups all-purpose flour
- ½ cup ground walnuts
- 1 tsp. baking powder
- ½ tsp. salt
- ⅛ tsp. baking soda
- 1 cup chopped walnuts, toasted
- 1 cup semisweet chocolate chunks

1. Preheat oven to 350°. Grease three 6½-in. cast-iron skillets.
2. In a large bowl, mix butter, brown sugar and vanilla until blended. Add eggs, 1 at a time, whisking to blend after each addition. In another bowl, mix flour, ground walnuts, baking powder, salt and baking soda; stir into butter mixture. Fold in the walnuts and the chocolate chunks.
3. Spread into skillets. Bake until a toothpick inserted in center comes out with moist crumbs and top is golden, 30-35 minutes. Cool slightly; serve warm.
1 serving: 262 cal., 15g fat (7g sat. fat), 36mg chol., 149mg sod., 32g carb. (22g sugars, 1g fiber), 3g pro.

CHOCOLATE-DIPPED PHYLLO STICKS
—Peggy Woodward, Senior Food Editor

Prep: 30 min. • **Bake:** 5 min.
Makes: 20 sticks

- 4 sheets phyllo dough (14x9-in. size)
- 2 Tbsp. butter, melted
- 1 Tbsp. sugar
- ¼ tsp. ground cinnamon
  Cooking spray
- 2 oz. semisweet chocolate, finely chopped
- ½ tsp. shortening
- ½ oz. white baking chocolate, melted

1. Preheat oven to 425°. Place 1 sheet of phyllo dough on a work surface; brush with butter. Cover with a second sheet of phyllo; brush with butter. (Keep remaining phyllo dough covered with plastic wrap and a damp towel to prevent it from drying out.) Cut phyllo lengthwise in half; cut each half crosswise into 5 rectangles (4½x2¾ in.). Tightly roll up rectangles jelly-roll style, starting with a long side.
2. Mix the sugar and cinnamon. Lightly coat sticks with cooking spray; sprinkle with 1½ tsp. sugar mixture. Place on an ungreased baking sheet. Bake until lightly browned, 3-5 minutes. Remove to a wire rack to cool. Repeat with the remaining ingredients.
3. In a microwave, melt the semisweet chocolate and shortening; stir until smooth. Dip 1 end of each phyllo stick in semisweet chocolate; allow extra to drip off. Place on waxed paper; let stand until set. Drizzle with white chocolate.
1 phyllo stick: 42 cal., 3g fat (2g sat. fat), 3mg chol., 19mg sod., 3g carb. (2g sugars, 0 fiber), 0 pro.

DISHING WITH

Peggy Woodward
Senior Food Editor

Looking for something light yet special to bake up for snack time? Try these crunchy treats. They're great with coffee and alongside sorbet or sherbet.

CHOCOLATE-DIPPED PHYLLO STICKS

CHOCOLATE BALLOON BOWLS

—Sarah Farmer, Executive Culinary Director

- -

Prep: 20 min. + chilling • **Makes:** 8 bowls

- 8 small balloons, filled with air and tied
- 24 oz. bittersweet chocolate, chopped, melted and cooled
- 6 oz. white baking chocolate, chopped, melted and cooled
  Optional: Mousse, ice cream, sorbet, assorted fresh fruit and assorted candies

1. Clean balloons with a damp paper towel. Drop chocolate, 1 Tbsp. at a time, 2-3 in. apart on a parchment-lined baking sheet to make 8 circles. Pour remaining bittersweet chocolate into a medium bowl.

2. Drizzle 1 Tbsp. white chocolate over bittersweet chocolate in bowl. Gently swirl with a toothpick or wooden skewer. Holding the tied end, dip 1 balloon halfway into bowl of melted chocolate, rolling back and forth to coat; allow excess to drip off. Repeat with remaining balloons, adding 1 Tbsp. white chocolate and gently swirling before dipping each balloon.

3. To secure balloons, lightly press each, dipped side down, onto a chocolate circle; wait a few seconds before releasing the pressure. Refrigerate until set, 5-10 minutes. Gently pop balloons; discard. Fill bowl as desired, with mousse, ice cream, sorbet, fresh fruit or candy.

1 bowl: 592 cal., 36g fat (23g sat. fat), 0 chol., 15mg sod., 26g carb. (22g sugars, 4g fiber), 8g pro.

TEST KITCHEN TIP

Almost any treat can be served in these bowls, just so long as it's not hot. Heck, you could even use them for your morning cereal; we won't judge!

DISHING WITH

Sarah Farmer
Executive Culinary Director

Enlist the kids to help make these DIY dessert bowls. They can be made ahead, so they're perfect for birthday parties and holiday dinners.

CHOCOLATE
BALLOON BOWLS

JIMMY'S BANG BANG
CHICKEN SLIDERS

DISHING WITH

James Schend
Deputy Editor, Culinary

I simmer chicken thighs in a spicy-sweet sauce, shred them and then pile 'em high on pretzel buns to create an incredibly addictive party food.

JIMMY'S BANG BANG CHICKEN SLIDERS

—James Schend, Deputy Editor, Culinary

- -

Prep: 20 min. • **Bake:** 45 min.
Makes: 1 dozen

- 3 lbs. boneless skinless chicken thighs
- 3 Tbsp. olive oil, divided
- ½ cup ketchup
- ½ cup Sriracha chili sauce
- ½ cup plus 2 Tbsp. honey, divided
- ½ cup water
- 3 Tbsp. lime juice
- 2 tsp. grated lime zest
- 2 tsp. minced garlic
- 1 tsp. ground ginger
- ¼ tsp. pepper
- 12 mini pretzel buns, split
- 12 slices part-skim mozzarella cheese, halved
- ¼ to ½ tsp. crushed red pepper flakes
  Coarse salt, optional

SRIRACHA-LIME DIPPING SAUCE
- 1 cup reduced-fat mayonnaise
- 2 Tbsp. Sriracha chili sauce
- 2 Tbsp. lime juice
- 2 tsp. grated lime zest
- 2 green onions, chopped

1. In a Dutch oven over medium heat, brown chicken in 1 Tbsp. olive oil, about 5 minutes.
2. Meanwhile, stir together ketchup, chili sauce, ½ cup honey, water, lime juice and zest, garlic, ginger and pepper. Pour over browned chicken and bring to a boil. Reduce heat to low and cook, covered, stirring occasionally, until the chicken is tender, 25-30 minutes. Remove chicken and bring sauce back to a simmer; cook until thick, about 5 minutes. Shred with 2 forks; toss with reduced sauce.
3. Preheat oven to 375°. Place bottom buns in a greased 13x9-in. baking dish. Place half a slice of cheese on each bun; spoon chicken mixture over cheese. Top with remaining cheese slices and bun tops. Stir together the remaining olive oil and honey and the pepper flakes. Brush over buns. Sprinkle with coarse salt, if desired.
4. Bake until the tops are golden and cheese has melted, 10-15 minutes. Garnish with the chopped green onions.
5. For sauce, stir together all ingredients.
1 slider: 516 cal., 26g fat (7g sat. fat), 100mg chol., 892mg sod., 40g carb. (18g sugars, 1g fiber), 31g pro.

ROOT BEER PULLED PORK NACHOS

ROOT BEER PULLED PORK NACHOS

I count on my slow cooker to do the honors when I have a house full of summer guests. Teenagers especially love DIY nachos. Try cola, ginger ale or lemon-lime soda if you're not into root beer.

—James Schend, Deputy Editor, Culinary

- -

Prep: 20 min. • **Cook:** 8 hours
Makes: 12 servings

- 1 boneless pork shoulder butt roast (3 to 4 lbs.)
- 1 can (12 oz.) root beer or cola
- 12 cups tortilla chips
- 2 cups shredded cheddar cheese
- 2 medium tomatoes, chopped
  Optional: Pico de gallo, chopped green onions and sliced jalapeno peppers

1. In a 4- or 5-qt. slow cooker, combine pork roast and root beer. Cook, covered, on low 8-9 hours, until meat is tender.
2. Remove roast; cool slightly. When cool enough to handle, shred meat with 2 forks. Return to slow cooker; keep warm.
3. To serve, drain pork. Layer tortilla chips with pork, cheese, tomatoes and optional toppings as desired. Serve immediately.
1 serving: 391 cal., 23g fat (8g sat. fat), 86mg chol., 287mg sod., 20g carb. (4g sugars, 1g fiber), 25g pro.

MAPLE & BACON SWIRL BREAD

MAPLE & BACON SWIRL BREAD
—Alicia Rooker, Recipe Editor/Tester

Prep: 50 min. + rising
Bake: 35 min. + cooling
Makes: 2 loaves (12 pieces each)

- 2 pkg. (¼ oz. each) active dry yeast
- ½ cup warm water (110° to 115°)
- 5 cups all-purpose flour
- ¾ cup sugar
- ½ tsp. salt
- ½ cup cold butter
- ½ cup sour cream
- 2 large eggs, lightly beaten, room temperature
- 2 large egg yolks, lightly beaten, room temperature
- 1 tsp. vanilla extract

FILLING
- 2 Tbsp. butter, melted
- 2 Tbsp. maple syrup
- 1 tsp. maple flavoring
- ½ cup packed brown sugar
- 8 bacon strips, cooked and crumbled
- ¼ cup raisins

1. In a small bowl, dissolve yeast in warm water. In a large bowl, mix flour, sugar and salt; cut in butter until crumbly. Add sour cream, eggs, yolks, vanilla and yeast mixture; stir to form a soft dough (dough will be sticky). Turn onto a floured surface; knead until smooth and elastic, 6-8 minutes. Do not let rise. Divide in half. Roll out into two 12-in. squares; cover.
2. In a small bowl, combine melted butter, maple syrup and flavoring. Spread over each square to within ½ in. of edges. Sprinkle with brown sugar, bacon and raisins. Roll up each square jelly-roll style; pinch seams to seal.
3. Place on a parchment-lined rimmed baking sheet. Cover and let rise until nearly doubled, about 45 minutes. Preheat oven to 350°. Bake until golden brown, 35-40 minutes. Remove from pan to a wire rack to cool.
1 piece: 225 cal., 8g fat (4g sat. fat), 48mg chol., 147mg sod., 34g carb. (13g sugars, 1g fiber), 5g pro.

DISHING WITH

Alicia Rooker
Recipe Editor/Tester

Swirled with maple syrup, raisins, bacon and brown sugar, this craveworthy bread is one they'll remember. The dough is easy to work with, and it rolls out nicely.

STRAWBERRY CRUNCH
ICE CREAM CAKE

HOT CHOCOLATE COOKIES
—Lisa Kaminski, Associate Digital Editor

Prep: 15 min. • **Bake:** 10 min./batch + cooling
Makes: 5 dozen

- ¾ cup butter, softened
- ¾ cup sugar
- ¾ cup packed brown sugar
- 2 large eggs, room temperature
- 1 tsp. vanilla extract
- 2¼ cups all-purpose flour
- ½ cup instant hot cocoa mix
    (about 3 packets)
- 3 Tbsp. baking cocoa
- 1 tsp. salt
- 1 tsp. baking soda
- ½ tsp. baking powder
- 1 cup vanilla marshmallow bits
    (not miniature marshmallows)
- 1 cup semisweet chocolate chips

1. Preheat oven to 375°. In a large bowl, cream butter and sugars until light and fluffy, 5-7 minutes. Beat in the eggs and vanilla. In another bowl, whisk flour, cocoa mix, baking cocoa, salt, baking soda and baking powder; gradually beat into creamed mixture. Gently stir in marshmallow bits and chocolate chips.
2. Drop dough by tablespoonfuls 2 in. apart onto greased baking sheets. Bake until set, 10-12 minutes. Remove to wire racks to cool completely.
1 cookie: 81 cal., 4g fat (2g sat. fat), 12mg chol., 95mg sod., 12g carb. (8g sugars, 0 fiber), 1g pro.

DISHING WITH

Lisa Kaminski
Associate Digital Editor

Using hot chocolate mix and marshmallow bits in the cookie dough really makes these cookies taste like hot cocoa.

STRAWBERRY CRUNCH ICE CREAM CAKE

Growing up, I loved all the treats from the ice cream truck that rolled through my neighborhood. This ice cream cake is inspired by one of those crunchy, yummy strawberry novelties.
—Lisa Kaminski, Associate Digital Editor

Prep: 20 min. + freezing
Bake: 25 min. + cooling • **Makes:** 9 servings

- 36 Golden Oreo cookies, divided
- 4 Tbsp. butter, melted
- 3 cups vanilla ice cream, softened
- 5 cups strawberry ice cream, softened
- 1 carton (8 oz.) frozen
    whipped topping, thawed
- 1 pkg. (1 oz.) freeze-dried
    strawberries, coarsely crushed
    Fresh strawberries, optional

1. Line a 9x9-in. baking pan with parchment, letting paper extend over sides. Preheat oven to 350°. Finely crush 24 cookies. In a small bowl, mix crumbs and butter. Press onto bottom of prepared pan. Bake until firm, 25-30 minutes. Cool on a wire rack.
2. Spread vanilla ice cream onto crust; freeze, covered, until firm. Spread with strawberry ice cream and then whipped topping; freeze, covered, until firm.
3. Coarsely crush remaining cookies. Combine cookie crumbs and freeze-dried strawberries; sprinkle over topping. Freeze, covered, until firm, 8 hours or overnight. Remove cake from freezer. Lifting with parchment, remove cake from pan. Peel off paper. Let stand 10 minutes before cutting. If desired, garnish with fresh strawberries.
1 piece: 584 cal., 30g fat (16g sat. fat), 54mg chol., 280mg sod., 72g carb. (33g sugars, 2g fiber), 6g pro.

HERB-BRINED CORNISH GAME HENS
—Shannon Norris, Senior Food Stylist

- -

Prep: 35 min. + chilling • **Bake:** 35 min. + standing • **Makes:** 8 servings

- ⅔ cup kosher salt
- ¼ cup packed brown sugar
- 12 whole peppercorns
- 5 fresh sage leaves
- 2 garlic cloves
- 1 fresh thyme sprig
- 1 fresh rosemary sprig
- 1 qt. water
- 1½ qt. cold water
- 2 large turkey-sized oven roasting bags
- 4 Cornish game hens (20 oz. each)

HERB BUTTER

- 14 whole peppercorns
- 2 garlic cloves
- ¾ cup butter, softened
- 3 Tbsp. plus 1 tsp. olive oil, divided
- ⅓ cup packed fresh parsley sprigs
- 3 Tbsp. fresh sage leaves
- 1 Tbsp. fresh rosemary leaves
- 2 Tbsp. fresh thyme leaves
- 2 lbs. fresh Brussels sprouts, trimmed and halved
- 2 small red onions, cut into wedges
- ½ tsp. kosher salt
- ½ tsp. coarsely ground pepper

DISHING WITH

Shannon Norris
Senior Food Stylist

Instead of a turkey or a big roast, why not serve individual Cornish game hens for the holidays? They cook in a fraction of the time and they're guaranteed to impress all your guests.

1. In a saucepan, combine the salt, brown sugar, peppercorns, sage, garlic, thyme, rosemary and 1 qt. water. Bring to a boil. Cook and stir until the salt and sugar are dissolved. Remove from the heat. Carefully add the cold water to cool the brine to room temperature.

2. Place a turkey-sized oven roasting bag inside a second roasting bag; add hens. Carefully pour cooled brine into bag. Squeeze out as much air as possible; seal bags and turn to coat. Place in a roasting pan. Refrigerate for 1-2 hours, turning occasionally. Drain and discard brine; pat hens dry.

3. Meanwhile, place the peppercorns and garlic in a food processor; cover and pulse until coarsely chopped. Add the butter, 3 Tbsp. olive oil and herbs; cover and process until smooth. With fingers, carefully loosen the skin from hens; rub half the butter mixture under skin. Secure skin to underside of breast with toothpicks; tie drumsticks together. Rub remaining butter mixture over skin.

4. In a 15x10x1-in. baking pan, toss Brussels sprouts and onions with remaining olive oil, salt and pepper. Arrange in a single layer. Place hens, breast side up, on top of the vegetables. Bake at 450° until thermometer inserted in breast reads 165°, 35-40 minutes. Cover loosely with aluminum foil if hens brown too quickly.

5. Remove hens and vegetables to a serving platter; cover and let stand for 10 minutes before carving. If desired, garnish with additional herbs.

1 serving: 592 cal., 39g fat (16g sat. fat), 199mg chol., 474mg sod., 12g carb. (3g sugars, 4g fiber), 49g pro.

HERB-BRINED
CORNISH GAME HENS

YETI COOKIES

RAINBOW FRUIT TOAST

Nothing will brighten up your morning more than one of these colorful and tasty toasts.
—Shannon Norris, Senior Food Stylist

- -

Takes: 15 minutes • **Makes:** 5 servings

  5 slices sourdough or
      multigrain bread, toasted
  1 cup reduced-fat cream cheese
STRAWBERRY BASIL TOAST
  1 cup sliced fresh strawberries
  1 Tbsp. fresh basil leaves, sliced
 ⅛ tsp. sea salt
MANGO CHILI TOAST
 ½ medium mango, peeled and sliced
 ½ tsp. grated lime zest
 ¼ tsp. chili powder
KIWI MINT TOAST
  1 medium kiwifruit, peeled and sliced
 ¼ cup green grapes, halved
  2 tsp. minced fresh mint
TANGERINE-THYME
  1 tangerine, peeled and sectioned
  1 Tbsp. coarsely chopped pistachios
 ½ tsp. minced fresh thyme
BERRY SERRANO TOAST
 ⅓ cup fresh blueberries
 ⅓ cup fresh blackberries, halved
  1 tsp. honey
 ¼ serrano pepper, sliced
MIXED BERRY TOAST
 ¼ cup sliced fresh strawberries
  2 Tbsp. fresh blueberries
  2 Tbsp. fresh blackberries, halved
  1 tsp. honey
AVOCADO TOMATO TOAST
 ½ medium ripe avocado,
      peeled and sliced
 ¼ cup heirloom cherry
      tomatoes, halved
      Coarsely ground pepper
RASPBERRY PEACH TOAST
 ⅓ cup sliced peaches
 ¼ cup fresh raspberries

Spread toasted bread with cream cheese.
Top as desired.

1 piece of toast with cream cheese: 172 cal., 10g fat (7g sat. fat), 33mg chol., 324mg sod., 13g carb. (3g sugars, 0 fiber), 7g pro.

YETI COOKIES

When the weather outside is frightful, these smiley guys are so delightful. And they really know how to celebrate the season. What a fun way to use gingerbread-men cookie cutters. Let it snow!
—Shannon Norris, Senior Food Stylist

- -

Prep: 45 min. + chilling • **Bake:** 10 min./batch + cooling • **Makes:** 1½ dozen

 ½ cup butter, softened
 ½ cup sugar
  1 large egg, room temperature
 ¾ tsp. vanilla extract
 ¼ tsp. almond extract
1¾ cups all-purpose flour
 ½ tsp. ground cinnamon
 ¼ tsp. salt
 ¼ tsp. baking powder
  1 can (16 oz.) vanilla frosting
  1 cup white sprinkles
 ¾ cup blue decorating icing
 ¼ cup black decorating icing
 36 candy eyes
      Additional sprinkles and candies

1. In a large bowl, cream butter and sugar until light and fluffy, 5-7 minutes. Beat in egg and extracts. In another bowl, whisk flour, cinnamon, salt and baking powder; gradually beat into creamed mixture. Shape into a disk; cover and refrigerate until firm enough to roll, about 1 hour.
2. Preheat oven to 350°. On a lightly floured surface, roll dough to ⅛-in. thickness. Cut with a floured 4-in. cookie cutter. Place 1 in. apart on ungreased baking sheets. Bake until light brown, 9-11 minutes. Remove from pans to wire racks to cool completely.
3. Spread cookies with vanilla frosting and decorate with sprinkles. Add face, hands and feet with blue icing; add mouth with black icing. Use additional sprinkles for teeth; add eyes. If desired, add additional sprinkles or candies for decoration.
To make ahead: Dough can be made 2 days in advance. Place in an airtight container. Store in the refrigerator.
Freeze option: Freeze undecorated cookies in airtight freezer containers. To use, thaw in covered containers and decorate as desired.
1 cookie: 345 cal., 14g fat (6g sat. fat), 24mg chol., 173mg sod., 52g carb. (36g sugars, 0 fiber), 2g pro.

MOM'S BEST
PUMPKIN CHEESECAKE

DISHING WITH

Jami Geittmann
Senior Art Director

Pumpkin swirls not only turn this fall cheesecake into a showstopper, but also seem to make it more delicious.

MOM'S BEST PUMPKIN CHEESECAKE
—Jami Geittmann, Senior Art Director

- -

Prep: 35 min. • **Bake:** 55 min. + chilling
Makes: 12 servings

- 1½ cups graham cracker crumbs
- ¼ cup sugar
- ⅓ cup butter, melted

FILLING
- 4 pkg. (8 oz. each) cream cheese, softened
- 1½ cups sugar
- 2 Tbsp. cornstarch
- 2 tsp. vanilla extract
- 4 large eggs, room temperature, lightly beaten
- 1 cup canned pumpkin
- 2 tsp. ground cinnamon
- 1½ tsp. ground nutmeg

OPTIONAL TOPPINGS
- Whipped cream, additional ground cinnamon and caramel syrup

1. Preheat oven to 325°. Place a greased 9-in. springform pan on a double thickness of heavy-duty foil (about 18 in. square). Securely wrap foil around pan.
2. Combine crumbs and ¼ cup sugar; stir in butter. Press onto bottom and 1½ in. up the sides of prepared pan. Place on a baking sheet. Bake until set, 10-15 minutes. Cool on a wire rack.
3. For filling, beat 1 package of cream cheese, ½ cup sugar and cornstarch until smooth, about 2 minutes. Beat in remaining cream cheese, 1 package at a time, until smooth. Beat in remaining sugar and the vanilla. Add eggs; beat on low speed just until combined. Place 2 cups filling in a small bowl; stir in pumpkin, cinnamon and nutmeg.
4. Pour half of plain filling over crust; dollop with half of pumpkin filling. Cut through with a knife to swirl. Repeat layers and swirling.
5. Place springform pan in a large baking pan; add 1 in. hot water to larger pan. Bake until center is just set and top appears dull, 55-65 minutes. Remove springform pan from water bath. Cool on a wire rack 10 minutes. Carefully run a knife around edge of pan to loosen; cool 1 hour longer. Refrigerate overnight, covering when completely cooled. Remove rim from pan. If desired, top with whipped cream and cinnamon or caramel sauce.

1 slice: 518 cal., 34g fat (19g sat. fat), 152mg chol., 361mg sod., 47g carb. (36g sugars, 1g fiber), 8g pro.

MANGO CREAM TART

MANGO CREAM TART
This fresh, luscious tart makes me happy!
—Jami Geittmann, Senior Art Director

- -

Prep: 30 min.
Bake: 15 min. + cooling
Makes: 10 servings

- 2 cups crumbled soft coconut macaroons (about 12 cookies)
- 1 cup ground almonds
- 3 Tbsp. butter, melted
- ½ cup heavy whipping cream
- 1 pkg. (8 oz.) reduced-fat cream cheese, softened
- ¼ cup plus 2 Tbsp. honey, divided
- 2 tsp. orange juice
- ¼ tsp. almond extract
- ¼ cup apricot preserves
- 2 medium mangoes, peeled and thinly sliced
- 2 Tbsp. lemon juice
- ½ cup sliced fresh strawberries
- ½ cup fresh blackberries

1. Preheat oven to 350°. Place the cookies, ground almonds and melted butter in a food processor; process until blended. Press onto bottom and up sides of an ungreased 11-in. fluted tart pan with removable bottom. Place pan on a baking sheet.
2. Bake until crust is golden brown, 12-14 minutes. Cool completely on a wire rack.
3. For filling, in a small bowl, beat whipping cream until soft peaks form. In another bowl, beat cream cheese and ¼ cup honey until combined. Beat in orange juice and extract. Fold in whipped cream. Spread over crust.
4. For glaze, in a small saucepan, mix apricot preserves and remaining honey. Cook and stir over low heat until melted; press through a strainer. Toss mangoes with lemon juice. Arrange mango slices over the filling; add strawberries and blackberries to form the eyes and mouth. Brush with glaze. Store in the refrigerator.

1 piece: 311 cal., 18g fat (9g sat. fat), 39mg chol., 155mg sod., 34g carb. (26g sugars, 3g fiber), 6g pro.

PIZZA STROMBOLI
PAGE 32

Snacks & Appetizers

Everyone loves a savory snack, and the staffers at *Taste of Home* are no exception! These party starters all got thumbs-up reviews from the team in our Test Kitchen.

HOLIDAY APPETIZER MEATBALLS

These beefy meatballs are a perennial staple at our holiday parties. You won't believe how easy these savory appetizers are to make. Yum!
—Pat Waymire, Yellow Springs, OH

Prep: 15 min. • **Bake:** 50 min.
Makes: about 3 dozen

- 1 large egg, lightly beaten
- ½ cup soft bread crumbs
- ¼ cup 2% milk
- ⅓ cup finely chopped onion
- 1 tsp. salt
- ½ tsp. Worcestershire sauce
- 1 lb. ground beef

SAUCE
- ½ cup ketchup
- ½ cup chopped onion
- ⅓ cup sugar
- ⅓ cup vinegar
- 1 Tbsp. Worcestershire sauce
- ⅛ tsp. pepper

1. In a bowl, combine the first 6 ingredients. Crumble beef over mixture and mix well. Shape into 1-in. balls.

2. In a large skillet over medium heat, brown meatballs; drain. Place in a 2½-qt. baking dish. Combine the sauce ingredients. Pour over meatballs. Bake, uncovered, at 350° for 50-60 minutes or until meatballs are no longer pink.

Note: To make soft bread crumbs, tear bread into pieces and place in a food processor or blender. Cover and pulse until crumbs form. One slice of bread yields ½-¾ cup crumbs.

2 meatballs: 84 cal., 4g fat (1g sat. fat), 29mg chol., 245mg sod., 7g carb. (5g sugars, 0 fiber), 6g pro.

> "These are a family favorite at my house. They are easy to make and can be doubled or tripled. And you can also make them ahead and serve them from a slow cooker."
>
> —PEGGY WOODWARD, SENIOR FOOD EDITOR

MANGO & HABANERO GUACAMOLE

For the ultimate sweet-spicy combo, pair mango with fresh habanero chili peppers. Depending on your preferences, you can control the guac's heat with the number of pepper seeds you use.
—*Taste of Home* Test Kitchen

Takes: 15 min. • **Makes:** 6 servings

- 3 medium ripe avocados, peeled and cubed
- 2 to 3 Tbsp. fresh lime juice
- ½ to 1 tsp. kosher salt
- 1 medium mango, peeled and chopped
- ½ to 1 habanero pepper, seeded and chopped

In a bowl, mash avocados until almost smooth. Stir in lime juice and ½ tsp. salt. Let stand 10 minutes to allow flavors to blend. Adjust seasoning with additional lime juice and salt if desired. Top with the mango and habanero.

Note: Wear disposable gloves when cutting hot peppers; the oils can burn skin. Avoid touching your face.

¼ cup: 150 cal., 11g fat (2g sat. fat), 0 chol., 166mg sod., 15g carb. (8g sugars, 6g fiber), 2g pro. **Diabetic exchanges:** 2 fat, 1 starch.

HOLIDAY APPETIZER MEATBALLS

ASIAN WRAPS

This recipe is just like any other Asian wrap, but with more delicious and healthy flavor. Instead of ordering Chinese, you'll be making these yourself!
—Melissa Hansen, Ellison Bay, WI

- -

Prep: 30 min. • **Cook:** 3½ hours
Makes: 1 dozen

- 2 lbs. boneless skinless chicken breast halves
- ¼ cup reduced-sodium soy sauce
- ¼ cup ketchup
- ¼ cup honey
- 2 Tbsp. minced fresh gingerroot
- 2 Tbsp. sesame oil
- 1 small onion, finely chopped
- 2 Tbsp. cornstarch
- 2 Tbsp. cold water
- 12 round rice papers (8 in.)
- 3 cups broccoli coleslaw mix
- ¾ cup crispy chow mein noodles

1. Place chicken in a 3-qt. slow cooker. In a small bowl, whisk the soy sauce, ketchup, honey, ginger and oil; stir in onion. Pour over chicken. Cook, covered, on low 3-4 hours or until chicken is tender. Remove chicken; shred with 2 forks and refrigerate until ready to assemble.

2. Meanwhile, in a small bowl, mix cornstarch and water until smooth; gradually stir into honey mixture. Cook, covered, on high until sauce is thickened, 20-30 minutes. Toss chicken with ¾ cup sauce; reserve remaining sauce for serving.

3. Fill a large shallow dish partway with water. Dip a rice paper wrapper into water just until pliable, about 45 seconds (do not soften completely); allow excess water to drip off.

4. Place wrapper on a flat surface. Layer ¼ cup coleslaw, ⅓ cup chicken mixture and 1 Tbsp. noodles across bottom third of wrapper. Fold in both sides of wrapper; fold bottom over filling, then roll up tightly. Place on a serving plate, seam side down. Repeat with remaining ingredients. Serve with reserved sauce.

1 wrap with 1 tsp. sauce: 195 cal., 5g fat (1g sat. fat), 42mg chol., 337mg sod., 21g carb. (8g sugars, 1g fiber), 17g pro. **Diabetic exchanges:** 2 lean meat, 1½ starch, ½ fat.

ASIAN WRAPS

CANDIED WALNUTS

Turn ordinary walnuts into a taste sensation with this simple recipe that's prepared on the stovetop. With plenty of brown sugar and a hint of pepper, the crunchy candied nuts are a nice complement to a fruit and cheese tray. But they can stand on their own as well, because they're so munchable!
—*Taste of Home* Test Kitchen

- -

Takes: 20 min. • **Makes:** 2 cups

- 2 Tbsp. canola oil
- 2 Tbsp. balsamic vinegar
- ⅛ tsp. pepper
- 2 cups walnut halves
- ½ cup packed brown sugar

1. In a large heavy skillet, combine the oil, vinegar and pepper. Cook and stir over medium heat until blended. Add walnuts and cook over medium heat until nuts are toasted, about 4 minutes.

2. Sprinkle with brown sugar. Cook and stir until the sugar is melted, 2-4 minutes. Spread on foil to cool. Store walnuts in an airtight container.

2 Tbsp.: 124 cal., 10g fat (1g sat. fat), 0 chol., 3mg sod., 9g carb. (7g sugars, 1g fiber), 2g pro.

CARAMEL CHEX MIX

This wonderfully crunchy snack is loaded with cereal, pretzels and nuts—and coated with a not-too-sweet brown sugar mixture. Set out a bowl at your party and watch it disappear by the handful.
—Samantha Moyer, Oskaloosa, IA

- -

Prep: 10 min. • **Bake:** 15 min. + cooling
Makes: 3 qt.

- 2 cups each Rice Chex, Corn Chex and Wheat Chex
- 2 cups miniature pretzels
- 2 cups pecan halves
- 2 cups salted cashews
- ¾ cup butter, cubed
- ¾ cup packed brown sugar

1. In a large bowl, combine the cereal, pretzels and nuts. In a small saucepan, combine butter and brown sugar. Bring to a boil; cook and stir until thickened, about 2 minutes. Pour over cereal; toss to coat.
2. Spread mixture into 2 greased 15x10x1-in. baking pans. Bake at 350° for 8 minutes. Stir; bake 6 minutes longer. Transfer to waxed paper-lined baking sheets. Cool completely. Store in airtight containers.
¾ cup: 383 cal., 27g fat (8g sat. fat), 23mg chol., 333mg sod., 34g carb. (14g sugars, 3g fiber), 6g pro.

ASK SARAH

LIKE IT HOT?

Add a new flavor to this snack by stirring a dash of cayenne pepper, curry powder or even ground coriander into the butter-brown sugar mixture.

CARAMEL CHEX MIX

OVEN-FRIED PICKLES

Like deep-fried pickles? You'll love this unfried version even more. Dill pickle slices are coated with panko bread crumbs and spices, then baked until crispy. Dip them with ranch dressing for an appetizer you won't soon forget.
—Nick Iverson, Denver, CO

- -

Prep: 20 min. + standing • **Bake:** 20 min.
Makes: 8 servings

- 32 dill pickle slices
- ½ cup all-purpose flour
- ½ tsp. salt
- 2 large eggs, lightly beaten
- 2 Tbsp. dill pickle juice
- ½ tsp. cayenne pepper
- ½ tsp. garlic powder
- ½ cup panko bread crumbs
- 1 Tbsp. snipped fresh dill

1. Preheat oven to 500°. Let pickle slices stand on a paper towel until liquid is almost absorbed, about 15 minutes.
2. Meanwhile, in a shallow bowl, combine the flour and salt. In another shallow bowl, whisk the eggs, pickle juice, cayenne and garlic powder. Combine the panko and dill in a third shallow bowl.
3. Dip pickles in flour mixture to coat both sides; shake off excess. Dip in egg mixture, then in crumb mixture, patting to help coating adhere. Transfer to a greased wire rack in a rimmed baking sheet.
4. Bake until pickles are golden brown and crispy, 20-25 minutes.
4 pickle slices: 65 cal., 2g fat (0 sat. fat), 47mg chol., 421mg sod., 9g carb. (1g sugars, 1g fiber), 3g pro.

CHEESY SKILLET PIZZA DIP

This creamy dip is oozing with cheesy goodness thanks to the combination of cream cheese and mozzarella. We topped ours with pepperoni slices, but you can easily customize it with your favorite pizza toppings. This is just one more delicious way to use your cast-iron skillet.
—*Taste of Home* Test Kitchen

- -

Prep: 25 min. + rising • **Bake:** 25 min.
Makes: 18 servings

- 6 Tbsp. butter
- 1 tsp. garlic powder, divided
- ¼ tsp. crushed red pepper flakes
- 1 pkg. (16 oz.) frozen bread dough dinner rolls, thawed
- 1 pkg. (8 oz.) cream cheese, softened
- 1½ cups shredded part-skim mozzarella cheese, divided
- 1 cup mayonnaise
- 1 tsp. Italian seasoning
- ½ cup pizza sauce
- ¼ cup (¾ oz.) sliced pepperoni
- 2 Tbsp. shredded Parmesan cheese
- 2 Tbsp. minced fresh basil

1. Microwave butter, ½ tsp. garlic powder and red pepper flakes, covered, until butter is melted. Cut each dinner roll into thirds; roll each piece into a ball. Dip the dough balls in butter mixture; place along the outer edge of a 10-in. cast-iron skillet, leaving center open. Gently stack the remaining balls on top of bottom layer, leaving some space in between them. Cover; let rise until almost doubled, about 30 minutes.
2. Preheat oven to 400°. Bake until the dough balls are set and beginning to brown, 15-18 minutes.
3. Meanwhile, combine cream cheese, 1 cup mozzarella, mayonnaise, Italian seasoning and remaining garlic powder; spoon into center of skillet. Layer with ¼ cup mozzarella and pizza sauce. Top with remaining 1¼ cups mozzarella and pepperoni. Brush rolls with some of remaining butter mixture; sprinkle with Parmesan.
4. Bake until dip is heated through and the rolls are golden brown, about 10 minutes, covering loosely with foil as needed to prevent rolls from becoming too dark. Sprinkle with basil.
1 serving: 258 cal., 20g fat (7g sat. fat), 29mg chol., 372mg sod., 15g carb. (2g sugars, 1g fiber), 6g pro.

CHEESY SKILLET PIZZA DIP

A KICK & A TWIST
ARTICHOKE DIP

BUFFALO CHICKEN CRESCENT ROLLS

My husband loves Buffalo wings, but they are so messy! These chicken rolls are mess-free and always disappear fast at parties—and they're much tastier than regular Buffalo wings, if you ask me.
—Tiffinie Cichon, Gulfport, MS

- -

Prep: 20 min. • **Bake:** 15 min.
Makes: 16 rolls

- 1 **cup shredded cooked chicken**
- 4 **oz. cream cheese, cubed**
- ½ **cup shredded cheddar cheese**
- 2 **Tbsp. prepared ranch salad dressing**
- 2 **Tbsp. Buffalo wing sauce**
- 2 **tubes (8 oz. each) refrigerated crescent rolls**
- ⅓ **cup crumbled blue cheese**

1. Preheat oven to 375°. In a small saucepan, combine chicken, cream cheese, cheddar cheese, ranch dressing and wing sauce. Cook and stir over low heat until cheeses are melted, about 5 minutes. Remove from the heat.
2. Unroll tubes of crescent dough; separate into 16 triangles. Place 1 Tbsp. chicken mixture in the center of each triangle; sprinkle with 1 tsp. blue cheese. Bring corners of dough over filling and twist; pinch seams to seal (the filling will not be completely enclosed). Place on ungreased baking sheets.
3. Bake until golden brown, 15-20 minutes. Serve warm.
1 appetizer: 175 cal., 11g fat (3g sat. fat), 21mg chol., 372mg sod., 13g carb. (3g sugars, 0 fiber), 6g pro.

TEST KITCHEN TIP
Add a dash of hot pepper sauce to the filling if you want to add some heat. This ingredient is prepared from red chili peppers, vinegar and salt, and is often aged in wooden casks like wine and specialty vinegars.

A KICK & A TWIST ARTICHOKE DIP

Some warm cream cheese-based dips are too salty for me. This one has a nice balance. I developed the recipe for a co-worker's going-away party. Adding black pepper or lemon pepper can add more zing if you'd like to spice it up a bit.
—Susan Hein, Burlington, WI

- -

Takes: 25 min. • **Makes:** 8 cups

- 1 **Tbsp. olive oil**
- 10 **to 12 green onions, chopped**
- 6 **garlic cloves, pureed**
- 1 **jalapeno pepper, seeded and chopped**
- ¼ **cup minced fresh parsley**
- 3 **Tbsp. lemon juice**
- 4 **pkg. (8 oz. each) cream cheese, softened**
- 1 **cup sour cream**
- 1 **cup mayonnaise**
- 2 **tsp. cracked fennel seed**
- 1 **to 2 tsp. crushed red pepper flakes**
- 2 **cups shredded Parmesan cheese**
- 2 **cans (14 oz. each) water-packed artichoke hearts, drained and coarsely chopped French bread baguette, sliced**

1. In a large skillet, heat oil over medium heat. Add onions, garlic and jalapeno; cook and stir until soft, 4-6 minutes. Reduce heat; stir in parsley and lemon juice.
2. Add cream cheese and cover, stirring every few minutes, until melted. Stir in sour cream, mayonnaise, fennel and pepper flakes. Remove from heat. Add Parmesan cheese and artichoke hearts, stirring gently to prevent artichokes from breaking up.
3. Transfer to a 3- or 4-qt. slow cooker; turn heat to low. Serve warm on baguette slices. May be refrigerated until serving.
¼ cup: 197 cal., 18g fat (8g sat. fat), 34mg chol., 275mg sod., 4g carb. (2g sugars, 0 fiber), 5g pro.

BUFFALO CHICKEN
CRESCENT ROLLS

BEST DEVILED EGGS

Herbs lend amazing flavor to these deviled eggs, which truly are the best you can make!
—Jesse and Anne Foust, Bluefield, WV

- -

Takes: 15 min. • **Makes:** 2 dozen

- ½ cup mayonnaise
- 2 Tbsp. 2% milk
- 1 tsp. dried parsley flakes
- ½ tsp. dill weed
- ½ tsp. minced chives
- ½ tsp. ground mustard
- ¼ tsp. salt
- ¼ tsp. paprika
- ⅛ tsp. garlic powder
- ⅛ tsp. pepper
- 12 hard-boiled large eggs
  Minced fresh parsley and additional paprika

In a bowl, combine the first 10 ingredients. Cut eggs lengthwise in half; remove yolks and set whites aside. In another bowl, mash yolks; add to the mayonnaise mixture, mixing well. Spoon or pipe filling into egg whites. Sprinkle with parsley and additional paprika. Refrigerate until serving.

1 stuffed egg half: 73 cal., 6g fat (1g sat. fat), 108mg chol., 81mg sod., 0 carb. (0 sugars, 0 fiber), 3g pro.

WASABI CRAB CAKES

With wasabi in both the crab cakes and the dipping sauce, this festive appetizer brings its own heat to the party.
—Marie Rizzio, Interlochen, MI

- -

Prep: 35 min. • **Bake:** 15 min.
Makes: 2 dozen (½ cup sauce)

- 1 medium sweet red pepper, finely chopped
- 1 celery rib, finely chopped
- ⅓ cup plus ½ cup dry bread crumbs, divided
- 3 green onions, finely chopped
- 2 large egg whites
- 3 Tbsp. fat-free mayonnaise
- ¼ tsp. prepared wasabi
- 1½ cups lump crabmeat, drained
  Cooking spray

SAUCE
- 1 celery rib, finely chopped
- ⅓ cup fat-free mayonnaise
- 1 green onion, finely chopped
- 1 Tbsp. sweet pickle relish
- ½ tsp. prepared wasabi

1. Preheat oven to 425°. Combine red pepper, celery, ⅓ cup bread crumbs, green onions, egg whites, mayonnaise and wasabi. Fold in crab.

2. Place remaining bread crumbs in a shallow bowl. Drop a heaping tablespoonful of crab mixture into crumbs. Gently coat and shape into a ¾-in.-thick patty; place on a baking sheet coated with cooking spray. Repeat with remaining mixture.

3. Spritz the crab cakes with cooking spray. Bake until golden brown, 15-18 minutes, turning once. Meanwhile, combine the sauce ingredients. Serve with the crab cakes.

1 crab cake with 1 tsp. sauce: 31 cal., 1g fat (0 sat. fat), 8mg chol., 148mg sod., 4g carb. (1g sugars, 1g fiber), 2g pro.

DID YOU KNOW?
Wasabi is a Japanese version of horseradish. It is traditionally used as a condiment with sushi.

WASABI CRAB CAKES

BEST EVER FRIED CHICKEN WINGS

HONEY BUFFALO MEATBALL SLIDERS

These little sliders deliver big Buffalo chicken flavor. Frozen meatballs make them easy! The spicy-sweet sliders are always a hit with kids and adults alike.
—Julie Peterson, Crofton, MD

Prep: 10 min. • **Cook:** 2 hours
Makes: 6 servings

- ¼ cup packed brown sugar
- ¼ cup Louisiana-style hot sauce
- ¼ cup honey
- ¼ cup apricot preserves
- 2 Tbsp. cornstarch
- 2 Tbsp. reduced-sodium soy sauce
- 1 pkg. (24 oz.) frozen fully cooked Italian turkey meatballs, thawed
  Additional hot sauce, optional
  Bibb lettuce leaves
- 12 mini buns
  Crumbled blue cheese
  Ranch salad dressing, optional

1. In a 3- or 4-qt. slow cooker, mix the first 6 ingredients until smooth. Stir in meatballs until coated. Cook, covered, on low 2-3 hours, until meatballs are heated through.
2. If desired, stir in additional hot sauce. Serve meatballs on lettuce-lined buns; top with cheese and, if desired, dressing.
2 sliders: 524 cal., 21g fat (6g sat. fat), 110mg chol., 1364mg sod., 61g carb. (29g sugars, 1g fiber), 28g pro.

BEST EVER FRIED CHICKEN WINGS

For game days, I shake up these saucy wings. When I run out, friends hover by the snack table until I bring out more. When they ask me how to fry chicken wings, they never believe it's so easy!
—Nick Iverson, Denver, CO

Prep: 10 min. + chilling • **Cook:** 20 min.
Makes: about 4 dozen

- 4 lbs. chicken wings
- 2 tsp. kosher salt
  Oil for deep-fat frying

BUFFALO WING SAUCE
- ¾ cup Louisiana-style hot sauce
- ¼ cup unsalted butter, cubed
- 2 Tbsp. molasses
- ¼ tsp. cayenne pepper

SPICY THAI SAUCE
- 1 Tbsp. canola oil
- 1 tsp. grated fresh gingerroot
- 1 garlic clove, minced
- 1 minced Thai chile pepper or ¼ tsp. crushed red pepper flakes
- ¼ cup packed dark brown sugar
- 2 Tbsp. lime juice
- 2 Tbsp. minced fresh cilantro
- 1 Tbsp. fish sauce

SPICY BARBECUE SAUCE
- ¾ cup barbecue sauce
- 2 chipotle peppers in adobo sauce, finely chopped
- 2 Tbsp. honey
- 1 Tbsp. cider vinegar
  Thinly sliced green onions, optional

1. Using a sharp knife, cut through the 2 wing joints; discard wing tips. Pat chicken dry with paper towels. Toss wings with kosher salt. Place on a wire rack in a 15x10x1-in. baking pan. Refrigerate at least 1 hour or overnight.
2. In an electric skillet or deep-fat fryer, heat oil to 375°. Fry wings in batches until skin is crisp and meat is tender, 8-10 minutes. Drain on paper towels.
3. For Buffalo wing sauce, bring hot sauce just to a boil in a small saucepan. Remove from heat; whisk in butter 1 piece at a time. Stir in molasses and cayenne pepper.
4. For Thai sauce, heat oil in a small saucepan over medium heat. Add ginger, garlic and chile pepper; cook and stir until fragrant, about 2 minutes. Stir in brown sugar and lime juice. Bring to a boil; cook until slightly thickened, about 5 minutes. Stir in cilantro and fish sauce.
5. For barbecue sauce, heat prepared barbecue sauce in a small saucepan over medium heat. Stir in chipotle peppers, honey and vinegar. Bring to a boil; cook and stir until slightly thickened, about 5 minutes.
6. Toss wings with 1 of the sauces. If desired, sprinkle with green onion slices.
Note: Uncooked chicken wing sections (wingettes) may be substituted for whole chicken wings.
1 piece: 87 cal., 8g fat (2g sat. fat), 15mg chol., 218mg sod., 1g carb. (1g sugars, 0 fiber), 4g pro.

SAVORY POTATO SKINS

For a simple hot snack on your next party buffet, put together a plate of these addictive potato skins.
—Andrea Holcomb, Torrington, CT

Prep: 1¼ hours • **Broil:** 5 min.
Makes: 32 appetizers

- 4 large baking potatoes (about 12 oz. each)
- 3 Tbsp. butter, melted
- 1 tsp. salt
- 1 tsp. garlic powder
- 1 tsp. paprika
- Optional: Sour cream and chives

1. Preheat oven to 375°. Scrub potatoes; pierce several times with a fork. Place on a greased baking sheet; bake until tender, 1-1¼ hours. Cool slightly.
2. Cut each potato lengthwise in half. Scoop out pulp, leaving ¼-in.-thick shells (save pulp for another use).
3. Cut each half shell lengthwise into quarters; return to baking sheet. Brush insides with butter. Mix seasonings; sprinkle over butter.
4. Broil 4-5 in. from heat until golden brown, 5-8 minutes. If desired, mix sour cream and chives and serve with potato skins.
1 piece: 56 cal., 2g fat (1g sat. fat), 6mg chol., 168mg sod., 8g carb. (0 sugars, 1g fiber), 1g pro.

PIZZA STROMBOLI

PIZZA STROMBOLI

I used to own a bakery, and this bread was one of our customers' favorites. Once they smelled the aroma of pizza and sampled these tempting spiral slices, they just couldn't resist taking some home.
—John Morcom, Oxford, MI

Prep: 25 min. + rising • **Bake:** 25 min.
Makes: 1 loaf (12 pieces)

- 1 pkg. (¼ oz.) active dry yeast
- ¾ cup warm water (110° to 115°)
- 4½ tsp. honey
- 1 Tbsp. nonfat dry milk powder
- 2 cups bread flour
- ½ cup whole wheat flour
- 2 tsp. Italian seasoning
- 1 tsp. salt
- 4½ tsp. pizza sauce
- ¾ cup chopped pepperoni
- ½ cup shredded cheddar cheese, divided
- ¼ cup shredded Parmesan cheese
- ¼ cup shredded part-skim mozzarella cheese, divided
- 2 Tbsp. finely chopped onion
- 1 Tbsp. each chopped ripe olives, chopped pimiento-stuffed olives and chopped canned mushrooms

1. In a large bowl, dissolve yeast in warm water. Stir in honey and milk powder until well blended. In a small bowl, combine 1 cup bread flour, whole wheat flour, seasoning and salt. Add to yeast mixture; beat until smooth. Stir in pizza sauce. Stir in enough remaining bread flour to form a soft dough.
2. Turn onto a floured surface; knead until smooth and elastic, 6-8 minutes. Place in a greased bowl, turning once to grease top. Cover; let rise in a warm place until doubled, about 1 hour.
3. Preheat oven to 350°. Punch dough down. Turn onto a lightly floured surface; roll into a 14x12-in. rectangle. Sprinkle pepperoni, ¼ cup cheddar cheese, Parmesan cheese, 2 Tbsp. mozzarella cheese, onion, olives and mushrooms to within ½ in. of edges.
4. Roll up jelly-roll style, starting with a long side; pinch seam to seal and tuck ends under. Place seam side down on a greased baking sheet. Cover and let rise for 45 minutes.
5. Sprinkle with remaining cheddar and mozzarella cheeses. Bake until golden brown, 25-30 minutes. Carefully remove from the pan to a wire rack. Serve warm. Refrigerate leftovers.
1 piece: 192 cal., 7g fat (3g sat. fat), 15mg chol., 478mg sod., 24g carb. (3g sugars, 1g fiber), 8g pro.

BUFFALO-STYLE CHICKEN CHILI DIP

Longing for that Buffalo wing thing without the bones? This do-ahead dip freezes well in individual containers, so you can pull them out when you want to a special snack.
—Brenda Calandrillo, Mahwah, NJ

Prep: 30 min. • **Cook:** 30 min.
Makes: 11 cups

- 3 celery ribs, finely chopped
- 1 large onion, chopped
- 1 large carrot, finely chopped
- 5 garlic cloves, minced
- 2 Tbsp. butter
- 2 lbs. ground chicken
- 1 Tbsp. olive oil
- 2 cups chicken broth
- 1 can (16 oz.) kidney beans, rinsed and drained
- 1 can (15 oz.) cannellini beans, rinsed and drained
- 1 can (15 oz.) crushed tomatoes
- 1 can (15 oz.) tomato sauce
- 1 can (6 oz.) tomato paste
- ¼ cup Louisiana-style hot sauce
- 3 tsp. smoked paprika
- 1 bay leaf
- ¾ tsp. salt
- ¼ tsp. pepper
   Crumbled blue cheese, optional
   Celery stalks and tortilla chips

1. In a Dutch oven, saute the celery, onion, carrot and minced garlic in butter until tender. Remove and set aside. In the same pan, cook chicken in olive oil until no longer pink; drain.

2. Stir in the broth, beans, tomatoes, tomato sauce, tomato paste, hot sauce, paprika, bay leaf, salt, pepper and vegetable mixture. Bring to a boil; reduce the heat. Simmer, uncovered, for 12-15 minutes or until slightly thickened. Discard bay leaf.

3. Serve desired amount of dip; if desired, sprinkle with cheese. Serve with celery and chips. Cool the remaining dip; transfer to freezer containers. Cover and freeze for up to 3 months.

To use frozen dip: Thaw in the refrigerator. Place in a saucepan; heat through. If desired, sprinkle with cheese. Serve dip with celery and chips.

¼ cup: 64 cal., 3g fat (1g sat. fat), 15mg chol., 192mg sod., 6g carb. (1g sugars, 1g fiber), 5g pro.

BUFFALO-STYLE
CHICKEN CHILI DIP

BRIE PUFF PASTRY

My husband was in the Air Force, so we have entertained guests all over the United States. I acquired this recipe while we were in California. It's one of my all-time favorite special appetizers.
—Sandra Twait, Tampa, FL

- -

Prep: 15 min. • **Bake:** 20 min. + standing
Makes: 10 servings

- 1 round (13.2 oz.) Brie cheese
- ½ cup crumbled blue cheese
- 1 sheet frozen puff pastry, thawed
- ¼ cup apricot jam
- ½ cup slivered almonds, toasted
- 1 large egg, lightly beaten
  Assorted crackers

1. Preheat oven to 400°. Cut the Brie horizontally in half. Sprinkle bottom half with blue cheese; replace top.
2. On a lightly floured surface, roll pastry into a 14-in. square. Trim corners to make a circle. Spoon jam onto center of pastry; sprinkle with almonds. Top with Brie.
3. Lightly brush edges of pastry with beaten egg. Fold pastry over cheese, pinching edges to seal; trim excess pastry as desired.
4. Transfer to an ungreased baking sheet, seam side down. Brush pastry with beaten egg. Bake until golden brown, 20-25 minutes.
5. Immediately remove from pan to a serving plate; let stand 45 minutes before serving. Serve with crackers.
Note: To toast nuts, bake in a shallow pan in a 350° oven for 5-10 minutes or cook in a skillet over low heat until lightly browned, stirring occasionally.
1 serving: 328 cal., 22g fat (10g sat. fat), 64mg chol., 424mg sod., 20g carb. (3g sugars, 2g fiber), 13g pro.

> "The moment I tasted this in our Test Kitchen, I knew I had to make the recipe at home. It's an impressive appetizer with loads of flavor. Best of all, it comes together easily."
> —MARK HAGEN, EXECUTIVE EDITOR

EASY TACO CUPS

These zesty little cups rank high on my list of standbys because they combine three qualities I look for in a recipe: fast, easy and delicious! They make a fantastic finger food for game-day parties, and guests have fun selecting their desired toppings.
—Ashley Jarvies, Manassa, CO

- -

Prep: 30 min. • **Bake:** 15 min.
Makes: 12 servings

- 1 lb. ground beef
- ½ cup chopped onion
- 1 envelope taco seasoning
- 1 can (16 oz.) refried beans
- 2 tubes (8 oz. each) refrigerated seamless crescent dough sheet
- 1½ cups shredded cheddar cheese
  Optional toppings: Chopped tomatoes, sliced ripe olives, shredded lettuce, sour cream, guacamole and salsa

1. Preheat oven to 375°. In a large skillet, cook beef and onion over medium heat 6-8 minutes or until no longer pink, breaking meat into crumbles; drain. Stir in the taco seasoning and refried beans; heat through.
2. Unroll each tube of dough into a long rectangle. Cut each rectangle into 12 pieces; press lightly onto bottoms and up sides of 24 ungreased muffin cups.
3. Fill each muffin cup with a rounded tablespoon of beef mixture; sprinkle each with 1 Tbsp. cheese. Bake 14-16 minutes or until dough is golden brown. Cool taco cups in pans 10 minutes before removing. Serve with toppings as desired.
2 taco cups: 291 cal., 15g fat (7g sat. fat), 37mg chol., 819mg sod., 25g carb. (4g sugars, 2g fiber), 15g pro.

EASY TACO CUPS

BAKED
EGG ROLLS

BARBECUE &
BEER MEATBALLS

Sauce up your meatballs with Asian flavors for an out-of-the-jar twist.
—James Schend, Deputy Editor, Culinary

Takes: 30 min. • **Makes:** 20 servings

    1 **pkg. (22 oz.) frozen fully cooked
       Angus beef meatballs**
    1 **cup barbecue sauce**
    ⅓ **cup beer**
       **Thinly sliced jalapeno pepper,
       optional**

1. Prepare the meatballs according to the package directions.
2. Meanwhile, in a small saucepan, combine barbecue sauce and beer; heat through. Add meatballs; stir to coat. If desired, top with jalapenos to serve.
1 meatball: 106 cal., 6g fat (3g sat. fat), 17mg chol., 338mg sod., 7g carb. (5g sugars, 0 fiber), 4g pro.

BAKED EGG ROLLS

These egg rolls are low in fat but the crispiness from baking will fool you into thinking they were fried!
—Barbara Lierman, Lyons, NE

Prep: 30 min. • **Bake:** 10 min.
Makes: 16 servings

    2 **cups grated carrots**
    1 **can (14 oz.) bean sprouts, drained**
    ½ **cup chopped water chestnuts**
    ¼ **cup chopped green pepper**
    ¼ **cup chopped green onions**
    1 **garlic clove, minced**
    2 **cups finely diced cooked chicken**
    4 **tsp. cornstarch**
    1 **Tbsp. water**
    1 **Tbsp. light soy sauce**
    1 **tsp. canola oil**
    1 **tsp. brown sugar**
       Pinch cayenne pepper
   16 **egg roll wrappers**
       Cooking spray

1. Coat a large skillet with cooking spray; heat pan over medium heat. Add the first 6 ingredients; cook and stir until vegetables are crisp-tender, about 3 minutes. Add the chicken; heat through.
2. In a small bowl, combine the cornstarch, water, soy sauce, oil, brown sugar and cayenne until smooth; stir into chicken mixture. Bring to a boil. Cook and stir for 2 minutes or until thickened; remove from the heat.
3. Spoon ¼ cup chicken mixture on the bottom third of 1 egg roll wrapper; fold the sides toward center and roll tightly. (Keep remaining wrappers covered with a damp paper towel until ready to use.) Place seam side down on a baking sheet coated with cooking spray. Repeat.
4. Spritz tops of egg rolls with cooking spray. Bake at 425° for 10-15 minutes or until lightly browned.
Freeze option: Freeze cooled egg rolls in a freezer container, separating layers with waxed paper. To use, reheat rolls on a baking sheet in a preheated 350° oven until crisp and heated through.
1 egg roll: 146 cal., 2g fat (0 sat. fat), 18mg chol., 250mg sod., 22g carb. (1g sugars, 1g fiber), 9g pro. **Diabetic exchanges:** 1½ starch, 1 lean meat, ½ fat.

CHEESY MEATBALL SLIDERS

These sliders are a fun way to serve up meatballs at your party without using a slow cooker. Served on mini Hawaiian rolls, they have a hint of sweetness to balance out all the great Italian seasonings.
—*Taste of Home* Test Kitchen

- -

Prep: 1 hour • **Bake:** 30 min.
Makes: 12 servings

- 2 lbs. lean ground beef (90% lean)
- 1 cup Italian-style bread crumbs
- 3 Tbsp. prepared pesto
- 1 large egg, lightly beaten
- 1 jar (24 oz.) pasta sauce
- 1 pkg. (18 oz.) Hawaiian sweet rolls
- 12 slices part-skim mozzarella cheese
- ½ tsp. dried oregano
- ¼ cup melted butter
- 1 Tbsp. olive oil
- 3 garlic cloves, minced
- 1 tsp. Italian seasoning
- ½ tsp. crushed red pepper flakes
- 2 Tbsp. grated Parmesan cheese
- 1 cup shredded part-skim mozzarella cheese or shredded Italian cheese blend
  Minced fresh basil

1. Preheat oven to 350°. Combine ground beef, bread crumbs, pesto and egg; mix lightly. Shape into 12 meatballs; place on a greased rack in a 15x10x1-in. baking pan. Bake until browned and a thermometer reads 160°, about 35 minutes. Toss the meatballs with sauce; set aside.
2. Meanwhile, without separating rolls, cut horizontally in half; arrange bottom halves in a greased 13x9-in. baking dish. Place half the cheese slices over roll bottoms; sprinkle with oregano. Add meatballs and sauce. Top with remaining cheese slices and bun tops.
3. Combine butter, olive oil, garlic, Italian seasoning and red pepper flakes; brush over buns. Bake, covered, for 20 minutes. Uncover; sprinkle with Parmesan and shredded mozzarella.
4. Bake, uncovered, until cheese is melted, 10-15 minutes longer. Sprinkle with basil before serving.
1 slider: 514 cal., 25g fat (12g sat. fat), 120mg chol., 856mg sod., 39g carb. (15g sugars, 3g fiber), 33g pro.

CAJUN CRAB POPPERS

CAJUN CRAB POPPERS

My brother moved to New Orleans, and I love visiting him and his family there. These easy jalapeno poppers are stuffed with crab, Cajun seasonings and bacon. They're a little hot and spicy, just like a visit to New Orleans!
—Elizabeth Lubin, Huntington Beach, CA

- -

Prep: 20 min. • **Bake:** 15 min.
Makes: 16 appetizers

- 4 oz. cream cheese, softened
- 1 large egg, lightly beaten
- 2 Tbsp. minced fresh parsley
- 1 garlic clove, minced
- ½ tsp. Cajun seasoning
- 1½ cups shredded sharp cheddar cheese
- 1 can (8 oz.) lump crabmeat, drained
- 2 bacon strips, cooked and crumbled
- 8 jalapeno peppers

Preheat oven to 375°. In a small bowl, beat the first 5 ingredients until blended. Stir in shredded cheese, crab and bacon. Cut the jalapenos in half lengthwise and remove seeds. Spoon filling into pepper halves. Place on an ungreased baking sheet. Bake until lightly browned, 15-20 minutes. Sprinkle with additional parsley.
Note: Wear disposable gloves when cutting hot peppers; the oils can burn skin. Avoid touching your face.
1 popper: 88 cal., 7g fat (4g sat. fat), 41mg chol., 187mg sod., 1g carb. (1g sugars, 0 fiber), 6g pro.

CHICKEN CORDON BLEU STROMBOLI

If chicken cordon bleu and stromboli had a baby, this would be it. Serve with jarred Alfredo sauce, homemade Alfredo sauce or classic Mornay sauce on the side if desired.
—Cyndy Gerken, Naples, FL

Takes: 30 min. • **Makes:** 6 servings

- 1   tube (13.8 oz.) refrigerated pizza crust
- 4   thin slices deli ham
- 1½ cups shredded cooked chicken
- 6   slices Swiss cheese
- 1   Tbsp. butter, melted
     Roasted garlic Alfredo sauce, optional

1. Preheat oven to 400°. Unroll pizza dough onto a baking sheet. Layer with ham, chicken and cheese to within ½ in. of edges. Roll up jelly-roll style, starting with a long side; pinch seam to seal and tuck ends under. Brush with melted butter.

2. Bake until crust is dark golden brown, 18-22 minutes. Let stand 5 minutes before slicing. If desired, serve with Alfredo sauce for dipping.

1 piece: 298 cal., 10g fat (4g sat. fat), 53mg chol., 580mg sod., 32g carb. (4g sugars, 1g fiber), 21g pro.

PATATAS BRAVAS

PATATAS BRAVAS

Patatas bravas ("spicy potatoes") is the ultimate Spanish comfort food. Served tapas-style, the crispy potatoes and smoky sauce are difficult to resist. Add a drizzle of garlic aioli for an even richer flavor.
—*Taste of Home* Test Kitchen

Prep: 45 min. • **Bake:** 25 min.
Makes: 6 servings

- 2   garlic cloves, minced
- ¼   tsp. salt
- ½   cup mayonnaise
- 1   Tbsp. lemon juice
- 1   Tbsp. olive oil

BRAVAS SAUCE
- 2   Tbsp. olive oil
- 1   small onion, chopped
- 2   garlic cloves, minced
- 1   Tbsp. all-purpose flour
- 2   tsp. sweet smoked paprika
- 1   tsp. hot smoked paprika
- 1   cup chicken broth
- 1   bay leaf

POTATOES
- 1½ lbs. russet potatoes, peeled
     Oil for deep-fat frying
- ¾   tsp. salt

1. Place garlic on a cutting board; sprinkle with salt. Mash garlic with flat side of knife blade, forming a smooth paste. Transfer to a small bowl. Whisk in mayonnaise, lemon juice and oil until smooth. Cover; refrigerate until serving.

2. For bravas sauce, in a small saucepan, heat oil over medium heat. Add onion; cook and stir until tender, 2-3 minutes. Add garlic; cook 1 minute longer. Stir in the flour and paprika until smooth; gradually stir in chicken broth. Add bay leaf. Bring to a boil, stirring constantly; cook and stir until thickened, 6-8 minutes.

3. Remove from heat; cool slightly. Remove and discard bay leaf. Puree sauce using an immersion blender. Or, cool slightly and puree sauce in a blender; return to pan and heat through. Keep warm.

4. Cut potatoes into 1½-in. cubes; soak in cold water for 30 minutes. Drain potatoes; pat dry with paper towels. In an electric skillet or deep-fat fryer, heat oil to 250°. Fry potatoes until tender, 8-10 minutes. Remove with a slotted spoon; drain on paper towels and cool completely.

5. Increase heat of oil to 375°. Fry potatoes again until crisp and golden brown, 3-4 minutes, turning frequently. Drain on paper towels; sprinkle with salt. Serve with bravas sauce and aioli.

1 cup potatoes with about 2 Tbsp. sauce and 1 Tbsp. aioli: 452 cal., 42g fat (5g sat. fat), 2mg chol., 654mg sod., 19g carb. (2g sugars, 2g fiber), 2g pro.

SLOW-COOKER CHEESEBURGER DIP

This fun dip recipe uses ingredients I always have in the fridge, so it's easy to throw together on short notice.
—Cindi DeClue, Anchorage, AK

Prep: 25 min. • **Cook:** 1¾ hours
Makes: 16 servings

- 1 lb. lean ground beef (90% lean)
- 1 medium onion, chopped
- 1 pkg. (8 oz.) cream cheese, cubed
- 2 cups shredded cheddar cheese, divided
- 1 Tbsp. Worcestershire sauce
- 2 tsp. prepared mustard
- ¼ tsp. salt
- ⅛ tsp. pepper
- 1 medium tomato, chopped
- ¼ cup chopped dill pickles
  Tortilla chips or crackers

1. In a large skillet, cook beef and onion over medium-high heat until beef is no longer pink and onion is tender, breaking up beef into crumbles, 6-8 minutes; drain. Transfer to a greased 1½- or 3-qt. slow cooker. Stir in the cream cheese, 1½ cups cheddar cheese, Worcestershire, mustard, salt and pepper. Sprinkle with remaining cheese.
2. Cook, covered, on low 1¾-2¼ hours or until mixture is heated through and cheese is melted. Top with tomatoes and pickles. Serve with tortilla chips.
¼ cup: 157 cal., 12g fat (6g sat. fat), 46mg chol., 225mg sod., 2g carb. (1g sugars, 0 fiber), 10g pro.

CHEESY ONION ROLL-UPS

These roll-ups are very fast to whip up. You can make them ahead and keep them wrapped in the refrigerator until you're ready to serve them.
—Barbara Keith, Faucett, MO

Prep: 20 min. + chilling
Makes: about 5 dozen

- 1 cup sour cream
- 1 pkg. (8 oz.) cream cheese, softened
- ½ cup finely shredded cheddar cheese
- ¾ cup sliced green onions
- 1 Tbsp. lime juice
- 1 Tbsp. minced seeded jalapeno pepper
- 1 pkg. (10 oz.) flour tortillas (6 in.), warmed
  Picante sauce

In a large bowl, combine first 6 ingredients. Spread over each tortilla and roll up tightly. Wrap and refrigerate for at least 1 hour. Slice into 1-in. pieces. Serve with picante sauce.
3 roll-ups: 119 cal., 8g fat (4g sat. fat), 23mg chol., 169mg sod., 8g carb. (1g sugars, 0 fiber), 3g pro.

> "My family (and even my neighbors) have been known to hover around while I'm cutting and plating these, so they can eat all of the cut ends that don't present as well."
>
> —RAEANN THOMPSON, SENIOR ART DIRECTOR

SLOW-COOKER CHEESEBURGER DIP

**BLUE CHEESE
POTATO CHIPS**

BLUE CHEESE POTATO CHIPS

Movie nights call for something fun. I top potato chips with tomatoes, bacon and tangy blue cheese. I make two big pans, and the chips always disappear.
—Bonnie Hawkins, Elkhorn, WI

- -

Takes: 15 min. • **Makes:** 10 servings

- 1 pkg. (8½ oz.) kettle-cooked potato chips
- 2 medium tomatoes, seeded and chopped
- 8 bacon strips, cooked and crumbled
- 6 green onions, chopped
- 1 cup crumbled blue cheese

1. Preheat broiler. In a 15x10x1-in. baking pan, arrange potato chips in an even layer. Top with remaining ingredients.
2. Broil 4-5 in. from heat until cheese begins to melt, 2-3 minutes. Serve immediately.
1 serving: 215 cal., 14g fat (5g sat. fat), 17mg chol., 359mg sod., 16g carb. (2g sugars, 1g fiber), 6g pro.

EASY PIMIENTO CHEESE

Every good Southerner has their own version of pimiento cheese. It's wonderful on crackers, in a sandwich with a fresh summer tomato, inside a grilled cheese sandwich or plain with some crackers.
—Josh Carter, Birmingham, AL

- -

Prep: 15 min. + chilling • **Makes:** 16 servings

- 1⅓ cups mayonnaise
- 2 jars (4 oz. each) pimiento strips, chopped
- 1½ tsp. Worcestershire sauce
- ¼ tsp. cayenne pepper
- ¼ tsp. pepper
- 1 block (8 oz.) sharp cheddar cheese, shredded
- 1 block (8 oz.) extra-sharp cheddar cheese, shredded

In a large bowl, combine first 5 ingredients. Add the cheeses and stir to combine. Refrigerate, covered, at least 1 hour.
¼ cup: 238 cal., 23g fat (7g sat. fat), 29mg chol., 286mg sod., 2g carb. (1g sugars, 0 fiber), 7g pro.

FRUIT & CHEESE BOARD

Who says cheese and sausage get to have all the fun? Make this a party favorite with any fruits that are in season.
—*Taste of Home* Test Kitchen

Takes: 25 minutes • **Makes:** 14 servings

- 10 fresh strawberries, halved
- 8 fresh or dried figs, halved
- 2 small navel oranges, thinly sliced
- 12 oz. seedless red grapes (about 1½ cups)
- 1 medium mango, halved and scored
- ½ cup fresh blueberries
- 1 cup fresh blackberries
- ½ cup dried banana chips
- 2 large kiwifruit, peeled, halved and thinly sliced
- 12 oz. seedless watermelon (about 6 slices)
- ½ cup unblanched almonds
- 8 oz. Brie cheese
- 8 oz. mascarpone cheese
- ½ cup honey

On a large platter or cutting board, arrange fruit, almonds and cheeses. Place honey in a small jar; tuck jar among fruit.

1 serving: 304 cal., 17g fat (8g sat. fat), 36mg chol., 116mg sod., 36g carb. (30g sugars, 4g fiber), 7g pro.

FRUIT & CHEESE BOARD

BROCCOLI & CHIVE STUFFED MINI PEPPERS

Crunchy peppers perfectly balance the creamy filling in these party appetizers. Fresh chives help them stand out.
—Jean McKenzie, Vancouver, WA

Takes: 30 min. • **Makes:** 2 dozen

- 12 miniature sweet peppers
- 1 pkg. (8 oz.) cream cheese, softened
- ⅓ cup minced fresh chives
- ⅛ tsp. salt
- ⅛ tsp. pepper
- ⅔ cup finely chopped fresh broccoli
- ⅔ cup shredded cheddar cheese

1. Preheat oven to 400°. Cut peppers lengthwise in half; remove seeds. In a bowl, mix cream cheese, chives, salt and pepper; stir in broccoli. Spoon into pepper halves.
2. Place on a foil-lined baking sheet; bake until heated through, 9-11 minutes. Sprinkle with cheddar cheese. Bake until cheese is melted, 3-4 minutes longer. Cool slightly before serving.
1 stuffed pepper half: 48 cal., 4g fat (2g sat. fat), 14mg chol., 68mg sod., 1g carb. (1g sugars, 0 fiber), 1g pro.

COLORFUL BRUNCH
FRITTATA, PAGE 59

Breakfasts

Rise and shine! Before they open the Test Kitchen every day, our staff members kick things off at home with a sunny breakfast. Turn here for some of the eye-opening recipes they rely on most!

LEMON BLACKBERRY TORTILLA FRENCH TOAST

This twist on crepes is tart-sweet with a creamy lemon filling and juicy blackberries. Think of this as a cross between thin French toast, light crepes and crispy quesadillas.
—Arlene Erlbach, Morton Grove, IL

- -

Prep: 25 min. • **Cook:** 5 min./batch
Makes: 6 servings

- 1 pkg. (8 oz.) cream cheese, softened
- 6 Tbsp. lemon curd, divided
- 2 tsp. grated lemon zest
- ⅛ tsp. almond extract
- 2 large eggs
- 2 Tbsp. heavy whipping cream
- 1 Tbsp. poppy seeds
- 3 Tbsp. butter
- 6 flour tortillas (6 in.)
- 1⅓ cups fresh blackberries
- ¼ cup seedless blackberry spreadable fruit
  Additional grated lemon zest, optional

1. In a small bowl, beat cream cheese, 3 Tbsp. lemon curd, lemon zest and extract until fluffy. Set aside.
2. In a shallow bowl, whisk eggs, cream and remaining lemon curd until blended; stir in poppy seeds. In a large cast-iron or other heavy skillet, heat 1 Tbsp. butter over medium heat. Dip both sides of a tortilla in egg mixture, allowing excess to drip off. Place in skillet; toast until golden brown, 2-3 minutes on each side. Remove to a wire rack. Repeat with remaining tortillas, adding butter to grease the skillet as needed.
3. Spread about 3 Tbsp. cream cheese mixture over each tortilla to within ¼ in. of edges. Fold tortillas in half over filling. In a microwave-safe bowl, combine blackberries and spreadable fruit; microwave, covered, at 50% power until warmed, 2-3 minutes, stirring once. Serve with tortillas and, if desired, additional lemon zest.
1 filled tortilla: 445 cal., 27g fat (15g sat. fat), 134mg chol., 403mg sod., 42g carb. (21g sugars, 3g fiber), 8g pro.

ORANGE-GLAZED BACON

Just when you thought bacon couldn't get any tastier, we jazz it up with the flavors of citrus, Dijon, ginger and honey.
—*Taste of Home* Test Kitchen

- -

Prep: 20 min. • **Bake:** 25 min.
Makes: 8 servings

- ¾ cup orange juice
- ¼ cup honey
- 1 Tbsp. Dijon mustard
- ¼ tsp. ground ginger
- ⅛ tsp. pepper
- 1 lb. bacon strips

1. In a small saucepan, combine the first 5 ingredients. Bring to a boil; cook until liquid is reduced to ⅓ cup.
2. Place bacon on a rack in an ungreased 15x10x1-in. baking pan. Bake at 350° for 10 minutes; drain.
3. Drizzle half of glaze over bacon. Bake for 10 minutes. Turn bacon and drizzle with remaining glaze. Bake until golden brown, 5-10 minutes longer. Place bacon on waxed paper until set. Serve warm.
3 glazed bacon strips: 146 cal., 8g fat (3g sat. fat), 21mg chol., 407mg sod., 12g carb. (11g sugars, 0 fiber), 7g pro.

LEMON BLACKBERRY TORTILLA FRENCH TOAST

SAUSAGE & EGGS OVER CHEDDAR-PARMESAN GRITS

These creamy grits topped with Italian sausage, peppers, onions and a fried egg on top are total comfort food. Perfect for brunch or even dinner, they are easy to put together and will satisfy a hungry crew.
—Debbie Glasscock, Conway, AR

- -

Prep: 20 min. • **Cook:** 20 min.
Makes: 6 servings

- 1 **lb. bulk Italian sausage**
- 1 **large sweet onion, chopped**
- 1 **medium sweet yellow pepper, chopped**
- 1 **medium sweet red pepper, chopped**
- 6 **cups water**
- 1½ **cups quick-cooking grits**
- 1 **cup shredded sharp cheddar cheese**
- ½ **cup shredded Parmesan cheese**
- 2 **Tbsp. half-and-half cream**
- ½ **tsp. salt**
- ¼ **tsp. pepper**
- 2 **tsp. olive oil**
- 6 **large eggs**
   Hot pepper sauce, optional

1. In a Dutch oven, cook sausage, onion, yellow pepper and red pepper over medium heat until sausage is no longer pink and vegetables are tender, 6-8 minutes, breaking up sausage into crumbles; drain.
2. Meanwhile, in a large saucepan, bring water to a boil. Slowly stir in grits. Reduce heat to medium-low; cook, covered, until thickened, about 5 minutes, stirring occasionally. Remove from heat. Stir in cheeses, cream, salt and pepper; keep warm.
3. In a large skillet, heat oil over medium-high heat. Break the eggs, 1 at a time, into pan; reduce heat to low. Cook until whites are set and yolks begin to thicken, turning once if desired. Divide grits among 6 serving bowls; top with the sausage mixture and eggs. If desired, serve with pepper sauce.
1 serving: 538 cal., 32g fat (12g sat. fat), 253mg chol., 972mg sod., 38g carb. (5g sugars, 3g fiber), 26g pro.

TEST KITCHEN TIP
Save a little time by omitting the eggs, and topping each serving with a spoonful of salsa for extra no-fuss flair.

SAUSAGE & EGGS OVER
CHEDDAR-PARMESAN GRITS

BUTTERMILK PANCAKES

You just can't beat a basic buttermilk pancake for a down-home hearty breakfast. Pair it with sausage and fresh fruit for a mouthwatering morning meal.
—Betty Abrey, Imperial, SK

Prep: 10 min. • **Cook:** 5 min./batch
Makes: 2½ dozen

- 4 **cups all-purpose flour**
- ¼ **cup sugar**
- 2 **tsp. baking soda**
- 2 **tsp. salt**
- 1½ **tsp. baking powder**
- 4 **large eggs, room temperature**
- 4 **cups buttermilk**

1. In a large bowl, combine the flour, sugar, baking soda, salt and baking powder. In another bowl, whisk the eggs and buttermilk until blended; stir into dry ingredients just until moistened.
2. Pour batter by ¼ cupfuls onto a lightly greased hot griddle; turn when bubbles form on top. Cook until second side is golden brown.
Freeze option: Freeze cooled pancakes between layers of waxed paper in a freezer container. To use, place pancakes on an ungreased baking sheet, cover with foil and reheat in a preheated 375° oven for 6-10 minutes. Or stack 3 pancakes on a microwave-safe plate and microwave on high until heated through, 45-90 seconds.
3 pancakes: 270 cal., 3g fat (1g sat. fat), 89mg chol., 913mg sod., 48g carb. (11g sugars, 1g fiber), 11g pro.

> "These are a traditional staple. They turn out super fluffy and flavorful every time I make them."

—JESS SORENSON, MANAGER, BOOKS MARKETING

SAVORY WAFFLES WITH ASPARAGUS, GRUYERE & ONION

SAVORY WAFFLES WITH ASPARAGUS, GRUYERE & ONION

I took one of our family's favorite puff pastry recipes, which uses a similar mix of ingredients, and translated it to savory waffles. It's a change of pace from sweeter fare. Served with a ham steak and fried eggs, it makes a fabulous meal. Feel free to add maple syrup or a spicy glaze.
—Leslie Ponce, Miami, FL

Prep: 35 min. • **Bake:** 25 min.
Makes: 6 servings

- 1 **bunch green onions, finely chopped**
- 16 **fresh asparagus spears, trimmed and cut into ¼-in. pieces**
- ¾ **tsp. salt, divided**
- ¼ **tsp. pepper**
- 9 **large eggs, room temperature, divided use**
- 2 **cups all-purpose flour**
- 1 **Tbsp. baking powder**
- ¼ **tsp. cayenne pepper**
- 1½ **cups 2% milk**
- 6 **Tbsp. butter, melted**
- 1 **cup Gruyere cheese, shredded**
- 1 **fully cooked boneless ham steak (12 oz.), cubed**

1. Preheat oven to 350°. Arrange onions and asparagus on a greased 15x10x1-in. baking pan; toss with ¼ tsp. salt and pepper. Roast until lightly browned, 10-12 minutes. Cool slightly; reserve ¼ cup vegetable mixture for topping.
2. Preheat a greased waffle iron. Separate 3 eggs. Whisk flour, baking powder, cayenne pepper and remaining salt. Add milk, 3 egg yolks and melted butter; mix gently but thoroughly. Stir in the remaining onion and asparagus mixture and ¾ cup of the shredded cheese
3. In another bowl, beat 3 egg whites on high until soft peaks form. Fold into the waffle mixture. Bake waffles according to manufacturer's directions until they are golden brown.
4. Meanwhile, in a large skillet coated with cooking spray, cook the ham steak until heated through; keep warm. In same skillet, fry remaining eggs until yolks are set. To serve, top waffle with ham and 1 egg. Sprinkle with the reserved onion and asparagus, and remaining ¼ cup cheese.
1 serving: 544 cal., 29g fat (15g sat. fat), 364mg chol., 1493mg sod., 38g carb. (4g sugars, 2g fiber), 33g pro.

REUBEN & RYE STRATA

This make-ahead dish is wonderful for brunch, lunch or supper. It's also great for a potluck because it travels well and is so easy to prepare. If you prefer it, substitute turkey pastrami for the corned beef.
—Mary Louise Lever, Rome, GA

Prep: 25 min. + chilling • **Bake:** 50 min.
Makes: 10 servings

- 10 slices rye bread, cubed (about 6 cups)
- 1¼ lbs. thinly sliced deli corned beef, chopped
- 2 cups shredded Gruyere cheese or Swiss cheese
- 1 cup sauerkraut, rinsed, drained and patted dry
- ¼ cup chopped dill pickles
- 6 large eggs
- 2 cups 2% milk
- ⅔ cup Thousand Island salad dressing
  Dash garlic powder
- ¼ cup shredded Parmesan cheese
  Chopped fresh parsley

1. Place bread cubes in a greased 13x9-in. baking dish. Top with corned beef, Gruyere, sauerkraut and pickles. In a large bowl, whisk eggs, milk, dressing and garlic powder. Pour over bread. Refrigerate, covered, overnight.
2. Preheat oven to 350°. Remove strata from the refrigerator while oven heats. Bake, uncovered, for 45 minutes. Sprinkle with Parmesan. Bake until a knife inserted in the center comes out clean, 5-10 minutes longer. Let stand 10-15 minutes before cutting. Sprinkle with parsley.
1 piece: 382 cal., 22g fat (9g sat. fat), 175mg chol., 1377mg sod., 21g carb. (6g sugars, 2g fiber), 25g pro.

REUBEN & RYE STRATA

PEANUT BUTTER BANANA OVERNIGHT OATS

Talk about wholesome and quick! You'll be satisfied right up until lunchtime with these easy, creamy overnight oats.
—*Taste of Home* Test Kitchen

Prep: 10 min. + chilling • **Makes:** 1 serving

- ⅓ cup old-fashioned oats
- ¼ cup mashed ripe banana
- 3 Tbsp. fat-free milk
- 1 Tbsp. honey
- 1 Tbsp. creamy peanut butter, warmed
  Sliced ripe banana and honey, optional

In a small container or Mason jar, combine oats, banana, milk, honey and peanut butter. Seal; refrigerate overnight. If desired, top with sliced bananas and drizzle with honey.
1 serving: 325 cal., 10g fat (2g sat. fat), 1mg chol., 89mg sod., 54g carb. (29g sugars, 5g fiber), 9g pro.

**POACHED EGG
BUDDHA BOWLS**

APPLE PIE RICOTTA WAFFLES

I had apples and ricotta cheese to use up, so instead of making a pie I decided to do something different. The result was these fluffy, tender golden waffles with just a hint of sweetness.
—Teri Rasey, Cadillac, MI

Prep: 25 min. • **Cook:** 10 min./batch
Makes: 6 servings

¼ cup butter
6 medium apples, peeled and chopped
2 Tbsp. sugar
1 Tbsp. honey
1 tsp. ground cinnamon
1 tsp. vanilla extract
WAFFLES
2 cups all-purpose flour
2 Tbsp. quick-cooking grits
1 Tbsp. cornstarch
1 tsp. baking soda
½ tsp. salt
2 large eggs, room temperature
2 cups buttermilk
1 cup reduced-fat ricotta cheese
½ cup canola oil
2 tsp. vanilla extract
1½ cups fat-free vanilla Greek yogurt
Fresh blueberries, optional

1. In a large skillet, melt the butter over medium-high heat. Add apples, sugar, honey, cinnamon and vanilla; cook and stir until apples are crisp-tender, 10-12 minutes. Remove from heat and keep warm.
2. Preheat waffle iron. In a large bowl, whisk flour, grits, cornstarch, baking soda and salt. In another bowl, whisk the eggs, buttermilk, ricotta, oil and vanilla until blended. Add to dry ingredients; stir just until moistened.
3. Bake waffles according to manufacturer's directions until golden brown. Serve with the apple topping, vanilla yogurt and, if desired, fresh blueberries.
1 waffle: 633 cal., 31g fat (8g sat. fat), 96mg chol., 709mg sod., 70g carb. (31g sugars, 4g fiber), 18g pro.

POACHED EGG BUDDHA BOWLS

My husband and I celebrate the arrival of spring with this dish, enjoying it in the backyard. I often include fresh peas and other spring delights.
—Amy McDonough, Carlton, OR

Prep: 10 min. • **Cook:** 65 min.
Makes: 2 servings

¾ cup wheat berries
3½ cups water, divided
2 Tbsp. olive oil
2 Tbsp. lemon juice
1 Tbsp. thinly sliced fresh mint leaves
¼ tsp. salt
⅛ tsp. freshly ground pepper
½ cup quartered cherry tomatoes
½ cup reduced-fat ricotta cheese
2 Tbsp. sliced Greek olives
2 large eggs
Optional: Additional olive oil and pepper

1. Place wheat berries and 2½ cups water in a large saucepan; bring to a boil. Reduce heat; simmer, covered, until tender, about 1 hour. Drain; transfer to a bowl. Cool berries slightly.
2. Stir in oil, lemon juice, mint, salt and pepper; divide between 2 bowls. Top with tomatoes, ricotta cheese and olives.
3. To poach each egg, place ½ cup water in a small microwave-safe bowl or glass measuring cup. Break an egg into water. Microwave, covered, on high 1 minute. Microwave in 10-second intervals until the white is set and yolk begins to thicken; let stand 1 minute.
4. Using a slotted spoon, transfer egg to 1 of the bowls. Repeat. If desired, drizzle egg with additional olive oil and sprinkle with more pepper.
1 serving: 526 cal., 24g fat (5g sat. fat), 201mg chol., 563mg sod., 58g carb. (5g sugars, 10g fiber), 21g pro.

SAUSAGE PANCAKE MUFFINS

My kids love sausage and pancakes but making them during the week was out of the question. I purchased the frozen variety on a stick but wasn't keen on the calories, additives or price. This version of pigs in a blanket is a great alternative that's much more cost effective.
—Lisa Dodd, Greenville, SC

- -

Prep: 25 min. • **Bake:** 15 min.
Makes: about 4 dozen

- 2 pkg. (7 oz. each) frozen fully cooked breakfast sausage links
- 2 cups all-purpose flour
- ¼ cup sugar
- 3 tsp. baking powder
- 1 tsp. salt
- ½ tsp. ground cinnamon
- ¼ tsp. ground nutmeg
- 1 large egg, lightly beaten
- 2 cups 2% milk
- 2 Tbsp. canola oil
- 2 Tbsp. honey
  Maple syrup, optional

1. Preheat oven to 350°. Coat 48 mini muffin cups with cooking spray. Microwave the sausages according to package directions; drain. Cut into small chunks; divide evenly among muffin cups.
2. Whisk next 6 ingredients. In another bowl, whisk egg, milk, canola oil and honey until blended. Add to the flour mixture; stir just until moistened. Pour batter over sausage chunks in prepared muffin cups.
3. Bake until lightly browned, 15-20 minutes. Cool 5 minutes before removing from pans to wire racks. Serve warm, adding syrup if desired.
4 mini muffins: 280 cal., 16g fat (5g sat. fat), 39mg chol., 658mg sod., 26g carb. (10g sugars, 1g fiber), 9g pro.

TEST KITCHEN TIP
Remember these savory bites the next time you need to bring a dish to a brunch or even a pancake breakfast potluck!

**SAUSAGE
PANCAKE MUFFINS**

MIXED FRUIT WITH LEMON-BASIL DRESSING

A slightly savory dressing compliments the sweet fruit in this quick recipe. I also use the dressing on salad greens.
—Dixie Terry, Goreville, IL

- -

Takes: 15 min. • **Makes:** 8 servings

2	Tbsp. lemon juice
½	tsp. sugar
¼	tsp. salt
¼	tsp. ground mustard
⅛	tsp. onion powder
	Dash pepper
6	Tbsp. olive oil
4½	tsp. minced fresh basil
1	cup cubed fresh pineapple
1	cup sliced fresh strawberries
1	cup sliced peeled kiwifruit
1	cup seedless watermelon balls
1	cup fresh blueberries
1	cup fresh raspberries

1. Place the lemon juice, sugar, salt, mustard, onion powder and pepper in a blender; cover and pulse until blended. While processing, gradually add oil in a steady stream. Stir in the basil.

2. In a large bowl, combine the fruit. Drizzle with dressing and toss to coat. Refrigerate until serving.

¾ cup: 145 cal., 11g fat (1g sat. fat), 0 chol., 76mg sod., 14g carb. (9g sugars, 3g fiber), 1g pro. **Diabetic exchanges:** 2 fat, 1 fruit.

ROASTED VEGETABLE & CHEVRE QUICHE

ROASTED VEGETABLE & CHEVRE QUICHE

Roasting the veggies in this rich yet bright quiche intensifies their flavors. And the addition of fresh goat cheese lends a wonderful creamy tanginess.
—Laura Davis, Chincoteague, VA

- -

Prep: 45 min. + chilling
Bake: 25 min. + standing • **Makes:** 6 servings

1	sheet refrigerated pie crust
1	small eggplant, cut into 1-in. pieces
1	poblano pepper, cut into 1-in. pieces
1	medium tomato, cut into 1-in. pieces
2	garlic cloves, minced
1	Tbsp. olive oil
2	large eggs plus 2 large egg yolks
¾	cup half-and-half cream
1	tsp. kosher salt
½	tsp. pepper
1	log (4 oz.) fresh goat cheese, crumbled

1. Unroll pie crust into an ungreased 9-in. tart pan. Refrigerate 30 minutes. Preheat oven to 425°.

2. Line unpricked crust with a double thickness of foil. Fill with pie weights, dried beans or uncooked rice. Bake on a lower oven rack until edges are golden brown, 10-12 minutes. Remove foil and weights; bake until the bottom is golden brown, 3-5 minutes longer. Cool on a wire rack.

3. In a large bowl, combine the eggplant, pepper, tomato and garlic. Add oil; toss to coat. Transfer to a greased 15x10x1-in. baking pan. Roast until vegetables are tender, 15-20 minutes, stirring halfway.

4. Reduce oven setting to 375°. Spoon roasted vegetables into crust. In a large bowl, whisk eggs, egg yolks, cream, salt and pepper until blended; pour over top. Sprinkle with goat cheese.

5. Bake on a lower oven rack on a baking sheet until a knife inserted near the center comes out clean, 25-30 minutes. Cover edges with foil if they begin to get too dark. Let stand 10 minutes before cutting.

1 piece: 219 cal., 14g fat (7g sat. fat), 83mg chol., 471mg sod., 19g carb. (2g sugars, 0 fiber), 3g pro.

HARD-BOILED EGGS

Here's a foolproof technique for making hard-boiled eggs to eat plain or to use in various recipes.
—*Taste of Home* Test Kitchen

Prep: 20 min. + cooling • **Makes:** 12 servings

12 **large eggs**
Cold water

1. Place eggs in a single layer in a large saucepan; add enough cold water to cover by 1 in. Cover and quickly bring to a boil. Remove from the heat. Let stand for 15 minutes for large eggs (18 minutes for extra-large eggs and 12 minutes for medium eggs).
2. Rinse the eggs in cold water and place in ice water until completely cooled. Drain and refrigerate.
Note: The green ring around the yolk of hard-boiled eggs is unattractive but harmless. It is caused by a reaction between the iron in the yolks and the sulfur in the whites. Cooking the eggs too long, or at a temperature that's too high, can cause this.
1 egg: 75 cal., 5g fat (2g sat. fat), 213mg chol., 63mg sod., 1g carb. (1g sugars, 0 fiber), 6g pro. **Diabetic exchanges:** 1 medium-fat meat.

SLOW-COOKER
CINNAMON ROLL

SLOW-COOKER CINNAMON ROLL

Come home to the heavenly aroma of fresh-baked cinnamon rolls! This healthier version tastes just as decadent as a regular cinnamon roll, but smartly sneaks in some whole grains.
—Nick Iverson, Denver, CO

Prep: 15 min. + rising • **Cook:** 3½ hours
Makes: 12 servings

1 **pkg. (¼ oz.) active dry yeast**
¾ **cup warm water (110° to 115°)**
½ **cup quick-cooking oats**
½ **cup whole wheat flour**
¼ **cup packed brown sugar**
2 **Tbsp. butter, melted**
1 **large egg, room temperature**
1 **tsp. salt**
1¾ **to 2¼ cups all-purpose flour**
FILLING
3 **Tbsp. butter, softened**
⅓ **cup sugar**
2 **tsp. ground cinnamon**
ICING
1 **cup confectioners' sugar**
2 **Tbsp. half-and-half cream**
4 **tsp. butter, softened**

1. Dissolve yeast in warm water. Add next 6 ingredients plus 1 cup all-purpose flour. Beat on medium speed until smooth. Stir in enough remaining flour to form a soft dough (dough will be sticky).
2. Turn onto a lightly floured surface; knead until smooth and elastic, 6-8 minutes. Roll into an 18x12-in. rectangle. For filling, spread dough with butter, then combine sugar and cinnamon; sprinkle over dough to within ½ in. of edges.
3. Roll up jelly-roll style, starting with a long side; pinch seam to seal. Cut crosswise in half to form 2 rolls. Place rolls side by side; pinch top ends together to seal. Using a sharp knife, cut rolls lengthwise in half; loosely twist strips around each other. Pinch bottom ends together to seal. Shape into a coil; place on parchment. Transfer to a 6-qt. slow cooker. Let rise until doubled, about 1 hour.
4. Cook, covered, on low until bread is lightly browned, 3½-4 hours. Remove from slow cooker and cool slightly. For the icing, beat ingredients until smooth. Spread over the warm roll.
1 slice: 240 cal., 7g fat (4g sat. fat), 33mg chol., 254mg sod., 41g carb. (20g sugars, 2g fiber), 4g pro.

CHOCOLATE CHERRY CREPES

One of the reasons we like this impressive-looking recipe is that it's easy to make. We prepare the crepes and filling in advance, then assemble them and add the toppings just before serving.
—*Taste of Home* Test Kitchen

Takes: 20 min. • **Makes:** 6 servings

- 1 can (21 oz.) cherry pie filling
- 1 tsp. almond extract
- ⅔ cup 2% milk
- 2 large eggs
- 2 Tbsp. butter, melted
- ¼ cup blanched almonds, ground
- ¼ cup all-purpose flour

FILLING
- 1 cup heavy whipping cream
- 3 oz. semisweet chocolate, melted and cooled
- ¼ cup slivered almonds, toasted

1. In a small bowl, combine pie filling and almond extract; cover and refrigerate until chilled. For crepes, place the milk, eggs, butter, almonds and flour in a blender; cover and process until smooth.

2. Heat a lightly greased 8-in. nonstick skillet; pour about 2 Tbsp. batter into center of skillet. Lift and tilt pan to coat bottom evenly. Cook until top appears dry and bottom is golden brown; turn and cook 15-20 seconds longer. Remove to a wire rack. Repeat with remaining batter, greasing skillet as needed. Stack cooled crepes with waxed paper or paper towels in between.

3. For the filling, in a mixing bowl, beat cream and melted chocolate until soft peaks form. Spoon about 2 Tbsp. over each crepe; roll up. Top with cherry mixture and sprinkle with slivered almonds.

2 filled crepes with toppings: 433 cal., 28g fat (14g sat. fat), 139mg chol., 108mg sod., 39g carb. (29g sugars, 2g fiber), 7g pro.

CHOCOLATE CHERRY CREPES

PRESSURE-COOKER CARROT CAKE OATMEAL

This warm breakfast cereal made in the pressure cooker is a great way to get your veggies in the morning and keep a healthy diet! For extra crunch, I garnish individual servings with ground walnuts or pecans.
—Debbie Kain, Colorado Springs, CO

Prep: 10 min. • **Cook:** 10 min. + releasing
Makes: 8 servings

- 4½ cups water
- 1 can (20 oz.) crushed pineapple, undrained
- 2 cups shredded carrots
- 1 cup steel-cut oats
- 1 cup raisins
- 2 tsp. ground cinnamon
- 1 tsp. pumpkin pie spice
  Brown sugar, optional

In a 6-qt. electric pressure cooker coated with cooking spray, combine the first 7 ingredients. Lock lid; make sure vent is closed. Select manual setting; adjust pressure to high, and set time for 10 minutes. When finished cooking, allow pressure to naturally release for 10 minutes, then quick-release any remaining pressure. If desired, sprinkle with brown sugar.

Note: Steel-cut oats are also known as Scotch oats or Irish oatmeal.

1 serving: 197 cal., 2g fat (0 sat. fat), 0 chol., 46mg sod., 46g carb. (26g sugars, 4g fiber), 4g pro.

THE BEST FRENCH TOAST

There's no question that this is the best French toast recipe. The caramelized exterior meets a soft, custardlike center that practically melts in your mouth. Not only that, but it's quick and easy, too!
—Audrey Rompon, Milwaukee, WI

- -

Takes: 15 min. • **Makes:** 4 servings

- 1½ **cups half-and-half cream**
- 3 **large egg yolks**
- 3 **Tbsp. brown sugar**
- 2 **tsp. vanilla extract**
- ¾ **tsp. ground cinnamon**
- ½ **tsp. salt**
- ¼ **tsp. ground nutmeg**
- 8 **slices day-old brioche bread (1 in. thick)**
  Optional toppings: Butter, maple syrup, fresh berries, whipped cream and confectioners' sugar

1. In a shallow dish, whisk together the first 7 ingredients. Preheat a greased griddle over medium heat.
2. Dip bread in egg mixture, letting it soak 5 seconds on each side. Cook on griddle until golden brown on both sides. Serve with toppings as desired.
2 pieces: 546 cal., 24g fat (15g sat. fat), 263mg chol., 786mg sod., 64g carb. (25g sugars, 2g fiber), 13g pro.

ASK SARAH

WHAT IF I DON'T LIKE VANILLA?
Swap out the vanilla extract for banana, coconut or almond extract and make this recipe your own.

MAKE-AHEAD EGGS
BENEDICT TOAST CUPS

MAKE-AHEAD EGGS BENEDICT TOAST CUPS

When I was growing up, we had a family tradition of having eggs Benedict with champagne and orange juice for our Christmas breakfast. But now that I'm cooking, a fussy breakfast isn't my style. I wanted to come up with a dish I could make ahead that would mimic the flavors of traditional eggs Benedict and would also freeze well. Friends, all I can say is, this one fits the bill!
—Lyndsay Wells, Ladysmith, BC

- -

Prep: 30 min. • **Bake:** 10 min.
Makes: 1 dozen

- 6 **English muffins, split**
- 1 **envelope hollandaise sauce mix**
- 12 **slices Canadian bacon, quartered**
- 1 **tsp. pepper**
- 1 **Tbsp. olive oil**
- 6 **large eggs**
- 1 **Tbsp. butter**

1. Preheat oven to 375°. Flatten muffin halves with a rolling pin; press into greased muffin cups. Bake until lightly browned, about 10 minutes.
2. Meanwhile, prepare hollandaise sauce according to package directions; cool slightly. Sprinkle the bacon with pepper. In a large skillet, cook bacon in oil over medium heat until partially cooked but not crisp. Remove to paper towels to drain. Divide the bacon among muffin cups. Wipe skillet clean.
3. Whisk eggs and ½ cup cooled hollandaise sauce until blended. In the same skillet, heat butter over medium heat. Pour in egg mixture; cook and stir until the eggs are thickened and no liquid egg remains. Divide egg mixture among muffin cups; top with remaining hollandaise sauce.
4. Bake until heated through, 8-10 minutes. Serve warm.
Overnight option: Refrigerate unbaked cups, covered, overnight. Bake until golden brown, 10-12 minutes.
Freeze option: Cover and freeze unbaked cups in muffin cups until firm. Transfer to an airtight container; return to freezer. To use, bake cups in muffin tin as directed, increasing time to 25-30 minutes. Cover loosely with foil if needed to prevent overbrowning.
1 toast cup: 199 cal., 11g fat (5g sat. fat), 114mg chol., 495mg sod., 15g carb. (2g sugars, 1g fiber), 9g pro.

SWEET POTATO & EGG SKILLET

I try to incorporate nutritious sweet potatoes in my meals as often as possible, especially with breakfast! This recipe originated with the purpose of feeding my family a healthy yet hearty breakfast, and it worked on both counts!
—Jeanne Larson, Rancho Santa Margarita, CA

Takes: 25 min. • **Makes:** 4 servings

2 Tbsp. butter
2 medium sweet potatoes, peeled and shredded (about 4 cups)
1 garlic clove, minced
½ tsp. salt, divided
⅛ tsp. dried thyme
2 cups fresh baby spinach
4 large eggs
⅛ tsp. coarsely ground pepper

1. In a large cast-iron or other heavy skillet, heat the butter over low heat. Add sweet potatoes, garlic, ¼ tsp. salt and thyme; cook, covered, until potatoes are almost tender, 4-5 minutes, stirring occasionally. Stir in spinach just until wilted, 2-3 minutes.
2. With the back of a spoon, make 4 wells in the potato mixture. Break an egg into each well. Sprinkle eggs with pepper and the remaining ¼ tsp. salt. Cook, covered, on medium-low until egg whites are completely set and yolks begin to thicken but are not hard, 5-7 minutes.
1 serving: 224 cal., 11g fat (5g sat. fat), 201mg chol., 433mg sod., 24g carb. (10g sugars, 3g fiber), 8g pro. **Diabetic exchanges:** 1½ starch, 1½ fat, 1 medium-fat meat.

FESTIVE CRANBERRY FRUIT SALAD

This fruit salad is always a tradition on my Christmas table. It goes together quickly, which is a plus on such a busy day.
—Rousheen Arel Wolf, Delta Junction, AK

Takes: 25 min. • **Makes:** 14 servings

1 pkg. (12 oz.) fresh or frozen cranberries
¾ cup water
½ cup sugar
5 medium apples, diced
2 medium firm bananas, sliced
1½ cups fresh or frozen blueberries, thawed
1 can (11 oz.) mandarin oranges, undrained
1 cup fresh or frozen raspberries, thawed
¾ cup fresh strawberries, halved

1. In a large saucepan, combine cranberries, water and sugar. Cook and stir over medium heat until berries pop, about 15 minutes. Remove from the heat; cool slightly.
2. In a large bowl, combine the remaining ingredients. Add cranberry mixture; stir gently. Refrigerate until serving.
Note: If using frozen blueberries, use without thawing to avoid discoloring the salad.
¾ cup: 105 cal., 0 fat (0 sat. fat), 0 chol., 2mg sod., 27g carb. (21g sugars, 4g fiber), 1g pro.

SWEET POTATO & EGG SKILLET

BLUEBERRY
MAPLE SUGAR PANCAKES

BREAKFAST WRAPS

We like quick and simple morning meals during the week, and these wraps can be prepped ahead of time. With just a minute in the microwave, breakfast is ready to go.
—Betty Kleberger, Florissant, MO

Takes: 15 min. • **Makes:** 4 servings

6	large eggs
2	Tbsp. 2% milk
¼	tsp. pepper
1	Tbsp. canola oil
1	cup shredded cheddar cheese
¾	cup diced fully cooked ham
4	flour tortillas (8 in.), warmed

1. In a small bowl, whisk the eggs, milk and pepper. In a large skillet, heat oil. Add egg mixture; cook and stir over medium heat until eggs are completely set. Stir in cheese and ham.
2. Spoon egg mixture down the center of each tortilla; roll up.
Freeze option: Wrap cooled egg wrap in foil and freeze in a freezer container. To use, thaw in refrigerator overnight. Remove foil; wrap tortilla in a moist paper towel. Microwave on high until heated through, 30-60 seconds. Serve immediately.
1 serving: 436 cal., 24g fat (10g sat. fat), 364mg chol., 853mg sod., 28g carb. (1g sugars, 0 fiber), 25g pro.

BLUEBERRY MAPLE SUGAR PANCAKES

We use maple sugar made at our farm, Bonhomie Acres, in these pancakes, and then we top them with 100 percent maple syrup, too. The delicious flavor demands nothing less!
—Katherine Brown, Fredericktown, OH

Prep: 15 min. • **Cook:** 5 min./batch
Makes: 1 batch (about 2 cups mix)

2	cups all-purpose flour
4	tsp. baking powder
½	tsp. salt
⅓	cup maple sugar
⅔	cup dried blueberries

ADDITIONAL INGREDIENTS

2	large eggs
1⅓	cups 2% milk
¼	cup butter, melted

1. Whisk together flour, baking powder and salt. Transfer to a 1-pt. glass jar. Top with maple sugar; cover. Place dried blueberries in a small plastic bag; attach to jar. Store in a cool dry place or in freezer up to 3 months.
2. To prepare pancakes: Preheat lightly greased griddle over medium heat. In a small bowl, mix flour mixture and maple sugar. Whisk in eggs, milk and melted butter. Stir in blueberries.
3. Pour batter by scant ¼ cupfuls onto griddle; cook until bubbles on top begin to pop and bottoms are golden brown. Turn; cook until second side is golden brown.
3 pancakes: 437 cal., 13g fat (7g sat. fat), 104mg chol., 757mg sod., 69g carb. (24g sugars, 3g fiber), 10g pro.

BAKED FRENCH TOAST

Any day is special when Mom makes this do-ahead baked French toast.
—Jill Baughman, New York, NY

Prep: 20 min. + chilling
Bake: 40 min. + standing • Makes: 8 servings

- 8 oz. day-old French bread, unsliced
- 4 large eggs
- 2 Tbsp. sugar
- 1 Tbsp. brown sugar
- 2 tsp. vanilla extract
- 1 tsp. maple extract
- ¼ tsp. kosher salt
- 2 cups whole milk
- ½ cup heavy whipping cream

TOPPING
- ¼ cup all-purpose flour
- 3 Tbsp. brown sugar
- 3 Tbsp. unsalted butter, cut into ¼-in. cubes
- 1 tsp. ground cinnamon

Freshly grated nutmeg, optional
Fresh blueberries or raspberries
Confectioners' sugar

1. Cut bread into 1-in.-thick slices. Arrange in a single layer in a greased 13x9-in. baking dish. Lightly beat next 6 ingredients; stir in milk and cream. Pour egg mixture over bread, turning once to coat. Refrigerate, covered, overnight.
2. Preheat oven to 375°. Turn bread again to coat. For topping, combine flour, brown sugar, butter, cinnamon and, if desired, nutmeg. Sprinkle flour mixture over bread.
3. Bake, uncovered, until a knife inserted in center comes out clean and topping is golden brown, 40-45 minutes. Let stand 10 minutes before cutting. Top with the blueberries or raspberries; sprinkle with confectioners' sugar.
1 serving: 297 cal., 15g fat (8g sat. fat), 128mg chol., 299mg sod., 32g carb. (15g sugars, 1g fiber), 9g pro.

CALICO SCRAMBLED EGGS

When you're short on time and scrambling to get a meal on the table, this recipe is just what you need. There's a short ingredient list, cooking is kept to a minimum, and the green pepper and tomato make it colorful.
—*Taste of Home* Test Kitchen

Takes: 15 min. • Makes: 4 servings

- 8 large eggs
- ¼ cup 2% milk
- ⅛ to ¼ tsp. dill weed
- ⅛ to ¼ tsp. salt
- ⅛ to ¼ tsp. pepper
- 1 Tbsp. butter
- ½ cup chopped green pepper
- ¼ cup chopped onion
- ½ cup chopped fresh tomato

1. In a bowl, whisk first 5 ingredients until blended. In a 12-in. nonstick skillet, heat butter over medium-high heat. Add green pepper and onion; cook and stir until tender. Remove from pan.
2. In same pan, pour in egg mixture; cook and stir over medium heat until the eggs begin to thicken. Add tomato and pepper mixture; cook until heated through and no liquid egg remains, stirring gently.
1 cup: 188 cal., 13g fat (5g sat. fat), 381mg chol., 248mg sod., 4g carb. (3g sugars, 1g fiber), 14g pro. **Diabetic exchanges:** 2 medium-fat meat, ½ fat.

BAKED FRENCH TOAST

COLORFUL BRUNCH FRITTATA

A friend called and asked me for a special recipe that could be served at his daughter's wedding brunch. I created this recipe for the occasion. It's loaded with colorful veggies and looks beautiful on a buffet.
—Kristin Arnett, Elkhorn, WI

- -

Prep: 15 min. • **Bake:** 50 min. + standing
Makes: 12 servings

- 1 lb. fresh asparagus, trimmed and cut into 1-in. pieces
- ½ lb. sliced fresh mushrooms
- 1 medium sweet red pepper, diced
- 1 medium sweet yellow pepper, diced
- 1 small onion, chopped
- 3 green onions, chopped
- 3 Tbsp. olive oil
- 2 garlic cloves, minced
- 3 plum tomatoes, seeded and chopped
- 14 large eggs, lightly beaten
- 2 cups half-and-half cream
- 2 cups shredded Colby-Monterey Jack cheese
- 3 Tbsp. minced fresh parsley
- 3 Tbsp. minced fresh basil
- ½ tsp. salt
- ¼ tsp. pepper
- ½ cup shredded Parmesan cheese

1. Preheat oven to 350°. In a large skillet, saute asparagus, mushrooms, peppers and onions in oil until tender. Add garlic; cook 1 minute longer. Add tomatoes; set aside.
2. In a large bowl, whisk the eggs, cream, Colby-Monterey Jack cheese, parsley, basil, salt and pepper; stir into vegetable mixture.
3. Pour into a greased 13x9-in. baking dish. Bake, uncovered, 45 minutes.
4. Sprinkle with the Parmesan cheese. Bake 5 minutes longer or until a knife inserted in the center comes out clean. Let stand at least 10 minutes before cutting.
1 piece: 270 cal., 19g fat (10g sat. fat), 256mg chol., 377mg sod., 7g carb. (4g sugars, 1g fiber), 16g pro.

COLORFUL
BRUNCH FRITTATA

RAISED YEAST WAFFLES

These terrific waffles are crispy on the outside and tender on the inside. Never too filling, they leave room for sampling the rest of the brunch buffet.
—Helen Knapp, North Pole, AK

- -

Prep: 15 min. + rising • **Bake:** 5 min./batch
Makes: 10 waffles

1	pkg. (¼ oz.) active dry yeast
1	tsp. sugar
½	cup warm water (110° to 115°)
2	cups warm 2% milk (110° to 115°)
2	large eggs
½	cup butter, melted
2¼	cups all-purpose flour
1	tsp. salt
⅛	tsp. baking soda

Dissolve yeast and sugar in warm water; let stand for 5 minutes. Beat in milk, eggs and butter. In another bowl, combine flour, salt and baking soda; stir into yeast mixture just until combined. Cover and let rise in a warm place until doubled, about 45 minutes. Stir batter. Bake in a preheated waffle iron according to manufacturer's directions until golden brown.

2 waffles: 453 cal., 23g fat (14g sat. fat), 131mg chol., 726mg sod., 49g carb. (6g sugars, 2g fiber), 12g pro.

SOUTHERN HASH BROWNS
& HAM SHEET-PAN BAKE

SOUTHERN HASH BROWNS & HAM SHEET-PAN BAKE

Why not take the convenience of sheet-pan cooking and apply it to breakfast? I love how easily this meal comes together.
—Colleen Delawder, Herndon, VA

- -

Prep: 15 min. • **Bake:** 35 min.
Makes: 4 servings

1	pkg. (20 oz.) refrigerated shredded hash brown potatoes
3	Tbsp. olive oil
½	tsp. salt
½	tsp. pepper
¼	cup apple jelly
¼	cup apricot preserves
1	Tbsp. horseradish sauce
1	tsp. Dijon mustard
¼	tsp. garlic powder
¼	tsp. onion powder
2	cups cubed fully cooked ham
4	large eggs
2	green onions, finely chopped

1. Preheat oven to 400°. Place potatoes in a greased 15x10x1-in. baking pan. Drizzle with oil; sprinkle with salt and pepper. Toss to coat. Bake until edges are golden brown, 25-30 minutes.

2. In a small bowl, combine jelly, preserves, horseradish sauce, Dijon, garlic powder and onion powder. Pour over potatoes; add ham. Toss to coat.

3. With the back of a spoon, make 4 wells in potato mixture. Break an egg into each well. Bake until the egg whites are completely set and yolks begin to thicken but are not hard, 10-12 minutes. Sprinkle with green onions and additional pepper.

1 serving: 483 cal., 19g fat (4g sat. fat), 228mg chol., 1340mg sod., 55g carb. (23g sugars, 3g fiber), 24g pro.

TEST KITCHEN TIP
Not sure the horseradish sauce will fly with younger taste buds? Simply leave it out.

AIR-FRYER FRENCH TOAST STICKS

Learn how to make French toast sticks with this quick and easy recipe. They're nice to have handy in the freezer for a hearty breakfast in an instant. You'll find them great for buffets, too.
—*Taste of Home* Test Kitchen

- -

Prep: 20 min. + freezing • **Cook:** 10 min.
Makes: 1½ dozen

- 6   slices day-old Texas toast
- 4   large eggs
- 1   cup 2% milk
- 2   Tbsp. sugar
- 1   tsp. vanilla extract
- ¼   to ½ tsp. ground cinnamon
- 1   cup crushed cornflakes, optional
      Confectioners' sugar, optional
      Maple syrup

1. Cut each piece of bread into thirds; place in an ungreased 13x9-in. dish. In a large bowl, whisk eggs, milk, sugar, vanilla extract and cinnamon. Pour over the bread; soak for 2 minutes, turning once. If desired, coat bread with cornflake crumbs on all sides.
2. Place in a greased 15x10x1-in. baking pan. Freeze until firm, about 45 minutes. Transfer to an airtight freezer container.
3. To use frozen French toast sticks: Preheat air fryer to 350°. Place desired number on greased tray in air-fryer basket. Cook for 3 minutes. Turn; cook until golden brown, 2-3 minutes longer. Sprinkle sticks with confectioners' sugar if desired. Serve with maple syrup.
3 sticks: 184 cal., 6g fat (2g sat. fat), 128mg chol., 253mg sod., 24g carb. (8g sugars, 1g fiber), 8g pro.

AIR-FRYER FRENCH TOAST STICKS

ITALIAN CLOUD EGGS

Drop egg yolks on nests of whipped Italian-seasoned egg whites, then bake in a cast-iron skillet. Dreamy!
—Matthew Hass, Ellison Bay, WI

- -

Takes: 25 min. • **Makes:** 4 servings

- 4   large eggs, separated
- ¼   tsp. Italian seasoning
- ⅛   tsp. salt
- ⅛   tsp. pepper
- ¼   cup shredded Parmesan cheese
- 1   Tbsp. minced fresh basil
- 1   Tbsp. finely chopped oil-packed sun-dried tomatoes

1. Preheat oven to 450°. Separate eggs; place whites in a large bowl and yolks in 4 separate small bowls. Beat egg whites, Italian seasoning, salt and pepper until stiff peaks form.
2. In a 9-in. cast-iron skillet generously coated with cooking spray, drop egg white mixture into 4 mounds. With the back of a spoon, create a small well in the center of each mound. Sprinkle with cheese. Bake until light brown, about 5 minutes. Gently slip an egg yolk into each of the mounds. Bake until yolks are set, 3-5 minutes longer. Sprinkle with basil and tomatoes. Serve immediately.
1 serving: 96 cal., 6g fat (2g sat. fat), 190mg chol., 234mg sod., 1g carb. (0 sugars, 0 fiber), 8g pro. **Diabetic exchanges:** 1 medium-fat meat.

HEAVENLY CHEESE
DANISH, PAGE 66

Breads, Biscuits & More

With more people flexing their baking muscles these days, the *Taste of Home* Test Kitchen receives more recipes for rolls, loaves, muffins and scones than ever before. Take a look at some of the treats our pros think are the best of the best, then bake up a golden delight today.

PARMESAN-SAGE BEER BREAD

I'm asked to bring this savory loaf to nearly every function I attend. It's great as a side dish, but if you're just in the mood for an extraordinary sandwich, start with two slices of this beer bread.
—Elizabeth King, Duluth, MN

Prep: 10 min. • **Bake:** 45 min.
Makes: 1 loaf (12 pieces)

- 2½ **cups all-purpose flour**
- 1 **cup grated Parmesan cheese**
- 2 **Tbsp. sugar**
- 3 **tsp. baking powder**
- 1 **Tbsp. chopped fresh sage**
- 1 **tsp. salt**
- 1½ **cups beer**
- ¼ **cup melted butter, divided**

1. Preheat oven to 375°. In a small bowl, whisk the first 6 ingredients. Add the beer and 3 Tbsp. melted butter; stir just until moistened.

2. Transfer to a greased 8x4-in. loaf pan. Drizzle with the remaining butter. Bake 45-50 minutes or until a toothpick inserted in center comes out clean. Cool in pan 5 minutes before removing to a wire rack to cool.

1 piece: 177 cal., 6g fat (4g sat. fat), 16mg chol., 469mg sod., 24g carb. (3g sugars, 1g fiber), 5g pro.

ASK SARAH

WHICH BEER IS BEST?

When baking a beer bread, it's best to stay away from dark beers and ales unless the recipe specifically calls for it.

SWIRL CINNAMON BREAD

If you like cinnamon, you'll love this quick bread! It's crusty on top, soft and moist inside. Consider making extra loaves for the holidays and give them to family and friends.
—*Taste of Home* Test Kitchen

- -

Prep: 25 min. • **Bake:** 45 min. + cooling
Makes: 1 loaf (12 pieces)

- 2 cups all-purpose flour
- ¾ cup sugar
- ½ tsp. baking soda
- ½ tsp. plus 1½ tsp. ground cinnamon, divided
- ¼ tsp. salt
- 1 large egg, room temperature
- 1 cup reduced-fat plain yogurt
- ¼ cup canola oil
- 1 tsp. vanilla extract
- ¼ cup packed brown sugar

1. Preheat oven to 350°. In a large bowl, combine flour, sugar, baking soda, ½ tsp. cinnamon and salt. In a small bowl, whisk egg, yogurt, oil and vanilla. Stir into dry ingredients just until moistened. In a small bowl, combine the brown sugar and the remaining 1½ tsp. cinnamon.

2. Spoon a third of the batter into an 8x4-in. loaf pan coated with cooking spray. Top with a third of the brown sugar mixture. Repeat layers twice. Cut through batter with a knife to swirl the brown sugar mixture.

3. Bake 45-55 minutes or until a toothpick inserted in the center comes out clean. Cool 10 minutes before removing from pan to a wire rack.

1 slice: 203 cal., 6g fat (1g sat. fat), 19mg chol., 124mg sod., 35g carb. (19g sugars, 1g fiber), 4g pro.

ONE-DISH NO-KNEAD BREAD

Here's a very easy way to have homemade bread for dinner tonight. Don't worry if you're new to baking. Anyone who can stir can make this a success!
—Heather Chambers, Largo, FL

- -

Prep: 15 min. + rising • **Bake:** 40 min.
Makes: 1 loaf (12 pieces)

- 1 tsp. active dry yeast
- 1½ cups warm water (110° to 115°)
- 2¾ cups all-purpose flour
- 2 Tbsp. sugar
- 2 Tbsp. olive oil
- 1½ tsp. salt

1. In a large bowl, dissolve yeast in warm water. Stir in remaining ingredients to form a wet dough; transfer to a greased 2½-qt. baking dish. Cover; let stand in a warm place 1 hour.

2. Stir down dough. Cover; let stand 1 hour. Preheat oven to 425°.

3. Bake 20 minutes. Reduce oven setting to 350°. Bake until the top is golden brown and a thermometer reads 210°, about 20 minutes longer.

4. Remove bread from baking dish to a wire rack to cool. Serve warm.

1 piece: 133 cal., 3g fat (0 sat. fat), 0 chol., 296mg sod., 24g carb. (2g sugars, 1g fiber), 3g pro. **Diabetic exchanges:** 1½ starch, ½ fat.

Health tip: Some packaged breads have more than 20 ingredients! This loaf includes just six easy-to-pronounce ones.

SWIRL CINNAMON BREAD

NEW ENGLAND
PUMPKIN-WALNUT
BREAD

HEAVENLY CHEESE DANISH

This tempting cheese Danish is baked to flaky perfection and made to shine with a simple egg wash gloss. It tastes just as decadent as any breakfast pastry you'd find in a bakery or coffee shop.
—Josephine Triton, Lakewood, OH

Prep: 50 min. + chilling • **Bake:** 15 min.
Makes: 16 rolls

- 2 pkg. (¼ oz. each) active dry yeast
- ½ cup warm water (110° to 115°)
- 4 cups all-purpose flour
- ⅓ cup sugar
- 2 tsp. salt
- 1 cup cold butter, cubed
- 1 cup 2% milk
- 4 large egg yolks, room temperature

ASSEMBLY
- 3 tsp. ground cinnamon, divided
- 12 oz. cream cheese, softened
- ⅓ cup sugar
- 1 large egg, separated, room temperature
- 1 Tbsp. water
- 2 Tbsp. maple syrup

1. Dissolve yeast in warm water. In another bowl, mix flour, sugar and salt; cut in butter until crumbly. Add the milk, egg yolks and yeast mixture; stir to form a soft dough (dough will be sticky). Cover and refrigerate 8-24 hours.
2. To assemble, punch down dough; divide into 4 portions. On a lightly floured surface, pat each portion into a 9x4-in. rectangle; sprinkle each with ¾ tsp. cinnamon. Cut each rectangle lengthwise into four 9x1-in. strips. Twist each strip, then loosely wrap strip around itself to form a coil; tuck end under and pinch to seal. Place rolls 3 in. apart on greased baking sheets.
3. Beat cream cheese, sugar and egg yolk until smooth. Press an indentation in center of each roll; fill with 1 rounded Tbsp. cream cheese mixture. Cover; let rise in a warm place until doubled, about 45 minutes. Preheat oven to 350°.
4. Whisk egg white with water; brush over rolls. Bake until golden brown, 15-20 minutes. Remove to wire racks; brush with syrup. Serve warm. Refrigerate leftovers.
1 roll: 359 cal., 21g fat (12g sat. fat), 111mg chol., 468mg sod., 37g carb. (12g sugars, 1g fiber), 7g pro.

NEW ENGLAND PUMPKIN-WALNUT BREAD

Pumpkin bread is for chilly mornings when you long for some homestyle New England food. I like to enjoy slices with a warm and soothing beverage.
—Kimberly Forni, Laconia, NH

Prep: 25 min. • **Bake:** 1 hour + cooling
Makes: 2 loaves (16 pieces each)

- ½ cup old-fashioned oats
- ¼ tsp. sugar
- ⅛ tsp. ground cinnamon

BREAD
- 1 can (15 oz.) solid-pack pumpkin
- 4 large eggs, room temperature
- ¾ cup canola oil
- ⅔ cup water
- 2 cups sugar
- 1 cup honey
- 1½ tsp. vanilla extract
- 3½ cups all-purpose flour
- 2 tsp. baking soda
- 1½ tsp. salt
- 1½ tsp. ground cinnamon
- 1 tsp. ground nutmeg
- ½ tsp. ground cloves
- ½ tsp. ground ginger
- 1 cup coarsely chopped walnuts, toasted

1. Preheat oven to 350°. In a small skillet, combine oats, sugar and cinnamon; cook and stir over medium heat 4-6 minutes or until oats are toasted. Remove from heat.
2. For bread, in a large bowl, beat pumpkin, eggs, oil, water, sugar, honey and vanilla until well blended. In another bowl, whisk flour, baking soda, salt and spices; gradually beat into pumpkin mixture. Fold in walnuts.
3. Transfer to 2 greased 9x5-in. loaf pans. Sprinkle tops with oat mixture.
4. Bake 60-70 minutes or until a toothpick inserted in center comes out clean. Cool in pan 10 minutes before removing to a wire rack to cool.
Note: To toast nuts, bake in a shallow pan in a 350° oven for 5-10 minutes or cook in a skillet over low heat until lightly browned, stirring occasionally.
1 piece: 220 cal., 9g fat (1g sat. fat), 23mg chol., 200mg sod., 34g carb. (22g sugars, 1g fiber), 3g pro.

HEAVENLY
CHEESE DANISH

SOUR CREAM & CHEDDAR BISCUITS

Here's my go-to recipe for biscuits. Brushing them with the garlic-butter topping before baking seals the deal!
—Amy Martin, Vancouver, WA

Prep: 25 min. • **Bake:** 15 min.
Makes: 1½ dozen

2½ cups all-purpose flour
3 tsp. baking powder
2 tsp. sugar
1 tsp. garlic powder
½ tsp. cream of tartar
¼ tsp. salt
¼ tsp. cayenne pepper
½ cup cold butter, cubed
1½ cups shredded cheddar cheese
¾ cup 2% milk
½ cup sour cream
TOPPING
6 Tbsp. butter, melted
1½ tsp. garlic powder
1 tsp. minced fresh parsley

1. Preheat oven to 450°. In a large bowl, whisk the first 7 ingredients. Cut in cold butter until mixture resembles coarse crumbs; stir in cheese. Add milk and sour cream; stir just until moistened.
2. Drop by ¼ cupfuls 2 in. apart onto greased baking sheets. Mix the topping ingredients; brush over tops. Bake 12-15 minutes or until light brown. Serve warm.
1 biscuit: 206 cal., 14g fat (8g sat. fat), 36mg chol., 256mg sod., 15g carb. (2g sugars, 1g fiber), 5g pro.

VANILLA-GLAZED GINGER SCONES

Gingerbread is a flavor that works with all sorts of delicious holiday baked goods. To glaze these ginger scones, just dip a fork or spoon into the glaze mixture and then drizzle over the tops.
—Colleen Delawder, Herndon, VA

Prep: 25 min. • **Bake:** 15 min.
Makes: 12 servings

2 cups all-purpose flour
¼ cup packed light brown sugar
2½ tsp. baking powder
1½ tsp. ground cinnamon
1 tsp. ground ginger
¼ tsp. salt
6 Tbsp. cold butter
¾ cup heavy whipping cream
1 large egg, room temperature
¼ cup molasses
1 Tbsp. maple syrup

GLAZE
1 cup confectioners' sugar
¼ cup heavy whipping cream
1 tsp. vanilla extract
Dash salt
¼ cup finely chopped crystallized ginger

1. Preheat oven to 400°. In a large bowl, whisk the first 6 ingredients. Cut in butter until mixture resembles coarse crumbs. In another bowl, whisk cream, egg, molasses and syrup until blended; stir into crumb mixture just until moistened.
2. Drop the dough by ¼ cupfuls onto a parchment-lined baking sheet. Bake until golden brown, 12-15 minutes. In a small bowl, combine confectioners' sugar, cream, vanilla and salt; stir until smooth. Drizzle over scones; sprinkle with ginger. Serve warm.
1 scone: 299 cal., 14g fat (8g sat. fat), 53mg chol., 226mg sod., 42g carb. (23g sugars, 1g fiber), 3g pro.

VANILLA-GLAZED GINGER SCONES

HONEY
BEET BREAD

HONEY BEET BREAD

If you have any of this colorful bread left over from dinner, you'll find it makes great sandwiches, too.
—Nancy Zimmerman,
Cape May Court House, NJ

Prep: 30 min. + rising • **Bake:** 30 min.
Makes: 2 loaves (16 pieces each)

- 2   pkg. (¼ oz. each) active dry yeast
- 1½ cups warm water (110° to 115°)
- 2   Tbsp. honey
- 1½ cups grated uncooked fresh beets, squeezed dry
- 1   cup warm 2% milk (110° to 115°)
- 2   Tbsp. butter, softened
- 2½ tsp. salt
- 6¼ to 6¾ cups all-purpose flour
- 1   large egg white, lightly beaten
      Toasted sesame seeds
      Optional: Honey and butter

1. In a large bowl, dissolve yeast in warm water. Add honey; let stand for 5 minutes. Add the beets, milk, butter, salt and 3 cups flour. Beat until smooth. Stir in enough remaining flour to form a soft dough.
2. Turn onto a floured surface; knead until smooth and elastic, 6-8 minutes. Place in a greased bowl, turning once to grease top. Cover; let rise in a warm place until doubled, about 50 minutes.

3. Punch dough down. Turn onto a lightly floured surface; divide dough in half. Shape into 2 loaves. Place in 2 greased 9x5-in. loaf pans. Cover and let rise until doubled, about 40 minutes.
4. Brush loaves with egg white; sprinkle with sesame seeds. Bake at 350° until top begins to brown, 30-35 minutes. Remove from pans to wire racks to cool. If desired, serve with honey and butter.
1 piece: 108 cal., 1g fat (1g sat. fat), 3mg chol., 203mg sod., 21g carb. (2g sugars, 1g fiber), 3g pro.

> "This unusual yeast bread is from one of our most prolific contributors, so I knew it had to be good! If you have a juicer, this is great way to use up your beet pulp, rather than grating the beets as Nancy does in her recipe."
>
> —CHRISTINE RUKAVENA, EDITOR

SOFT BUTTERMILK DINNER ROLLS

Warm, buttery dinner rolls are absolutely irresistible. I save time and use a stand mixer to make my dough.
—Jennifer Patterson, Shoshone, ID

Prep: 40 min. + rising
Bake: 20 min. + cooling • **Makes:** 20 servings

- 1   pkg. (¼ oz.) active dry yeast
- ¼   cup warm water (110° to 115°)
- 1   cup plus 2 Tbsp. warm buttermilk (110° to 115°), divided
- ½   cup plus 1 tsp. softened butter, divided
- 1   large egg, room temperature
- ⅓   cup sugar
- 1   tsp. salt
- 4   cups bread flour

1. Dissolve yeast in warm water until foamy. In a large bowl, combine 1 cup buttermilk, ½ cup butter, egg, sugar, salt and yeast mixture, then add 3 cups flour; beat on medium speed until smooth, 1 minute. Add remaining flour, ¼ cup at a time, to form a soft dough.
2. Turn dough onto a lightly floured surface; knead until smooth and elastic, 6-8 minutes. Place in a greased bowl, turning once to grease the top. Cover and let rise in a warm place until doubled, about 1 hour.
3. Punch down dough. Turn onto a lightly floured surface; divide and shape into 20 balls. Place in a greased 13x9-in. pan. Cover with a kitchen towel; let rise in a warm place until almost doubled, about 45 minutes.
4. Preheat oven to 350°. Brush rolls lightly with remaining buttermilk and butter. Bake until golden brown, 20-25 minutes. Cool in pan 20 minutes. Remove to a wire rack; serve rolls warm.
Note: To substitute for 1 cup of buttermilk, use 1 Tbsp. white vinegar or lemon juice plus enough milk to measure 1 cup. Stir, then let stand 5 min. Or, use 1 cup plain yogurt or 1¾ tsp. cream of tartar plus 1 cup milk.
1 roll: 165 cal., 6g fat (3g sat. fat), 23mg chol., 187mg sod., 24g carb. (4g sugars, 1g fiber), 4g pro.

CRANBERRY ORANGE ALMOND QUICK BREAD

The beauty of this bread is that you can customize it to your family's specific tastes. Try dried apricots and pecans, or dried blueberries and hazelnuts.
—*Taste of Home* Test Kitchen

- -

Prep: 15 min. • **Bake:** 40 min. + cooling
Makes: 1 loaf (12 pieces)

- 3 cups all-purpose flour
- 3 Tbsp. sugar
- 1 Tbsp. baking powder
- ½ tsp. salt
- 1 cup dried cranberries
- ½ cup sliced almonds, toasted
- 1 large egg, room temperature
- 1 cup fat-free milk
- ⅓ cup canola oil
- ¾ tsp. grated orange zest
- ¾ tsp. almond extract

1. Preheat oven to 350°. In a large bowl, whisk together first 4 ingredients; stir in cranberries and almonds. In another bowl, whisk together egg, milk, oil, zest and extract. Add to flour mixture; stir just until moistened.

2. Transfer to a 9x5-in. loaf pan coated with cooking spray. Bake until a toothpick inserted in center of loaf comes out clean, 40-50 minutes. Cool in pan 10 minutes before removing to a wire rack to cool.

1 piece: 258 cal., 9g fat (1g sat. fat), 16mg chol., 234mg sod., 40g carb. (14g sugars, 2g fiber), 5g pro.

CARAWAY RYE DINNER ROLLS

CARAWAY RYE DINNER ROLLS

Caraway seeds give these rye dinner rolls a delicate nutty flavor. Denser than most, these onion-infused buns are ideal for dipping in hearty stews.
—Deborah Maki, Kamloops, BC

- -

Prep: 35 min. + rising • **Bake:** 15 min.
Makes: 1½ dozen

- 1¼ cups rye flour
- ½ cup wheat germ
- 2 Tbsp. caraway seeds
- 1 pkg. (¼ oz.) active dry yeast
- 1 tsp. salt
- 3 cups all-purpose flour
- 1 cup 2% milk
- ½ cup water
- 3 Tbsp. butter
- 2 Tbsp. honey
- ⅓ cup finely chopped onion

EGG WASH
- 1 large egg
- 2 tsp. water

1. In a large bowl, mix the first 5 ingredients and 1 cup all-purpose flour. In a small saucepan, heat milk, water, butter and honey to 120°-130°. Add to dry ingredients; beat on medium speed 3 minutes. Stir in onion and enough remaining all-purpose flour to form a soft dough (dough will be sticky).

2. Turn dough onto a floured surface; knead until smooth and elastic, 6-8 minutes. Place in a greased bowl, turning once to grease the top. Cover; let rise in a warm place until doubled, about 1 hour.

3. Punch down dough. Turn onto a lightly floured surface; divide and shape into 18 balls. Place 2 in. apart on greased baking sheets. Cover with a kitchen towel; let rise in a warm place until almost doubled, about 45 minutes. Preheat oven to 400°.

4. For egg wash, in a small bowl, whisk egg and water; brush over rolls. Bake until lightly browned, 11-14 minutes. Remove to wire racks to cool.

1 roll: 152 cal., 3g fat (2g sat. fat), 17mg chol., 158mg sod., 26g carb. (3g sugars, 2g fiber), 5g pro.

JAVA MUFFINS

I look to these muffins to get me going in the morning. They're especially satisfying with a cup of coffee.
—Zainab Ahmed, Mountlake Terrace, WA

Takes: 30 min. • **Makes:** 1 dozen

- ¼ cup butter, softened
- 1 cup packed brown sugar
- 2 large eggs, room temperature
- ¼ cup unsweetened applesauce
- ½ cup buttermilk
- ½ cup strong brewed coffee
- 1 Tbsp. instant coffee granules
- ½ tsp. vanilla extract
- 1 cup all-purpose flour
- ¾ cup whole wheat flour
- 1½ tsp. baking powder
- ½ tsp. baking soda
- ½ tsp. ground cinnamon
- ¼ tsp. salt
- ½ cup finely chopped pecans, divided

1. Preheat oven to 375°. In a large bowl, beat butter and brown sugar until crumbly, about 2 minutes. Add the eggs; mix well. Beat in applesauce. In a small bowl, whisk buttermilk, coffee, coffee granules and vanilla until granules are dissolved; gradually add to butter mixture.

2. In another bowl, whisk flours, baking powder, baking soda, cinnamon and salt. Add to butter mixture; stir just until moistened. Fold in ¼ cup pecans.

3. Coat 12 muffin cups with cooking spray or use paper liners; fill three-fourths full. Sprinkle with the remaining pecans. Bake 15-20 minutes or until a toothpick inserted in center comes out clean. Cool 5 minutes before removing from pan to a wire rack. Serve warm.

1 muffin: 220 cal., 9g fat (3g sat. fat), 46mg chol., 209mg sod., 33g carb. (19g sugars, 2g fiber), 4g pro. **Diabetic exchanges:** 2 starch, 1½ fat.

GARLIC-DILL SODA BREAD

It's amazing how bread can be made in a slow cooker, which is why this recipe is so awesome—who knew it could be so simple! Let the inviting aroma of dill and cheese fill your kitchen.
—Melissa Hansen, Ellison Bay, WI

Prep: 15 min. • **Cook:** 1½ hours
Makes: 1 loaf (12 pieces)

- 4 cups all-purpose flour
- 2 Tbsp. dried parsley flakes
- 1 Tbsp. dried minced onion
- 2 tsp. garlic powder
- 1½ tsp. dill weed
- 1 tsp. salt
- 1 tsp. baking soda
- 1 tsp. ground mustard
- 1¾ cups buttermilk
- 1 cup shredded sharp cheddar cheese

1. In a large bowl, whisk first 8 ingredients. Add buttermilk and cheese; stir just until moistened. Turn onto a lightly floured surface; knead gently 6-8 times or just until dough comes together. Shape dough into a 6-in. round loaf. Using a sharp knife, score surface with 1-in.-deep cuts in a crisscross pattern. Place in a greased 5-qt. slow cooker.

2. Cook, covered, on high 1½-2 hours or until a thermometer reads 190°-200°.

3. Preheat broiler. Remove bread; place on a baking sheet. Broil 6-8 in. from heat 2-3 minutes or until golden brown. Remove to a wire rack to cool completely.

1 piece: 209 cal., 4g fat (2g sat. fat), 11mg chol., 434mg sod., 35g carb. (2g sugars, 1g fiber), 8g pro.

JAVA MUFFINS

CHALLAH

CHALLAH

Eggs lend to the richness of this traditional challah bread. The attractive golden color and delicious flavor make it hard to resist.
—*Taste of Home* Test Kitchen

Prep: 30 min. + rising • **Bake:** 30 min.
Makes: 2 loaves (16 pieces each)

- 2 pkg. (¼ oz. each) active dry yeast
- 1 cup warm water (110° to 115°)
- ½ cup canola oil
- ⅓ cup sugar
- 1 Tbsp. salt
- 4 large eggs, room temperature
- 6 to 6½ cups all-purpose flour

TOPPING
- 1 large egg
- 1 tsp. cold water
- 1 Tbsp. sesame or poppy seeds, optional

1. In a large bowl, dissolve yeast in warm water. Add oil, sugar, salt, eggs and 4 cups flour. Beat until smooth. Stir in enough remaining flour to form a firm dough. Turn onto a floured surface; knead until smooth and elastic, 6-8 minutes. Place in a greased bowl, turning once to grease top. Cover and let rise in a warm place until doubled, about 1 hour.
2. Punch dough down. Turn onto a lightly floured surface; divide in half. Divide each portion into thirds. Shape each piece into a 15-in. rope.
3. Place 3 ropes on a greased baking sheet and braid; pinch ends to seal and tuck under. Repeat with remaining dough. Cover and let rise until doubled, about 1 hour.
4. Preheat oven to 350°. Beat egg and cold water; brush over the braids. Sprinkle with sesame or poppy seeds if desired. Bake until golden brown, 30-40 minutes. Remove to wire racks to cool.
1 piece: 139 cal., 5g fat (1g sat. fat), 29mg chol., 233mg sod., 20g carb. (2g sugars, 1g fiber), 4g pro.

DID YOU KNOW?
Traditional challah calls for several eggs to give it a rich color and flavor. Some recipes also include raisins or honey.

CRANBERRY CHIP MONKEY BREAD

CRANBERRY CHIP MONKEY BREAD

Monkey bread is no stranger at our house, but I wanted a holiday version. This one with cranberries and eggnog is a breakfast treat or knockout dessert.
—Katherine Wollgast, Troy, MO

Prep: 15 min. • **Bake:** 40 min.
Makes: 16 servings

- ¾ cup sugar, divided
- 4 tsp. ground cinnamon
- 4 tubes (7½ oz. each) refrigerated buttermilk biscuits
- ½ cup white baking chips
- ½ cup dried cranberries
- ¼ cup chopped walnuts or pecans
- ¼ cup butter, cubed
- ½ cup eggnog

GLAZE
- 1 cup confectioners' sugar
- ½ tsp. rum or vanilla extract
- 2 to 3 Tbsp. eggnog
  Optional toppings: Additional dried cranberries, white baking chips and chopped nuts

1. Preheat oven to 350°. In a large bowl, mix ½ cup sugar and cinnamon. Cut each biscuit into quarters; add to sugar mixture and toss to coat. Arrange half of the biscuits in a greased 10-in. tube pan. Sprinkle with baking chips, cranberries and walnuts. Top with remaining biscuits.
2. In a microwave, melt butter. Stir in eggnog and remaining sugar until blended; pour over the biscuits.
3. Bake 40-45 minutes or until golden brown. Cool in pan 5 minutes before inverting onto a serving plate.
4. For the glaze, in a small bowl, mix the confectioners' sugar, extract and enough eggnog to reach a drizzling consistency. Spoon over warm bread. Sprinkle with toppings as desired.
1 serving: 310 cal., 13g fat (5g sat. fat), 15mg chol., 596mg sod., 47g carb. (26g sugars, 1g fiber), 4g pro.

PEANUT BUTTER & JELLY DOUGHNUTS

A classic jelly doughnut gets a fun twist with peanut butter glaze. No one will be able to resist these fluffy peanut butter and jelly doughnuts that instantly take you back to your childhood.
—*Taste of Home* Test Kitchen

- -

Prep: 25 min. + rising • **Cook:** 30 min.
Makes: 15 doughnuts

1   pkg. (¼ oz.) active dry yeast
1   cup warm 2% milk (110° to 115°)
3½ cups all-purpose flour, divided
1   large egg, room temperature
2   large egg yolks, room temperature
¼   cup sugar
½   tsp. salt
¼   cup butter, melted
     Oil for deep-fat frying
½   cup grape or strawberry jelly
GLAZE
3   Tbsp. creamy peanut butter
1½ cups confectioners' sugar
⅛   tsp. salt
7   to 8 Tbsp. heavy whipping cream

1. In a large bowl, dissolve yeast in warm milk. Add 1 cup flour; mix well. Let stand in a warm place for 30 minutes. Add the egg, egg yolks, sugar and salt; mix well. Beat in butter and remaining flour. Do not knead. Cover and let rise in a warm place until doubled, about 45 minutes.
2. Punch dough down. On a lightly floured surface, roll out to ½-in. thickness. Cut with a 2½-in. biscuit cutter. Place on lightly greased baking sheets. Cover and let rise until nearly doubled, about 35 minutes.
3. In a deep-fat fryer or electric skillet, heat oil to 375°. Fry doughnuts, a few at a time, for 1½-2 minutes on each side or until browned. Drain on paper towels.
4. Cool for 2-3 minutes; cut a small slit with a sharp knife on 1 side of each doughnut. Cut a small hole in the corner of a pastry bag; insert a very small round tip. Fill bag with jelly. Fill each doughnut with about 1 tsp. jelly.
5. In a small bowl, beat the peanut butter, confectioners' sugar and salt until smooth. Gradually beat in enough whipping cream to reach desired glaze consistency. Dip doughnuts in frosting.

1 doughnut: 343 cal., 15g fat (4g sat. fat), 47mg chol., 199mg sod., 47g carb. (23g sugars, 1g fiber), 5g pro.

SOUR CREAM CUT-OUT BISCUITS

After trying different ways to make biscuits without being completely satisfied, I tried incorporating sour cream. Success! Split while warm, butter, and enjoy.
—Lorraine Caland, Shuniah, ON

- -

Takes: 30 min. • **Makes:** 10 biscuits

2   cups all-purpose flour
2   Tbsp. sugar
3   tsp. baking powder
½   tsp. salt
½   tsp. baking soda
1   cup sour cream
1   Tbsp. butter, melted

1. Preheat oven to 425°. In a large bowl, whisk the flour, sugar, baking powder, salt and baking soda. Stir in sour cream just until moistened.
2. Turn onto a lightly floured surface; knead gently 8-10 times. Pat or roll dough to ½-in. thickness; cut with a floured 2¼-in. biscuit cutter. Place 1 in. apart on an ungreased baking sheet. Bake until golden brown, 10-12 minutes. Brush biscuits with butter; serve warm.

1 biscuit: 159 cal., 6g fat (4g sat. fat), 9mg chol., 343mg sod., 22g carb. (3g sugars, 1g fiber), 3g pro.

PEANUT BUTTER & JELLY DOUGHNUTS

PULL-APART BACON BREAD

I stumbled across this recipe while looking for something different to take to a brunch. Boy, am I glad I did! Everyone asked for the recipe and was surprised it only called for five ingredients. It's the perfect treat to bake for an informal get-together.
—Traci Collins, Cheyenne, WY

- -

Prep: 20 min. + rising • **Bake:** 55 min.
Makes: 16 servings

- 12 bacon strips, diced
- 1 loaf (1 lb.) frozen bread dough, thawed
- 2 Tbsp. olive oil, divided
- 1 cup shredded part-skim mozzarella cheese
- 1 envelope (1 oz.) ranch salad dressing mix

1. In a large skillet, cook bacon over medium heat for 5 minutes or until partially cooked; drain on paper towels. Roll out dough to ½-in. thickness; brush with 1 Tbsp. of oil. Cut into 1-in. pieces; place in a large bowl. Add the bacon, cheese, dressing mix and remaining oil; toss to coat.

2. Arrange pieces in a 9x5-in. oval on a parchment-lined baking sheet, layering as needed. Cover and let rise in a warm place for 30 minutes or until doubled.

3. Bake at 350° for 40 minutes. Cover with aluminum foil; bake 15 minutes longer or until golden brown.

1 serving: 149 cal., 6g fat (2g sat. fat), 8mg chol., 621mg sod., 17g carb. (1g sugars, 1g fiber), 6g pro.

"I love this no-fuss bread. It's great with chili or with a casserole or simply set out on an appetizer buffet. It's a nice addition for a brunch with friends, too."

—MARK HAGEN, EXECUTIVE EDITOR

PULL-APART BACON BREAD

CREOLE CORNBREAD

Cornbread is a staple of Cajun and Creole cuisine. This version is an old favorite, and it really tastes wonderful. I found the recipe in the bottom of my recipe drawer.
—Enid Hebert, Lafayette, LA

Prep: 15 min. • **Bake:** 45 min.
Makes: 12 servings

- 2 cups cooked rice
- 1 cup yellow cornmeal
- ½ cup chopped onion
- 1 to 2 Tbsp. seeded chopped jalapeno pepper
- 1 tsp. salt
- ½ tsp. baking soda
- 2 large eggs, room temperature
- 1 cup 2% milk
- ¼ cup canola oil
- 1 can (16½ oz.) cream-style corn
- 3 cups shredded cheddar cheese
  Additional cornmeal

1. In a large bowl, combine rice, cornmeal, onion, peppers, salt and baking soda.
2. In another bowl, beat eggs, milk and oil. Add corn; mix well. Stir into rice mixture until blended. Fold in cheese. Sprinkle a well-greased 10-in. ovenproof skillet with cornmeal. Pour batter into skillet.
3. Bake at 350° for 45-50 minutes or until the bread tests done. Cut into wedges and serve warm.
Note: Wear disposable gloves when cutting hot peppers; the oils can burn skin. Avoid touching your face.
1 piece: 272 cal., 14g fat (7g sat. fat), 68mg chol., 551mg sod., 26g carb. (3g sugars, 2g fiber), 10g pro.

SOFT BEER PRETZEL NUGGETS

What goes together better than beer and pretzels? Not much that I can think of. That's why I put them together into one recipe. I'm always looking for new ways to combine fun flavors. I love the way this recipe turned out!
—Alyssa Wilhite, Whitehouse, TX

Prep: 1 hour + rising • **Bake:** 10 min./batch
Makes: 8 dozen

- 1 bottle (12 oz.) amber beer or nonalcoholic beer
- 1 pkg. (¼ oz.) active dry yeast
- 2 Tbsp. unsalted butter, melted
- 2 Tbsp. sugar
- 1½ tsp. salt
- 4 to 4½ cups all-purpose flour
- 10 cups water
- ⅔ cup baking soda
TOPPING
- 1 large egg yolk
- 1 Tbsp. water
  Coarse salt, optional

1. In a small saucepan, heat beer to 110°-115°; remove from heat. Stir in yeast until dissolved. In a large bowl, combine butter, sugar, salt, yeast mixture and 3 cups flour; beat on medium speed until smooth.

Stir in enough remaining flour to form a soft dough (dough will be sticky).
2. Turn dough onto a floured surface; knead until smooth and elastic, 6-8 minutes. Place in a greased bowl, turning once to grease the top. Cover and let rise in a warm place until doubled, about 1 hour.
3. Preheat oven to 425°. Punch dough down. Turn onto a lightly floured surface; divide and shape into 8 balls. Roll each into a 12-in. rope. Cut each rope into 1-in. pieces.
4. In a Dutch oven, bring 10 cups water and baking soda to a boil. Drop the nuggets, 12 at a time, into boiling water. Cook for 30 seconds. Remove with a slotted spoon; drain well on paper towels.
5. Place on greased baking sheets. In a small bowl, whisk the egg yolk and 1 Tbsp. water; brush over pretzels. Sprinkle with coarse salt if desired. Bake 10-12 minutes or until golden brown. Remove from baking pans to a wire rack to cool.

Freeze option: Freeze cooled pretzel nuggets in airtight containers. To use, thaw at room temperature or, if desired, microwave on high 20-30 seconds or until heated through.
6 pretzel nuggets: 144 cal., 2g fat (1g sat. fat), 8mg chol., 302mg sod., 26g carb. (2g sugars, 1g fiber), 4g pro.

SOFT BEER PRETZEL NUGGETS

GIANT
CINNAMON
ROLL

ONE-BOWL CHOCOLATE CHIP BREAD

My family of chocoholics hops out of bed on Valentine's Day because they know I'm baking this indulgent quick bread for breakfast. But don't wait for a special occasion to enjoy it. It hits the spot any time of year.
—Angela Lively, Conroe, TX

Prep: 20 min. • **Bake:** 65 minutes
Makes: 1 loaf (16 pieces)

- 3 large eggs, room temperature
- 1 cup sugar
- 2 cups sour cream
- 3 cups self-rising flour
- 2 cups semisweet chocolate chips

1. Preheat oven to 350°. Beat eggs, sugar and sour cream until well blended. Gradually stir in flour. Fold in chocolate chips. Transfer to a greased 9x5-in. loaf pan.
2. Bake until a toothpick comes out clean, 65-75 minutes. Cool in pan 5 minutes before removing to a wire rack to cool.
1 piece: 306 cal., 13g fat (8g sat. fat), 42mg chol., 305mg sod., 44g carb. (25g sugars, 2g fiber), 5g pro.

GIANT CINNAMON ROLL

This must-try cinnamon roll is all about the pillowy texture, the sweet spices and the homemade caramel drizzle.
—Leah Rekau, Milwaukee, WI

Prep: 30 min. + rising • **Bake:** 30 min.
Makes: 12 servings

- 1 pkg. (¼ oz.) active dry yeast
- ½ cup warm water (110° to 115°)
- ½ cup heavy whipping cream, warmed (110° to 115°)
- ½ cup sugar
- ½ tsp. sea salt
- 3 to 4 cups all-purpose flour
- 1 large egg, room temperature, beaten
- 3 Tbsp. butter, melted

FILLING
- ¼ cup butter, softened
- ¼ cup sugar
- 1 Tbsp. ground cinnamon

TOPPING
- 1 cup sugar
- 2 Tbsp. water
- 6 Tbsp. butter
- ½ cup heavy whipping cream
- 1 tsp. sea salt

1. Dissolve the yeast in warm water and whipping cream until foamy. In another bowl, combine sugar and salt; add 3 cups flour, yeast mixture, egg and melted butter. Stir until moistened. Add enough remaining flour to form a soft dough.
2. Turn onto a lightly floured surface; knead until smooth and elastic, 3-4 minutes. Place in a greased bowl, turning once to grease top. Cover; let rise in a warm place until doubled, about 30 minutes.
3. Punch down dough. Turn onto a lightly floured surface; roll into a 15x12-in. rectangle. Spread softened butter over dough. Sprinkle with sugar and cinnamon. Using a pizza cutter, cut into 2-in.-wide strips. Roll up 1 strip and place in the center of a greased 9-in. deep-dish pie plate; wrap remaining strips around center to form 1 giant roll. Cover with greased foil; let rise until doubled, about 1 hour. Meanwhile, preheat oven to 350°.
4. Bake until golden brown, 30-40 minutes. If dough starts browning too quickly, cover lightly with foil. Cool on a wire rack.
5. To prepare topping, combine sugar and water in a small saucepan; cook over medium heat until it turns light amber. Add butter, stirring vigorously. Remove from heat; add cream while continuing to stir vigorously. Cool slightly. Pour ¾ cup sauce over warm roll; sprinkle with the salt. Serve with the remaining sauce.
1 piece: 416 cal., 21g fat (13g sat. fat), 76mg chol., 354mg sod., 55g carb. (30g sugars, 1g fiber), 5g pro.

BEST EVER POTATO
SOUP PAGE 81

Soups, Salads & Sandwiches

Looking for a no-fuss meal? Turn to the popular pairing of soup and salad! Toss in a sammie for extra flair and you have a comforting lineup no one can resist.

VEGETARIAN SPLIT PEA SOUP

Even the pickiest soup lover will request this version time and again. Well-seasoned and thick, it's a nutritional powerhouse packed with fiber and protein. It's wonderful served with a slice of crusty French bread.
—Michele Doucette, Stephenville, NL

Prep: 15 min. • **Cook:** 1½ hours
Makes: 7 servings

- 6 cups vegetable broth
- 2 cups dried green split peas, rinsed
- 1 medium onion, chopped
- 1 cup chopped carrots
- 2 celery ribs with leaves, chopped
- 2 garlic cloves, minced
- ½ tsp. dried marjoram
- ½ tsp. dried basil
- ¼ tsp. ground cumin
- ½ tsp. salt
- ¼ tsp. pepper
  Optional: Shredded carrots and sliced green onions

1. In a large saucepan, combine the first 9 ingredients; bring to a boil. Reduce heat; cover and simmer until peas are tender, about 1 hour, stirring occasionally.
2. Add salt and pepper; simmer 10 minutes longer. Remove soup from heat; cool slightly. Process in batches in a blender or food processor until smooth; return to pan and heat through. If desired, garnish with carrots and green onions.
1 cup: 227 cal., 1g fat (0 sat. fat), 0 chol., 771mg sod., 42g carb. (7g sugars, 15g fiber), 14g pro.

BBQ BACON PULLED CHICKEN SANDWICHES

This simple recipe tastes amazing. We prefer putting mayo on the bun and adding cheddar or Muenster cheese, lettuce, tomato and onion. Several of us put ranch dressing on our sandwiches, too.
—Jennifer Darling, Ventura, CA

Prep: 20 min. • **Cook:** 3 hours
Makes: 12 servings

- 1 bottle (18 oz.) barbecue sauce
- ½ cup amber beer or root beer
- ¼ cup cider vinegar
- 2 green onions, chopped
- 2 Tbsp. dried minced onion
- 2 Tbsp. Dijon mustard
- 2 Tbsp. Worcestershire sauce
- 4 garlic cloves, minced
- 1 Tbsp. dried parsley flakes
- 2 lbs. boneless skinless chicken breasts
- 12 hamburger buns, split and toasted
- 24 cooked bacon strips
- 12 lettuce leaves

1. In a bowl, combine the first 9 ingredients. Place chicken in a greased 4- or 5-qt. slow cooker; pour sauce over top. Cook, covered, on low 3-4 hours or until tender.
2. Remove chicken; shred with 2 forks. Return chicken to slow cooker; heat through. Serve on buns with bacon and lettuce.
Freeze option: Freeze cooled, cooked chicken mixture in freezer containers. To use, partially thaw in refrigerator overnight. Heat through in a saucepan, stirring occasionally and adding a little water if necessary.
1 sandwich: 401 cal., 12g fat (4g sat. fat), 65mg chol., 1175mg sod., 43g carb. (19g sugars, 2g fiber), 28g pro.

BBQ BACON PULLED CHICKEN SANDWICHES

BEST EVER POTATO SOUP

CURRIED EGG SALAD

A curry kick gives this egg salad big appeal. We love it when the weather gets warm.
—Joyce McDowell, West Union, OH

- -

Takes: 15 min. • **Makes:** 6 sandwiches

- ½ cup mayonnaise
- ½ tsp. ground curry
- ½ tsp. honey
  Dash ground ginger
- 6 hard-boiled large eggs, coarsely chopped
- 3 green onions, sliced
- 6 slices whole wheat bread
  Optional: Tomato slices and cracked pepper

Mix the first 4 ingredients; stir in eggs and green onions. Spread on bread. If desired, top with tomato and sprinkle with pepper.
1 open-faced sandwich: 273 cal., 20g fat (4g sat. fat), 188mg chol., 284mg sod., 14g carb. (2g sugars, 2g fiber), 10g pro.
Health tip: Switch to low-fat mayonnaise to save 100 calories and more than 10 grams of fat per serving.

BEST EVER POTATO SOUP

You'll be surprised at the taste of this rich, cheesy concoction—it's not your typical potato soup. I came up with the recipe after enjoying baked potato soup at one of our favorite restaurants. I added bacon, and we think that makes it even better.
—Coleen Morrissey, Sweet Valley, PA

- -

Takes: 30 min. • **Makes:** 8 servings (2 qt.)

- 6 bacon strips, diced
- 3 cups cubed peeled potatoes
- 1 small carrot, grated
- ½ cup chopped onion
- 1 Tbsp. dried parsley flakes
- ½ tsp. salt
- ½ tsp. pepper
- ½ tsp. celery seed
- 1 can (14½ oz.) chicken broth
- 3 Tbsp. all-purpose flour
- 3 cups 2% milk
- 8 oz. Velveeta, cubed
- 2 green onions, thinly sliced, optional

1. In a large saucepan, cook bacon over medium heat until crisp, stirring occasionally; drain drippings. Add vegetables, seasonings and broth; bring to a boil. Reduce heat; simmer, covered, until potatoes are tender, 10-15 minutes.
2. Mix flour and milk until smooth; stir into soup. Bring to a boil, stirring constantly; cook and stir until soup is thickened, about 2 minutes. Stir in cheese until melted. If desired, serve with green onions.
1 cup: 250 cal., 13g fat (7g sat. fat), 35mg chol., 823mg sod., 22g carb. (8g sugars, 2g fiber), 12g pro.

TEST KITCHEN TIP

Before you peel potatoes, scrub them with a vegetable brush under cold water. Remove any eyes or sprouts. If you have a lot of potatoes, place them in cold water after peeling to prevent them from discoloring.

FESTIVE TOSSED SALAD

I owe my discovery of this salad to my sister-in-law, a Louisiana native and a fabulous cook. It's always a hit.
—Ruby Williams, Bogalusa, LA

- -

Takes: 15 min. • **Makes:** 2 servings

- 2   Tbsp. canola oil
- 1   Tbsp. lemon juice
- 1   Tbsp. honey
- ¼   tsp. sugar
- ¼   tsp. garlic powder
-     Dash salt
- 2   to 3 cups torn salad greens
- 1   celery rib, sliced
- 1   medium carrot, shredded
- 2   green onions, sliced
- ½   cup mandarin oranges
- 1   Tbsp. sliced almonds, toasted

In a small bowl, whisk the first 6 ingredients; set aside. In a salad bowl, toss the greens, celery, carrot, onions and oranges. Add dressing and toss to coat; sprinkle with almonds. Serve immediately.
1½ cups: 243 cal., 15g fat (2g sat. fat), 0 chol., 122mg sod., 28g carb. (22g sugars, 4g fiber), 3g pro.

> "I like to double or triple this salad for special nights with guest. It is so refreshing and so easy. I just love how the honey, oranges and almonds taste together."

—MARK HAGEN, EXECUTIVE EDITOR

MEXICAN CHICKEN CORN CHOWDER

MEXICAN CHICKEN CORN CHOWDER

I like to make this smooth, creamy soup when company comes to visit. Its zippy flavor is full of southwestern flair. My family enjoys dipping slices of homemade bread in this chowder to soak up every bite!
—Susan Garoutte, Georgetown, TX

- -

Takes: 30 min. • **Makes:** 8 servings (2 qt.)

- 1½ lbs. boneless skinless chicken breasts, cut into 1-in. pieces
- ½   cup chopped onion
- 3   Tbsp. butter
- 1   to 2 garlic cloves, minced
- 1   cup hot water
- 2   tsp. chicken bouillon granules
- ½   to 1 tsp. ground cumin
- 2   cups half-and-half cream
- 2   cups shredded Monterey Jack cheese
- 1   can (14¾ oz.) cream-style corn
- 1   can (4 oz.) chopped green chiles, undrained
- ¼   to 1 tsp. hot pepper sauce
- 1   medium tomato, chopped
-     Optional: Minced fresh cilantro and fried tortilla strips

1. In a Dutch oven, brown chicken and onion in butter until chicken is no longer pink. Add garlic; cook 1 minute longer. Add the water, bouillon and cumin; bring to a boil. Reduce heat; cover and simmer for 5 minutes.
2. Stir in the cream, cheese, corn, chiles and hot pepper sauce. Cook and stir over low heat until cheese is melted; add tomato. If desired, top with cilantro and tortilla strips.
1 cup: 368 cal., 21g fat (13g sat. fat), 114mg chol., 753mg sod., 14g carb. (5g sugars, 1g fiber), 28g pro.

GRILLED CHEESE, HAM & APPLE SANDWICH

In this stepped-up version of a ham and cheese sandwich, melty cheeses, crispy apples and smoky ham make for the ultimate combination.
—Josh Rink, Food Stylist

Takes: 25 min. • **Makes:** 4 servings

- 6   Tbsp. butter, softened, divided
- 8   slices sourdough bread
- 3   Tbsp. mayonnaise
- 3   Tbsp. finely shredded Manchego or Parmesan cheese
- ⅛   tsp. onion powder
- ½   cup shredded sharp white cheddar cheese
- ½   cup shredded Monterey Jack cheese
- ½   cup shredded Gruyere cheese
- 4   oz. Brie cheese with rind removed, sliced
- 12 slices deli ham
- 1   tart apple, thinly sliced

1. Spread 3 Tbsp. butter on 1 side of bread slices. Toast bread, butter side down, in a large skillet or an electric griddle over medium-low heat until golden brown, 2-3 minutes; remove. In a small bowl, mix together mayonnaise, Manchego cheese, onion powder and remaining 3 Tbsp. butter. In another bowl, combine the cheddar, Monterey Jack and Gruyere.

2. To assemble sandwiches, top toasted side of 4 bread slices with sliced Brie. Sprinkle cheddar cheese mixture evenly over Brie. Layer ham and apple slices over Brie; top with remaining bread slices, toasted side facing inward. Spread mayonnaise mixture on the outsides of each sandwich. Place in same skillet and cook until bread is golden brown and cheese is melted, 5-6 minutes on each side. Serve immediately.

1 sandwich: 725 cal., 50g fat (27g sat. fat), 141mg chol., 1415mg sod., 37g carb. (9g sugars, 2g fiber), 32g pro.

MANDARIN-BERRY STEAK SALAD

Here's a salad even meat lovers will ask for time and again. Sirloin steak, strawberries, pecans and goat cheese work extremely well together. Give it a try!
—*Taste of Home* Test Kitchen

Takes: 25 min.
Makes: 4 servings (1 cup vinaigrette)

- 3   Tbsp. olive oil
- ¼   cup cider vinegar
- ¼   cup orange juice
- 2   Tbsp. minced fresh parsley
- 2   Tbsp. honey
- 1   garlic clove, minced
- 1   tsp. chili sauce
- ½   tsp. salt
- 8   cups torn romaine
- ½   lb. cooked beef sirloin steak, sliced
- 3   cups sliced fresh strawberries
- 1   small red onion, sliced
- 1   can (11 oz.) mandarin oranges, drained
- ½   cup chopped pecans, toasted
- 2   oz. fresh goat cheese, crumbled

In a small bowl, whisk the first 8 ingredients; set aside. Divide romaine among 4 plates; top with steak, strawberries, onion, oranges, pecans and cheese. Serve with vinaigrette.

1 serving: 443 cal., 24g fat (4g sat. fat), 46mg chol., 367mg sod., 40g carb. (31g sugars, 7g fiber), 21g pro.

GRILLED CHEESE, HAM & APPLE SANDWICH

TURKEY SOUP

I like making this soup around the holidays after a big turkey dinner. It's especially good on cold winter nights when it's snowing—which happens a lot where I live!
—Carol Brethauer, Denver, CO

- -

Prep: 30 min. • **Cook:** 4 hours
Makes: 12 servings (5 qt.)

- 1 leftover turkey carcass (from a 14-lb. turkey)
- 3 qt. water
- 2 cans (14½ oz. each) reduced-sodium chicken broth
- ½ cup uncooked long grain rice
- 1 medium onion, finely chopped
- 4 celery ribs, finely chopped
- 2 medium carrots, grated
- 1 bay leaf

Dash poultry seasoning
- ½ tsp. onion powder
- ½ tsp. garlic powder
- ¼ tsp. pepper
  Salt, optional

1. In a stockpot, place turkey carcass, water and broth. Bring to a boil. Reduce heat; cover and simmer for 4-5 hours.

2. Remove carcass from stock. Remove any meat and dice. Return to stock along with rice, onion, celery, carrots, bay leaf and poultry seasoning. Add the remaining seasonings to taste. Cover and simmer over medium-low heat until the rice is cooked. Discard bay leaf.

1⅔ cups: 147 cal., 2g fat (0 sat. fat), 28mg chol., 412mg sod., 15g carb. (3g sugars, 1g fiber), 12g pro. **Diabetic exchanges:** 1 starch, 1 lean meat.

EASY GRILLED HAMBURGERS

These easy hamburgers always come together in a snap. Grill and then add your favorite toppings.
—James Schend, Deputy Editor, Culinary

- -

Prep: 20 min. • **Grill:** 15 min.
Makes: 6 servings

- 1⅓ lbs. ground beef
- ¾ tsp. salt
- ¼ tsp. pepper
- 4 hamburger buns, split and toasted
  Optional toppings: Lettuce leaves, sliced tomato, sliced onion, bacon and mayonnaise

Shape ground beef into four ¾-in.-thick patties. Just before grilling, sprinkle with salt and pepper. Grill burgers, covered, over medium heat until a thermometer reads 160°, 5-7 minutes on each side. Top bun bottoms with burgers. If desired, serve with lettuce, tomato, onion, bacon and mayonnaise.

1 burger: 265 cal., 13g fat (5g sat. fat), 62mg chol., 495mg sod., 15g carb. (2g sugars, 1g fiber), 21g pro.

Pan-Fried Burgers: In a large skillet, heat 1 Tbsp. butter or oil over medium heat. Add burgers; cook until a thermometer reads 160°, 6-8 minutes on each side.

Oven-Baked Burgers: Place patties on a lightly greased baking sheet. Bake at 350° until a thermometer reads 160°, 15-20 minutes, turning once.

Air-Fried Burgers: Place burgers in a single layer on tray in air-fryer basket. Air-fry at 350° until a thermometer reads 160°, 8-10 minutes, turning halfway through cooking.

TEST KITCHEN TIP

Keep beef in the refrigerator until you're ready to form the patties (and then again until you're ready to grill). When the fat is kept cold, it rapidly expands when it hits the heat of the grill, creating delicious flavor pockets inside the patty.

TURKEY SOUP

EASY GRILLED
HAMBURGERS

REFRESHING SHRIMP SALAD

Avocado, strawberries and shrimp are wonderful together in this filling yet light salad. Balsamic or raspberry vinaigrette dressings go well with the salad, as do any Asian-inspired dressings.
—*Taste of Home* Test Kitchen

- -

Takes: 15 min. • **Makes:** 4 servings

- 1   pkg. (5 oz.) spring mix salad greens
- 1   lb. cooked medium shrimp, peeled and deveined
- 1   large navel orange, peeled and sectioned
- 1   medium ripe avocado, peeled and chopped
- 1   cup fresh strawberries, quartered
- ½   cup thinly sliced green onions
     Salad dressing of your choice

On each of 4 serving plates, arrange the salad greens, shrimp, orange, avocado, strawberries and onions. Drizzle with the dressing.

3 cups: 239 cal., 9g fat (1g sat. fat), 172mg chol., 181mg sod., 16g carb. (7g sugars, 6g fiber), 25g pro. **Diabetic exchanges:** 3 lean meat, 1½ fat, 1 vegetable, ½ fruit.

TURKEY SANDWICH WITH RASPBERRY-MUSTARD SPREAD

TURKEY SANDWICH WITH RASPBERRY-MUSTARD SPREAD

My hearty sandwich has different yet complementary flavors and textures. It is filled with flavor and nutrients, without all the unhealthy fats, sodium and added sugar many other sandwiches have. And it's absolutely delicious!
—Sarah Savage, Buena Vista, VA

- -

Takes: 25 min. • **Makes:** 2 servings

- 1   Tbsp. honey
- 1   Tbsp. spicy brown mustard
- 1   tsp. red raspberry preserves
- ¼   tsp. mustard seed
- 1   Tbsp. olive oil
- 4   oz. fresh mushrooms, thinly sliced
- 1   cup fresh baby spinach, coarsely chopped
- 1   garlic clove, minced
- ½   tsp. chili powder
- 4   slices multigrain bread, toasted
- 6   oz. sliced cooked turkey breast
- ½   medium ripe avocado, sliced

1. Combine the honey, mustard, preserves and mustard seed; set aside. In a large skillet, heat oil over medium-high heat. Add the mushrooms; cook and stir until tender, 4-5 minutes. Add spinach, garlic and chili powder; cook and stir until spinach is wilted, 3-4 minutes.

2. Spread half of the mustard mixture over 2 slices of toast. Layer with the turkey, mushroom mixture and avocado. Spread remaining mustard mixture over remaining toast; place over top.

1 sandwich: 449 cal., 16g fat (3g sat. fat), 68mg chol., 392mg sod., 40g carb. (14g sugars, 7g fiber), 35g pro.

QUICK & EASY CHILI

Your busy schedule doesn't always allow you to have chili simmer all day long on the stove. But you don't have to wait until the weekend to make some. This chili can be made in a flash and is easily doubled or tripled to satisfy any famished family.
—*Taste of Home* Test Kitchen

Prep: 10 min. • **Cook:** 30 min.
Makes: 6 servings

1 lb. ground beef
1 medium onion, chopped
1 medium green pepper, chopped
2 to 3 tsp. chili powder
1 tsp. ground cumin
1 tsp. salt
1 can (14½ oz.) Mexican stewed tomatoes
1 can (16 oz.) chili beans, undrained
1 cup frozen corn
    Shredded cheddar cheese, optional

In a large saucepan, cook the beef, onion and green pepper over medium heat until meat is no longer pink; drain. Add next 6 ingredients; cover and simmer for 20 minutes. Serve with cheese if desired.

1 cup: 249 cal., 8g fat (3g sat. fat), 37mg chol., 947mg sod., 26g carb. (6g sugars, 6g fiber), 19g pro.

PINA COLADA CARROT SALAD

This carrot salad with pina colada yogurt, green grapes and macadamia nuts has a tropical theme. Just mix and chill out.
—Emily Tyra, Lake Ann, MI

Takes: 10 min. • **Makes:** 4 servings

1 pkg. (10 oz.) julienned carrots
1 cup green grapes, halved
¾ cup pina colada yogurt
⅓ cup salted dry roasted macadamia nuts, chopped
    Lemon wedges

In a large bowl, combine carrots, grapes, yogurt and macadamia nuts; toss to coat. Squeeze the lemon wedges over salad before serving.

¾ cup: 184 cal., 9g fat (2g sat. fat), 2mg chol., 157mg sod., 24g carb. (19g sugars, 3g fiber), 3g pro. **Diabetic exchanges:** 1½ fat, 1 starch, 1 vegetable.

QUICK & EASY CHILI

ASK SARAH

HOW CAN I JAZZ UP THIS TROPICAL SALAD?

Drain a small can of pineapple chunks or crushed pineapple into the salad for a little extra tropical flair.

TEX-MEX POTATO SALAD

I created this recipe for one of my Tex-Mex cooking classes, and it was a hit. It is perfect for a cookout or potluck. The secret is in the pickled jalapenos—they add interest and flavor! Add a drained can of black beans for more protein.
—Dianna Ackerley, Cibolo, TX

Prep: 20 min. • Cook: 20 min. + chilling
Makes: 12 servings

- 2   medium ears sweet corn
- 1   large sweet red pepper
- 2   lbs. small red potatoes
- 1   medium ripe avocado, peeled and cubed
- 1   cup grape tomatoes, halved
- 2   green onions, cut into ½-in. slices
- ¼   cup reduced-fat sour cream or fat-free plain Greek yogurt
- ¼   cup reduced-fat mayonnaise
- ¼   cup salsa
- 2   Tbsp. lime juice
- 1   Tbsp. red wine vinegar
- 2   tsp. chopped pickled jalapeno slices
- ½   tsp. salt
- ¼   tsp. garlic powder
- ¼   tsp. onion powder
- ¼   tsp. ground cumin
- ¼   tsp. pepper
      Dash cayenne pepper
      Fresh cilantro leaves

1. Preheat oven to 400°. Place corn and red pepper on a greased baking sheet. Roast until lightly charred, 20-25 minutes, turning once. Let cool. Peel off and discard skin from pepper. Remove the stems and seeds. Cut pepper into ½-in pieces. Cut corn from cobs; set aside.
2. Place potatoes in a large saucepan; add water to cover. Bring to a boil. Reduce heat; cook, uncovered, until tender, 10-12 minutes. Drain and cool. Cut potatoes in half; place in a large bowl. Add sliced red pepper, corn, avocado, tomatoes and green onions.
3. Place sour cream, mayonnaise, salsa, lime juice, vinegar, jalapenos and spices in a blender. Cover and process until blended. Pour over potato mixture; toss to coat. Refrigerate, covered, until chilled. Serve with cilantro.

¾ cup: 120 cal., 4g fat (1g sat. fat), 2mg chol., 168mg sod., 19g carb. (4g sugars, 3g fiber), 3g pro. Diabetic exchanges: 1 starch, 1 fat.

SWEET & SPICY PINEAPPLE CHICKEN SANDWICHES

My kids often ask for chicken sloppy joes, and this version has a bonus of sweet pineapple. It is a perfect recipe to double for a potluck. Try topping the sandwiches with smoked Gouda cheese.
—Nancy Heishman, Las Vegas, NV

Prep: 15 min. • Cook: 2¾ hours
Makes: 8 servings

- 2½ lbs. boneless skinless chicken breasts
- 1   bottle (18 oz.) sweet and spicy barbecue sauce, divided
- 2   Tbsp. honey mustard
- 1   can (8 oz.) unsweetened crushed pineapple, undrained
- 8   hamburger buns, split and toasted
      Optional: Bibb lettuce leaves and thinly sliced red onion

1. Place chicken breasts in a 4-qt. slow cooker. Combine ¼ cup barbecue sauce and mustard; pour over chicken. Cover and cook on low 2½-3 hours or until chicken is tender.
2. Remove chicken; discard liquid. Shred chicken with 2 forks and return to slow cooker. Add the crushed pineapple and remaining barbecue sauce; cover and cook on high for 15 minutes.
3. Serve on toasted buns with lettuce and onion if desired.

Freeze option: Place shredded chicken in freezer containers. Cool and freeze. To use, partially thaw in the refrigerator overnight. Heat through in a covered saucepan, stirring gently; add broth if necessary.

1 sandwich: 415 cal., 6g fat (1g sat. fat), 78mg chol., 973mg sod., 56g carb. (30g sugars, 2g fiber), 34g pro.

TEX-MEX POTATO SALAD

CREAM OF TURKEY & WILD RICE SOUP

A dear friend brought me some of this soup when I was ill—and it instantly hit the spot. I asked her for the recipe and I've made it several times since, especially when I have leftover turkey to use up. Now I like to take it to friends myself when they're not feeling well. It's filling, and really warms you up on a chilly winter day!

—Doris Cox, New Freedom, PA

- -

Prep: 15 min. • **Cook:** 20 min.
Makes: 6 servings

- 1   medium onion, chopped
- 1   can (4 oz.) sliced mushrooms, drained
- 2   Tbsp. butter
- 3   cups water
- 2   cups chicken broth
- 1   pkg. (6 oz.) long grain and wild rice mix
- 2   cups diced cooked turkey
- 1   cup heavy whipping cream
     Minced fresh parsley

In a large saucepan, saute onion and mushrooms in butter until onion is tender. Add water, chicken broth and rice mix with seasoning; bring to a boil. Reduce heat; simmer for 20-25 minutes or until rice is tender. Stir in turkey and cream; heat through. Sprinkle with parsley.

1 cup: 364 cal., 21g fat (12g sat. fat), 100mg chol., 857mg sod., 25g carb. (3g sugars, 1g fiber), 19g pro.

TEST KITCHEN TIP
Cream soups don't always freeze particularly well, so it might be best to enjoy this comforting dish right away.

CREAM OF TURKEY & WILD RICE SOUP

PITCHFORK PULLED PORK

Pile the spaghetti squash on top of these Italian-style pulled pork sandwiches so it looks like a haystack. It's so fun, your kids won't know they're eating vegetables.
—Matthew Hass, Ellison Bay, WI

- -

Prep: 15 min. • **Cook:** 6 hours
Makes: 12 servings

- 1   boneless pork shoulder butt roast (3 to 4 lbs.)
- 4½ tsp. Italian seasoning, divided
- 2½ tsp. salt, divided
- 1   cup water, divided
- 1   Tbsp. olive oil
- 1   medium onion, chopped
- 4   garlic cloves, minced
- 1   can (28 oz.) crushed tomatoes in puree
- 1   can (6 oz.) tomato paste
- 2   tsp. sugar
- ½   tsp. pepper
- 2   bay leaves
- 1   medium spaghetti squash (about 4 lbs.)
- 12 kaiser rolls, split

1. Sprinkle roast with 1½ tsp. Italian seasoning and 1½ tsp. salt. Place in a 4- or 5-qt. slow cooker; add ½ cup water. Cook, covered, on low 6-8 hours or until the meat is tender.

2. Meanwhile, in a large saucepan, heat oil over medium heat. Add onion; cook and stir 4-5 minutes or until tender. Add garlic; cook 1 minute longer. Stir in tomatoes, tomato paste, sugar, pepper, bay leaves and the remaining Italian seasoning, salt and water; bring to a boil. Reduce the heat; simmer, uncovered, 15-20 minutes to allow flavors to blend. Discard bay leaves.

3. Cut squash lengthwise in half; discard seeds. Place squash on a microwave-safe plate, cut side down. Microwave, uncovered, on high 15-20 minutes or until tender. When squash is cool enough to handle, use a fork to separate strands.

4. Remove roast; discard cooking juices. When cool enough to handle, shred meat with 2 forks. Return meat to slow cooker. Stir in sauce; heat through.

5. Using tongs, place meat mixture on bun bottoms; top with squash. Replace tops.

1 sandwich: 450 cal., 16g fat (5g sat. fat), 67mg chol., 1030mg sod., 50g carb. (6g sugars, 5g fiber), 28g pro.

INDIAN-SPICED CHICKPEA WRAPS

INDIAN-SPICED CHICKPEA WRAPS

Raita, an Indian condiment made with yogurt, elevates this vegetarian dish into a satisfying gourmet wrap. I sometimes substitute diced mango or cucumber for the pineapple and add fresh herbs like cilantro or even mint.
—Jennifer Beckman, Falls Church, VA

- -

Takes: 30 min. • **Makes:** 4 servings

- 1   cup reduced-fat plain yogurt
- ½   cup unsweetened pineapple tidbits
- ¼   tsp. salt
- ¼   tsp. ground cumin

WRAPS
- 2   tsp. canola oil
- 1   small onion, chopped
- 1   Tbsp. minced fresh gingerroot
- 2   garlic cloves, minced
- ½   tsp. curry powder
- ¼   tsp. salt
- ¼   tsp. ground coriander
- ¼   tsp. ground cumin
- ¼   tsp. cayenne pepper, optional
- 1   can (15 oz.) chickpeas or garbanzo beans, rinsed and drained
- 1   cup canned crushed tomatoes
- 3   cups fresh baby spinach
- 4   whole wheat tortillas (8 in.), warmed

1. For pineapple raita, mix first 4 ingredients.

2. For wraps, in a large nonstick skillet, heat oil over medium-high heat; saute onion until tender. Add ginger, garlic and seasonings; cook and stir until fragrant, about 1 minute. Stir in chickpeas and tomatoes; bring to a boil. Reduce heat; simmer, uncovered, until slightly thickened, 5-8 minutes, stirring occasionally.

3. Place the spinach and chickpea mixture on tortillas. Top with raita and roll up.

1 wrap: 321 cal., 7g fat (1g sat. fat), 3mg chol., 734mg sod., 55g carb. (15g sugars, 10g fiber), 13g pro.

Health tip: This handheld has it all—fruit, veggies, whole grains, reduced-fat dairy and protein-packed pulses.

RAMEN-VEGGIE CHICKEN SALAD

Like a salad with plenty of crunch? Then this refreshing recipe is sure to please. Toasted noodles, almonds and a few sesame seeds provide the crunchy topping. The chicken makes it a main dish.
—Linda Gearhart, Greensboro, NC

Prep: 30 min. • **Grill:** 10 min.
Makes: 2 servings

- ¼ cup sugar
- ¼ cup canola oil
- 2 Tbsp. cider vinegar
- 1 Tbsp. reduced-sodium soy sauce
- 1 pkg. (3 oz.) ramen noodles
- 1 Tbsp. butter
- ⅓ cup sliced almonds
- 1 Tbsp. sesame seeds
- 1 boneless skinless chicken breast half (6 oz.)
- 4 cups shredded Chinese or napa cabbage
- ½ large sweet red pepper, thinly sliced
- 3 green onions, thinly sliced
- 1 medium carrot, julienned

1. In a small saucepan, combine the sugar, oil, vinegar and soy sauce. Bring to a boil, cook and stir until sugar is dissolved, about 1 minute; set aside to cool.
2. Meanwhile, break noodles into small pieces (save seasoning packet for another use). In a small skillet, melt butter over medium heat. Add the noodles, almonds and sesame seeds; cook and stir until lightly toasted, 1-2 minutes.
3. Grill chicken, covered, over medium heat until a thermometer reads 170°, 4-6 minutes on each side.
4. Meanwhile, arrange the cabbage, red pepper, onions and carrot on 2 serving plates. Slice chicken; place on salad. Top with noodle mixture; drizzle with dressing.
1 serving: 865 cal., 53g fat (11g sat. fat), 62mg chol., 574mg sod., 68g carb. (32g sugars, 7g fiber), 29g pro.

RAMEN-VEGGIE CHICKEN SALAD

AIR-FRYER REUBEN CALZONES

I love a Reuben sandwich, so I tried the fillings in a pizza pocket instead of on rye bread. This hand-held dinner is a big-time winner at our house.
—Nickie Frye, Evansville, IN

Prep: 15 min. • **Cook:** 10 min./batch
Makes: 4 servings

- 1 tube (13.8 oz.) refrigerated pizza crust
- 4 slices Swiss cheese
- 1 cup sauerkraut, rinsed and well drained
- ½ lb. sliced cooked corned beef
  Thousand Island salad dressing

1. Preheat air fryer to 400°. On a lightly floured surface, unroll pizza crust dough and pat into a 12-in. square. Cut into 4 squares. Layer 1 slice cheese and a fourth of the sauerkraut and corned beef diagonally over half of each square to within ½ in. of edges. Fold 1 corner over filling to the opposite corner, forming a triangle; press edges with a fork to seal. Place 2 calzones in a single layer on greased tray in air-fryer basket.
2. Cook until golden brown, 8-12 minutes, flipping halfway through cooking. Serve with salad dressing.
1 calzone: 430 cal., 17g fat (6g sat. fat), 66mg chol., 1471mg sod., 49g carb. (7g sugars, 2g fiber), 21g pro.

PASTA
FAGIOLI SOUP

PASTA FAGIOLI SOUP

My husband enjoys my version of this soup so much that he stopped ordering it at restaurants. He'd rather savor the version we can have at home. It's so easy to make, yet hearty enough to be a full dinner.
—Brenda Thomas, Springfield, MO

- -

Takes: 30 min. • **Makes:** 5 servings

- ½ lb. Italian turkey sausage links, casings removed, crumbled
- 1 small onion, chopped
- 1½ tsp. canola oil
- 1 garlic clove, minced
- 2 cups water
- 1 can (15½ oz.) great northern beans, rinsed and drained
- 1 can (14½ oz.) diced tomatoes, undrained
- 1 can (14½ oz.) reduced-sodium chicken broth
- ¾ cup uncooked elbow macaroni
- ¼ tsp. pepper
- 1 cup fresh spinach leaves, cut as desired
- 5 tsp. shredded Parmesan cheese

1. In a large saucepan, cook the sausage over medium heat until no longer pink; drain, remove from pan and set aside. In the same pan, saute onion in oil until tender. Add the garlic; saute 1 minute longer.
2. Add the water, beans, tomatoes, broth, macaroni and pepper; bring to a boil. Cook, uncovered, until the macaroni is tender, 8-10 minutes.
3. Reduce heat to low; stir in sausage and spinach. Cook until the spinach is wilted, 2-3 minutes. Garnish with cheese.
1⅓ cups: 228 cal., 7g fat (1g sat. fat), 29mg chol., 841mg sod., 27g carb. (4g sugars, 6g fiber), 16g pro. **Diabetic exchanges:** 1½ starch, 1 lean meat, 1 vegetable, ½ fat.

COLORFUL AVOCADO SALAD

I appreciate the crisp, fresh vegetables and bright colors in this nutritious salad. The avocado adds a delightful creaminess. A friend gave me the idea for this recipe while we were discussing salads.
—Bev Lehrman, Jijoca, Brazil

- -

Takes: 20 min. • **Makes:** 2 servings

- 1 medium tomato, cut into eighths
- ½ small cucumber, thinly sliced
- 1 small red onion, halved and thinly sliced
- ⅓ cup julienned green pepper
- 2 Tbsp. Italian salad dressing
- 1 medium ripe avocado, peeled and cubed

In a bowl, combine the first 4 ingredients. Add dressing and toss to coat. Chill until serving. Just before serving, add avocado and toss gently.
¾ cup: 176 cal., 13g fat (2g sat. fat), 0 chol., 161mg sod., 14g carb. (5g sugars, 6g fiber), 3g pro. **Diabetic exchanges:** 2½ fat, 1 vegetable.

CHEESY WILD RICE SOUP

We often eat easy-to-make soups when there's not a lot of time to cook. I replaced the wild rice specified in the original recipe with a boxed rice mix.
—Lisa Hofer, Hitchcock, SD

- -

Takes: 30 min. • **Makes:** 8 servings

- 1 pkg. (6.2 oz.) fast-cooking long grain and wild rice mix
- 4 cups 2% milk
- 1 can (10¾ oz.) condensed cream of potato soup, undiluted
- 8 oz. Velveeta, cubed
- ½ lb. bacon strips, cooked and crumbled
  Optional: Minced chives and oyster crackers

In a large saucepan, prepare the rice mix according to package directions. Add the milk, soup and cheese. Cook and stir until the cheese is melted. Garnish with bacon and, if desired, minced fresh chives and oyster crackers.
1 cup: 464 cal., 29g fat (14g sat. fat), 70mg chol., 1492mg sod., 29g carb. (9g sugars, 1g fiber), 21g pro.

MUSHROOM BACON TURKEY BURGERS

If you ask me, a good burger needs some mushrooms on top, but they tend to slide around and fall off. I decided to put finely chopped mushrooms right into the patties—problem solved!
—Melissa Obernesser, Oriskany, NY

- -

Takes: 30 min. • **Makes:** 4 servings

- 1 cup finely chopped fresh mushrooms (about 4 medium)
- 3 Tbsp. soft bread crumbs
- 3 Tbsp. barbecue sauce
- ¾ tsp. onion powder
- ½ tsp. garlic powder
- ¼ tsp. pepper
- 1 lb. extra-lean ground turkey
- 4 turkey bacon strips, halved
- 4 thin slices cheddar cheese
- 4 whole wheat hamburger buns, split
  Additional barbecue sauce
  Dill pickle slices, optional

1. Combine first 6 ingredients. Add turkey; mix lightly but thoroughly. Shape into four ½-in.-thick patties.
2. Place the burgers on an oiled grill rack over medium heat; grill, covered, until a thermometer reads 165°, 4-5 minutes per side. Grill bacon strips, covered, until crisp, 2-3 minutes per side. Top burgers with the cheese and bacon; grill, covered, until cheese is melted, about 30 seconds.
3. Serve on buns. Top with additional barbecue sauce and, if desired, pickles.
Note: To make soft bread crumbs, tear bread into pieces and place in a food processor or blender. Cover and pulse until crumbs form. One slice of bread yields ½-¾ cup crumbs.
1 burger: 389 cal., 17g fat (4g sat. fat), 95mg chol., 727mg sod., 30g carb. (9g sugars, 4g fiber), 32g pro. **Diabetic exchanges:** 4 lean meat, 2 starch, 2 fat.

EASY CITRUS SEAFOOD SALAD

This super simple, deceptively delicious recipe was inspired by a seafood salad in the Bahamas that featured conch. I substitute crab and shrimp and like this version even more!
—Cindy Heyd, Edmond, OK

- -

Takes: 15 min. • **Makes:** 4 servings

- 1 medium orange
- 1 medium lemon
- 1 medium lime
- ½ lb. peeled and deveined cooked shrimp (31-40 per lb.), coarsely chopped
- ½ lb. refrigerated fresh or imitation crabmeat, coarsely chopped
- 2 Tbsp. finely chopped sweet onion
- 2 Tbsp. finely chopped sweet red pepper
  Shredded lettuce
  Assorted crackers

Finely grate zest from orange. Cut orange crosswise in half; squeeze juice from orange. Transfer zest and juice to a large bowl. Repeat with lemon and lime. Add shrimp, crab, onion and pepper; toss to coat. Serve on lettuce with crackers.
¾ cup: 128 cal., 2g fat (0 sat. fat), 141mg chol., 309mg sod., 6g carb. (3g sugars, 1g fiber), 22g pro. **Diabetic exchanges:** 3 lean meat.

SWEET & SPICY SLOPPY JOES

These sandwiches have been the go-to meal for my son's basketball team. Turkey is a wonderful change from ground beef and really absorbs all the flavors. I've also used this for a Friday the 13th celebration at work, calling it 13-ingredient sloppy joes.
—Karen Hildebrand, Labelle, FL

- -

Prep: 30 min. • **Cook:** 4 hours
Makes: 12 servings

- 2 tsp. canola oil
- 3 lbs. ground turkey
- 1 large onion, chopped
- ½ medium green pepper, chopped
- 3 garlic cloves, minced
- 2 Tbsp. Worcestershire sauce
- 1 tsp. crushed red pepper flakes
- 3 cups ketchup
- ⅔ cup water
- ⅓ cup packed brown sugar
- 3 Tbsp. spicy brown mustard
- ½ tsp. salt
- ¼ tsp. pepper
- 12 hamburger buns, split
  Optional: Coleslaw and dill pickle slices

1. Heat oil in a large nonstick skillet over medium-high heat. Cook turkey in batches until no longer pink, breaking into crumbles, 8-10 minutes per batch. Transfer meat to a 5- or 6-qt. slow cooker. In the same skillet, cook the onion and green pepper until tender, 2-3 minutes. Add minced garlic, Worcestershire and red pepper flakes; cook 1 minute longer. Transfer to slow cooker.
2. In a bowl, combine ketchup, water, brown sugar, mustard, salt and pepper; pour over meat. Cover and cook on low 4-5 hours or until flavors are blended. Serve on buns with toppings as desired.
1 sandwich: 390 cal., 11g fat (3g sat. fat), 75mg chol., 1206mg sod., 46g carb. (26g sugars, 1g fiber), 27g pro.

SWEET & SPICY SLOPPY JOES

TURKEY PINTO BEAN SALAD WITH SOUTHERN MOLASSES DRESSING

THAI CHICKEN NOODLE SOUP

This slow-cooker soup is a semi-homemade version that coaxes all the flavor out of a rotisserie chicken. All the prep work for this can be done the day before so you can toss it into the slow cooker with ease.
—Beth Jacobson, Milwaukee, WI

Prep: 20 min. • **Cook:** 6 hours
Makes: 8 servings

- 1 large onion, halved
- 1 piece fresh gingerroot (3 to 4 in.), halved lengthwise
- 1 Tbsp. canola oil
- 1 rotisserie chicken
- 1 cinnamon stick (3 in.)
- 5 whole cloves
- 3 whole star anise
- 1 tsp. coriander seeds
- 1 tsp. fennel seed
- 3 qt. reduced-sodium chicken broth
- 1 pkg. (8.8 oz.) rice noodles
- 2 Tbsp. brown sugar
- 2 Tbsp. fish sauce
- 1 Tbsp. lime juice
  Optional: Bean sprouts, fresh basil leaves, fresh cilantro leaves, thinly sliced green onions, chili garlic sauce, fish sauce and lime wedges

1. Preheat broiler. Place onion and ginger in a foil-lined 15x10x1-in. baking pan; drizzle with oil. Broil 3-4 in. from heat 8-10 minutes or until well browned. Meanwhile, remove chicken from bones; reserve carcass and shred meat. Place carcass, onion, ginger, spices and broth in a 6-qt slow cooker. Cook on low 6-8 hours.
2. Cook noodles according to package instructions. Strain soup and keep warm; discard carcass, vegetables and spices. Stir in brown sugar, fish sauce and lime juice. Place noodles and chicken in soup bowls. Ladle broth into the bowls and add toppings of your choice.
2½ cups: 398 cal., 15g fat (4g sat. fat), 78mg chol., 1321mg sod., 32g carb. (6g sugars, 1g fiber), 32g pro.

TURKEY PINTO BEAN SALAD WITH SOUTHERN MOLASSES DRESSING

This salad is a welcome alternative to the usual post-Thanksgiving fare. It's a tasty main dish loaded with good-for-you protein.
—Lily Julow, Lawrenceville, GA

Prep: 35 min. + chilling • **Makes:** 6 servings

- ½ cup oil-packed sun-dried tomatoes
- 1 garlic clove, peeled and halved
- ½ cup molasses
- 3 Tbsp. cider vinegar
- 1 tsp. prepared mustard
- ½ tsp. salt
- ¼ tsp. coarsely ground pepper
- 3 cups cubed cooked turkey breast
- 2 cans (15 oz. each) pinto beans, rinsed and drained
- 1 medium green pepper, diced
- 2 celery ribs, diced
- 1 cup chopped sweet onion
- ¼ cup minced fresh parsley
  Lettuce leaves, optional

1. Drain tomatoes, reserving 2 Tbsp. oil. Place the garlic and tomatoes in a food processor; cover and process until chopped. Add the molasses, vinegar, mustard, salt, pepper and reserved oil. Cover and process until smooth.
2. In a large bowl, combine the turkey, beans, green pepper, celery, onion and parsley. Add the dressing and toss to coat. Cover and refrigerate for at least 2 hours. If desired, serve with lettuce leaves.
1⅓ cups: 379 cal., 7g fat (1g sat. fat), 60mg chol., 483mg sod., 49g carb. (19g sugars, 7g fiber), 29g pro. **Diabetic exchanges:** 4 lean meat, 2½ starch, 1 vegetable, 1 fat.

TEST KITCHEN TIP
Sun-dried tomatoes are sold either packed in oil or dry-packed. Dry-packed sun-dried tomatoes are usually soaked in a liquid to soften them before use. As the name indicates, sun-dried tomatoes have been dried to remove most of their water content, producing a chewy, intensely flavored product.

RAMEN SLIDERS

RAMEN SLIDERS

I grew up eating ramen and love it to this day. A fun spin on my favorite type of noodle soup, these sliders are topped with an egg and kimchi.
—Julie Teramoto, Los Angeles, CA

- -

Prep: 40 min. • **Bake:** 20 min.
Makes: 10 servings

- 1 pkg. (3 oz.) beef or pork ramen noodles
- 1 lb. ground beef
- 4 green onions, thinly sliced
- 2 hard-boiled large eggs, sliced
  Sriracha chili sauce
  Kimchi, optional

1. Preheat oven to 350°. Grease 20 muffin cups. Cook noodles according to package directions, saving seasoning packet for meat mixture. Drain; divide the noodles among prepared muffin cups. Bake until crisp and light golden brown, 20-25 minutes. Remove from pans to wire racks to cool.
2. Meanwhile, combine beef, green onions and reserved seasoning packet, mixing lightly but thoroughly. Shape the beef into ten 2½-in.-round patties.
3. In a large nonstick skillet, cook burgers over medium heat until a thermometer reads 160°, 4-6 minutes on each side. Cut each egg into 5 slices. Serve burgers on ramen buns with egg slices, chili sauce and, if desired, kimchi.
1 slider: 137 cal., 8g fat (3g sat. fat), 65mg chol., 185mg sod., 6g carb. (0 sugars, 0 fiber), 10g pro.

"I made these last summer, and they're so tasty, different and fun."

—JAMES SCHEND, DEPUTY EDITOR, CULINARY

CAPRESE MACARONI SALAD

When fresh tomatoes and basil are abundant in the summer, I like to do everything I can with these wonderful ingredients. This is a favorite!
—Debbie Glasscock, Conway, AR

Takes: 20 min. • **Makes:** 7 servings

- 2 cups uncooked elbow macaroni
- 1 cup mayonnaise
- 1 Tbsp. Italian salad dressing mix
- 2 tsp. sugar
- ¾ tsp. ground mustard
- ¼ tsp. salt
- ⅛ tsp. pepper
- 1 pint cherry tomatoes, halved
- 1 cup fresh mozzarella cheese pearls
- ¼ cup fresh basil leaves, slivered
- 2 Tbsp. grated Parmesan cheese

1. Cook macaroni according to package directions; drain and rinse with cold water. Cool completely.
2. For dressing, in a small bowl, combine mayonnaise, dressing mix, sugar, mustard, salt and pepper. In a large bowl, combine tomatoes, mozzarella and macaroni. Add dressing; gently toss to coat. Refrigerate until serving. Top with basil and Parmesan before serving.
¾ cup: 397 cal., 31g fat (8g sat. fat), 29mg chol., 458mg sod., 20g carb. (4g sugars, 1g fiber), 10g pro.

EASY WHITE CHICKEN CHILI

Chili is one of our best cold-weather strategies. We use chicken and white beans for a twist on the regular bowl of red. It's soothing comfort food.
—Rachel Lewis, Danville, VA

Takes: 30 min. • **Makes:** 6 servings

- 1 lb. lean ground chicken
- 1 medium onion, chopped
- 2 cans (15 oz. each) cannellini beans, rinsed and drained
- 1 can (4 oz.) chopped green chiles
- 1 tsp. ground cumin
- ½ tsp. dried oregano
- ¼ tsp. pepper
- 1 can (14½ oz.) reduced-sodium chicken broth
  Optional toppings: Reduced-fat sour cream, shredded cheddar cheese and chopped fresh cilantro

1. In a large saucepan, cook chicken and onion over medium-high heat until chicken is no longer pink, 6-8 minutes, breaking up chicken into crumbles.
2. Pour 1 can of beans in a small bowl; mash slightly. Stir the mashed beans, remaining can of beans, chiles, seasonings and broth into chicken mixture; bring to a boil. Reduce heat; simmer, covered, until the flavors are blended, 12-15 minutes. Serve with toppings as desired.
Freeze option: Freeze cooled chili in freezer containers. To use, partially thaw in the refrigerator overnight. Heat through in a saucepan, stirring occasionally; add broth if necessary.
1 cup: 228 cal., 5g fat (1g sat. fat), 54mg chol., 504mg sod., 23g carb. (1g sugars, 6g fiber), 22g pro. **Diabetic exchanges:** 3 lean meat, 1½ starch.

EASY WHITE CHICKEN CHILI

STRAWBERRY TARRAGON CHICKEN SALAD

After thinking about creating this salad for some time, this past spring I used my homegrown strawberries and fresh tarragon to do a little experimenting. It didn't take me long to come up with a winner! My husband enjoyed my creation as much as I did, and we can't wait for strawberry season to come around again!
—Sue Gronholz, Beaver Dam, WI

Takes: 30 min. • **Makes:** 5 servings

- ½ cup mayonnaise
- 2 tsp. sugar
- 2 tsp. minced fresh tarragon or 1 tsp. dried tarragon
- ¼ tsp. salt
- ⅛ tsp. pepper
- 2½ cups cubed cooked chicken breast
- 2 cups quartered fresh strawberries
- 1 cup fresh shelled peas or frozen peas, thawed
- ½ cup chopped celery
- 2 Tbsp. chopped sweet onion
  Torn mixed salad greens
- ½ cup chopped pecans, toasted

In a large bowl, whisk the first 5 ingredients until blended. Stir in chicken, strawberries, peas, celery and onion. Serve over salad greens; sprinkle with pecans.
1 cup: 378 cal., 26g fat (4g sat. fat), 56mg chol., 285mg sod., 13g carb. (7g sugars, 4g fiber), 23g pro.

GRANDMA'S CHICKEN & DUMPLING SOUP

GRANDMA'S CHICKEN & DUMPLING SOUP

I've enjoyed making this rich soup for over 40 years. Every time I serve it, I remember my grandma, who was very special to me and was known as a great cook.
—Paulette Balda, Prophetstown, IL

Prep: 20 min. + cooling • **Cook:** 2¾ hours
Makes: 12 servings (3 qt.)

- 1 broiler/fryer chicken (3½ to 4 lbs.), cut up
- 2¼ qt. cold water
- 5 chicken bouillon cubes
- 6 whole peppercorns
- 3 whole cloves
- 1 can (10¾ oz.) condensed cream of chicken soup, undiluted
- 1 can (10¾ oz.) condensed cream of mushroom soup, undiluted
- 1½ cups chopped carrots
- 1 cup fresh or frozen peas
- 1 cup chopped celery
- 1 cup chopped peeled potatoes
- ¼ cup chopped onion
- 1½ tsp. seasoned salt
- ¼ tsp. pepper
- 1 bay leaf

DUMPLINGS
- 2 cups all-purpose flour
- 4 tsp. baking powder
- 1 tsp. salt
- ¼ tsp. pepper
- 1 large egg, beaten
- 2 Tbsp. butter, melted
- ¾ to 1 cup 2% milk
  Snipped fresh parsley, optional

1. Place the chicken, water, bouillon, peppercorns and cloves in a stockpot. Cover and bring to a boil; skim foam. Reduce heat; cover and simmer 45-60 minutes or until chicken is tender. Strain the broth; return to stockpot.

2. Remove chicken and set aside until cool enough to handle. Remove meat from bones; discard the bones and skin and cut chicken into chunks. Cool broth and skim off the fat.

3. Return chicken to stockpot with soups, vegetables and seasonings; bring to a boil. Reduce heat; cover and simmer for 1 hour. Uncover; increase heat to a gentle boil. Discard bay leaf.

4. For dumplings, combine dry ingredients in a medium bowl. Stir in egg, butter and enough milk to make a moist stiff batter. Drop by teaspoonfuls into soup. Cover and cook without lifting the lid for 18-20 minutes. Sprinkle with parsley if desired.
1 cup: 333 cal., 14g fat (5g sat. fat), 79mg chol., 1447mg sod., 28g carb. (4g sugars, 3g fiber), 22g pro.

"This is absolutely loaded with comforting flavor, including the dumplings!"

—JESS SORENSON, MANAGER, BOOKS MARKETING

ROASTED SWEET POTATO & CHICKPEA PITAS

Here's a hearty take on Mediterranean food, this time with sweet potatoes tucked inside. These unique pockets are delicious for lunch or dinner.
—Beth Jacobson, Milwaukee, WI

Takes: 30 min. • **Makes:** 6 servings

- 2 medium sweet potatoes (about 1¼ lbs.), peeled and cubed
- 2 cans (15 oz. each) chickpeas or garbanzo beans, rinsed and drained
- 1 medium red onion, chopped
- 3 Tbsp. canola oil, divided
- 2 tsp. garam masala
- ½ tsp. salt, divided
- 2 garlic cloves, minced
- 1 cup plain Greek yogurt
- 1 Tbsp. lemon juice
- 1 tsp. ground cumin
- 2 cups arugula or baby spinach
- 12 whole wheat pita pocket halves, warmed
- ¼ cup minced fresh cilantro

1. Preheat oven to 400°. Place potatoes in a large microwave-safe bowl; microwave, covered, on high 5 minutes. Stir in chickpeas and red onion; toss with 2 Tbsp. oil, garam masala and ¼ tsp. salt.
2. Spread into a 15x10x1-in. pan. Roast until the potatoes are tender, about 15 minutes. Cool slightly.
3. Place the garlic and remaining oil in a small microwave-safe bowl; microwave on high until garlic is lightly browned, 1-1½ minutes. Stir in yogurt, lemon juice, cumin and remaining salt.
4. Toss potato mixture with arugula. Spoon into pitas; top with sauce and cilantro.
2 filled pita halves: 462 cal., 15g fat (3g sat. fat), 10mg chol., 662mg sod., 72g carb. (13g sugars, 12g fiber), 14g pro.

CINCINNATI CHILI

Cinnamon and cocoa give a rich brown color to hearty Cincinnati chili. This dish will warm you up on a cold day.
—Edith Joyce, Parkman, OH

Prep: 20 min. • **Cook:** 1¾ hours
Makes: 8 servings

- 1 lb. ground beef
- 1 lb. ground pork
- 4 medium onions, chopped
- 6 garlic cloves, minced
- 2 cans (16 oz. each) kidney beans, rinsed and drained
- 1 can (28 oz.) crushed tomatoes
- ¼ cup white vinegar
- ¼ cup baking cocoa
- 2 Tbsp. Worcestershire sauce
- 2 tsp. hot pepper sauce
- 1 tsp. sugar
- 2 Tbsp. chili powder
- 4 tsp. ground cinnamon
- 3 tsp. dried oregano
- 2 tsp. ground cumin
- 2 tsp. ground allspice
- 3 bay leaves
  Salt and pepper to taste
  Hot cooked spaghetti
  Optional: Shredded cheddar cheese, sour cream, chopped tomatoes and green onions

1. In a Dutch oven, cook the beef, pork and onions over medium heat until meat is no longer pink, breaking meat into crumbles. Add garlic; cook 1 minute longer. Drain. Add the beans, tomatoes, vinegar, cocoa, sauces, sugar and seasonings; bring to a boil. Reduce heat; cover and simmer for 1½ hours.
2. Discard bay leaves. Serve with spaghetti. If desired, garnish with cheese, sour cream, tomatoes and onions.
1 cup: 421 cal., 16g fat (6g sat. fat), 75mg chol., 443mg sod., 38g carb. (7g sugars, 11g fiber), 32g pro.

ROASTED SWEET POTATO & CHICKPEA PITAS

LIME & DILL CHIMICHURRI SHRIMP
PAGE 108

Fish, Seafood & Meatless

Whether you enjoy fish and seafood occasionally or you've made meatless meals a way of life, you've come to the right spot!

LENTIL BURRITOS

I'm constantly trying to incorporate healthy but tasty meals into our menus. Kids and adults alike love these mildly spiced burritos that combine filling lentils with zucchini. They're healthy, satisfying, fast and tasty!
—Pam Masters, Wickenburg, AZ

Takes: 30 min. • **Makes:** 8 burritos

- 2 cups water
- 1 cup dried brown lentils
- 2 Tbsp. dried minced onion
- ½ tsp. dried minced garlic
- ½ tsp. ground cumin
- ⅛ tsp. hot pepper sauce
- 1 small zucchini, chopped
- 1 cup taco sauce
- 1 cup shredded part-skim mozzarella cheese
- 8 flour tortillas (8 in.), warmed

1. Place the first 6 ingredients in a large saucepan; bring to a boil. Reduce heat; simmer, covered, until lentils are tender, 15-20 minutes. Drain if necessary.
2. Stir zucchini, taco sauce and cheese into lentils. To serve, place about ½ cup lentil mixture on each tortilla and roll up.
1 burrito: 313 cal., 7g fat (3g sat. fat), 9mg chol., 452mg sod., 47g carb. (4g sugars, 5g fiber), 14g pro. **Diabetic exchanges:** 3 starch, 2 lean meat, 1 fat.

LENTIL BURRITOS

AIR-FRYER PRETZEL-CRUSTED CATFISH

I love the flavor of this air-fryer catfish recipe. I'm not a big fish lover, so any concoction that has me loving fish is a keeper in my book. This is wonderful served with a nice herb rice pilaf and corn muffins with butter and honey.
—Kelly Williams, Forked River, NJ

Prep: 15 min. • **Cook:** 10 min./batch
Makes: 4 servings

- 4 catfish fillets (6 oz. each)
- ½ tsp. salt
- ½ tsp. pepper
- 2 large eggs
- ⅓ cup Dijon mustard
- 2 Tbsp. 2% milk
- ½ cup all-purpose flour
- 4 cups honey mustard miniature pretzels, coarsely crushed
  Cooking spray
  Lemon slices, optional

1. Preheat air fryer to 325°. Sprinkle catfish with salt and pepper. Whisk eggs, mustard and milk in a shallow bowl. Place flour and pretzels in separate shallow bowls. Coat the fillets with flour, then dip in egg mixture and coat with pretzels.
2. In batches, place fillets in a single layer on greased tray in air-fryer basket; spritz with cooking spray. Cook until fish flakes easily with a fork, 10-12 minutes. If desired, serve with lemon slices.
1 fillet: 466 cal., 14g fat (3g sat. fat), 164mg chol., 1580mg sod., 45g carb. (2g sugars, 2g fiber), 33g pro.

CLASSIC CRAB CAKES

Our region is known for good seafood, and crab cakes are a traditional favorite. I learned to make them from a chef in a restaurant where they were a bestseller. The crabmeat's sweet and mild flavor is sparked by the blend of other ingredients.
—Debbie Terenzini, Lusby, MD

Takes: 20 min. • **Makes:** 8 servings

- 1 lb. fresh or canned crabmeat, drained, flaked and cartilage removed
- 2 to 2½ cups soft bread crumbs
- 1 large egg, beaten
- ¾ cup mayonnaise
- ⅓ cup each chopped celery, green pepper and onion
- 1 Tbsp. seafood seasoning
- 1 Tbsp. minced fresh parsley
- 2 tsp. lemon juice
- 1 tsp. Worcestershire sauce
- 1 tsp. prepared mustard
- ¼ tsp. pepper
- ⅛ tsp. hot pepper sauce
- 2 to 4 Tbsp. vegetable oil, optional
  Lemon wedges, optional

In a large bowl, combine the crab, bread crumbs, egg, mayonnaise, vegetables and seasonings. Shape into 8 patties. Broil or cook the patties in a cast-iron or other ovenproof skillet in oil for 4 minutes on each side or until golden brown. If desired, serve with lemon.

Freeze option: Freeze cooled crab cakes in freezer containers, separating layers with waxed paper. To use, reheat crab cakes on a baking sheet in a preheated 325° oven until heated through.

1 crab cake: 282 cal., 22g fat (3g sat. fat), 85mg chol., 638mg sod., 7g carb. (1g sugars, 1g fiber), 14g pro.

TEST KITCHEN TIP
Serve crab cakes on their own or top them with deli coleslaw for a special sandwich.

CLASSIC
CRAB CAKES

SHRIMP SCAMPI

This shrimp scampi recipe looks elegant enough to serve to company, but it's easy to prepare. The bright flavors of lemon and herbs enhance the shrimp. Serve it over pasta and wait for the compliments.
—Lori Packer, Omaha, NE

Takes: 20 min. • **Makes:** 4 servings

- 3 to 4 garlic cloves, minced
- ¼ cup butter, cubed
- ¼ cup olive oil
- 1 lb. uncooked medium shrimp, peeled and deveined
- ¼ cup lemon juice
- ½ tsp. pepper
- ¼ tsp. dried oregano
- ½ cup grated Parmesan cheese
- ¼ cup dry bread crumbs
- ¼ cup minced fresh parsley
  Hot cooked angel hair pasta

1. In a 10-in. ovenproof skillet, saute garlic in butter and oil until fragrant. Add the shrimp, lemon juice, pepper and oregano; cook and stir until shrimp turn pink. Sprinkle with the cheese, bread crumbs and parsley.
2. Broil 6 in. from the heat for 2-3 minutes or until the topping is golden brown. Serve with pasta.
1 cup: 395 cal., 30g fat (11g sat. fat), 177mg chol., 420mg sod., 9g carb. (1g sugars, 1g fiber), 24g pro.

> "This dish is guaranteed to make everyone happy. It's extremely tasty, even for those who don't always love shrimp, and has lots of fresh lemon flavor."
>
> —JESS SORENSON, MANAGER, BOOKS MARKETING

SHEET-PAN TILAPIA & VEGETABLE MEDLEY

SHEET-PAN TILAPIA & VEGETABLE MEDLEY

Unlike some one-pan dinners that require precooking in a skillet or pot, this one uses just the sheet pan, period.
—Judy Batson, Tampa, FL

Prep: 15 min. • **Bake:** 25 min.
Makes: 2 servings

- 2 medium Yukon Gold potatoes, cut into wedges
- 3 large fresh Brussels sprouts, thinly sliced
- 3 large radishes, thinly sliced
- 1 cup fresh sugar snap peas, cut into ½-in. pieces
- 1 small carrot, thinly sliced
- 2 Tbsp. butter, melted
- ½ tsp. garlic salt
- ½ tsp. pepper
- 2 tilapia fillets (6 oz. each)
- 2 tsp. minced fresh tarragon or ½ tsp. dried tarragon
- ⅛ tsp. salt
- 1 Tbsp. butter, softened
  Optional: Lemon wedges and tartar sauce

1. Preheat oven to 450°. Line a 15x10x1-in. baking pan with foil; grease foil.
2. In a bowl, combine first 5 ingredients. Add melted butter, garlic salt and pepper; toss to coat. Place the vegetables in a single layer in prepared pan; bake until potatoes are tender, about 20 minutes.
3. Remove from oven; preheat broiler. Arrange vegetables on 1 side of sheet pan. Add fish to other side. Sprinkle fillets with tarragon and salt; dot with softened butter. Broil 4-5 in. from heat until fish flakes easily with a fork, about 5 minutes. If desired, serve with lemon wedges and tartar sauce.
1 serving: 555 cal., 20g fat (12g sat. fat), 129mg chol., 892mg sod., 56g carb. (8g sugars, 8g fiber), 41g pro.

RAVIOLI WITH SNAP PEAS & MUSHROOMS

Topped with the toasty texture and flavor of hazelnuts, this pasta makes an easy, earthy weeknight dinner. I serve it with an herb and lettuce salad and white wine.
—Charlene Chambers, Ormond Beach, FL

- -

Takes: 30 min. • **Makes:** 8 servings

- 1 pkg. (20 oz.) refrigerated cheese ravioli
- 1 lb. fresh sugar snap peas, trimmed
- 1 Tbsp. butter
- ½ lb. sliced fresh mushrooms
- 3 shallots, finely chopped
- 2 garlic cloves, minced
- 2 cups fat-free evaporated milk
- 8 fresh sage leaves, thinly sliced or 2 tsp. rubbed sage
- 1 tsp. grated lemon zest
- 1 tsp. lemon-pepper seasoning
- ¼ tsp. white pepper
- ¼ cup shredded Parmesan cheese
- ¼ cup hazelnuts, coarsely chopped and toasted

1. In a large saucepan, cook ravioli according to package directions, adding snap peas during the last 3 minutes of cooking; drain.
2. Meanwhile, in a large skillet, heat butter over medium-high heat. Add mushrooms, shallots and garlic; cook and stir until the mushrooms are tender. Stir in milk, sage, zest, lemon pepper and white pepper; bring to a boil. Reduce heat; simmer, uncovered, until slightly thickened, about 2 minutes.
3. Add ravioli and snap peas to sauce; heat through. Sprinkle with cheese and hazelnuts.
Note: To toast nuts, bake in a shallow pan in a 350° oven for 5-10 minutes or cook in a skillet over low heat until lightly browned, stirring occasionally.
1 cup: 347 cal., 11g fat (5g sat. fat), 36mg chol., 470mg sod., 44g carb. (11g sugars, 4g fiber), 20g pro. **Diabetic exchanges:** 2½ starch, 1 medium-fat meat, 1 vegetable, 1 fat.

BLACK BEAN BURRITOS

My neighbor and I discovered these fabulous low-fat burritos a few years ago. On nights my husband or I have a meeting, we can have a satisfying supper on the table in minutes.
—Angela Studebaker, Goshen, IN

- -

Takes: 10 min. • **Makes:** 4 servings

- 1 Tbsp. canola oil
- 3 Tbsp. chopped onion
- 3 Tbsp. chopped green pepper
- 1 can (15 oz.) black beans, rinsed and drained
- 4 flour tortillas (8 in.), warmed
- 1 cup shredded Mexican cheese blend
- 1 medium tomato, chopped
- 1 cup shredded lettuce
  Optional toppings: Salsa, sour cream, minced fresh cilantro and cubed avocado

1. In a nonstick skillet, heat oil over medium heat; saute onion and green pepper until tender. Stir in beans; heat through.
2. Spoon about ½ cup of vegetable mixture off center on each tortilla. Sprinkle with the cheese, tomato and lettuce. Fold the sides and ends over filling and roll up. Serve with optional toppings as desired.
1 burrito: 395 cal., 16g fat (6g sat. fat), 25mg chol., 610mg sod., 46g carb. (2g sugars, 7g fiber), 16g pro. **Diabetic exchanges:** 2½ starch, 1 vegetable, 1 lean meat, 1 fat.

RAVIOLI WITH SNAP PEAS & MUSHROOMS

PINEAPPLE SHRIMP TACOS

Taste the tropics with our cool and crispy take on shrimp tacos. Wrapping the shells in lettuce adds even more crunch and keeps the tacos tidy after you take a bite.
—*Taste of Home* Test Kitchen

Takes: 25 min. • **Makes:** 4 servings

- 1 lb. uncooked large shrimp, peeled and deveined
- 3 tsp. olive oil, divided
- 1 large sweet orange pepper, sliced
- 1 large sweet red pepper, sliced
- 1 small onion, halved and sliced
- 1 cup pineapple tidbits
- 1 envelope fajita seasoning mix
- ⅓ cup water
- 8 corn tortillas (6 in.), warmed
- ½ cup shredded Cotija or mozzarella cheese
- 8 large romaine lettuce leaves

1. Cook shrimp in 2 tsp. oil in a large cast-iron or other heavy skillet over medium heat until shrimp turn pink, 4-6 minutes. Remove and keep warm.
2. In the same skillet, saute the peppers, onion and pineapple in remaining oil until vegetables are tender. Add seasoning mix and water. Bring to a boil; cook and stir for 2 minutes. Return shrimp to the skillet; heat through. Spoon onto tortillas; top with shredded cheese. Wrap the lettuce around tortillas to serve.
2 tacos: 382 cal., 11g fat (4g sat. fat), 153mg chol., 1123mg sod., 44g carb. (13g sugars, 6g fiber), 27g pro.

HEARTY CHICKPEA POTPIE

You simply won't miss the meat in this savory veggie potpie! The spring veggies, easy prep and impressive presentation make this a perfect addition to special family dinners.
—Deanna Wolfe, Muskegon, MI

Prep: 35 min. • **Cook:** 25 min.
Makes: 6 servings

- 1 pkg. (14.1 oz.) refrigerated pie crust
- 3 Tbsp. butter
- 1 cup diced onions
- 1 cup diced celery
- 1 cup diced carrots
- 1 cup diced potatoes
- 1 cup (4 oz.) frozen peas, thawed
- ¼ cup all-purpose flour
- 1 tsp. poultry seasoning
- ½ tsp. ground turmeric
- ¼ tsp. salt
- ¼ tsp. pepper
- 2 cups vegetable broth
- 1 can (15 oz.) chickpeas or garbanzo beans, rinsed and drained

1. Preheat oven to 400°. Unroll 1 crust into a 9-in. pie plate; trim even with rim. Line unpricked crust with parchment. Fill with pie weights or dried beans. Bake on a lower oven rack until edges are light golden brown, 15-20 minutes. Remove parchment and weights; bake until bottom is golden brown, 3-6 minutes longer. Cool on a wire rack.
2. Meanwhile, in a large skillet, melt butter over medium heat. Add onions, celery and carrots; cook and stir until onions are translucent, about 5 minutes. Stir in the potatoes and peas, cooking until vegetables are tender, 5-7 minutes. Whisk in the next 5 ingredients. Increase heat to medium-high; gradually whisk in vegetable broth. Bring to a boil; cook, stirring constantly, until thickened, 4-6 minutes. Stir in chickpeas. Remove from heat.
3. Spoon vegetable filling over bottom crust. Unroll remaining crust; place over filling. Trim; cut slits in top.
4. Bake until the top crust is golden, about 15 minutes. Cool 5 minutes before serving.
1 serving: 496 cal., 25g fat (11g sat. fat), 28mg chol., 760mg sod., 61g carb. (8g sugars, 6g fiber), 8g pro.

HEARTY CHICKPEA POTPIE

AIR-FRYER
FISH & CHIPS

SOUTHWESTERN VEGETABLES & RICE

Short on time? Here's a spicy, satisfying supper that comes together in minutes.
—*Taste of Home* Test Kitchen

Takes: 20 min. • **Makes:** 4 servings

- 1 can (14½ oz.) fire-roasted diced tomatoes, undrained
- 1 pkg. (12 oz.) frozen vegetarian meat crumbles, thawed
- 1 pkg. (10.8 oz.) frozen southwestern corn, thawed
- 1 can (10¾ oz.) condensed tomato soup, undiluted
- 1 cup water
- 1 tsp. ground cumin
- ¼ tsp. salt
- 1 cup uncooked instant rice
- 1 cup shredded Monterey Jack cheese

In a Dutch oven, combine first 7 ingredients. Bring to a boil. Stir in rice. Remove from the heat; cover and let stand for 5-7 minutes or until rice is tender. Sprinkle with cheese.
1½ cups: 502 cal., 15g fat (6g sat. fat), 25mg chol., 1629mg sod., 62g carb. (16g sugars, 7g fiber), 29g pro.

AIR-FRYER FISH & CHIPS

Looking for an easy air-fryer recipe? Try my simple fish and chips. The fillets have a fuss-free coating that's healthier than the deep-fried kind, but just as crunchy and golden. Simply seasoned, the crispy fries are perfect on the side.
—Janice Mitchell, Aurora, CO

Prep: 15 min. • **Cook:** 25 min.
Makes: 2 servings

- 1 medium potato
- 1 Tbsp. olive oil
- ⅛ tsp. pepper
- ⅛ tsp. salt

FISH

- 3 Tbsp. all-purpose flour
- ⅛ tsp. pepper
- 1 large egg
- 2 Tbsp. water
- ⅓ cup crushed cornflakes
- 1½ tsp. grated Parmesan cheese
   Dash cayenne pepper
- ⅛ tsp. salt
- ½ lb. haddock or cod fillets
   Tartar sauce, optional

1. Preheat air fryer to 400°. Peel and cut potato lengthwise into ½-in.-thick slices; cut slices into ½-in.-thick sticks.
2. In a large bowl, toss potato with oil, pepper and salt. Place potato pieces in a single layer in air-fryer basket; cook until just tender, 5-10 minutes Toss potatoes in basket to redistribute; continue to cook until lightly browned and crisp, 5-10 minutes longer.
3. Meanwhile, in a shallow bowl, mix flour and pepper. In another shallow bowl, whisk the egg with water. In a third bowl, toss the cornflakes with cheese and cayenne. Sprinkle fish with salt; dip into flour mixture to coat both sides and shake off excess. Dip in egg mixture, then in cornflake mixture, patting to help coating adhere.
4. Remove fries from basket; keep warm. Place fish in a single layer in air-fryer basket. Cook until fish is lightly browned and just beginning to flake easily with a fork, turning halfway through cooking, 8-10 minutes. Do not overcook. Return fries to basket to heat through. Serve immediately. If desired, serve with tartar sauce.
1 serving: 304 cal., 9g fat (2g sat. fat), 84mg chol., 503mg sod., 33g carb. (3g sugars, 1g fiber), 23g pro. **Diabetic exchanges:** 3 lean meat, 2 starch, 1½ fat..

GARLIC & HERB
ARTICHOKE SALMON

LIME & DILL
CHIMICHURRI SHRIMP

Chimichurri is a very popular condiment in Argentina and Uruguay and is often used as a dipping sauce or a marinade for meats. My chimichurri shrimp version incorporates both dill and lime, which give it a brighter flavor and make it ideal for spring and summer entertaining.
—Bonnie Landy, Castro Valley, CA

Prep: 25 min. + standing • **Grill:** 10 min.
Makes: 4 servings

- ½ cup extra virgin olive oil
- ½ cup packed fresh parsley sprigs
- ¼ cup snipped fresh dill
- ¼ cup fresh cilantro leaves
- 3 Tbsp. lime juice
- 3 garlic cloves, halved
- ½ tsp. salt
- ¼ tsp. pepper
- 1 lb. uncooked shrimp (26-30 per lb.), peeled and deveined
- 1 medium red onion, cut into thick wedges
- 1 medium zucchini, cut into ½-in. pieces
- 1 medium yellow summer squash, cut into ½-in. pieces
- 8 cherry tomatoes
  Crusty bread

1. Place the first 8 ingredients in a food processor; process until pureed. Reserve 6 Tbsp. mixture for serving. Place remaining mixture in a bowl; toss with the shrimp and vegetables. Let stand 15 minutes.
2. Alternately thread shrimp and vegetables onto 8 metal or soaked wooden skewers. Grill, covered, over medium heat or broil 4 in. from heat until shrimp turn pink, 3-4 minutes per side. Serve on bed of additional herbs with crusty bread and reserved sauce.
2 kabobs: 316 cal., 22g fat (3g sat. fat), 138mg chol., 371mg sod., 10g carb. (4g sugars, 2g fiber), 21g pro.

GARLIC & HERB
ARTICHOKE SALMON

If you're new to cooking fish (or even if you're a pro), this no-fail salmon recipe is one you have to try. It's easy enough for everyday, but also wows at dinner parties.
—Margee Berry, White Salmon, WA

Takes: 25 min. • **Makes:** 4 servings

- 4 salmon fillets (6 oz. each)
- 2 tsp. grated lemon zest
- ¼ tsp. salt
- ¼ tsp. pepper
- 2 green onions, white and green portions separated and sliced
- ¼ cup marinated quartered artichoke hearts
- 1 Tbsp. lemon juice
- ⅓ cup garlic-herb spreadable cheese (about half of a 6.5-oz. pkg.)

1. Place salmon fillets on a large piece of heavy-duty foil (about 18x12 in.), skin side down. Sprinkle with lemon zest, salt and pepper; top with white portion of green onions. Fold foil around fish, sealing tightly. Grill, covered, over medium-high heat until the salmon just begins to flake easily with a fork, 7-9 minutes.

2. Meanwhile, place the artichoke hearts, lemon juice and cheese in a food processor; process until smooth. To serve, open foil carefully to allow steam to escape. Remove salmon to serving plates, leaving skin on foil. Top fillets with artichoke mixture; sprinkle with remaining green onion.
1 serving: 379 cal., 27g fat (10g sat. fat), 109mg chol., 409mg sod., 3g carb. (1g sugars, 0 fiber), 30g pro.

ASK SARAH

WHAT'S THE ADVANTAGE OF
USING LEMON ZEST?

Lemon zest is a great way to punch up flavor, particularly in fish dishes. When zesting a lemon, don't cut into the white pith—it can taste bitter.

LIME & DILL
CHIMICHURRI SHRIMP

AIR-FRYER SPINACH FETA TURNOVERS

These quick and easy turnovers are one of my wife's favorite entrees. The refrigerated pizza dough makes preparation a snap!
—David Baruch, Weston, FL

Takes: 30 min. • **Makes:** 4 servings

- 2 large eggs
- 1 pkg. (10 oz.) frozen spinach, thawed, squeezed dry and chopped
- ¾ cup crumbled feta cheese
- 2 garlic cloves, minced
- ¼ tsp. pepper
- 1 tube (13.8 oz.) refrigerated pizza crust
  Refrigerated tzatziki sauce, optional

1. Preheat air fryer to 425°. In a bowl, whisk eggs; set aside 1 Tbsp. of eggs. Combine spinach, feta cheese, garlic, pepper and remaining beaten eggs.
2. Unroll pizza crust; roll into a 12-in. square. Cut into four 6-in. squares. Top each square with about ⅓ cup spinach mixture. Fold into a triangle and pinch edges to seal. Cut slits in top; brush with reserved egg.
3. In batches, place triangles in a single layer on greased tray in air-fryer basket. Cook until golden brown, 10-12 minutes. If desired, serve with tzatziki sauce.
1 turnover: 361 cal., 9g fat (4g sat. fat), 104mg chol., 936mg sod., 51g carb. (7g sugars, 4g fiber), 17g pro.

FISH TACOS WITH GUACAMOLE

FISH TACOS WITH GUACAMOLE

Fish tacos are my new favorite thing. They are lighter and so much healthier than beef tacos smothered in cheese. Try adding tomatoes, green onions and chopped jalapeno on top.
—Deb Perry, Traverse City, MI

Prep: 25 min. • **Cook:** 10 min.
Makes: 4 servings

- 2 cups angel hair coleslaw mix
- 1½ tsp. canola oil
- 1½ tsp. lime juice

GUACAMOLE

- 1 medium ripe avocado, peeled and quartered
- 2 Tbsp. fat-free sour cream
- 1 Tbsp. finely chopped onion
- 1 Tbsp. minced fresh cilantro
- ⅛ tsp. salt
  Dash pepper

TACOS

- 1 lb. tilapia fillets, cut into 1-in. pieces
- ¼ tsp. salt
- ⅛ tsp. pepper
- 2 tsp. canola oil
- 8 corn tortillas (6 in.), warmed
  Optional toppings: Hot pepper sauce, chopped tomatoes, green onions and jalapeno pepper

1. In a small bowl, toss the coleslaw mix with oil and lime juice; refrigerate until serving. In another bowl, the mash avocado with a fork; stir in sour cream, onion, cilantro, salt and pepper.
2. Sprinkle tilapia with salt and pepper. In a large nonstick skillet, heat canola oil over medium-high heat. Add tilapia; cook until fish just begins to flake easily with a fork, 3-4 minutes per side. Serve in tortillas with coleslaw, guacamole and desired toppings.
2 tacos: 308 cal., 12g fat (2g sat. fat), 56mg chol., 299mg sod., 28g carb. (2g sugars, 6g fiber), 25g pro. **Diabetic exchanges:** 3 lean meat, 2 starch, 2 fat.

SHRIMP PASTA PRIMAVERA

They say the way to a man's heart is through his stomach. So when I invite that special guy to dinner, I like to prepare something that's equally wonderful. This well-seasoned pasta dish has tons of flavor.
—Shari Neff, Takoma Park, MD

- -

Takes: 15 min. • **Makes:** 2 servings

- 4 oz. uncooked angel hair pasta
- 8 jumbo shrimp, peeled and deveined
- 6 fresh asparagus spears, trimmed and cut into 2-in. pieces
- ¼ cup olive oil
- 2 garlic cloves, minced
- ½ cup sliced fresh mushrooms
- ½ cup chicken broth
- 1 small plum tomato, peeled, seeded and diced
- ¼ tsp. salt
- ⅛ tsp. crushed red pepper flakes
- 1 Tbsp. each minced fresh basil, oregano, thyme and parsley
- ¼ cup grated Parmesan cheese

1. Cook the pasta according to package directions. Meanwhile, in a large skillet, saute shrimp and asparagus in oil until shrimp turn pink, 3-4 minutes. Add garlic; cook 1 minute longer. Add the mushrooms, broth, tomato, salt and pepper flakes; simmer, uncovered, for 2 minutes.

2. Drain pasta. Add the pasta and seasonings to skillet; toss to coat. Sprinkle with cheese.

1 serving: 581 cal., 32g fat (6g sat. fat), 89mg chol., 783mg sod., 49g carb. (4g sugars, 3g fiber), 24g pro.

RAVIOLI WITH CREAMY SQUASH SAUCE

Store-bought ravioli speeds assembly of this cozy, restaurant-quality dish that tastes so good, your family won't notice it's meatless.
—*Taste of Home* Test Kitchen

- -

Takes: 20 min. • **Makes:** 4 servings

- 1 pkg. (9 oz.) refrigerated cheese ravioli
- 3 garlic cloves, minced
- 2 Tbsp. butter
- 1 pkg. (10 oz.) frozen cooked winter squash, thawed
- 1 pkg. (6 oz.) fresh baby spinach
- 1 cup heavy whipping cream
- ⅓ cup vegetable broth
- ¼ tsp. salt
- 1 cup chopped walnuts, toasted

1. Cook the ravioli according to package directions. Meanwhile, in a Dutch oven, saute garlic in butter for 1 minute. Add the squash and spinach; cook 2-3 minutes longer or until spinach is wilted. Stir in the cream, vegetable broth and salt. Bring to a gentle boil; cook for 6-8 minutes or until slightly thickened.

2. Drain ravioli; add to squash mixture. Toss to coat. Sprinkle with walnuts.

1¼ cups: 671 cal., 51g fat (22g sat. fat), 122mg chol., 578mg sod., 42g carb. (2g sugars, 7g fiber), 18g pro.

SHRIMP PASTA PRIMAVERA

LENTIL LOAF

This lentil loaf is so flavorful, you won't even miss the meat. Best of all, it's packed with fiber and nutrients.
—Tracy Fleming, Phoenix, AZ

Prep: 35 min. • **Bake:** 45 min. + standing
Makes: 6 servings

¾ cup brown lentils, rinsed
1 can (14½ oz.) vegetable broth
1 Tbsp. olive oil
1¾ cups shredded carrots
1 cup finely chopped onion
1 cup chopped fresh mushrooms
2 Tbsp. minced fresh basil
   or 2 tsp. dried basil
1 Tbsp. minced fresh parsley
1 cup shredded part-skim
   mozzarella cheese
½ cup cooked brown rice
1 large egg
1 large egg white
½ tsp. salt
½ tsp. garlic powder
¼ tsp. pepper
2 Tbsp. tomato paste
2 Tbsp. water

1. Place lentils and broth in a small saucepan; bring to a boil. Reduce the heat; simmer, covered, until tender, about 30 minutes.
2. Preheat oven to 350°. Line a 9x5-in. loaf pan with parchment, letting ends extend up sides. Coat paper with cooking spray.
3. In a large skillet, heat oil over medium heat; saute carrots, onion and mushrooms until tender, about 10 minutes. Stir in herbs. Transfer to a large bowl; cool slightly.
4. Add cheese, brown rice, egg, egg white, seasonings and lentils to vegetables; mix well. Mix tomato paste and water; spread over loaf.
5. Bake until a thermometer inserted into the center reads 160°, 45-50 minutes. Let stand 10 minutes before slicing.
1 slice: 213 cal., 5g fat (3g sat. fat), 43mg chol., 580mg sod., 29g carb. (5g sugars, 5g fiber), 14g pro. **Diabetic exchanges:** 2 lean meat, 1½ starch, 1 vegetable, ½ fat.

LENTIL
LOAF

CRISPY RICE
PATTIES WITH
VEGETABLES & EGGS

ROSEMARY GARLIC SHRIMP

Delicate shrimp take on fabulous flavor when simmered in a chicken broth mixed with garlic and ripe olives.
—*Taste of Home* Test Kitchen

- -

Takes: 20 min. • **Makes:** 8 servings

- 1¼ cups chicken or vegetable broth
- 3 Tbsp. chopped ripe olives
- 1 small cayenne or other fresh red chili pepper, finely chopped
- 2 Tbsp. lemon juice
- 1 Tbsp. minced fresh rosemary or 1 tsp. dried rosemary, crushed
- 4 garlic cloves, minced
- 2 tsp. Worcestershire sauce
- 1 tsp. paprika
- ½ tsp. salt
- ¼ to ½ tsp. pepper
- 2 lbs. uncooked shrimp (31-40 per lb.), peeled and deveined

1. In a large skillet, combine all ingredients except shrimp; bring to a boil. Cook, uncovered, until liquid is reduced by half.
2. Stir in shrimp; return just to a boil. Reduce heat; simmer, uncovered, until shrimp turn pink, 3-4 minutes, stirring occasionally.
Note: Wear disposable gloves when cutting hot peppers; the oils can burn skin. Avoid touching your face.
½ cup: 110 cal., 2g fat (0 sat. fat), 139mg chol., 473mg sod., 3g carb. (1g sugars, 0 fiber), 19g pro. **Diabetic exchanges:** 3 lean meat.

CRISPY RICE PATTIES WITH VEGETABLES & EGGS

Serve these patties at any time of day. The recipe features vegetables, protein and grains all in one dish. It's also a great way to use leftover rice.
—Megumi Garcia, Milwaukee, WI

- -

Takes: 30 min. • **Makes:** 4 servings

- 2 pkg. (7.4 oz. each) ready-to-serve white sticky rice
- 1 Tbsp. plus 2 tsp. canola oil, divided
- 1 tsp. reduced-sodium soy sauce
- 2 cups thinly sliced Brussels sprouts
- 1 cup julienned carrots
- 1 medium sweet red pepper, julienned
- ½ tsp. sesame oil
- ½ tsp. salt
- ⅛ tsp. freshly ground pepper
- 1 Tbsp. water
- 4 large eggs
  Minced fresh chives
  Additional pepper

1. Cook rice according to package directions; cool slightly. Press one-fourth of the rice into a ½-cup measuring cup that has been moistened lightly with water; invert onto a large sheet of plastic wrap. Fold plastic around rice; shape rice into a ½-in.-thick patty. Repeat 3 times.
2. In a large nonstick skillet, heat 1 Tbsp. canola oil over medium-high heat. Cook patties until crisp, 3-5 minutes per side; brush tops with soy sauce after turning. Remove from pan; keep warm.
3. In same pan, cook and stir vegetables over medium-high heat until lightly browned. Stir in sesame oil, salt and pepper. Add water; reduce heat to medium. Cook, covered, until vegetables are crisp-tender, 1-2 minutes. Remove from pan; keep warm.
4. In same pan, heat remaining canola oil over medium heat. Break eggs, 1 at a time, into pan; immediately reduce heat to low. Cook, uncovered, until whites are completely set and the yolks just begin to thicken, about 5 minutes. To serve, top rice patties with vegetables and eggs. Sprinkle with chives and additional pepper.
1 serving: 320 cal., 11g fat (2g sat. fat), 186mg chol., 447mg sod., 43g carb. (4g sugars, 3g fiber), 11g pro. **Diabetic exchanges:** 3 starch, 1 medium-fat meat, 1 fat.

LEMONY SCALLOPS WITH ANGEL HAIR PASTA

This delicate dish tastes so bright with a touch of lemon and tender sauteed scallops. Serve with crusty whole grain bread, and you have an impressive dinner that comes together in a flash.
—Thomas Faglon, Somerset, NJ

Takes: 25 min. • **Makes:** 4 servings

- 8 oz. uncooked multigrain angel hair pasta
- 3 Tbsp. olive oil, divided
- 1 lb. sea scallops, patted dry
- 2 cups sliced radishes (about 1 bunch)
- 2 garlic cloves, sliced
- ½ tsp. crushed red pepper flakes
- 6 green onions, thinly sliced
- ½ tsp. kosher salt
- 1 Tbsp. grated lemon zest
- ¼ cup lemon juice

1. In a 6-qt. stockpot, cook pasta according to the package directions; drain and return to pot.
2. Meanwhile, in a large skillet, heat 2 Tbsp. oil over medium-high heat; sear scallops in batches until opaque and edges are golden brown, about 2 minutes per side. Remove from skillet; keep warm.
3. In the same skillet, saute radishes, garlic and pepper flakes in remaining oil until the radishes are tender, 2-3 minutes. Stir in green onions and salt; cook 1 minute. Add to pasta; toss to combine. Sprinkle with lemon zest and juice. Top with scallops to serve.
1½ cups: 404 cal., 13g fat (2g sat. fat), 27mg chol., 737mg sod., 48g carb. (4g sugars, 6g fiber), 25g pro.

GARDEN-FRESH GRILLED VEGGIE PIZZA

I have four gardens, including one just for herbs, so I always have a pretty wonderful spread of produce. I created this loaded-up pizza as a fun summer appetizer using some of my top garden goodies.
—Dianna Wara, Washington, IL

Prep: 30 min. • **Grill:** 15 min.
Makes: 6 servings

- 3 Tbsp. olive oil
- 3 garlic cloves, minced
- 3 medium tomatoes, cut into ½-in. slices
- 1 large sweet red pepper, halved, stemmed and seeded
- 1 small zucchini, cut lengthwise into ¼-in. slices
- 1 small onion, cut crosswise into ½-in. slices
- 1 tsp. coarsely ground pepper
- 1 prebaked 12-in. pizza crust
- ⅓ cup spreadable garden vegetable cream cheese
- 8 slices smoked provolone cheese, divided
- ½ cup minced fresh basil, divided
- ¼ cup shredded carrots
- 1 Tbsp. minced fresh oregano
- 1 tsp. minced fresh thyme

1. Mix oil and garlic; brush onto both sides of the vegetables. Sprinkle with the pepper. Grill, covered, over medium heat until tender, 4-5 minutes per side for pepper and onion, 3-4 minutes per side for zucchini, 2-3 minutes per side for tomatoes.
2. Coarsely chop pepper, onion and zucchini. Spread pizza crust with cream cheese; layer with 4 slices provolone and tomato slices. Sprinkle with ¼ cup basil, carrots, oregano and thyme. Top with grilled vegetables, then the remaining cheese.
3. Grill the pizza, covered, over medium heat until the bottom is golden brown and the cheese is melted, 5-7 minutes. Top with the remaining basil.
1 piece: 395 cal., 22g fat (8g sat. fat), 23mg chol., 618mg sod., 36g carb. (6g sugars, 3g fiber), 16g pro.

GARDEN-FRESH GRILLED VEGGIE PIZZA

BLEND OF
THE BAYOU

SPEEDY SALMON STIR-FRY

Salmon is a staple where I live, so I tried it in a stir-fry. My recipe has an orange glaze, but I like it with lime, too.
—Joni Hilton, Rocklin, CA

- -

Takes: 30 min. • **Makes:** 4 servings

- ¼ cup reduced-fat honey mustard salad dressing
- 2 Tbsp. orange juice
- 1 Tbsp. minced fresh gingerroot
- 1 Tbsp. reduced-sodium soy sauce
- 1 Tbsp. molasses
- 1 tsp. grated orange zest
- 4 tsp. canola oil, divided
- 1 lb. salmon fillets, skinned and cut into 1-in. pieces
- 1 pkg. (16 oz.) frozen stir-fry vegetable blend
- 2⅔ cups hot cooked brown rice
- 1 Tbsp. sesame seeds, toasted

1. In a small bowl, whisk first 6 ingredients. In a large skillet, heat 2 tsp. canola oil over medium-high heat. Add salmon; cook and gently stir 3-4 minutes or until fish just begins to flake easily with a fork. Remove from pan.

2. In same pan, heat remaining oil. Add vegetable blend; stir-fry until crisp-tender. Add salad dressing mixture. Return salmon to skillet. Gently combine; heat through. Serve with rice; sprinkle with sesame seeds.

1 cup stir-fry with ⅔ cup rice: 498 cal., 19g fat (3g sat. fat), 57mg chol., 394mg sod., 54g carb. (11g sugars, 5g fiber), 26g pro.

BLEND OF THE BAYOU

My sister-in-law shared this recipe with me when I first moved to Louisiana. It's been handed down in my husband's family for generations. It's quick to prepare, nutritious and beautiful. I've passed it on to my adult children, too.
—Ruby Williams, Bogalusa, LA

- -

Prep: 20 min. • **Bake:** 25 min.
Makes: 8 servings

- 1 pkg. (8 oz.) cream cheese, cubed
- 4 Tbsp. butter, divided
- 1 large onion, chopped
- 2 celery ribs, chopped
- 1 large green pepper, chopped
- 1 lb. cooked medium shrimp, peeled and deveined
- 2 cans (6 oz. each) crabmeat, drained, flaked and cartilage removed
- 1 can (10¾ oz.) condensed cream of mushroom soup, undiluted
- ¾ cup cooked rice
- 1 jar (4½ oz.) sliced mushrooms, drained
- 1 tsp. garlic salt
- ¾ tsp. hot pepper sauce
- ½ tsp. cayenne pepper
- ¾ cup shredded cheddar cheese
- ½ cup crushed butter-flavored crackers (about 12 crackers)

1. Preheat oven to 350°. In a small saucepan, cook and stir cream cheese and 2 Tbsp. butter over low heat until mixture is melted and smooth.

2. In a large cast-iron or other ovenproof skillet, saute onion, celery and green pepper in remaining butter until tender. Stir in shrimp, crab, soup, rice, mushrooms, garlic salt, pepper sauce, cayenne and cream cheese mixture.

3. Combine cheddar cheese and cracker crumbs; sprinkle over top. Bake, uncovered, until bubbly, 25-30 minutes.

1 cup: 366 cal., 23g fat (13g sat. fat), 164mg chol., 981mg sod., 17g carb. (3g sugars, 2g fiber), 23g pro.

"This instantly became a favorite in my home. I've never had a seafood dish this comforting. I also love that I can make it in my cast-iron skillet!"

—MARK HAGEN, EXECUTIVE EDITOR

VEGETARIAN
SKILLET ENCHILADAS

VEGETARIAN SKILLET ENCHILADAS

Whether it's for meatless Monday or your family's everyday vegetarian meal, everyone will be satisfied with these unconventional enchiladas. Garnish with optional toppings or other favorites like tortilla chips and extra shredded cheese.
—Susan Court, Pewaukee, WI

- -

Takes: 25 min. • **Makes:** 4 servings

- 1 Tbsp. canola oil
- 1 medium onion, chopped
- 1 medium sweet red pepper, chopped
- 2 garlic cloves, minced
- 1 can (15 oz.) black beans, rinsed and drained
- 1 can (10 oz.) enchilada sauce
- 1 cup frozen corn
- 2 tsp. chili powder
- ½ tsp. ground cumin
- ⅛ tsp. pepper
- 8 corn tortillas (6 in.), cut into ½-in. strips
- 1 cup shredded Mexican cheese blend
  Optional: Chopped fresh cilantro, sliced avocado, sliced radishes, sour cream and lime wedges

1. Preheat oven to 400°. Heat oil in a 10-in. cast-iron or other ovenproof skillet over medium-high heat. Add onion and pepper; cook and stir until tender, 2-3 minutes. Add garlic; cook 1 minute longer. Stir in beans, enchilada sauce, corn, chili powder, cumin and pepper. Stir in tortillas.
2. Bring to a boil. Reduce heat; simmer, uncovered, until tortillas are softened, 3-5 minutes. Sprinkle with cheese. Bake, uncovered, until sauce is bubbly and cheese is melted, 3-5 minutes. If desired, garnish with optional ingredients.
1½ cups: 307 cal., 14g fat (5g sat. fat), 25mg chol., 839mg sod., 33g carb. (5g sugars, 7g fiber), 14g pro.

TEST KITCHEN TIP
We love these deconstructed enchiladas as a zesty meatless entree, but they're also a great way to use up leftover cooked beef, chicken or even pork. Simply chop up the meat and stir in with the beans.

POACHED SALMON WITH CHIMICHURRI

POACHED SALMON WITH CHIMICHURRI

Tender, flaky poached salmon is treated to a flavorful sauce in this elegant dish. Though the entree may take a little extra prep time, the impressive main course will please everyone at the table.
—*Taste of Home* Test Kitchen

- -

Prep: 40 min. • **Cook:** 10 min.
Makes: 4 servings

- 4 cups water
- ½ cup white wine or reduced-sodium chicken broth
- ½ cup white wine vinegar
- 1 medium carrot, coarsely chopped
- 1 celery rib with leaves, coarsely chopped
- 1 medium onion, coarsely chopped
- 4 sprigs fresh parsley
- 4 whole peppercorns
- 1 bay leaf
- 4 salmon fillets (4 oz. each)

CHIMICHURRI
- 2 Tbsp. lemon juice
- 1 Tbsp. white wine vinegar
- 1 Tbsp. olive oil
- 3 Tbsp. finely chopped onion
- 3 Tbsp. minced fresh parsley
- 1 garlic clove, minced
- ⅛ tsp. pepper
- ⅛ tsp. cayenne pepper

1. In a large Dutch oven, bring the first 9 ingredients to a boil. Reduce heat; simmer, uncovered, for 15 minutes. Strain, reserving liquid (discard vegetables and spices).
2. Return liquid to the pan and bring to a boil. Reduce heat; add salmon. Poach, uncovered, until fish just begins to flake easily with a fork, 8-10 minutes.
3. Meanwhile, in a small bowl, whisk the lemon juice, vinegar and oil. Stir in the onion, parsley, garlic, pepper and cayenne. Serve with salmon.
1 fillet with 1 Tbsp. chimichurri: 246 cal., 16g fat (3g sat. fat), 67mg chol., 69mg sod., 2g carb. (1g sugars, 0 fiber), 23g pro.

TRUE SHRIMP CREOLE

An authentic Cajun dish, this tastes even better if refrigerated overnight to allow all the flavors to blend.
—Johnnie McLeod, Bastrop, LA

Prep: 10 min. • **Cook:** 25 min.
Makes: 6 servings

- ¼ cup all-purpose flour
- ½ cup canola oil
- 1 medium onion, chopped
- 1 medium green pepper, chopped
- 1 celery rib, chopped
- 1 garlic clove, minced
- 1 can (14½ oz.) stewed tomatoes
- 1 can (6 oz.) tomato paste
- 4 bay leaves
- 1 Tbsp. Worcestershire sauce
- ½ tsp. hot pepper sauce
  Salt and pepper to taste
- 2 lbs. fresh or frozen uncooked medium shrimp, peeled and deveined
  Hot cooked rice

1. In a large heavy skillet, combine flour and oil until smooth. Cook and stir over medium heat until flour is a rich deep brown. Add onion, green pepper and celery; cook until vegetables are tender, 5-6 minutes. Add minced garlic; cook 1 minute longer. Stir in next 6 ingredients. Cover and simmer until heated through, 4-5 minutes.
2. Add shrimp. Simmer, uncovered, until shrimp turn pink, 5-6 minutes. Discard bay leaves. Serve with rice.
1 serving: 358 cal., 19g fat (3g sat. fat), 224mg chol., 440mg sod., 20g carb. (10g sugars, 3g fiber), 27g pro.

CRAWFISH ETOUFFEE

CRAWFISH ETOUFFEE

I like to serve this Cajun sensation when I entertain. Etouffee is typically served with shellfish over rice and is similar to gumbo. This dish has its roots in New Orleans and the bayou country of Louisiana.
—Tamra Duncan, Lincoln, AR

Prep: 15 min. • **Cook:** 50 min.
Makes: 8 servings

- ½ cup butter, cubed
- ½ cup plus 2 Tbsp. all-purpose flour
- 1¼ cups chopped celery
- 1 cup chopped green pepper
- ½ cup chopped green onions
- 1 can (14½ oz.) chicken broth
- 1 cup water
- ¼ cup minced fresh parsley
- 1 Tbsp. tomato paste
- 1 bay leaf
- ½ tsp. salt
- ¼ tsp. pepper
- ¼ tsp. cayenne pepper
- 2 lbs. frozen cooked crawfish tail meat, thawed
  Hot cooked rice

1. In a large heavy skillet, melt butter; stir in flour. Cook and stir over low heat until mixture is a caramel-colored paste, about 20 minutes. Add the celery, pepper and onions; stir until coated. Add the broth, water, parsley, tomato paste, bay leaf, salt, pepper and cayenne pepper. Bring to a boil.
2. Reduce heat; cover and simmer for 30 minutes, stirring occasionally. Discard bay leaf. Add crawfish and heat through. Serve with rice.
1 cup: 250 cal., 13g fat (7g sat. fat), 187mg chol., 579mg sod., 10g carb. (1g sugars, 1g fiber), 22g pro.

DECADENT SPINACH-STUFFED SHELLS

I created this comforting stuffed shells dish to serve on Christmas Eve, but it's so good that we enjoy it all year long. It can easily be assembled and frozen to bake at a later date. If you have any leftover cheese mixture, you can serve it as a dip, either cold or spooned into ramekins and baked until browned. If you don't like roasted red peppers, feel free to substitute chopped sun-dried tomatoes in the filling. You can also use any pasta sauce you have on hand.
—Crystal Schlueter, Northglenn, CO

Prep: 25 min. • **Cook:** 30 min.
Makes: 12 servings

- 1 pkg. (12 oz.) jumbo pasta shells
- 1 jar (24 oz.) roasted red pepper and garlic pasta sauce, divided
- 2 pkg. (8 oz. each) cream cheese, softened
- 1 cup roasted garlic Alfredo sauce
  Dash salt
  Dash pepper
  Dash crushed red pepper flakes, optional
- 2 cups shredded Italian cheese blend
- ½ cup grated Parmesan cheese
- 1 pkg. (10 oz.) frozen chopped spinach, thawed and squeezed dry
- ½ cup finely chopped water-packed artichoke hearts
- ¼ cup finely chopped roasted sweet red pepper
  Additional Parmesan cheese, optional

1. Preheat oven to 350°. Cook the pasta shells according to package directions for al dente. Drain.
2. Spread 1 cup sauce into a greased 13x9-in. baking dish. In a large bowl, beat cream cheese, Alfredo sauce and seasonings until blended. Stir in cheeses and vegetables. Spoon into shells. Arrange in prepared baking dish.
3. Pour remaining sauce over top. Bake, covered, 20 minutes. If desired, sprinkle with additional Parmesan cheese. Bake, uncovered, 10-15 minutes longer or until cheese is melted.

3 stuffed pasta shells: 389 cal., 22g fat (13g sat. fat), 70mg chol., 707mg sod., 33g carb. (7g sugars, 3g fiber), 14g pro.

EDAMAME & SOBA NOODLE BOWL

Toothsome soba noodles are made from buckwheat flour.
—Matthew Hass, Ellison Bay, WI

Takes: 30 min. • **Makes:** 6 servings

- 1 pkg. (12 oz.) uncooked Japanese soba noodles or whole wheat spaghetti
- 2 Tbsp. sesame oil
- 2 cups fresh small broccoli florets
- 1 medium onion, halved and thinly sliced
- 3 cups frozen shelled edamame, thawed
- 2 large carrots, cut into ribbons with a vegetable peeler
- 4 garlic cloves, minced
- 1 cup reduced-fat Asian toasted sesame salad dressing
- ¼ tsp. pepper
  Sesame seeds, toasted, optional

1. In a 6 qt. stockpot, cook soba noodles according to package directions; drain and return to pan.
2. Meanwhile, in a large skillet, heat oil over medium heat. Add the broccoli and onion; cook and stir until crisp-tender, 4-6 minutes. Add the edamame and carrots; cook and stir until tender, 6-8 minutes. Add the garlic; cook 1 minute longer. Add the vegetable mixture, dressing and pepper to noodles; toss to combine. Sprinkle with the sesame seeds if desired.

1⅓ cups: 414 cal., 12g fat (1g sat. fat), 0 chol., 867mg sod., 64g carb. (12g sugars, 4g fiber), 18g pro.

DECADENT SPINACH-STUFFED SHELLS

JAMAICAN SALMON WITH COCONUT CREAM SAUCE

We try to eat salmon a lot because it's so healthy, and I love thinking of new ways to make it different and delicious. This dazzler is easy and is my go-to meal for company.
—Joni Hilton, Rocklin, CA

Takes: 30 min. • **Makes:** 4 servings

- 4 salmon fillets (6 oz. each)
- 3 Tbsp. mayonnaise
- 4 tsp. Caribbean jerk seasoning
- ⅓ cup sour cream
- ¼ cup cream of coconut
- 1 tsp. grated lime zest
- ¼ cup lime juice
- ½ cup sweetened shredded coconut, toasted

1. Preheat oven to 350°. Place fillets in a greased 13x9-in. baking dish. Spread the mayonnaise over the fillets; sprinkle with jerk seasoning.
2. Bake until fish just begins to flake easily with a fork, 18-22 minutes. Meanwhile, for sauce, in a small saucepan, combine sour cream, cream of coconut, and lime zest and juice; cook and stir over medium-low heat until blended.
3. Drizzle the fillets with the sauce; sprinkle with coconut.
Note: To toast coconut, bake in a shallow pan in a 350° oven for 5-10 minutes or cook in a skillet over low heat until golden brown, stirring occasionally.
1 fillet with 3 Tbsp. sauce and 2 Tbsp. coconut: 497 cal., 34g fat (12g sat. fat), 102mg chol., 467mg sod., 16g carb. (14g sugars, 1g fiber), 30g pro.

MODERN TUNA CASSEROLE

I loved tuna casserole as a kid and found myself craving it as an adult. However, the massive amounts of fat and salt in the traditional recipe were a turnoff healthwise, and it didn't taste as good as I remembered. I reconfigured the recipe to include more vegetables and the result was delicious.
—Rebecca Blanton, St. Helena, CA

Prep: 20 min. • **Cook:** 20 min.
Makes: 6 servings

- 3 Tbsp. butter, divided
- 4 medium carrots, chopped
- 1 medium onion, chopped
- 1 medium sweet red pepper, chopped
- 1 cup sliced baby portobello mushrooms
- 2 cans (5 oz. each) albacore white tuna in water, drained and flaked
- 2 cups fresh baby spinach
- 1 cup frozen peas
- 3 cups uncooked spiral pasta
- 1 Tbsp. all-purpose flour
- ⅔ cup reduced-sodium chicken broth
- ⅓ cup half-and-half cream
- ½ cup shredded Parmesan cheese
- ¾ tsp. salt
- ¼ tsp. pepper

1. In a large skillet, heat 1 Tbsp. butter over medium-high heat. Add carrots, onion, red pepper and mushrooms. Cook and stir until tender, 8-10 minutes. Add tuna, baby spinach and peas; cook until spinach is just wilted, 2-3 minutes.
2. Meanwhile, cook the pasta according to package directions for al dente. Drain pasta, reserving 1 cup pasta water. In a large bowl, place the pasta and tuna mixture; toss to combine. Wipe skillet clean.
3. In the same skillet, melt remaining butter over medium heat. Stir in flour until smooth; gradually whisk in broth and cream. Bring to a boil, stirring constantly; cook and stir until thickened, 1-2 minutes, adding reserved pasta water if needed. Stir in cheese, salt and pepper. Pour over pasta; toss to coat.
1¾ cups: 372 cal., 11g fat (6g sat. fat), 47mg chol., 767mg sod., 44g carb. (7g sugars, 5g fiber), 23g pro. **Diabetic exchanges:** 3 lean meat, 2½ starch, 1½ fat, 1 vegetable.

MODERN TUNA CASSEROLE

FROGMORE STEW

This picnic-style medley of shrimp, smoked kielbasa, corn and spuds is a specialty of South Carolina cuisine. It's commonly dubbed Frogmore stew or Beaufort stew in recognition of both of the low country communities that lay claim to its origin. No matter what you call it, this one-pot wonder won't disappoint!
—*Taste of Home* Test Kitchen

Prep: 10 min. • **Cook:** 35 min.
Makes: 8 servings

- 16 cups water
- 1 large sweet onion, quartered
- 3 Tbsp. seafood seasoning
- 2 medium lemons, halved, optional
- 1 lb. small red potatoes
- 1 lb. smoked kielbasa or fully cooked hot links, cut into 1-in. pieces
- 4 medium ears sweet corn, cut into thirds
- 2 lbs. uncooked medium shrimp, peeled and deveined
  Seafood cocktail sauce
  Melted butter
  Additional seafood seasoning

1. In a stockpot, combine water, onion, seafood seasoning and, if desired, lemons; bring to a boil. Add the potatoes; cook, uncovered, 10 minutes. Add kielbasa and corn; return to a boil. Reduce heat; simmer, uncovered, 10-12 minutes or until potatoes are tender. Add shrimp; cook 2-3 minutes longer or until shrimp turn pink.

2. Drain; transfer to a bowl. Serve with cocktail sauce, butter and additional seasoning.

1 serving: 369 cal., 18g fat (6g sat. fat), 175mg chol., 751mg sod., 24g carb. (7g sugars, 2g fiber), 28g pro.

FROGMORE STEW

JALAPENO-LIME CHICKEN
DRUMSTICKS, PAGE 131

Beef, Chicken & Pork

Testing and tasting recipe submissions all day, our kitchen pros have long lists of entree recipes they've taken home to prepare for their own families. Here are just a few of the main courses they turn to most.

SLOW-COOKER TATER TOT CASSEROLE

What's not to love about classic Tater Tot casserole—especially when it's made easy in the slow cooker? You'll want to add this family-pleasing potluck favorite to your regular rotation.
—Nick Iverson, Denver, CO

- -

Prep: 25 min. • **Cook:** 6 hours + standing
Makes: 12 servings

- 2 lbs. ground beef
- 1 large onion, chopped
- 1 lb. sliced fresh mushrooms
- 3 garlic cloves, minced
- 2 cans (10¾ oz. each) condensed cream of mushroom soup, undiluted
- ½ tsp. salt
- ½ tsp. pepper
- 1 lb. frozen cut green beans
- 1 bag (32 oz.) frozen Tater Tots
- 1 cup shredded cheddar cheese

1. In a large skillet cook beef over medium-high heat until no longer pink, 5-6 minutes, breaking into crumbles; drain and transfer to a 5-qt. slow cooker. Add the onions and sliced mushrooms to skillet; cook over medium-high heat until vegetables are tender, 8-10 minutes. Add the garlic; cook 1 minute longer. Stir in condensed soup, salt and pepper. Place vegetable mixture in slow cooker; add green beans and stir to combine. Top with Tater Tots and cheese.
2. Cook, covered, on low 6 hours. Let stand, uncovered, 15 minutes before serving.

1 serving: 383 cal., 22g fat (7g sat. fat), 58mg chol., 941mg sod., 27g carb. (3g sugars, 4g fiber), 20g pro.

SLOW-COOKER TATER TOT CASSEROLE

HAM & SCALLOPED POTATOES

I fix this saucy skillet dish often, especially when I'm running late, because it's easy and it takes so little time to prepare. The recipe actually won first prize in our local paper some years back.
—Emma Magielda, Amsterdam, NY

- -

Takes: 30 min. • **Makes:** 4 servings

- 4 medium potatoes, peeled and thinly sliced
- 2 Tbsp. butter
- ⅓ cup water
- ½ cup 2% milk
- 2 to 3 Tbsp. onion soup mix
- 3 Tbsp. minced fresh parsley
- 1 cup cubed Velveeta
- 1 cup cubed fully cooked ham

1. In a large skillet, cook potatoes in butter until potatoes are lightly browned. Add water; bring to a boil. Reduce heat; cover and simmer for 14-15 minutes or until potatoes are tender.
2. Meanwhile in a small bowl, combine the milk, soup mix and parsley; stir in cheese. Pour over potatoes. Add ham; cook and stir gently over medium heat until cheese is melted and sauce is bubbly.

1 serving: 353 cal., 17g fat (10g sat. fat), 56mg chol., 1170mg sod., 36g carb. (6g sugars, 2g fiber), 16g pro.

MEAT & POTATO KABOBS

They're summery, but these kabobs really stick to your ribs. A microwave makes quick work of cooking the potatoes, so grilling is done in a flash.

—*Taste of Home* Test Kitchen

Takes: 30 min. • **Makes:** 4 servings

MEAT &
POTATO KABOBS

1	lb. beef top sirloin steak, cut into 1-in. cubes
1½	tsp. steak seasoning, divided
1	garlic clove, minced
1	cup cola
3	small red potatoes (about 8 oz.), cubed
1	Tbsp. water
1	cup cherry tomatoes
1	medium sweet orange pepper, cut into 1-in. pieces
1	tsp. canola oil
1	cup pineapple chunks

1. Sprinkle beef with 1 tsp. steak seasoning and garlic. Place cola in a large bowl. Add beef; toss to coat. Set aside.

2. Place potatoes and water in a microwave-safe bowl. Microwave, covered, on high for 4-5 minutes or just until tender; drain. Return to bowl. Add tomatoes, pepper, oil and remaining steak seasoning; gently toss to coat.

3. Drain beef, discarding the marinade. On 8 metal or soaked wooden skewers, alternately thread beef, vegetables and pineapple. Grill, covered, over medium heat or broil 4 in. from heat until beef reaches desired doneness and pepper is crisp-tender, 6-8 minutes, turning the skewers occasionally.

2 kabobs: 279 cal., 6g fat (2g sat. fat), 46mg chol., 321mg sod., 30g carb. (19g sugars, 3g fiber), 26g pro. **Diabetic exchanges:** 3 lean meat, 2 starch.

TEST KITCHEN TIP

Some cooks find it easier to thread the meat and the produce on separate skewers. This can make it easier to cook the meat to desired donesss without over- or undercooking the produce.

ASPARAGUS HAM DINNER

I've been making this light meal for my family for years now, and it's always well received. With asparagus, tomato, pasta and chunks of ham, it's a tempting blend of tastes and textures.
—Rhonda Zavodny, David City, NE

- -

Takes: 25 min. • **Makes:** 6 servings

- 2 cups uncooked corkscrew or spiral pasta
- ¾ lb. fresh asparagus, cut into 1-in. pieces
- 1 medium sweet yellow pepper, julienned
- 1 Tbsp. olive oil
- 6 medium tomatoes, diced
- 6 oz. boneless fully cooked ham, cubed
- ¼ cup minced fresh parsley
- ½ tsp. salt
- ½ tsp. dried oregano
- ½ tsp. dried basil
- ⅛ to ¼ tsp. cayenne pepper
- ¼ cup shredded Parmesan cheese

Cook pasta according to package directions. Meanwhile, in a large cast-iron or other heavy skillet, saute asparagus and yellow pepper in olive oil until crisp-tender. Add tomatoes and ham; heat through. Drain pasta; add to mixture. Stir in parsley and seasonings. Sprinkle with cheese.

1⅓ cups: 204 cal., 5g fat (1g sat. fat), 17mg chol., 561mg sod., 29g carb. (5g sugars, 3g fiber), 12g pro. **Diabetic exchanges:** 1½ starch, 1 lean meat, 1 vegetable, ½ fat.

LIME-CHIPOTLE
CARNITAS TOSTADAS

LIME-CHIPOTLE CARNITAS TOSTADAS

Here's a terrific recipe for your next party! Set out various toppings and garnishes so guests can customize their own tostadas with the lime-kissed shredded pork.
—Jan Valdez, Chicago, IL

- -

Prep: 20 min. • **Cook:** 8 hours
Makes: 16 servings

- ½ cup chicken broth
- 4 tsp. ground chipotle pepper
- 4 tsp. ground cumin
- 1 tsp. salt
- 1 boneless pork shoulder roast (4 to 5 lbs.), halved
- 1 large onion, peeled and halved
- 8 garlic cloves, peeled
- 1 to 2 limes, halved
- 16 tostada shells
  Optional toppings: Warmed refried beans, salsa, sour cream, shredded lettuce, sliced avocado, crumbled queso fresco and minced fresh cilantro
  Lime wedges

1. Add broth to a 5-qt. slow cooker. Mix seasonings; rub over all sides of pork. Place in slow cooker. Add onion and garlic cloves. Cook, covered, on low 8-10 hours, until meat is tender.

2. Remove pork; cool slightly. Strain cooking juices, reserving garlic cloves; discard onion. Skim fat from cooking juices. Mash garlic with a fork. Shred pork with 2 forks.

3. Return cooking juices, garlic and pork to slow cooker. Squeeze lime juice over pork; heat through, stirring to combine. Layer tostada shells with the pork mixture and toppings as desired. Serve with lime wedges.

1 tostada: 269 cal., 15g fat (5g sat. fat), 76mg chol., 279mg sod., 9g carb. (1g sugars, 1g fiber), 23g pro. **Diabetic exchanges:** 3 medium-fat meat, ½ starch.

SLOW-COOKED MEXICAN MEAT LOAF

Chopped onion and garlic plus a few spicy seasonings add outstanding flavor to this slow-cooked meat loaf.
—*Taste of Home* Test Kitchen

Prep: 25 min. • **Cook:** 4 hours
Makes: 8 servings

- 6   Tbsp. ketchup, divided
- 2   Tbsp. Worcestershire sauce
- 12 saltines, crushed
- 1   medium onion, finely chopped
- 6   garlic cloves, minced
- 1   tsp. paprika
- ½   tsp. salt
- ½   tsp. pepper
- ⅛   tsp. cayenne pepper
- 2   lbs. lean ground beef (90% lean)

1. Cut three 20x3-in. strips of heavy-duty foil; crisscross so they resemble spokes of a wheel. Place strips on the bottom and up the sides of a 3-qt. slow cooker. Coat strips with cooking spray.

2. In a large bowl, combine 2 Tbsp. ketchup, Worcestershire sauce, saltines, onion, garlic, paprika, salt, pepper and cayenne. Crumble beef over mixture and mix well.

3. Shape into a round loaf. Place in the center of the strips. Cover; cook on low 4-5 hours, until no pink remains and a thermometer reads 160°.

4. Using foil strips as handles, remove the meat loaf to a platter.

5. Spread remaining ketchup over top.

1 slice: 222 cal., 10g fat (4g sat. fat), 71mg chol., 447mg sod., 10g carb. (5g sugars, 1g fiber), 23g pro. **Diabetic exchanges:** 3 lean meat, ½ starch.

DID YOU KNOW?

Worcestershire is a thin, dark sauce used in meats, gravies, sauces and salad dressings, and as a condiment. It's made with white vinegar, garlic, molasses, tamarind extract, onions and anchovies. White wine Worcestershire sauce, which is pale in color, is also available.

CHICKEN CORDON BLEU BAKE

A friend shared this awesome hot dish recipe with me. I freeze several pans to share with neighbors or for days when I'm scrambling at mealtime.
—Rea Newell, Decatur, IL

Prep: 20 min. • **Bake:** 40 min.
Makes: 2 casseroles (6 servings each)

- 2   pkg. (6 oz. each) reduced-sodium stuffing mix
- 1   can (10¾ oz.) condensed cream of chicken soup, undiluted
- 1   cup 2% milk
- 8   cups cubed cooked chicken
- ½   tsp. pepper
- ¾   lb. sliced deli ham, cut into 1-in. strips
- 1   cup shredded Swiss cheese
- 3   cups shredded cheddar cheese

1. Preheat oven to 350°. Prepare stuffing mixes according to package directions. Meanwhile, whisk together soup and milk.

2. Toss chicken with pepper; divide between 2 greased 13x9-in. baking dishes. Layer with ham, Swiss cheese, 1 cup cheddar cheese, soup mixture and stuffing. Sprinkle with remaining cheddar cheese.

3. Bake, covered, 30 minutes. Uncover; bake until cheese is melted, 10-15 minutes.

Freeze option: Cover and freeze unbaked casserole. To use, partially thaw in the refrigerator overnight. Remove from refrigerator 30 minutes before baking. Preheat oven to 350°. Bake, covered, until dish is heated through and a thermometer inserted in the center reads 165°, about 45 minutes. Uncover; bake until cheese is melted, 10-15 minutes.

1 cup: 555 cal., 29g fat (15g sat. fat), 158mg chol., 1055mg sod., 26g carb. (5g sugars, 1g fiber), 46g pro.

SLOW-COOKED MEXICAN MEAT LOAF

HOMEMADE
CORNED BEEF

STEAK STROGANOFF

This slow-cooker recipe makes a traditional dinner completely fuss-free. Serve tender sirloin steak with a flavorful gravy over noodles for a homestyle meal that your whole family is sure to request again.
—Lisa VanEgmond, Annapolis, IL

- -

Prep: 25 min. • **Cook:** 7 hours
Makes: 12 servings

- 3 to 4 lbs. beef top sirloin steak, cubed
- 2 cans (14½ oz. each) chicken broth
- 1 lb. sliced fresh mushrooms
- 1 can (12 oz.) regular cola
- ½ cup chopped onion
- 1 envelope onion soup mix
- 1 to 2 tsp. garlic powder
- 2 tsp. dried parsley flakes
- ½ tsp. pepper
- 2 envelopes country gravy mix
- 2 cups sour cream
   Hot cooked noodles
   Minced fresh parsley, optional

1. In a 5-qt. slow cooker, combine the first 9 ingredients. Cover and cook on low for 7-8 hours or until beef is tender.
2. With a slotted spoon, remove beef and mushrooms. Place gravy mix in a large saucepan; gradually whisk in cooking liquid. Bring to a boil; cook and stir for 2 minutes or until thickened. Remove from the heat; stir in sour cream. Add beef and mushrooms to the gravy. Serve with noodles. If desired, sprinkle with parsley.
1 cup: 345 cal., 20g fat (11g sat. fat), 65mg chol., 840mg sod., 11g carb. (7g sugars, 1g fiber), 29g pro.

HOMEMADE CORNED BEEF

Here's a recipe you've gotta plan for, but you don't need to do much work to get this deli-quality corned beef.
—Nick Iverson, Denver, CO

- -

Prep: 30 min. + chilling • **Cook:** 3 hours
Makes: 12 servings

- 1 gallon water
- 1½ cups kosher salt
- ½ cup packed brown sugar
- ¼ cup mixed pickling spices, divided
- 4 tsp. pink curing salt #1
- 4 garlic cloves, minced
- 2 oven roasting bags
- 1 fresh beef brisket (4 to 5 lbs.)
- 2 large carrots, chopped
- 2 medium onions, chopped
- 2 celery ribs, chopped

1. In a large stockpot, combine water, kosher salt, brown sugar, 2 Tbsp. pickling spices, pink curing salt and garlic. Bring to a simmer, stirring until salt and sugar are dissolved.

Remove from the heat; cool to room temperature, then refrigerate until chilled.
2. Place 1 large oven roasting bag inside another. Place brisket inside inner bag; pour in cooled brine. Seal bags, pressing out as much air as possible; turn to coat meat. Refrigerate 10 days, turning occasionally to keep meat coated. Remove brisket from brine; rinse thoroughly. Place in a Dutch oven with water to cover. Add carrots, onions, celery and remaining pickling spices. Bring to a boil over high heat. Reduce heat; simmer, covered, adding water if necessary to keep brisket covered, until meat is tender, about 3 hours.
3. Serve warm or cool. Slice brisket thinly and serve in a sandwich or with additional vegetables simmered until tender in the cooking liquid.
To make ahead: Refrigerate meat in the cooking liquid for several days; reheat in the cooking liquid.
4 oz. cooked corned beef: 277 cal., 21g fat (7g sat. fat), 108mg chol., 1252mg sod., 1g carb. (0 sugars, 0 fiber), 20g pro.

STEAK
STROGANOFF

HAM & CHEESE POCKETS

These unique sandwich pockets are filled with ingredients most children like. But you'll find that adults enjoy them just as much as the kids do!
—Callie Myers, Rockport, TX

- -

Prep: 15 min. + rising • **Bake:** 15 min.
Makes: 10 servings

- 1 loaf (1 lb.) frozen bread dough, thawed
- 2½ cups finely chopped fully cooked ham
- 1 cup shredded Swiss cheese
- 1 large egg yolk
- 1 Tbsp. water

1. Let dough rise according to package directions. Punch down; divide into 10 pieces. On a lightly floured surface, roll each piece into a 5-in. circle.
2. Preheat oven to 375°. Place 1 circle on a greased baking sheet; top with about ¼ cup ham and 2 Tbsp. cheese to within ½ in. of edge. Press filling to flatten. Combine egg yolk and water; brush edges of dough. Fold dough over filling and pinch edges to seal. Repeat with remaining dough and filling. Brush tops with remaining egg yolk mixture.
3. Bake until golden brown, 15-20 minutes. Serve warm or cold.

1 pocket: 229 cal., 9g fat (3g sat. fat), 50mg chol., 729mg sod., 25g carb. (2g sugars, 1g fiber), 14g pro.

MUSHROOM PASTA CARBONARA

I absolutely love this creamy and cheesy recipe. I serve it with a side salad and rolls to make a complete meal.
—Cindi Bauer, Marshfield, WI

- -

Takes: 30 min. • **Makes:** 4 servings

- 2½ cups uncooked mostaccioli
- 8 bacon strips, diced
- 1 jar (4½ oz.) whole mushrooms, drained
- ¾ cup half-and-half cream
- ⅓ cup butter, cubed
- 1 tsp. dried parsley flakes
- 1 tsp. minced garlic
- 6 to 8 drops hot pepper sauce
- ¼ tsp. salt
- ⅓ cup grated Parmesan cheese
- ¼ cup sliced green onions

1. Cook mostaccioli according to the package directions.
2. Meanwhile, in a large skillet, cook bacon over medium heat until crisp. Using a slotted spoon, remove to paper towels to drain. Brown mushrooms in drippings; remove to paper towels. Drain drippings from pan.
3. Add the cream, butter, parsley, garlic, pepper sauce and salt to skillet; cook and stir over medium heat until butter is melted. Drain mostaccioli; add to cream mixture. Stir in bacon, mushrooms and cheese; heat through. Remove from the heat. Sprinkle with green onions.

1¼ cups: 511 cal., 33g fat (18g sat. fat), 78mg chol., 525mg sod., 43g carb. (4g sugars, 2g fiber), 11g pro.

HAM & CHEESE POCKETS

GARDEN-STUFFED
ZUCCHINI BOATS

JALAPENO-LIME CHICKEN DRUMSTICKS

Bottled hot sauce just isn't my thing, so I developed a fresh pepper glaze for grilled chicken. These drumsticks practically fly off the plate.
—Kristeen DeVorss, Farmington, NM

Takes: 25 min. • **Makes:** 6 servings

- 1 jar (10 oz.) red jalapeno pepper jelly
- ¼ cup lime juice
- 12 chicken drumsticks (about 3 lbs.)
- 1 tsp. salt
- ½ tsp. pepper

1. In a small saucepan, heat jelly and lime juice over medium heat until melted. Set aside ½ cup for serving.
2. Sprinkle chicken with salt and pepper. On a greased grill rack, grill chicken, covered, over medium heat 15-20 minutes or until a thermometer reads 170°-175°, turning occasionally and basting with remaining jelly mixture during the last 5 minutes of cooking. Serve with reserved jelly mixture.

2 chicken drumsticks: 361 cal., 12g fat (3g sat. fat), 95mg chol., 494mg sod., 34g carb. (24g sugars, 1g fiber), 29g pro.

GARDEN-STUFFED ZUCCHINI BOATS

These boats are not only healthy, they are basically a one-dish meal that covers all the bases. Just grab your favorite garden goodies and add any spices or mix-ins you and your family like.
—Janie Zirbser, Mullica Hill, NJ

Prep: 40 min. + cooling • **Bake:** 25 min.
Makes: 3 servings

- 3 medium zucchini
- ¾ lb. ground beef
- ¾ cup chopped onion
- ½ cup chopped green pepper
- 2 garlic cloves, minced
- 1½ cups water, divided
- ¾ cup canned fire-roasted diced tomatoes or chopped fresh tomatoes (with seeds and juices)
- ½ cup chopped roasted sweet red peppers
- ⅓ cup chopped fresh mushrooms
- ¼ cup uncooked ditalini or other small pasta
- 2 tsp. minced fresh thyme or 1 tsp. dried thyme
- ½ tsp. minced fresh oregano or ¼ tsp. dried oregano
- ¼ tsp. salt
- ¼ tsp. pepper
- ¼ cup grated Parmesan cheese
- 1 cup shredded Italian cheese blend, divided
  Pasta sauce, optional

1. Preheat oven to 350°. Halve zucchini lengthwise; place cut side down in an ungreased 13x9-in. baking dish. Bake for 10 minutes. When cool enough to handle, scoop out seeds, leaving a ¼-in. shell.
2. Meanwhile, in a large skillet, cook beef, onion, green pepper and garlic over medium heat 8-10 minutes or until beef is no longer pink, breaking up beef into crumbles; drain. Stir in 1 cup water, tomatoes, red peppers, mushrooms, pasta, thyme, oregano, salt and pepper. Cook until mixture is thickened and pasta is al dente, 12-15 minutes. Stir in the Parmesan cheese.
3. Spoon mixture into zucchini shells. Place in an ungreased 13x9-in. baking dish; sprinkle with ¾ cup Italian cheese blend. Pour the remaining water into bottom of dish. Bake, covered, 20 minutes. Sprinkle with remaining cheese. Bake, uncovered, until the zucchini is tender and cheese is melted, 5 minutes longer. Serve with pasta sauce if desired.
2 stuffed zucchini halves: 489 cal., 24g fat (12g sat. fat), 103mg chol., 992mg sod., 28g carb. (10g sugars, 4g fiber), 36g pro.

ASPARAGUS BEEF CASHEW STIR-FRY

As appealing to the eye as to the palate, this stovetop specialty features lots of vegetables, beef and crunchy cashews. A local restaurant once handed out asparagus recipes, including this one.
—Joyce Huebner, Marinette, WI

Prep: 20 min. • **Cook:** 25 min.
Makes: 6 servings

- 2 Tbsp. cornstarch
- 1 cup beef broth
- 3 Tbsp. soy sauce
- ½ tsp. sugar
- 2 Tbsp. canola oil
- 2 whole garlic cloves
- 2 lbs. fresh asparagus, trimmed and cut into 2½-in. pieces
- 2 medium onions, halved and thinly sliced
- 1 medium sweet red pepper, julienned
- 1 large carrot, cut into 2½-in. strips
- 2½ cups sliced cooked roast beef (2½-in. strips)
- 1 cup salted cashew halves Hot cooked rice

1. In a small bowl, combine cornstarch and broth until smooth. Stir in soy sauce and sugar; set aside. In a wok or large skillet, heat oil; add garlic cloves. Cook and stir until lightly browned, about 1 minute; discard garlic.
2. Stir-fry the asparagus, onions, red pepper and carrot until crisp-tender, 15-20 minutes. Add beef and heat through. Stir reserved sauce; add to the pan. Bring to a boil; cook and stir until thickened, about 2 minutes. Sprinkle with cashews. Serve with rice.
¾ cup: 382 cal., 21g fat (4g sat. fat), 54mg chol., 815mg sod., 18g carb. (7g sugars, 4g fiber), 30g pro.

ASPARAGUS BEEF CASHEW STIR-FRY

SWEET POTATO-CRUSTED CHICKEN NUGGETS

I was looking for ways to spice up traditional chicken nuggets and came up with this air-fryer recipe. The chips add crunch, while the meat is tender on the inside.
—Kristina Segarra, Yonkers, NY

Prep: 15 min. • **Cook:** 10 min./batch
Makes: 4 servings

- 1 cup sweet potato chips
- ¼ cup all-purpose flour
- 1 tsp. salt, divided
- ½ tsp. coarsely ground pepper
- ¼ tsp. baking powder
- 1 Tbsp. cornstarch
- 1 lb. chicken tenderloins, cut into 1½-in. pieces
  Cooking spray

1. Preheat air fryer to 400°. Place chips, flour, ½ tsp. salt, pepper and baking powder in a food processor; pulse until ground. Transfer to a shallow dish.
2. Mix cornstarch and remaining ½ tsp. salt; toss with chicken. Toss chicken with potato chip mixture, pressing to coat.
3. In batches, arrange chicken in a single layer on greased tray in air-fryer basket; spritz with cooking spray. Cook until golden brown, 3-4 minutes. Turn; spritz chicken with cooking spray. Cook until golden brown and chicken is no longer pink, 3-4 minutes longer.

3 oz. cooked chicken: 190 cal., 4g fat (0 sat. fat), 56mg chol., 690mg sod., 13g carb. (1g sugars, 1g fiber), 28g pro. **Diabetic exchanges:** 3 lean meat, 1 starch.

CIDER-GLAZED HAM

Here is a heartwarming and classic way to serve ham. I think the apple cider and mustard perfectly accent the ham's rich, smoky flavor.
—Jennifer Foos-Furer, Marysville, OH

Prep: 15 min. • **Cook:** 4 hours
Makes: 8 servings

- 1 boneless fully cooked ham (3 lbs.)
- 1¾ cups apple cider or juice
- ¼ cup packed brown sugar
- ¼ cup Dijon mustard
- ¼ cup honey
- 2 Tbsp. cornstarch
- 2 Tbsp. cold water

1. Place ham in a 5-qt. slow cooker. In a small bowl, combine cider, brown sugar, mustard and honey; pour over ham. Cover and cook on low for 4-5 hours or until heated through. Remove the ham and keep warm.
2. Pour cooking juices into a small saucepan. Combine cornstarch and water until smooth; stir into cooking juices. Bring to a boil; cook and stir for 2 minutes or until thickened. Serve with the ham.

4 oz. cooked ham with about ¼ cup glaze: 280 cal., 6g fat (2g sat. fat), 86mg chol., 1954mg sod., 26g carb. (21g sugars, 0 fiber), 31g pro.

SWEET POTATO-CRUSTED CHICKEN NUGGETS

QUICK GARLIC-LIME CHICKEN

After tending the farm and growing our own produce, I don't have much time left for cooking. This simple chicken dish is ideal for my many hectic days.
—Doris Carnahan, Lincoln, AR

Prep: 5 min. + marinating • **Grill:** 10 min.
Makes: 6 servings

- ⅓ cup soy sauce
- ¼ cup fresh lime juice
- 1 Tbsp. Worcestershire sauce
- ½ tsp. ground mustard
- 2 garlic cloves, minced
- 6 boneless skinless chicken breast halves (6 oz. each)
- ½ tsp. pepper

1. In a shallow dish, combine the first 5 ingredients; add chicken and turn to coat. Cover and refrigerate at least 30 minutes.
2. Drain and discard marinade. Sprinkle chicken with pepper. Grill, covered, over medium heat until a thermometer reads 165°, 7-8 minutes on each side.

1 chicken breast half: 191 cal., 4g fat (1g sat. fat), 94mg chol., 344mg sod., 1g carb. (0 sugars, 0 fiber), 35g pro. **Diabetic exchanges:** 5 lean meat.

PRESSURE-COOKER PORK CHOPS

PRESSURE-COOKER PORK CHOPS

Everyone will enjoy these fork-tender pork chops with a light gravy. Serve with a green vegetable or garden-fresh salad.
—Sue Bingham, Madisonville, TN

Prep: 15 min. • **Cook:** 5 min.
Makes: 4 servings

- ½ cup all-purpose flour, divided
- ½ tsp. ground mustard
- ½ tsp. garlic pepper blend
- ¼ tsp. seasoned salt
- 4 boneless pork loin chops (4 oz. each)
- 2 Tbsp. canola oil
- 1 can (14½ oz.) chicken broth, divided

1. In a shallow bowl, mix ¼ cup flour, ground mustard, garlic pepper and seasoned salt. Add pork chops, 1 at a time, and toss to coat; shake off excess.

2. Select saute or browning setting on a 6-qt. electric pressure cooker. Adjust for medium heat; add oil. When oil is hot, brown the pork in batches. Add 1½ cups broth to pressure cooker. Cook 30 seconds, stirring to loosen browned bits. Press cancel. Return all pork to pressure cooker.
3. Lock lid; close pressure-release valve. Adjust to pressure-cook on high for 3 minutes. Quick-release pressure. A thermometer inserted in pork should read at least 145°. Remove pork to a serving plate and keep warm.
4. In a small bowl, mix remaining ¼ cup flour and ¼ cup broth until smooth; stir into pressure cooker. Select saute setting and adjust for low heat. Simmer, stirring constantly, until thickened, 1-2 minutes. Serve with pork.

1 pork chop with ⅓ cup gravy: 257 cal., 14g fat (3g sat. fat), 57mg chol., 606mg sod., 8g carb. (0 sugars, 0 fiber), 23g pro. **Diabetic exchanges:** 3 lean meat, 1½ fat, ½ starch.

MATTHEW'S BEST EVER MEAT LOAF

This is comfort food at its best. Mushrooms, beef stock, tomato paste, Worcestershire and soy sauce help boost the meaty flavor of this classic diner staple.
—Matthew Hass, Ellison Bay, WI

- -

Prep: 30 min. • **Bake:** 1¼ hours + standing
Makes: 8 servings

- 3 slices white bread, torn into small pieces
- ½ cup beef stock
- 2 large portobello mushrooms (about 6 oz.), cut into chunks
- 1 medium onion, cut into wedges
- 1 medium carrot, cut into chunks
- 1 celery rib, cut into chunks
- 3 garlic cloves, halved
- 1 Tbsp. olive oil
- 2 Tbsp. tomato paste
- 2 large eggs, lightly beaten
- 1¼ lbs. ground beef
- ¾ lb. ground pork
- 1 Tbsp. Worcestershire sauce
- 1 Tbsp. reduced-sodium soy sauce
- 1¼ tsp. salt
- ¾ tsp. pepper

GLAZE
- ½ cup ketchup
- 2 Tbsp. tomato paste
- 2 Tbsp. brown sugar
- 1 tsp. ground mustard

1. Preheat oven to 350°. Combine bread and stock; let stand until liquid is absorbed.
2. Meanwhile, pulse mushrooms, onion, carrot, celery and garlic in a food processor until finely chopped. In a large skillet, heat olive oil over medium heat. Add mushroom mixture; cook and stir until vegetables are tender and liquid is evaporated, 5-6 minutes. Stir in the tomato paste; cook 1 minute longer. Cool mixture slightly.

3. Add the next 7 ingredients and cooked vegetables to bread mixture; mix thoroughly. Place a 12x7-in. piece of foil on a rack in a foil-lined rimmed baking pan. Transfer the meat mixture to the foil and shape into a 10x6-in. loaf.
4. Bake 1 hour. Mix glaze ingredients; spread over loaf. Bake until a thermometer reads 160°, 15-25 minutes longer. Let stand for 10 minutes before slicing.
Freeze option: Shape meat loaf on a plastic wrap-lined baking sheet; wrap and freeze until firm. Remove from pan and wrap securely in foil; return to freezer. To use, unwrap meat loaf and bake as directed, increasing initial baking time to 2 hours. Mix together glaze ingredients; spread over loaf. Bake until a thermometer inserted in center reads 160°, 15-25 minutes longer. Let stand 10 minutes before slicing.
1 piece: 341 cal., 18g fat (6g sat. fat), 119mg chol., 832mg sod., 19g carb. (11g sugars, 2g fiber), 25g pro.

SPICE-RUBBED RIBS

For grilling, here's the rub I recommend. If you have some left after making ribs, put it in a shaker and use it another day on pork or beef roasts, tenderloins, steaks and more. It's great alone or under sauce.
—Cheryl Ewing, Ellwood City, PA

- -

Prep: 10 min. • **Grill:** 1 hour
Makes: 10 servings

- 3 Tbsp. paprika
- 2 Tbsp. plus 1 tsp. salt
- 2 Tbsp. plus 1 tsp. garlic powder
- 2 Tbsp. cayenne pepper
- 4 tsp. onion powder
- 4 tsp. dried oregano
- 4 tsp. dried thyme
- 4 tsp. pepper
- 10 lbs. pork baby back ribs

1. In a small bowl, combine the seasonings; rub over ribs.
2. Prepare grill for indirect heat, using a drip pan. Grill ribs, covered, over indirect medium heat for 1 hour or until tender, turning occasionally.
1 serving: 792 cal., 62g fat (23g sat. fat), 245mg chol., 1864mg sod., 5g carb. (0 sugars, 2g fiber), 51g pro.

MATTHEW'S BEST EVER MEAT LOAF

AIR-FRYER
STEAK FAJITAS

AIR-FRYER STEAK FAJITAS

Zesty salsa and tender strips of steak make these traditional fajitas extra special.
—Rebecca Baird, Salt Lake City, UT

Takes: 30 min. • **Makes:** 6 servings

- 2 large tomatoes, seeded and chopped
- ½ cup diced red onion
- ¼ cup lime juice
- 1 jalapeno pepper, seeded and minced
- 3 Tbsp. minced fresh cilantro
- 2 tsp. ground cumin, divided
- ¾ tsp. salt, divided
- 1 beef flank steak (about 1½ lbs.)
- 1 large onion, halved and sliced
- 6 whole wheat tortillas (8 in.), warmed
  Optional: Sliced avocado and lime wedges

1. For salsa, place first 5 ingredients in a small bowl; stir in 1 tsp. cumin and ¼ tsp. salt. Let stand until serving.

2. Preheat air fryer to 400°. Sprinkle steak with the remaining cumin and salt. Place on greased tray in air-fryer basket. Cook until meat reaches desired doneness (for medium-rare, a thermometer should read 135°; medium, 140°; medium-well, 145°), 6-8 minutes per side. Remove from basket and let stand 5 minutes.

3. Meanwhile, place onion on tray in air-fryer basket. Cook until crisp-tender, 2-3 minutes, stirring once. Slice the steak thinly across the grain; serve in tortillas with onion and salsa. If desired, serve with avocado and lime wedges.

1 fajita: 309 cal., 9g fat (4g sat. fat), 54mg chol., 498mg sod., 29g carb. (3g sugars, 5g fiber), 27g pro. **Diabetic exchanges:** 4 lean meat, 2 starch.

TRADITIONAL LASAGNA

TRADITIONAL LASAGNA

My family tasted this rich lasagna at a friend's home on Christmas Eve, and it became our holiday tradition. My sister's Italian in-laws request it often.
—Lorri Foockle, Granville, IL

Prep: 30 min. + simmering
Bake: 70 min. + standing • **Makes:** 12 servings

- 1 lb. ground beef
- ¾ lb. bulk pork sausage
- 3 cans (8 oz. each) tomato sauce
- 2 cans (6 oz. each) tomato paste
- 2 garlic cloves, minced
- 2 tsp. sugar
- 1 tsp. Italian seasoning
- ½ to 1 tsp. salt
- ¼ to ½ tsp. pepper
- 3 large eggs
- 3 Tbsp. minced fresh parsley
- 3 cups 4% small-curd cottage cheese
- 1 cup ricotta cheese
- ½ cup grated Parmesan cheese
- 9 lasagna noodles, cooked and drained
- 6 slices provolone cheese (about 6 oz.)
- 3 cups shredded part-skim mozzarella cheese, divided

1. In a large skillet over medium heat, cook and crumble beef and sausage until no longer pink; drain. Add next 7 ingredients. Bring to a boil. Reduce heat; simmer, uncovered, 1 hour, stirring occasionally. Adjust seasoning with additional salt and pepper, if desired.

2. Meanwhile, in a large bowl, lightly beat eggs. Add parsley; stir in cottage cheese, ricotta and Parmesan cheese.

3. Preheat oven to 375°. Spread 1 cup meat sauce in an ungreased 13x9-in. baking dish. Layer with 3 noodles, the provolone cheese, 2 cups cottage cheese mixture, 1 cup mozzarella, 3 noodles, 2 cups meat sauce, remaining cottage cheese mixture and 1 cup mozzarella. Top with remaining noodles, meat sauce and mozzarella (dish will be full).

4. Cover; bake 50 minutes. Uncover; bake until heated through, about 20 minutes. Let stand 15 minutes before cutting.

1 piece: 503 cal., 27g fat (13g sat. fat), 136mg chol., 1208mg sod., 30g carb. (9g sugars, 2g fiber), 36g pro.

> "This lasagna is not only super cheesy, but the layers stay intact nicely!"
>
> —JESS SORENSON, MANAGER, BOOKS MARKETING

HEARTY PENNE BEEF

This is comfort food at its finest! The best of everything is found here—it's tasty, easy and a great way to sneak some spinach in for extra nutrition.
—*Taste of Home* Test Kitchen

- -

Takes: 30 min. • **Makes:** 4 servings

- 1¾ cups uncooked penne pasta
- 1 lb. ground beef
- 1 tsp. minced garlic
- 1 can (15 oz.) tomato puree
- 1 can (14½ oz.) beef broth
- 1½ tsp. Italian seasoning
- 1 tsp. Worcestershire sauce
- ¼ tsp. salt
- ¼ tsp. pepper
- 2 cups chopped fresh spinach
- 2 cups shredded part-skim mozzarella cheese

1. Cook the pasta according to package directions. Meanwhile, in a Dutch oven, cook beef over medium heat until no longer pink, breaking it into crumbles. Add garlic; cook 1 minute longer. Drain. Stir in tomato puree, broth, Italian seasoning, Worcestershire sauce, salt and pepper.

2. Bring to a boil. Reduce heat; simmer, uncovered, until mixture is slightly thickened, 10-15 minutes. Add chopped spinach; cook until wilted, 1-2 minutes.

3. Drain pasta; stir into the beef mixture. Sprinkle with cheese; cover and cook until cheese is melted, 3-4 minutes.

Freeze option: Freeze cooled pasta mixture in freezer containers. To use, partially thaw in refrigerator overnight. Heat through in a saucepan, stirring occasionally; add broth or water if necessary.

1½ cups: 482 cal., 20g fat (10g sat. fat), 88mg chol., 1001mg sod., 33g carb. (5g sugars, 2g fiber), 41g pro.

CRISPY FRIED CHICKEN

This fried chicken can be served hot or pulled out of the fridge the next day as leftovers. Either way, folks love it.
—Jeanne Schnitzler, Lima, MT

- -

Prep: 15 min. • **Cook:** 15 min./batch
Makes: 12 servings

- 4 cups all-purpose flour, divided
- 2 Tbsp. garlic salt
- 1 Tbsp. paprika
- 3 tsp. pepper, divided
- 2½ tsp. poultry seasoning
- 2 large eggs
- 1½ cups water
- 1 tsp. salt
- 2 broiler/fryer chickens (3½ to 4 lbs. each), cut up
  Oil for deep-fat frying

1. In a large shallow dish, combine 2⅔ cups flour, garlic salt, paprika, 2½ tsp. pepper and poultry seasoning. In another shallow dish, beat eggs and 1½ cups water; add 1 tsp. salt and the the remaining 1⅓ cup flour and ½ tsp. pepper. Dip chicken in egg mixture, then place in the flour mixture, a few pieces at a time. Turn to coat.

2. In a deep-fat fryer, heat oil to 375°. Working in batches, fry chicken, several pieces at a time, until skin is golden brown and a thermometer inserted into chicken reads 165°, about 7-8 minutes on each side. Drain on paper towels.

5 oz. cooked chicken: 543 cal., 33g fat (7g sat. fat), 137mg chol., 798mg sod., 17g carb. (0 sugars, 1g fiber), 41g pro.

HEARTY PENNE BEEF

CURRIED PORK & ORANGE KABOBS

I love the sweet flavor of red, yellow and orange peppers. I always go for these in the summer when they are inexpensive and plentiful. I think they taste a whole lot better than green peppers.
—Liv Vors, Peterborough, ON

- -

Takes: 30 min. • **Makes:** 4 servings

- ½ cup canola oil
- 2 Tbsp. dried minced onion
- 1 garlic clove, minced
- 1 to 2 Tbsp. curry powder
- ½ tsp. each ground cumin, coriander and cinnamon
- 1½ lbs. pork tenderloin
- 1 large sweet red pepper
- 1 large sweet yellow or orange pepper
- 1 small onion
- 1 large unpeeled navel orange

1. In a small bowl, mix oil, minced onion, garlic and spices; reserve half of mixture for basting kabobs while cooking. Cut the pork, peppers, onion and unpeeled orange into 1-in. pieces. On four metal or soaked wooden skewers, alternately thread pork, vegetables and orange; brush with remaining curry mixture.

2. Grill kabobs, covered, over medium heat 10-15 minutes or until vegetables and pork are tender, turning occasionally. Baste frequently with reserved curry mixture during the last 4 minutes of cooking.

1 kabob: 515 cal., 34g fat (4g sat. fat), 95mg chol., 73mg sod., 16g carb. (8g sugars, 4g fiber), 36g pro.

ASK SARAH

WHAT IF I'M OUT OF PORK?
You can easily swap out the pork in these kabobs for skinless chicken or turkey breasts.

CURRIED PORK & ORANGE KABOBS

PORK CHOPS WITH PARMESAN SAUCE

Tender skillet chops always make a speedy weeknight meal. These are finished with a creamy and flavorful Parmesan sauce. Here's a new family favorite!
—*Taste of Home* Test Kitchen

Takes: 20 min. • **Makes:** 4 servings

- 4   boneless pork loin chops (4 oz. each)
- ½   tsp. salt
- ¼   tsp. pepper
- 1   Tbsp. butter
- 2   Tbsp. all-purpose flour
- 1   cup fat-free milk
- ⅓   cup grated Parmesan cheese
- 2   Tbsp. grated onion
- 3   tsp. minced fresh parsley
- ¼   tsp. dried thyme
- ¼   tsp. ground nutmeg

1. Sprinkle pork chops with salt and pepper. In a large nonstick skillet, cook chops in butter over medium heat until meat juices run clear; remove and keep warm.
2. Combine flour and milk until smooth; stir into pan. Bring to a boil; cook and stir for 2 minutes or until thickened. Stir in the remaining ingredients; heat through. Serve with the chops.
1 pork chop with ¼ cup sauce: 244 cal., 11g fat (5g sat. fat), 69mg chol., 475mg sod., 7g carb. (3g sugars, 0 fiber), 27g pro. **Diabetic exchanges:** 3 lean meat, ½ starch, ½ fat.

MOM'S SWEDISH MEATBALLS

Mom fixed these meatballs for all sorts of family dinners, potluck suppers and PTA meetings. After smelling the aromas of browning meat and caramelized onions, everyone will be ready to eat.
—Marybeth Mank, Mesquite, TX

Prep: 30 min. • **Cook:** 40 min.
Makes: 6 servings

- ¾   cup seasoned bread crumbs
- 1   medium onion, chopped
- 2   large eggs, lightly beaten
- ⅓   cup minced fresh parsley
- 1   tsp. coarsely ground pepper
- ¾   tsp. salt
- 2   lbs. ground beef

GRAVY
- ½   cup all-purpose flour
- 2¾   cups 2% milk
- 2   cans (10½ oz. each) condensed beef consomme, undiluted
- 1   Tbsp. Worcestershire sauce
- 1   tsp. coarsely ground pepper
- ¾   tsp. salt

NOODLES
- 1   pkg. (16 oz.) egg noodles
- ¼   cup butter, cubed
- ¼   cup minced fresh parsley

1. In a large bowl, combine the first 6 ingredients. Add beef; mix lightly but thoroughly. Shape into 1½-in. meatballs (about 36). In a large skillet over medium heat, brown meatballs in batches. Using a slotted spoon, remove to paper towels to drain, reserving drippings in pan.
2. For gravy, stir flour into drippings; cook over medium-high heat until light brown (do not burn). Gradually whisk in milk until smooth. Stir in consomme, Worcestershire sauce, pepper and salt. Bring to a boil over medium-high heat; cook and stir until thickened, about 2 minutes.
3. Reduce heat to medium-low; return meatballs to pan. Cook, uncovered, until cooked through, 15-20 minutes longer, stirring occasionally.
4. Meanwhile, cook noodles according to package directions. Drain; toss with butter. Serve with meatball mixture; sprinkle with the parsley.
6 meatballs with 1¾ cups noodles and about ⅓ cup gravy: 837 cal., 33g fat (14g sat. fat), 256mg chol., 1744mg sod., 82g carb. (10g sugars, 4g fiber), 50g pro.

MOM'S SWEDISH MEATBALLS

PUFF PASTRY
CHICKEN POTPIE

BABY BACK RIBS

Slow-cook the ribs during the day and they
will be ready to finish on the grill when you
get home.
—*Taste of Home* Test Kitchen

- -

Prep: 5 min. • **Cook:** 6¼ hours
Makes: 4 servings

2½	lbs. pork baby back ribs, cut into 8 pieces
5	cups water
1	medium onion, sliced
2	celery ribs, cut in half
2	tsp. minced garlic, divided
1	tsp. whole peppercorns
½	cup barbecue sauce
¼	cup plum sauce
	Dash hot pepper sauce

1. Place the ribs in a 5-qt. slow cooker. Add
the water, onion, celery, 1 tsp. garlic and
peppercorns. Cover and cook on low for
6 hours, or until meat is tender.
2. In a small saucepan, combine barbecue
sauce, plum sauce, hot pepper sauce and
remaining 1 tsp. garlic. Cook and stir over
medium heat until heated through, about
5 minutes. Remove ribs. Discard cooking
juices and vegetables.
3. Brush ribs with sauce. Grill, covered, on
an oiled rack over medium-low heat until
browned, 8-10 minutes, turning and basting
occasionally with remaining sauce.
2 pieces: 555 cal., 39g fat (14g sat. fat),
153mg chol., 500mg sod., 15g carb. (11g
sugars, 1g fiber), 33g pro.

PUFF PASTRY
CHICKEN POTPIE

When my wife is craving comfort food,
I whip up my chicken potpie. It's easy to
make, sticks to your ribs and delivers
soul-satisfying flavor.
—Nick Iverson, Denver, CO

- -

Prep: 45 min. • **Bake:** 45 min. + standing
Makes: 8 servings

1	pkg. (17.3 oz.) frozen puff pastry, thawed
2	lbs. boneless skinless chicken breasts, cut into 1-in. pieces
1	tsp. salt, divided
1	tsp. pepper, divided
4	Tbsp. butter, divided
1	large onion, chopped
2	garlic cloves, minced
1	tsp. minced fresh thyme or ¼ tsp. dried thyme
1	tsp. minced fresh sage or ¼ tsp. rubbed sage
½	cup all-purpose flour
1½	cups chicken broth
1	cup plus 1 Tbsp. half-and-half cream, divided
2	cups frozen mixed vegetables (about 10 oz.)
1	Tbsp. lemon juice
1	large egg yolk

1. Preheat oven to 400°. On a lightly floured
surface, roll each puff pastry sheet into a
12x10-in. rectangle. Cut 1 sheet crosswise
into six 2-in. strips; cut remaining sheet
lengthwise into five 2-in. strips. On a baking
sheet, closely weave the strips to make a
12x10-in. lattice. Freeze while making filling.
2. Toss chicken with ½ tsp. each salt and
pepper. In a large skillet, heat 1 Tbsp. butter
over medium-high heat; saute chicken until
browned, 5-7 minutes. Remove from pan.
3. In same skillet, heat remaining butter over
medium-high heat; saute onion until tender,
5-7 minutes. Stir in garlic and herbs; cook
1 minute. Stir in flour until blended; cook
and stir 1 minute. Gradually stir in broth
and 1 cup cream. Bring to a boil, stirring
constantly; cook and stir until thickened,
about 2 minutes.
4. Stir in vegetables, lemon juice, chicken and
the remaining salt and pepper; return to a
boil. Transfer to a greased 2½-qt. oblong
baking dish. Top with lattice, trimming to fit.
5. Whisk together egg yolk and remaining
cream; brush over pastry. Bake, uncovered,
until filling is bubbly and pastry is golden
brown, 45-55 minutes. Cover loosely with
foil if pastry starts getting too dark. Let
stand 15 minutes before serving.
1 serving: 523 cal., 25g fat (10g sat. fat),
118mg chol., 768mg sod., 42g carb. (4g
sugars, 6g fiber), 30g pro.

BAVARIAN POT ROAST

All my grandparents were German, so it's no wonder so many Bavarian recipes have been handed down to me. In this classic European pot roast recipe, the tang of tomato sauce and vinegar is balanced by cinnamon and ginger.
—Susan Robertson, Hamilton, OH

- -

Prep: 15 min. • **Cook:** 2¾ hours
Makes: 10 servings

- 2 Tbsp. canola oil
- 1 boneless beef chuck roast (about 3 lbs.)
- 1¼ cups water
- ¾ cup beer or beef broth
- 1 can (8 oz.) tomato sauce
- ½ cup chopped onion
- 2 Tbsp. sugar
- 1 Tbsp. white vinegar
- 2 tsp. salt
- 1 tsp. ground cinnamon
- 1 bay leaf
- ½ tsp. pepper
- ½ tsp. ground ginger

1. In a Dutch oven, heat canola oil. Brown roast on all sides. Meanwhile, combine water, beer, tomato sauce, onion, sugar, vinegar, salt, cinnamon, bay leaf, pepper and ginger. Pour over meat and bring to a boil. Reduce heat; cover and simmer until meat is tender, 2½-3 hours.
2. Remove meat and slice. Discard bay leaf. If desired, thicken pan juices for gravy.
Freeze option: Place sliced pot roast in freezer containers; top with cooking juices. Cool and freeze. To use, partially thaw in refrigerator overnight. Microwave, covered, on high in a microwave-safe dish until heated through, gently stirring and adding a little broth if necessary.
4 oz. cooked beef: 281 cal., 16g fat (5g sat. fat), 88mg chol., 633mg sod., 5g carb. (4g sugars, 0 fiber), 27g pro.

SLOW-COOKED SOUTHWEST CHICKEN

SLOW-COOKED SOUTHWEST CHICKEN

This dish needs just 15 minutes of prep, so you'll be out of the kitchen in no time. The delicious low-fat chicken gets even better with a garnish of reduced-fat sour cream and fresh cilantro. Wrap leftovers in a tortilla for lunch the next day.
—Brandi Castillo, Santa Maria, CA

- -

Prep: 15 min. • **Cook:** 3 hours
Makes: 6 servings

- 2 cans (15 oz. each) black beans, rinsed and drained
- 1 can (14½ oz.) reduced-sodium chicken broth
- 1 can (14½ oz.) diced tomatoes with mild green chiles, undrained
- ½ lb. boneless skinless chicken breast
- 1 jar (8 oz.) chunky salsa
- 1 cup frozen corn
- 1 Tbsp. dried parsley flakes
- 1 tsp. ground cumin
- ¼ tsp. pepper
- 3 cups hot cooked rice
  Optional: Lime wedges and fresh cilantro leaves

1. In a 2- or 3-qt. slow cooker, combine the beans, broth, tomatoes, chicken, salsa, corn and seasonings. Cover and cook on low 3-4 hours or until a thermometer inserted in chicken reads 165°.
2. Shred the chicken with 2 forks and return to slow cooker; heat through. Serve over rice. If desired, serve with lime wedges and fresh cilantro.
Freeze option: After shredding chicken, freeze cooled mixture in freezer containers. To use, partially thaw in the refrigerator overnight. Heat through in a saucepan, stirring occasionally; add a little broth or water if necessary.
1 cup: 320 cal., 1g fat (0 sat. fat), 21mg chol., 873mg sod., 56g carb. (7g sugars, 8g fiber), 19g pro.

"As a working mom, I love this recipe because I always have the ingredients on hand and can put them all in the slow cooker before work. When the kids are coming and going at different times during the dinner hour, it can be served all evening without getting cold. The corn adds a nice twist. We top it with fresh cilantro and cheese."

—TERESA RUPPENTHAL, SENIOR MANAGER

ORANGE-GLAZED PORK LOIN

This is one of the best pork recipes I've ever tried. My family looks forward to this roast for dinner, and guests always want the recipe. The flavorful rub, and the glaze brightened with orange juice, are also outstanding on pork chops.
—Lynnette Miete, Alna, ME

Prep: 10 min.
Bake: 1 hour 20 min. + standing
Makes: 16 servings

- 1 tsp. salt
- 1 garlic clove, minced
- 2 to 3 fresh thyme sprigs
     or ¼ tsp. dried thyme
- ¼ tsp. ground ginger
- ¼ tsp. pepper
- 1 boneless pork loin roast (5 lbs.)

GLAZE

- 1 cup orange juice
- ¼ cup packed brown sugar
- 1 Tbsp. Dijon mustard
- ⅓ cup cold water
- 1 Tbsp. cornstarch

1. Preheat oven to 350°. Combine the first 5 ingredients; rub over roast. Place fat side up on a rack in a shallow roasting pan. Bake, uncovered, for 1 hour.
2. Meanwhile, in a saucepan over medium heat, combine orange juice, brown sugar and mustard. In a small bowl, mix the water and cornstarch until smooth. Add to the orange juice mixture. Bring to a boil; cook and stir 2 minutes. Reserve 1 cup glaze for serving; brush half of remaining glaze over roast.
3. Bake until a thermometer reads 145°, 20-40 minutes longer, brushing occasionally with remaining glaze. Let stand 10 minutes before slicing. Reheat reserved glaze; serve with roast.

4 oz. cooked pork with 1 Tbsp. glaze: 199 cal., 7g fat (2g sat. fat), 71mg chol., 212mg sod., 6g carb. (5g sugars, 0 fiber), 28g pro. **Diabetic exchanges:** 4 lean meat, ½ starch.

ORANGE-GLAZED
PORK LOIN

CHICKEN PARMESAN PIZZA

This tasty pizza is the perfect combo—quick and easy to make, and a winner with even picky eaters. It's a handy option for a family dinner on a busy night or for the center of the table at a kids' party.
—Karen Wittmeier, Parkland, FL

Prep: 25 min. • **Bake:** 15 min.
Makes: 6 pieces

- 8   frozen breaded chicken tenders
- 1   loaf (1 lb.) frozen pizza dough, thawed
- ½   cup marinara sauce
- ¼   tsp. garlic powder
- 2   cups (8 oz.) shredded part-skim mozzarella cheese
- ¼   cup shredded Parmesan cheese
- 2   Tbsp. thinly sliced fresh basil
      Additional warmed marinara sauce

1. Bake chicken tenders according to package directions. Remove from oven; increase oven setting to 450°.
2. Meanwhile, grease a 12-in. pizza pan. Roll dough to fit pan. In a small bowl, mix the marinara sauce and garlic powder; spread over dough.
3. Cut chicken into 1-in. pieces. Top pizza with chicken and mozzarella cheese. Bake on a lower oven rack 12-15 minutes or until crust is golden brown and cheese is melted. Sprinkle with Parmesan cheese and basil. Serve with additional marinara.
1 piece: 440 cal., 17g fat (6g sat. fat), 35mg chol., 774mg sod., 48g carb. (4g sugars, 3g fiber), 23g pro.

CARNITAS WITH ORZO & PEPPERS IN RED MOLE SAUCE

CARNITAS WITH ORZO & PEPPERS IN RED MOLE SAUCE

For a tasty way to stretch my grocery dollars, I combine pork shoulder roast with orzo, peppers and mole sauce to make this spicy Mexican comfort food.
—Kari Wheaton, South Beloit, IL

Prep: 1 hour 35 min. • **Bake:** 40 min.
Makes: 5 servings

- 1   boneless pork shoulder butt roast (1½ to 2 lbs.), cut into ½-in. cubes
- 1½ tsp. salt, divided
- ½   tsp. pepper
- 1   cup uncooked orzo pasta
- 1   each medium green, sweet red and yellow peppers, chopped
- 2   jalapeno peppers, seeded and chopped
- 1   medium onion, chopped
- 1   Tbsp. olive oil
- 1   cup chicken broth
- ¼   cup red mole sauce
- 2   Tbsp. tomato paste
- 1   cup quesadilla or Monterey Jack cheese, shredded
       Optional: Chopped cilantro and sour cream

1. Place pork in a 15x10x1-in. baking pan; sprinkle with 1 tsp. salt and ½ tsp. pepper. Bake at 325° until tender, about 1½ hours. Remove pork from oven. Increase oven setting to 350°.
2. Meanwhile, cook pasta according to package directions; drain and set aside. In a large skillet, saute peppers and onion in olive oil until crisp-tender. In a greased 13x9-in. baking pan, combine the orzo, peppers and onion.
3. In a small saucepan, whisk the chicken broth, mole sauce, tomato paste and remaining salt. Cook and stir until thickened and bubbly. Pour over orzo and vegetables. Stir in pork; sprinkle with cheese. Cover and bake until heated through, 35-40 minutes. Uncover; broil 3-4 in. from the heat until cheese is golden brown, 4-5 minutes. If desired, top with chopped cilantro and serve with sour cream.
Freeze option: Cool unbaked casserole; cover and freeze. To use, partially thaw in refrigerator overnight. Remove from the refrigerator 30 minutes before baking. Bake casserole as directed, increasing time as necessary to heat through.
Note: Wear disposable gloves when cutting hot peppers; the oils can burn skin. Avoid touching your face.
1⅓ cups: 559 cal., 26g fat (9g sat. fat), 105mg chol., 1509mg sod., 45g carb. (8g sugars, 5g fiber), 37g pro.

AIR-FRYER SPICED STEAKS WITH CHERRY SAUCE

Who needs to grill? These impressive steaks, topped with a rich cherry sauce, will delight your guests.
—*Taste of Home* Test Kitchen

Prep: 20 min. + chilling • **Cook:** 20 min.
Makes: 4 servings

- ½   cup dried cherries
- ¼   cup port wine, warmed
- 3½ tsp. coarsely ground pepper
- 1   tsp. brown sugar
- ¾   tsp. garlic powder
- ¾   tsp. paprika
- ¾   tsp. ground coffee
- ½   tsp. kosher salt
- ¼   tsp. ground cinnamon
- ¼   tsp. ground cumin
- ⅛   tsp. ground mustard
- 4   beef tenderloin steaks (1¼ in. thick and 6 oz. each)
- 1   Tbsp. butter
- 1   large shallot, finely chopped
- 1   cup reduced-sodium beef broth
- 1   tsp. minced fresh thyme
- ½   cup heavy whipping cream
      Crumbled blue cheese, optional

1. In a small bowl, combine cherries and wine; set aside. In a shallow dish, combine pepper, brown sugar, garlic powder, paprika, coffee, salt, cinnamon, cumin and mustard. Add steaks, 1 at a time, and turn to coat. Cover and refrigerate for 30 minutes.

2. In a small skillet, heat the butter over medium-high heat. Add shallot; cook and stir 2 minutes. Add broth and thyme. Bring to a boil; cook until liquid is reduced by half, about 8 minutes. Stir in cream; bring to a boil. Cook until thickened, about 8 minutes, stirring occasionally.

3. Meanwhile, preheat air fryer to 375°. In batches, arrange steaks on greased tray in air-fryer basket. Cook until meat reaches desired doneness (for medium-rare, a thermometer should read 135°; medium, 140°; medium-well, 145°), 3-6 minutes on each side.

4. Stir reserved cherry mixture into cream sauce; serve with steaks. If desired, sprinkle with blue cheese.

1 steak with 3 Tbsp. sauce: 488 cal., 24g fat (13g sat. fat), 117mg chol., 388mg sod., 24g carb. (17g sugars, 1g fiber), 39g pro.

PASTA WITH PROSCIUTTO, LETTUCE & PEAS

This elevated pasta dish will make your guests think you spent all day in the kitchen. It's a perfect holiday dish without requiring a lot of work.
—Amy White, Manchester, CT

Prep: 20 min. • **Cook:** 15 min.
Makes: 8 servings

- 1   lb. uncooked campanelle pasta
- 2   Tbsp. butter
- 3   Tbsp. olive oil, divided
- 12 green onions, sliced
- 1   shallot, finely chopped
- ½   cup white wine or reduced-sodium chicken broth
- ½   cup reduced-sodium chicken broth
- ¼   tsp. salt
- ⅛   tsp. pepper
- 1   head Boston lettuce, cut into ¾-in. slices
- 2   cups fresh or frozen peas
- 1   cup grated Parmesan cheese
- 4   oz. thinly sliced prosciutto or deli ham, cut into ½-in. strips

1. Cook the pasta according to package directions for al dente.

2. Meanwhile, in a large skillet, heat butter and 2 Tbsp. olive oil over medium-high heat. Add green onions and shallot; cook and stir until tender. Stir in white wine. Bring to a boil; cook and stir 6-8 minutes or until the liquid is almost evaporated.

3. Add broth, salt and pepper. Bring to a boil. Reduce heat; stir in lettuce and peas. Cook and stir until lettuce is wilted. Drain pasta; add to pan. Stir in cheese and prosciutto; drizzle with remaining oil. If desired, top with additional Parmesan cheese.

1¼ cups: 220 cal., 13g fat (5g sat. fat), 29mg chol., 629mg sod., 14g carb. (5g sugars, 5g fiber), 13g pro.

AIR-FRYER SPICED STEAKS WITH CHERRY SAUCE

LIME-GLAZED PORK CHOPS

A wonderful sweet-sour citrus glaze makes perfect, tender chops that are tangy and tasty. They're great for weeknight dinners and weekend barbecues alike.
—Jacqueline Correa, Landing, NJ

- -

Takes: 25 min. • **Makes:** 4 servings

⅓ cup orange marmalade
1 jalapeno pepper, seeded and finely chopped
2 Tbsp. lime juice
1 tsp. grated fresh gingerroot
4 bone-in pork loin chops (8 oz. each)
4 tsp. minced fresh cilantro
Lime wedges

1. For glaze, in a small saucepan, combine marmalade, jalapeno, lime juice and ginger; cook and stir over medium heat 4-6 minutes or until marmalade is melted.

2. Grill chops, covered, on an oiled rack over medium heat or broil 4 in. from heat until a thermometer reads 145°, 6-8 minutes on each side, brushing with glaze during the last 5 minutes. Let stand 5 minutes. Sprinkle with cilantro; serve with lime wedges.

Note: Wear disposable gloves when cutting hot peppers; the oils can burn skin. Avoid touching your face.

1 pork chop: 303 cal., 10g fat (4g sat. fat), 98mg chol., 87mg sod., 19g carb. (16g sugars, 0 fiber), 35g pro. **Diabetic exchanges:** 1 starch, 4 lean meat.

SLOW-COOKED PORK TACOS

Sometimes I'll substitute Bibb lettuce leaves for the tortillas to make crunchy lettuce wraps instead of tacos.
—Kathleen Wolf, Naperville, IL

- -

Prep: 20 min. • **Cook:** 4 hours
Makes: 10 servings

2 lbs. boneless pork sirloin chops, cut into 2-in. pieces
1½ cups salsa verde
1 medium sweet red pepper, chopped
1 medium onion, chopped
¼ cup chopped dried apricots
2 Tbsp. lime juice
2 garlic cloves, minced
1 tsp. ground cumin
½ tsp. salt
¼ tsp. white pepper
Dash hot pepper sauce
10 flour tortillas (8 in.), warmed
Optional toppings: Chopped tomatoes, cubed avocado, reduced-fat sour cream, shredded reduced-fat cheddar cheese and sliced green onions

1. In a 3-qt. slow cooker, combine all the ingredients except tortillas and toppings. Cook, covered, on high 4-5 hours or until meat is tender.

2. Shred pork with 2 forks. Serve in tortillas; top as desired.

1 taco: 310 cal., 9g fat (3g sat. fat), 55mg chol., 596mg sod., 34g carb. (4g sugars, 2g fiber), 23g pro. **Diabetic exchanges:** 3 lean meat, 2 starch.

LIME-GLAZED
PORK CHOPS

EASY
PAD THAI

SLOW-COOKER SPAGHETTI & MEATBALLS

I've been cooking for more than 50 years, and this classic is still one that guests ask for frequently. It also makes amazing meatball sandwiches, and the sauce works for any type of pasta.
—Jane Whittaker, Pensacola, FL

Prep: 50 min. • **Cook:** 5 hours
Makes: 12 servings

- 1   cup seasoned bread crumbs
- 2   Tbsp. grated Parmesan and Romano cheese blend
- 1   tsp. pepper
- ½   tsp. salt
- 2   large eggs, lightly beaten
- 2   lbs. ground beef

SAUCE
- 1   large onion, finely chopped
- 1   medium green pepper, finely chopped
- 3   cans (15 oz. each) tomato sauce
- 2   cans (14½ oz. each) diced tomatoes, undrained
- 1   can (6 oz.) tomato paste
- 6   garlic cloves, minced
- 2   bay leaves
- 1   tsp. each dried basil, oregano and parsley flakes
- 1   tsp. salt
- ½   tsp. pepper
- ¼   tsp. crushed red pepper flakes
      Hot cooked spaghetti

1. In a large bowl, mix bread crumbs, cheese, pepper and salt; stir in eggs. Add beef; mix lightly but thoroughly. Shape into 1½-in. balls. In a large skillet, brown meatballs in batches over medium heat; drain.
2. Place the first 5 sauce ingredients in a 6-qt. slow cooker; stir in minced garlic and seasonings. Add meatballs, stirring gently to coat. Cook, covered, on low 5-6 hours, until meatballs are cooked through.
3. Remove bay leaves. Serve with spaghetti.
3 meatballs with ¾ cup sauce: 250 cal., 11g fat (4g sat. fat), 79mg chol., 1116mg sod., 20g carb. (7g sugars, 4g fiber), 20g pro.

EASY PAD THAI

Skip the take-out restaurant and give this pad thai recipe a try if you need an easy and quick meal.
—James Schend, Deputy Editor, Culinary

Takes: 30 min. • **Makes:** 4 servings

- 4   oz. uncooked thick rice noodles
- ½   lb. pork tenderloin, cut into thin strips
- 2   tsp. canola oil
- 2   shallots, thinly sliced
- 2   garlic cloves, minced
- 1   large egg, lightly beaten
- 3   cups coleslaw mix
- 4   green onions, thinly sliced
- ⅓   cup rice vinegar
- ¼   cup sugar
- 3   Tbsp. reduced-sodium soy sauce
- 2   Tbsp. fish sauce or additional reduced-sodium soy sauce
- 1   Tbsp. chili garlic sauce
- 1   Tbsp. lime juice
- 2   Tbsp. chopped salted peanuts
      Chopped fresh cilantro leaves, lime wedges and fresh bean sprouts

1. Cook the rice noodles according to the package directions.
2. In a large nonstick skillet or wok, stir-fry the pork in oil over high heat until lightly browned; remove and set aside. Add shallot to pan and cook until tender, about 1 minute; add garlic and cook 30 seconds. Make a well in the center of the onion mixture; add egg. Stir-fry for 1-2 minutes or until the egg is completely set.
3. Add the coleslaw mix, green onions, vinegar, sugar, soy sauce, fish sauce, chili garlic sauce, lime juice and peanuts; heat through. Return pork to pan and heat through. Drain noodles; toss with pork mixture. Garnish with cilantro, additional peanuts, lime wedges and bean sprouts.
1¼ cups: 361 cal., 8g fat (2g sat. fat), 78mg chol., 1669mg sod., 53g carb. (23g sugars, 2g fiber), 19g pro.

"There aren't any Thai restaurants close to where I live, so finding a recipe that is easy to make and tastes close to something I'd find in a restaurant is wonderful. Sometimes I even make it meatless, with a little tofu or with shrimp."

—PEGGY WOODWARD, SENIOR FOOD EDITOR

FAVORITE

Side Dishes

When it's time to round out a meal, few things can steal the show like savory sides. From garden-fresh asparagus and corn cakes to crispy fries and popular pasta salads, you'll find nothing but best-of-the-best dinner accompaniments here!

FREEZER SWEET CORN
PAGE 158

GERMAN RED CABBAGE

Sunday afternoons were a time for family gatherings when I was a kid. While the uncles played cards, the aunts made German treats like this tasty, traditional red cabbage.
—Jeannette Heim, Dunlap, TN

- -

Prep: 10 min. • **Cook:** 65 min.
Makes: 10 servings

- 1 **medium onion, halved and sliced**
- 1 **medium apple, sliced**
- 1 **medium head red cabbage, shredded (about 8 cups)**
- ⅓ **cup sugar**
- ⅓ **cup white vinegar**
- ¾ **tsp. salt, optional**
- ¼ **tsp. pepper**

In a large Dutch oven coated with cooking spray, cook and stir onion and apple over medium heat until onion is tender, about 5 minutes. Stir in the remaining ingredients; cook, covered, until the cabbage is tender, about 1 hour, stirring occasionally. Serve warm or cold.

1 cup: 64 cal., 0 fat (0 sat. fat), 0 chol., 23mg sod., 16g carb. (12g sugars, 2g fiber), 1g pro.
Diabetic exchanges: 1 vegetable, ½ starch.

ZUCCHINI-CORNMEAL PANCAKES

My mom has made these treasured family hotcakes for ages. Try them as a breakfast-for-dinner meal with fresh fruit, yogurt and honey on top.
—Katherine Wollgast, Troy, MO

- -

Takes: 25 min. • **Makes:** 8 pancakes

- 2 **cups shredded zucchini**
- 1 **cup all-purpose flour**
- ½ **cup grated Parmesan cheese**
- ⅓ **cup yellow cornmeal**
- ¼ **cup sugar**
- 1½ **tsp. baking powder**
- 1 **tsp. salt**
- ¼ **tsp. pepper**
- 2 **large eggs**
- ⅓ **cup 2% milk**
- ¼ **cup finely chopped onion**
  Optional: Butter and maple syrup

1. Place the zucchini in a colander to drain; squeeze well to remove any excess liquid. Pat dry.
2. Whisk flour, cheese, cornmeal, sugar, baking powder, salt and pepper. In another bowl, whisk together eggs, milk and onion. Add to dry ingredients, stirring just until moistened. Fold in zucchini.
3. Lightly grease a griddle with cooking spray; preheat over medium heat. Pour batter by ¼ cupfuls onto griddle. Cook until bubbles on top begin to pop and bottoms are golden brown. Turn; cook until second side is golden brown. If desired, serve with butter and syrup.

2 pancakes: 314 cal., 6g fat (3g sat. fat), 103mg chol., 973mg sod., 52g carb. (16g sugars, 2g fiber), 12g pro.

"Here's one of my favorite ways to use fresh zucchini. I actually serve these without butter or syrup as a side dish for summer meals. It's wonderful with chicken or pork chops and sliced fresh tomatoes."

—CHRISTINE RUKAVENA, EDITOR

GERMAN
RED CABBAGE

BACON-CORN STUFFED PEPPERS

Filled with corn, salsa, green onions, mozzarella cheese and bacon, these grilled pepper halves are sure to liven up your next cookout. They have a wonderful taste and give a fun twist to the usual corn on the cob.
—Mitzi Sentiff, Annapolis, MD

Prep: 20 min. • **Grill:** 25 min.
Makes: 4 servings

- 2 **cups frozen corn, thawed**
- ⅓ **cup salsa**
- 6 **green onions, chopped**
- 1 **medium green pepper, halved and seeded**
- 1 **medium sweet red pepper, halved and seeded**
- ¼ **cup shredded part-skim mozzarella cheese**
- 2 **bacon strips, cooked and crumbled Additional salsa, optional**

1. In a large bowl, combine corn, salsa and onions. Spoon into pepper halves. Place each stuffed pepper half on a piece of heavy-duty foil (about 18x12 in.). Fold foil around peppers and seal tightly.
2. Grill, covered, over medium heat until peppers are crisp-tender, 25-30 minutes. Carefully open packets to allow steam to escape. Sprinkle with cheese and bacon. Return to the grill until cheese is melted, 3-5 minutes. Serve with additional salsa if desired.

1 stuffed pepper half: 130 cal., 4g fat (1g sat. fat), 9mg chol., 207mg sod., 21g carb. (5g sugars, 3g fiber), 6g pro. **Diabetic exchanges:** 1 starch, 1 vegetable, ½ fat.

BACON-CORN
STUFFED PEPPERS

SIMPLE SAUCY POTATOES

These rich and creamy potatoes are simple to prepare for potlucks, particulary since they're made in a slow cooker. The saucy side dish always gets rave reviews wherever I take it.

—Gloria Schroeder, Ottawa Lake, MI

Prep: 10 min. • **Cook:** 4 hours
Makes: 12 servings

- 4 cans (14½ oz. each) sliced potatoes, drained
- 2 cans (10¾ oz. each) condensed cream of celery soup, undiluted
- 2 cups sour cream
- 10 bacon strips, cooked and crumbled, divided
- 6 green onions, thinly sliced
Optional: Chopped chives and coarse cracked pepper

Place sliliced potatoes in a 3-qt. slow cooker. Combine remaining ingredients, reserving ⅓ cup bacon crumbles; pour over potatoes and mix well. Cover and cook on high for 4-5 hours. Top with reserved bacon and, if desired, chopped chives and coarse cracked pepper.

¾ cup: 144 cal., 10g fat (6g sat. fat), 32mg chol., 369mg sod., 7g carb. (2g sugars, 1g fiber), 4g pro.

EGGPLANT PARMESAN

We really like eggplant and would rather have it baked than fried. This can be served as a side dish or main dish.

—Donna Wardlow-Keating, Omaha, NE

Prep: 10 min. • **Bake:** 45 min. + cooling
Makes: 2 servings

- 2 Tbsp. olive oil
- 1 garlic clove, minced
- 1 small eggplant, peeled and cut into ¼-in. slices
- 1 Tbsp. minced fresh basil or 1 tsp. dried basil
- 1 Tbsp. grated Parmesan cheese
- 1 medium tomato, thinly sliced
- ½ cup shredded mozzarella cheese
Additional basil, optional

1. Combine oil and garlic; brush over both sides of eggplant slices. Place on a greased baking sheet. Bake at 425° for 15 minutes; turn. Bake until golden brown, 5 minutes longer. Cool on a wire rack.

2. Place half the eggplant in a greased 1-qt. baking dish. Sprinkle with half the basil and Parmesan cheese. Arrange tomato slices over top; sprinkle with remaining basil and Parmesan. Layer with half the mozzarella cheese and remaining eggplant; top with remaining mozzarella. Cover and bake at 350° for 20 minutes. Uncover; bake until the cheese is melted, 5-7 minutes longer. Garnish with additional basil, if desired.

1 serving: 275 cal., 21g fat (6g sat. fat), 24mg chol., 164mg sod., 16g carb. (9g sugars, 5g fiber), 9g pro.

SIMPLE SAUCY POTATOES

RUSTIC
SQUASH TARTS

SLOW-COOKED BROCCOLI

This crumb-topped side dish is quick to assemble and full of flavor. Since it simmers in a slow cooker, it frees up my oven for other things. This is a tremendous help when I'm preparing several items for a big meal at home.
—Connie Slocum, Antioch, TN

- -

Prep: 10 min. • **Cook:** 2¾ hours
Makes: 10 servings

- 6 **cups frozen chopped broccoli, partially thawed**
- 1 **can (10¾ oz.) condensed cream of celery soup, undiluted**
- 1½ **cups shredded sharp cheddar cheese, divided**
- ¼ **cup chopped onion**
- ½ **tsp. Worcestershire sauce**
- ¼ **tsp. pepper**
- 1 **cup crushed butter-flavored crackers (about 25)**
- 2 **Tbsp. butter**

1. In a large bowl, combine the broccoli, soup, 1 cup cheese, onion, Worcestershire sauce and pepper. Pour into a greased 3-qt. slow cooker. Sprinkle crackers on top; dot with butter.
2. Cover and cook on high for 2½-3 hours. Sprinkle with remaining cheese. Cook until the cheese is melted, 10 minutes longer.
½ cup: 159 cal., 11g fat (6g sat. fat), 25mg chol., 431mg sod., 11g carb. (2g sugars, 1g fiber), 6g pro.

RUSTIC SQUASH TARTS

Of all the delicious Thanksgiving side dishes we test, this recipe from Ann Marie Moch of Kintyre, North Dakota, was the biggest surprise. These flaky, rustic-looking pastry shells hold a sweet and spicy pecan layer under the squash slices.
—*Taste of Home* Test Kitchen

- -

Prep: 30 min. • **Bake:** 35 min.
Makes: 2 tarts (8 servings each)

- 1 **medium butternut squash, peeled, seeded and cut into ⅛-in. slices**
- 1 **medium acorn squash, peeled, seeded and cut into ⅛-in. slices**
- 2 **Tbsp. water**
- ¼ **cup olive oil**
- 1 **Tbsp. minced fresh thyme**
- 1 **Tbsp. minced fresh parsley**
- ½ **tsp. salt**
- ¼ **tsp. pepper**
- ½ **cup all-purpose flour**
- ½ **cup ground pecans**
- 6 **Tbsp. sugar**
- ½ **tsp. ground nutmeg**
- ½ **tsp. ground cinnamon**

- 1 **pkg. (17.3 oz.) frozen puff pastry, thawed**
- 1 **large egg, lightly beaten**
- 2 **Tbsp. butter**

1. In a large microwave-safe bowl, combine squash and water. Cover and microwave on high for 5 minutes or until crisp-tender. Drain; return to bowl. In a small bowl, combine oil, thyme, parsley, salt and pepper; drizzle onto squash and toss to coat. In another small bowl, combine flour, pecans, sugar, nutmeg and cinnamon; set aside.
2. Unfold pastry sheets on a lightly floured surface. Roll each pastry to ⅛-in. thickness; transfer each to an ungreased baking sheet. Sprinkle with pecan mixture. Arrange squash slices to within 1½ in. of edges, alternating slices of butternut and acorn squash.
3. Fold up edges of pastry over filling, leaving centers uncovered. Brush pastry with egg. Dot squash with butter. Bake at 375° for 35-40 minutes or until golden brown.
1 piece: 279 cal., 15g fat (4g sat. fat), 17mg chol., 196mg sod., 34g carb. (7g sugars, 5g fiber), 4g pro.

SPICY COWBOY BEANS

These beans are a perfect contribution to a potluck buffet any time of year. Instead of needing hours on the stove, they cook quickly in the pressure cooker and there's no need to pre-soak the beans.
—Joan Hallford, North Richland Hills, TX

- -

Prep: 25 min. • **Cook:** 1½ hours + releasing
Makes: 10 servings

- 4   bacon strips, chopped
- 1   medium onion, chopped
- 2   garlic cloves, minced
- 2   cups reduced-sodium beef broth
- 3   cups water
- 1   pkg. (16 oz.) 16-bean soup mix
- 1   can (10 oz.) diced tomatoes and green chiles, undrained
- 1   can (8 oz.) tomato sauce
- 1   poblano pepper, chopped
- ¼   cup packed brown sugar
- 1   envelope taco seasoning
      Optional: Chopped fresh cilantro, shredded cheddar cheese and sour cream

1. Select saute or browning setting on a 6-qt. electric pressure cooker; adjust for medium heat. Cook bacon until crisp, 4-5 minutes. Add onion and garlic; cook until tender, 5-6 minutes longer. Add broth to pressure cooker. Cook 30 seconds, stirring to loosen browned bits from pan. Press cancel.
2. Add water, soup mix, tomatoes and green chiles, tomato sauce, poblano pepper, brown sugar and taco seasoning. Lock lid; close pressure-release valve. Adjust to pressure-cook on high for 90 minutes. Let pressure release naturally.
3. If desired, select saute setting and adjust for low heat. Simmer, stirring constantly, until beans reach desired consistency. Press cancel. Serve with toppings of your choice.
Freeze option: Freeze cooled bean mixture in freezer containers. To use, partially thaw in refrigerator overnight. Heat through in a saucepan, stirring occasionally; add broth if necessary.
¾ cup: 245 cal., 6g fat (2g sat. fat), 10mg chol., 1823mg sod., 52g carb. (9g sugars, 21g fiber), 15g pro.

SPRING ASPARAGUS

This fresh and colorful side dish is delicious served warm or cold. I get compliments on the homemade dressing.
—Millie Vickery, Lena, IL

- -

Takes: 25 min. • **Makes:** 8 servings

- 1½ lbs. fresh asparagus, trimmed and cut into 2-in. pieces
- 2   small tomatoes, cut into wedges
- 3   Tbsp. cider vinegar
- ¾   tsp. Worcestershire sauce
- ⅓   cup sugar
- 1   Tbsp. grated onion
- ½   tsp. salt
- ½   tsp. paprika
- ⅓   cup canola oil
- ⅓   cup sliced almonds, toasted
- ⅓   cup crumbled blue cheese, optional

1. In a large saucepan, bring 1 cup water to a boil. Add the asparagus; cook, covered, until crisp-tender, 3-5 minutes. Drain; place in a large bowl. Add tomatoes; cover and keep warm.
2. Place vinegar, Worcestershire sauce, sugar, onion, salt and paprika in a blender; cover and process until smooth. While processing, gradually add oil in a steady stream. Toss with asparagus mixture. Top with almonds and, if desired, cheese.
Note: To toast nuts, bake in a shallow pan in a 350° oven for 5-10 minutes or cook in a skillet over low heat until lightly browned, stirring occasionally.
¾ cup: 154 cal., 11g fat (1g sat. fat), 0 chol., 159mg sod., 12g carb. (10g sugars, 1g fiber), 2g pro. **Diabetic exchanges:** 2 fat, 1 vegetable, ½ starch.

CRISPY BAKED ZUCCHINI FRIES

I coat zucchini strips with a mixture of panko bread crumbs, Parmesan cheese and spices. Then I bake them until they're crispy and golden brown. Delicious!
—Matthew Hass, Ellison Bay, WI

Prep: 25 min. • **Bake:** 20 min.
Makes: 4 servings

- 2 medium zucchini
- 1 cup panko bread crumbs
- ¾ cup grated Parmesan cheese
- 2 tsp. smoked paprika
- ½ tsp. garlic powder
- ¼ tsp. ground chipotle pepper
- ¼ tsp. salt
- ¼ tsp. pepper
- ⅓ cup all-purpose flour
- 2 large eggs, beaten
- 3 Tbsp. olive oil

1. Preheat oven to 425°. Cut each zucchini in half lengthwise and then in half crosswise. Cut each piece lengthwise into ¼-in. slices.
2. In a shallow bowl, mix the bread crumbs, cheese and seasonings. Place flour and eggs in separate shallow bowls. Dip zucchini slices in flour, then in egg and then in crumb mixture, patting to help coating adhere. Place on a greased rack in a foil-lined rimmed baking pan. Drizzle with oil. Bake until golden brown, 20-25 minutes.
1 serving: 289 cal., 18g fat (5g sat. fat), 106mg chol., 510mg sod., 21g carb. (3g sugars, 2g fiber), 12g pro.

CRISPY BAKED ZUCCHINI FRIES

LEMON GARLIC MUSHROOMS

I baste whole mushrooms with a lemony sauce to prepare this simple side dish. Using skewers or a basket makes it easy to turn them as they grill to perfection.
—Diane Hixon, Niceville, FL

Takes: 15 min. • **Makes:** 4 servings

- ¼ cup lemon juice
- 3 Tbsp. minced fresh parsley
- 2 Tbsp. olive oil
- 3 garlic cloves, minced
  Pepper to taste
- 1 lb. large fresh mushrooms

1. For dressing, whisk together the first 5 ingredients. Toss the mushrooms with 2 Tbsp. dressing.
2. Grill mushrooms, covered, over medium-high heat until tender, 5-7 minutes per side. Toss with remaining dressing before serving.
1 serving: 94 cal., 7g fat (1g sat. fat), 0 chol., 2mg sod., 6g carb. (0 sugars, 0 fiber), 3g pro.
Diabetic exchanges: 1½ fat, 1 vegetable.

SALSA CORN CAKES

CHERRY TOMATO PASTA WITH AVOCADO SAUCE

Heart-healthy avocado makes this pasta dish feel indulgent without being overly rich. The flavorful sauce is so luscious, you'll think there is cream hiding in there. It's guilt-free and dairy-free, but with a texture and consistency that's similar to traditional cream-based sauces.
—Julie Peterson, Crofton, MD

- -

Takes: 30 min. • **Makes:** 10 servings

1   pkg. (14½ oz.) protein-enriched rotini (about 3½ cups uncooked)
2   medium ripe avocados, peeled and pitted
1   cup fresh spinach
¼   cup loosely packed basil leaves
2   garlic cloves, halved
2   Tbsp. lime juice
½   tsp. kosher salt
¼   tsp. coarsely ground pepper
⅓   cup olive oil
1   cup assorted cherry tomatoes, halved
½   cup pine nuts
    Optional: Shredded Parmesan cheese, shredded mozzarella cheese and grated lime zest

1. Cook rotini according to package directions for al dente. Meanwhile, place avocados, spinach, basil, garlic, lime juice, salt and pepper in a food processor; pulse until chopped. Continue processing while gradually adding oil in a steady stream.
2. Drain rotini; transfer to a large bowl. Add avocado mixture and tomatoes; toss to coat. Top with the pine nuts and the toppings of your choice.
¾ cup: 314 cal., 18g fat (2g sat. fat), 0 chol., 125mg sod., 32g carb. (2g sugars, 5g fiber), 9g pro.

SALSA CORN CAKES

I whip up these patties to serve alongside nachos or tacos on hot summer evenings. The salsa is subtle but adds flavor. You can use fresh corn when it is in season.
—Lisa Boettcher, Rosebush, MI

- -

Takes: 20 min. • **Makes:** 8 servings

6   oz. cream cheese, softened
¼   cup butter, melted
6   large eggs
1   cup 2% milk
1½   cups all-purpose flour
½   cup cornmeal
1   tsp. baking powder
1   tsp. salt
1   can (15¼ oz.) whole kernel corn, drained
½   cup salsa, drained
¼   cup minced green onions
    Sour cream and additional salsa

1. In a large bowl, beat cream cheese and butter until smooth; add the eggs and mix well. Beat in the milk until smooth. Combine the flour, cornmeal, baking powder and salt; stir into cream cheese mixture just until moistened. Fold in corn, salsa and onions.
2. Pour batter by ¼ cupfuls into a large greased cast-iron skillet or hot griddle. Turn when bubbles form on top; cook until the second side is golden brown. Serve with sour cream and salsa.
1 serving: 324 cal., 15g fat (8g sat. fat), 191mg chol., 715mg sod., 34g carb. (5g sugars, 3g fiber), 11g pro.

CHERRY TOMATO PASTA
WITH AVOCADO SAUCE

FREEZER SWEET CORN

People ask me how to freeze corn on the cob because my frozen corn tastes as good as fresh! This method helps it stay very crisp-tender, and now I can have fresh corn any time of the year.
—Judy Oudekerk, St. Michael, MN

- -

Prep: 30 min. • **Cook:** 15 min. • **Makes:** 3 qt.

- 4 qt. fresh corn (cut from about 20 ears)
- 1 qt. hot water
- ⅔ cup sugar
- ½ cup butter, cubed
- 2 tsp. salt

In a stockpot, combine all ingredients; bring to a boil. Reduce heat; simmer, uncovered, 5-7 minutes, stirring occasionally. Transfer to large shallow containers to cool quickly, stirring occasionally. Freeze in airtight containers, allowing some headspace for expansion.

½ cup: 113 cal., 5g fat (2g sat. fat), 10mg chol., 245mg sod., 18g carb. (9g sugars, 2g fiber), 2g pro.

ASK SARAH

WHY SHOULD I FREEZE CORN?
The benefits of keeping containers of this corn in your freezer are endless. Simply thaw the corn overnight in the fridge; then use it in casseroles, chili or any recipe that calls for corn kernels. Or, simply heat it with melted butter and season to taste for a garden-fresh side you can enjoy in any season.

FREEZER
SWEET CORN

TOMATO COBBLER

I always make this recipe during the height of summer, when tomatoes are abundant and super flavorful. The topping is a cross between that of a crisp and a cobbler. It's a unique yet delightful way to use up fresh garden produce.

—Mohammed Abdullah, Fremont, CA

- -

Prep: 25 min. • **Bake:** 35 min.
Makes: 8 servings

- 1 cup plus 3 Tbsp. all-purpose flour, divided
- ½ cup grated Parmesan cheese, divided
- ¼ cup dry bread crumbs
- 2 Tbsp. sugar, divided
- 1 tsp. baking powder
- 1 tsp. salt, divided
- 1 tsp. dried basil, divided
- ½ tsp. garlic powder, divided
- ½ tsp. pepper, divided
- 2 large eggs, room temperature, lightly beaten
- 8 large tomatoes, skins and seeds removed, coarsely chopped
- ¼ cup butter, melted
    Minced fresh basil, optional

1. Preheat oven to 350°. For topping, in a small bowl, combine 1 cup flour, ¼ cup Parmesan cheese, bread crumbs, 1 Tbsp. sugar, baking powder, ½ tsp. salt, ½ tsp. basil, ¼ tsp. garlic powder and ¼ tsp. pepper. Gradually add eggs, tossing with a fork until the dough holds together when pressed (mixture will be sticky); set aside.
2. In a large bowl, combine remaining ¼ cup Parmesan cheese, 3 Tbsp. flour, 1 Tbsp. sugar, ½ tsp. salt, ½ tsp. basil, ¼ tsp. garlic powder and ¼ tsp. pepper. Add tomatoes; gently toss to coat. Transfer mixture to a greased 3-qt. baking dish. Sprinkle with topping; drizzle with melted butter.
3. Bake, uncovered, until filling is bubbly and topping is golden brown, 35-40 minutes. If desired, top with fresh basil. Serve warm.
1 serving: 217 cal., 9g fat (5g sat. fat), 66mg chol., 543mg sod., 28g carb. (8g sugars, 3g fiber), 7g pro.

CAULIFLOWER CASSEROLE

To dress up fresh cauliflower, Mom used a delightful mixture of a cheesy sauce, bright red and green pepper pieces and crushed cornflakes. We enjoyed this casserole so much that leftovers were rare.

—Linda McGinty, Parma, OH

- -

Prep: 15 min. • **Bake:** 30 min.
Makes: 8 servings

- 1 medium head cauliflower, broken into florets
- 1 cup sour cream
- 1 cup shredded cheddar cheese
- ½ cup crushed cornflakes
- ¼ cup chopped green pepper
- ¼ cup chopped sweet red pepper
- 1 tsp. salt
- ¼ cup grated Parmesan cheese
    Paprika

1. Preheat oven to 325°. Place 1 in. of water in a saucepan; add cauliflower. Bring to a boil. Reduce heat; cover and simmer until crisp-tender, 5-10 minutes. Drain.
2. In a large bowl, combine the cauliflower, sour cream, cheddar cheese, cornflakes, peppers and salt; transfer to a greased 2-qt. baking dish. Sprinkle with Parmesan cheese and paprika.
3. Bake, uncovered, until heated through, 30-35 minutes.
1 serving: 162 cal., 10g fat (7g sat. fat), 37mg chol., 503mg sod., 10g carb. (4g sugars, 2g fiber), 7g pro.

CAULIFLOWER CASSEROLE

CUCUMBER & HUMMUS BOATS

The refreshing combo of cucumber and hummus really brings this meatless meal together. It transports easily, making it a great option for weekday lunches.
—Matthew Hass, Ellison Bay, WI

- -

Takes: 30 min. • **Makes:** 6 servings

- 1 cup quinoa, rinsed
- 6 medium cucumbers
- 1 can (15 oz.) garbanzo beans or chickpeas, rinsed and drained
- 1 cup cherry tomatoes, halved
- 1 pkg. (4 oz.) crumbled tomato and basil feta cheese
- ½ cup pitted Greek olives, chopped
- ¼ cup lemon juice
- 3 Tbsp. honey
- 2 Tbsp. olive oil
- 2 garlic cloves, minced
- ¼ tsp. pepper
- 1 carton (14 oz.) roasted garlic hummus
  Minced fresh basil, optional

1. Cook quinoa according to the package directions. Transfer quinoa to a large bowl; cool slightly.

2. Meanwhile, cut each cucumber in half lengthwise. Scoop out pulp, leaving a ¼-in. shell. Add garbanzo beans, tomatoes, cheese and olives to quinoa. In a small bowl, whisk lemon juice, honey, oil, garlic and pepper until blended. Pour over quinoa mixture; gently toss to coat. Spread about 2 Tbsp. hummus inside each cucumber shell. Top each with about ⅓ cup quinoa mixture. Sprinkle with basil if desired.

2 stuffed cucumber halves: 482 cal., 21g fat (3g sat. fat), 10mg chol., 1026mg sod., 60g carb. (17g sugars, 11g fiber), 16g pro.

COLORFUL CRANBERRY SWEET POTATO BAKE

Sweet potatoes and tart cranberries are a feast for the eyes and the palate in this beautiful side dish.
—Patricia Kile, Elizabethtown, PA

- -

Prep: 25 min. • **Bake:** 35 min.
Makes: 8 servings

- 1½ lbs. sweet potatoes (about 3 medium), peeled and cut into 1-in. cubes
- 1½ cups fresh or frozen cranberries, thawed
- ⅔ cup sugar
- ⅓ cup orange juice
- 1 tsp. salt
- 1 Tbsp. butter
- 1½ cups granola without raisins

1. Preheat oven to 350°. Place potatoes in a large saucepan with water to cover; bring to a boil. Reduce heat; cook, uncovered, until tender, 10-15 minutes. Drain.

2. Toss cranberries with sugar, orange juice and salt; spread half of the mixture in a greased 11x7-in. baking dish. Top with half of the potatoes. Repeat layers. Dot with butter.

3. Bake, covered, until cranberries are tender, about 25 minutes. Uncover; sprinkle with granola. Bake 10 minutes.

½ cup: 261 cal., 5g fat (1g sat. fat), 4mg chol., 323mg sod., 54g carb. (29g sugars, 7g fiber), 5g pro.

CUCUMBER & HUMMUS BOATS

CHEESY STUFFED BAKED POTATOES

BACON-WRAPPED ASPARAGUS

My husband and I grill dinner almost every night, and I love grilling asparagus for a side dish. I serve these bacon-wrapped spears with grilled meat and sliced fresh tomatoes for a wonderful meal.
—Trisha Kitts, Dickinson, TX

Takes: 30 min. • **Makes:** 2 servings

- 10 fresh asparagus spears, trimmed
  Cooking spray
- ⅛ tsp. pepper
- 5 bacon strips, halved lengthwise

1. Place asparagus on a sheet of waxed paper; coat with cooking spray. Sprinkle with pepper; turn to coat. Wrap a bacon piece around each spear; secure the ends with toothpicks.
2. Grill, uncovered, over medium heat until bacon is crisp, 4-6 minutes on each side. Discard toothpicks.
5 pieces : 120 cal., 8g fat (3g sat. fat), 21mg chol., 372mg sod., 4g carb. (1g sugars, 1g fiber), 9g pro.

CHEESY STUFFED BAKED POTATOES

These special potatoes are a hit with my whole family, from the smallest grandchild on up. I often prepare them up to a week in advance, wrap them well and freeze. Their flavorful filling goes so nicely with juicy ham slices. Leftovers are great for lunch!
—Marge Clark, West Lebanon, IN

Prep: 1¼ hours • **Bake:** 20 min.
Makes: 6 servings

- 3 large baking potatoes (1 lb. each)
- 1½ tsp. canola oil, optional
- ½ cup sliced green onions
- ½ cup butter, cubed, divided
- ½ cup half-and-half cream
- ½ cup sour cream
- 1 tsp. salt
- ½ tsp. white pepper
- 1 cup shredded cheddar cheese
  Paprika

1. Preheat oven to 400°. Scrub and pierce potatoes. Rub with oil if desired. Bake until tender, 50-75 minutes. When cool enough to handle, cut each potato in half lengthwise. Scoop out pulp, leaving a thin shell; set aside. Reduce oven temperature to 375°.
2. In a small skillet, saute onions in ¼ cup butter until tender. In a large bowl, mash potato pulp. Stir in sauteed onions, cream, sour cream, salt and pepper. Fold in cheese. Stuff into potato shells.
3. Place on a baking sheet. Melt remaining butter; drizzle over potatoes. Sprinkle with paprika. Bake until heated through, about 20 minutes.
1 stuffed potato half: 416 cal., 26g fat (17g sat. fat), 84mg chol., 693mg sod., 36g carb. (4g sugars, 3g fiber), 9g pro.

CAULIFLOWER
AU GRATIN

CAULIFLOWER AU GRATIN

This is a lower-carb side dish that pairs well with pork, ham or beef. It's so creamy and delicious that even the kids will ask for seconds! If you like a little crunch, sprinkle buttered bread crumbs over the top for the last five minutes in the oven.
—Mary Zinchiak, Boardman, OH

- -

Prep: 25 min. • **Bake:** 45 min.
Makes: 8 servings

- 1 large head cauliflower, cut into florets
- 2 Tbsp. olive oil
- 1 tsp. salt, divided
- 1 tsp. pepper, divided
- 4 Tbsp. butter, cubed
- 3 Tbsp. all-purpose flour
- 2 cups 2% milk
- 1 cup shredded Swiss cheese
- ½ cup grated Parmesan cheese
- ½ tsp. onion powder
- ½ tsp. ground mustard
- ½ tsp. Worcestershire sauce
- ⅛ tsp. cayenne pepper
  Chopped fresh thyme, optional

1. Preheat oven to 375°. Place cauliflower on a rimmed baking sheet. Drizzle with oil; sprinkle with ½ tsp. salt and ½ tsp. pepper. Toss to coat. Bake 8 minutes. Stir; bake until crisp-tender and lightly browned, 7-8 minutes longer.
2. In a large saucepan, melt butter over medium heat. Stir in flour until smooth; gradually whisk in milk. Bring to a simmer, stirring constantly; cook and stir until thickened, 2-3 minutes. Remove from heat. Stir in next 6 ingredients and the remaining ½ tsp. salt and ½ tsp. pepper until smooth.
3. Pour ¾ cup cheese sauce into a greased 2-qt. baking dish. Top with cauliflower and remaining cheese sauce. Bake, uncovered, until bubbly and lightly browned, 30-35 minutes. If desired, top with the chopped fresh thyme.
¾ cup: 196 cal., 14g fat (7g sat. fat), 34mg chol., 291mg sod., 11g carb. (5g sugars, 2g fiber), 9g pro.

GLAZED RANCH CARROTS

GLAZED RANCH CARROTS

Ranch salad dressing mix flavors these tasty veggies in a flash. By using packages of baby carrots, there's no time-consuming peeling or slicing.
—Marion Reed, Omak, WA

- -

Takes: 25 min. • **Makes:** 12 servings

- 2 lbs. fresh baby carrots
- ½ cup butter, cubed
- ½ cup packed brown sugar
- 2 envelopes ranch salad dressing mix
  Minced fresh parsley, optional

1. Place carrots in a saucepan; add 1 in. of water. Bring to a boil. Reduce heat; cover and cook for 8-10 minutes or until crisp-tender. Drain and set aside.
2. In the same pan, combine the butter, brown sugar and salad dressing mix until blended. Add carrots. Cook and stir over medium heat for 5 minutes or until glazed. Sprinkle with parsley, if desired.
¾ cup: 156 cal., 8g fat (5g sat. fat), 20mg chol., 1067mg sod., 22g carb. (13g sugars, 1g fiber), 1g pro.

GRILLED SWEET CORN

Since we have plenty of fresh sweet corn available in our area, we use this recipe often in summer. Parsley, chili powder and cumin accent the corn's just-picked flavor.
—Connie Lou Hollister, Lake Odessa, MI

- -

Prep: 10 min. + soaking • **Grill:** 25 min.
Makes: 8 servings

- 8 large ears sweet corn in husks
- 6 Tbsp. butter, softened
- 1 Tbsp. minced fresh parsley
- 1 to 2 tsp. chili powder
- 1 tsp. garlic salt
- ½ to 1 tsp. ground cumin

1. Place corn in a stockpot; cover with cold water. Soak 20 minutes.
2. Mix remaining ingredients. Drain corn; carefully peel back husks to within 1 in. of bottoms and remove silk. Spread corn with butter mixture; rewrap in husks and secure with kitchen string.
3. Grill corn, covered, over medium heat until tender, 25-30 minutes, turning often. To serve, cut string and peel back husks.
1 ear of corn: 200 cal., 10g fat (6g sat. fat), 23mg chol., 338mg sod., 28g carb. (8g sugars, 4g fiber), 5g pro.

BUTTERY MASHED
POTATOES

BUTTERY MASHED POTATOES

These creamy, buttery mashed potatoes use simple ingredients. The tricks are to use Yukon Gold potatoes and then to warm the cream and butter just a bit before adding them to the potatoes.
—Rashanda Cobbins, Food Editor

- -

Takes: 30 min. • **Makes:** 6 servings

- 3 lbs. medium Yukon Gold potatoes, peeled
- ⅔ cup heavy whipping cream
- ½ cup butter, cubed
- 1 tsp. salt
- ¾ tsp. white pepper

1. Place potatoes in a Dutch oven; add water to cover. Bring to a boil. Reduce heat; cook, uncovered, until tender, 15-20 minutes. Meanwhile, in a small saucepan, heat cream, butter, salt and pepper until butter is melted.
2. Drain the potatoes; return to pan. Mash potatoes, gradually adding enough cream mixture to reach desired consistency.

¾ cup: 438 cal., 25g fat (16g sat. fat), 71mg chol., 534mg sod., 50g carb. (5g sugars, 3g fiber), 5g pro.

ASK SARAH

WHAT'S THE SECRET TO LUMP-FREE SPUDS?

If you're looking for extra creamy mashed spuds without any lumps, considering beating the final potato mixture with a handheld mixer.

SUMMER ZUCCHINI PASTA

I'm always experimenting when my garden cranks out zucchini and summer squash. This simple and healthy pasta dish is one of my latest wins. It's meatless, but you can add shredded chicken or grilled salmon for a heartier dish.

—Beth Berlin, Oak Creek, WI

- -

Takes: 25 min. • **Makes:** 10 servings

- 1 pkg. (16 oz.) pappardelle or tagliatelle pasta
- ¼ cup olive oil
- 2 small zucchini, cut into thin ribbons
- 2 small yellow summer squash, cut into thin ribbons
- 4 garlic cloves, thinly sliced
- 2 cans (14½ oz. each) diced tomatoes with roasted garlic, undrained
- ⅓ cup loosely packed basil leaves, torn
- 1 Tbsp. coarsely chopped fresh rosemary
- ½ tsp. salt
- ¼ tsp. crushed red pepper flakes

Cook pasta according to package directions. Meanwhile, in a Dutch oven, heat oil over medium-high heat. Add the zucchini and yellow squash; cook and stir until crisp-tender, 3-4 minutes. Add sliced garlic; cook 1 minute longer. Add tomatoes, basil leaves, fresh rosemary, salt and pepper flakes; heat through. Drain the pasta; serve with zucchini mixture. If desired, top with additional basil.

1 cup: 254 cal., 7g fat (1g sat. fat), 0 chol., 505mg sod., 42g carb. (8g sugars, 3g fiber), 7g pro.

SUMMER ZUCCHINI PASTA

SKILLET CABBAGE

I use this dish often when the schedule gets tight and I need a hurry-up vegetable to cook. It always adds plenty of substance to a simple meal.

—Charmaine Fricke, St. Charles, IL

- -

Takes: 25 min. • **Makes:** 6 servings

- 2 Tbsp. butter
- 4 cups shredded cabbage
- 1 green pepper, cut into thin strips
- 2 Tbsp. water
- ½ tsp. salt
- ¼ tsp. pepper
- 3 oz. cream cheese, cubed and softened

Melt butter in a large cast-iron or other heavy skillet; add shredded cabbage and green pepper and toss to coat. Stir in water, salt and pepper. Cover; simmer until cabbage is tender, 8-10 minutes. Add cream cheese; stir until melted.

½ cup: 100 cal., 9g fat (5g sat. fat), 26mg chol., 286mg sod., 4g carb. (2g sugars, 1g fiber), 2g pro.

CHEESY SLOW-COOKED CORN

Even those who usually don't eat much corn will ask for a second helping of this creamy, cheesy side dish. Folks love the flavor, but I love how easy it is to make with ingredients I usually have on hand.
—Mary Ann Truitt, Wichita, KS

Prep: 5 min. • **Cook:** 3 hours
Makes: 12 servings

- 9½ cups (48 oz.) frozen corn
- 11 oz. cream cheese, softened
- ¼ cup butter, cubed
- 3 Tbsp. water
- 3 Tbsp. 2% milk
- 2 Tbsp. sugar
- 6 slices American cheese, cut into small pieces

In a 4- or 5-qt. slow cooker, combine all ingredients. Cook, covered, on low, for 3-4 hours, until heated through and cheese is melted, stirring once.

1 cup: 265 cal., 16g fat (9g sat. fat), 39mg chol., 227mg sod., 27g carb. (6g sugars, 2g fiber), 7g pro.

"I've lost count of how many times I've made this recipe. It's perfect when you're hosting a party and need a side dish that simmers on its own. I've served it alongside Easter ham in spring as well as grilled meats in summer."

— MARK HAGEN, EXECUTIVE EDITOR

SAUCY SPROUTS & ORANGES

Expect compliments when you serve this mouthwatering Brussels sprouts dish. Citrus and mustard flavor the tasty sauce.
—Carolyn Hannay, Antioch, TN

Takes: 30 min. • **Makes:** 6 servings

- 3 medium navel oranges
- 1 lb. fresh Brussels sprouts, trimmed and halved
- 1 Tbsp. butter
- 2 tsp. cornstarch
- 2 Tbsp. honey mustard
- ¼ tsp. Chinese five-spice powder
- 2 Tbsp. slivered almonds, toasted

1. Finely grate zest of 1 orange; set zest aside. Cut that orange in half; squeeze juice into a 1-cup measuring cup. Add enough water to measure ½ cup; set aside. Peel and discard white membranes from remaining oranges; section them and set aside.

2. In a large saucepan, bring 1 in. water and Brussels sprouts to a boil. Cover and cook for 8-10 minutes or until crisp-tender.

3. Meanwhile, in a small saucepan, melt the butter. Whisk the cornstarch and reserved orange juice mixture until smooth; add to the butter. Stir in mustard and five-spice powder. Bring to a boil over medium heat; cook and stir for 1-2 minutes or until the mixture is thickened and bubbly.

4. Drain sprouts; gently stir in orange sections. Transfer to a serving bowl; drizzle with sauce. Sprinkle with almonds and grated orange zest.

¾ cup: 97 cal., 4g fat (1g sat. fat), 5mg chol., 81mg sod., 15g carb. (8g sugars, 3g fiber), 4g pro. **Diabetic exchanges:** 1 vegetable, 1 fat, ½ fruit.

SAUCY SPROUTS & ORANGES

SPAETZLE
DUMPLINGS

STIR-FRIED ZUCCHINI

I plant many vegetables to use in cooking. Zucchini is among our favorites and I often have it in abundance. That's why this dish is so popular at our house.
—Deborah Elliot, Ridge Spring, SC

- -

Takes: 10 min. • **Makes:** 8 servings

- 2 lbs. sliced zucchini
- 2 garlic cloves, minced
- ¼ cup olive oil
- 1 tsp. salt
- ½ tsp. Italian seasoning
- ¼ tsp. pepper

In a large skillet, saute the zucchini and garlic in oil until zucchini is crisp-tender, about 5 minutes. Sprinkle with the seasonings. Serve immediately.
½ cup: 77 cal., 7g fat (1g sat. fat), 0 chol., 299mg sod., 4g carb. (2g sugars, 1g fiber), 1g pro.

SPAETZLE DUMPLINGS

These tender homemade spaetzle noodles take only minutes to make and are a natural accompaniment to chicken. You can serve the spaetzle with chicken gravy or simply butter it and sprinkle with parsley.
—Pamela Eaton, Monclova, OH

- -

Takes: 15 min. • **Makes:** 6 servings

- 2 cups all-purpose flour
- 4 large eggs, lightly beaten
- ⅓ cup 2% milk
- 2 tsp. salt
- 8 cups water
- 1 Tbsp. butter
  Minced fresh parsley, optional

1. In a large bowl, stir the flour, eggs, milk and salt until smooth (dough will be sticky). In a large saucepan over high heat, bring water to a boil. Pour dough into a colander or spaetzle maker coated with cooking spray; place over boiling water.
2. With a wooden spoon, press dough until small pieces drop into boiling water. Cook for 2 minutes or until dumplings are tender and float. Remove with a slotted spoon; toss with butter. If desired, sprinkle with parsley.
1 cup: 223 cal., 6g fat (2g sat. fat), 130mg chol., 856mg sod., 33g carb. (1g sugars, 1g fiber), 9g pro.

CREAMY SWEET POTATOES

I took my mother's delicious sweet potato casserole and gave it a new twist by adding the tempting taste of orange, a fruit very abundant in our state. The flavors are wonderful together.
—Norma Poole, Auburndale, FL

- -

Prep: 15 min. • **Bake:** 40 min.
Makes: 12 servings

- 5 lbs. sweet potatoes, peeled and cooked
- 4 large eggs, lightly beaten
- ½ cup orange juice
- ½ cup butter, softened
- ½ cup sugar
- 1 tsp. vanilla extract
- ½ tsp. ground nutmeg
  Dash salt
- 1 cup miniature marshmallows

1. In a large bowl, mash sweet potatoes. Add the eggs, orange juice, butter, sugar, vanilla extract, nutmeg and salt; mix well. Transfer to a greased 3-qt. baking dish.
2. Bake at 350° until set, 35-40 minutes. Top with marshmallows; return to oven until they just begin to puff and melt, 5-10 minutes.
¾ cup: 312 cal., 10g fat (5g sat. fat), 82mg chol., 266mg sod., 53g carb. (41g sugars, 5g fiber), 4g pro.

HARVARD BEETS

This pretty side dish's bright, citrusy flavors are an ideal companion for down-to-earth entrees—and for people who usually shy away from beets.
—Jean Ann Perkins, Newburyport, MD

- -

Takes: 15 min. • **Makes:** 4 servings

- 1 can (16 oz.) sliced beets
- ¼ cup sugar
- 1½ tsp. cornstarch
- 2 Tbsp. vinegar
- 2 Tbsp. orange juice
- 1 Tbsp. grated orange zest

Drain beets, reserving 2 Tbsp. juice; set beets and juice aside. In a saucepan, combine sugar and cornstarch. Add vinegar, orange juice and beet juice; bring to a boil. Reduce heat and simmer for 3-4 minutes or until thickened. Add the beets and orange zest; heat through.
½ cup: 93 cal., 0 fat (0 sat. fat), 0 chol., 220mg sod., 23g carb. (19g sugars, 2g fiber), 1g pro.

TABBOULEH

Tabouleh, also known as tabbouleh, is a classic Middle Eastern salad. The fresh veggies and mint leaves make it light and refreshing on a hot day.
—Michael & Mathil Chebat, Lake Ridge, VA

Takes: 30 min. • **Makes:** 8 servings

- ¼   cup bulgur
- 3   bunches fresh parsley, minced (about 2 cups)
- 3   large tomatoes, finely chopped
- 1   small onion, finely chopped
- ¼   cup lemon juice
- ¼   cup olive oil
- 5   fresh mint leaves, minced
- ½   tsp. salt
- ½   tsp. pepper
- ¼   tsp. cayenne pepper

Prepare bulgur according to the package directions; cool. Transfer to a large bowl. Stir in remaining ingredients. If desired, chill before serving.

⅔ cup: 100 cal., 7g fat (1g sat. fat), 0 chol., 164mg sod., 9g carb. (3g sugars, 2g fiber), 2g pro. **Diabetic exchanges:** 1½ fat, ½ starch.

PASTA WITH ASPARAGUS

Many terrific recipes change hands at the monthly get-togethers of my ladies' bridge group. That's where I discovered this zippy, tempting dish. The garlic, asparagus, Parmesan cheese and red pepper flakes create an irresistible taste combination.
—Jean Fisher, Redlands, CA

Takes: 20 min. • **Makes:** 6 servings

- 5   garlic cloves, minced
- ¼   to ½ tsp. crushed red pepper flakes
- 2   to 3 dashes hot pepper sauce
- ¼   cup olive oil
- 1   Tbsp. butter
- 1   lb. fresh asparagus, cut into 1½-in. pieces
     Salt to taste
- ¼   tsp. pepper
- ¼   cup shredded Parmesan cheese
- ½   lb. mostaccioli or elbow macaroni, cooked and drained

In a large cast-iron or other heavy skillet, cook the garlic, red pepper flakes and hot pepper sauce in oil and butter for 1 minute. Add the asparagus, salt and pepper; saute until asparagus is crisp-tender, 8-10 minutes. Stir in cheese. Pour over hot pasta and toss to coat. Serve immediately.

1 cup: 259 cal., 13g fat (3g sat. fat), 8mg chol., 83mg sod., 30g carb. (2g sugars, 2g fiber), 7g pro.

TABBOULEH

MACARONI COLESLAW

My friend Peggy brought this coleslaw to one of our picnics, and everyone liked it so much, we all had to have the recipe.
—Sandra Matteson, Westhope, ND

Prep: 25 min. + chilling • **Makes:** 16 servings

- 1 pkg. (7 oz.) ring macaroni or ditalini
- 1 pkg. (14 oz.) coleslaw mix
- 2 medium onions, finely chopped
- 2 celery ribs, finely chopped
- 1 medium cucumber, finely chopped
- 1 medium green pepper, finely chopped
- 1 can (8 oz.) whole water chestnuts, drained and chopped

DRESSING
- 1½ cups Miracle Whip Light
- ⅓ cup sugar
- ¼ cup cider vinegar
- ½ tsp. salt
- ¼ tsp. pepper

1. Cook macaroni according to the package directions; drain and rinse in cold water. Transfer to a large bowl; add the coleslaw mix, onions, celery, cucumber, green pepper and water chestnuts.

2. In a small bowl, whisk the dressing ingredients. Pour over salad; toss to coat. Cover and refrigerate for at least 1 hour.

¾ cup: 150 cal., 5g fat (1g sat. fat), 6mg chol., 286mg sod., 24g carb. (12g sugars, 2g fiber), 3g pro. **Diabetic exchanges:** 1 starch, 1 vegetable, 1 fat.

> "Pasta salad or coleslaw? Make this for your next picnic and you won't have to choose. I love that this salad stands proudly alone on any picnic spread!"
>
> —CHRISTINE RUKAVENA, EDITOR

MACARONI COLESLAW

WATERMELON JELLY, PAGE 176

Odds & Ends

From beverages and broths to seasonings and salad dressings, it's the little things that amp up flavor and round out menus. Turn here for the extras we love for taking meals from ordinary to extraordinary.

STRAWBERRY-BASIL FROZEN MARGARITA

Fresh, fruity and oh, so cool, this may be the perfect summer cocktail.
—James Schend, Deputy Editor, Culinary

Takes: 10 min. • **Makes:** 1 serving

- 1 lime wedge
  Coarse sugar, optional
- 1½ oz. blanco tequila
- 1 oz. Triple Sec
- ½ oz. freshly squeezed lime juice
- 1 cup frozen unsweetened sliced strawberries
- 4 fresh basil leaves
  Fresh strawberries, optional

1. Moisten rim of 1 cocktail glass with lime wedge. If desired, sprinkle sugar on a plate; dip rim in sugar.
2. Place tequila, Triple Sec, lime juice, strawberries and basil in a blender; cover and process until smooth. Pour into prepared glass. Garnish with lime wedge, strawberries and, if desired, additional basil.
1 serving: 256 cal., 0 fat (0 sat. fat), 0 chol., 3mg sod., 28g carb. (18g sugars, 3g fiber), 0 pro.

HOMEMADE TACO
SEASONING MIX

HOMEMADE TACO SEASONING MIX

This seasoning mix is right on. It tastes like purchased mixes, but is cheaper and has nearly half the sodium. Your heart and wallet will surely thank you!
—*Taste of Home* Test Kitchen

Takes: 20 min. • **Makes:** 4 servings per batch

- ¼ cup all-purpose flour
- ¼ cup chili powder
- 3 Tbsp. dried minced onion
- 1 Tbsp. garlic powder
- 2½ tsp. salt
- 2 tsp. dried oregano
- 2 tsp. ground cumin
- 1½ tsp. cayenne pepper
- 1 tsp. ground coriander

ADDITIONAL INGREDIENTS
- 1 lb. lean ground beef (90% lean)
- ¾ cup water
- 4 whole wheat tortillas (8 in.), warmed

1. Combine the first 9 ingredients. Store in an airtight container in a cool, dry place for up to 1 year. **Yield:** 4 batches (about 1 cup total).
2. To prepare tacos: In a large skillet, cook beef over medium heat until no longer pink; drain. Add ¼ cup taco seasoning mix and water. Bring to a boil; cook and stir for 2 minutes. Fill each tortilla with ½ cup beef mixture.

1 prepared taco: 338 cal., 13g fat (4g sat. fat), 71mg chol., 619mg sod., 26g carb. (2g sugars, 3g fiber), 27g pro.

CAULIFLOWER PIZZA CRUST

Make your next pizza night a little healthier with our cauliflower pizza crust recipe. The herbs and cheese add a ton of flavor!
—*Taste of Home* Test Kitchen

Prep: 30 min. • **Bake:** 30 min+ cooling
Makes: 6 servings

- 1½ heads cauliflower (about 1½ lbs.), chopped (about 6 cups)
- ½ cup shredded part-skim mozzarella cheese
- ½ cup grated Parmesan cheese
- 1 large eggs, lightly beaten
- 1 tsp. dried oregano
- 1 tsp. garlic powder
- ½ tsp. salt

1. Preheat oven to 425°. Working in batches, place the cauliflower in food processor; process until finely ground. Transfer to a large microwave-safe bowl; repeat with the remaining cauliflower. Microwave, covered, until cauliflower is tender, about 8 minutes. When cool enough to handle, squeeze dry; return to bowl.
2. Stir in the remaining ingredients until combined. Line a baking sheet with parchment. Press and shape cauliflower mixture into an 10-in. circle or 13x6-in. oval.
3. Bake until edges of crust are browned, 20-25 minutes. Top as desired; bake until toppings are heated through, 10-12 minutes.
1 piece: 71 cal., 4g fat (2g sat. fat), 32mg chol., 316mg sod., 5g carb. (2g sugars, 2g fiber), 5g pro. **Diabetic exchanges:** 1 medium-fat meat, 1 vegetable.

CAULIFLOWER PIZZA CRUST

GERMAN BUTTERCREAM

This frosting is super silky and buttery. It's pleasantly sweet, but not overly sweet like some American buttercreams can be.
—Rashanda Cobbins, Food Editor

Takes: 25 min. • **Makes:** 4 cups

- ½ cup sugar
- 1 Tbsp. cornstarch
- 1 cup whole milk
- 4 large egg yolks, room temperature, beaten
- 1 tsp. vanilla extract

BUTTERCREAM
- 1½ cups butter, softened
  Optional: 3 Tbsp. confectioners' sugar and vanilla extract

1. For pastry cream, in a small saucepan, combine sugar and cornstarch. Stir in milk until smooth. Cook and stir over medium heat until thickened and bubbly. Reduce heat; cook and stir 2 minutes longer. Remove from the heat. Stir a small amount of hot filling into egg yolks; return all to the pan, stirring constantly. Bring to a gentle boil; cook and stir 2 minutes longer.
2. Remove from the heat. Gently stir in vanilla. Cool to room temperature without stirring. For buttercream, in a bowl, cream the butter until fluffy, about 5 minutes. Gradually beat in cooled pastry cream. If desired, beat in confectioners' sugar and additional vanilla extract until fluffy, about 5 minutes. If necessary, refrigerate until frosting reaches spreading consistency. Store in the refrigerator.
2 Tbsp.: 51 cal., 5g fat (3g sat. fat), 23mg chol., 36mg sod., 2g carb. (2g sugars, 0 fiber), 0 pro.

COLD-BREW COFFEE

COLD-BREW COFFEE

Cold brewing reduces the acidity of coffee, which enhances its natural sweetness and complex flavors. Even those who take hot coffee with sugar and cream might find themselves sipping cold brew plain.
—*Taste of Home* Test Kitchen

Prep: 10 min. + chilling • **Makes:** 8 servings

- 1 **cup coarsely ground medium-roast coffee**
- 1 **cup hot water (205°)**
- 6 **to 7 cups cold water**
  Optional: 2% milk or half-and-half cream

1. Place the coffee grounds in a clean glass container. Pour hot water over the grounds; let stand 10 minutes. Stir in cold water. Cover and refrigerate for 12-24 hours. (The longer the coffee sits, the stronger the flavor.)
2. Strain the coffee through a fine mesh sieve; discard grounds. Strain the coffee again through a coffee filter; discard grounds. Serve over ice, with milk or cream if desired. Store in the refrigerator for up to 2 weeks.
1 cup: 2 cal., 0 fat (0 sat. fat), 0 chol., 4mg sod., 0 carb. (0 sugars, 0 fiber), 0 pro.

TEST KITCHEN TIP
While many cold brew recipes don't use any hot water, we like it in this recipe. The near-boiling water releases carbon dioxide in the grounds, extracting more flavor from the beans.

PICKLED PEACHES

Fresh peaches soaked in vinegar, sugar and spices is a southern treat. Serve with ice cream, pound cake or roasted meat, or mix into your favorite salad greens.
—Nick Iverson, Denver, CO

- -

Prep: 20 min. • **Process:** 15 min.
Makes: 12 servings

- 6 cinnamon sticks (3 in.)
- 24 whole peppercorns
- 18 whole cloves
- 2 tsp. thinly sliced fresh gingerroot
- 12 medium peaches, peeled, pitted and quartered
- 3 cups sugar
- 1 cup white vinegar
- 1 cup water

1. Divide cinnamon sticks, peppercorns, cloves and ginger slices among 6 hot pint jars; add peaches.
2. In a large saucepan, bring sugar, vinegar and water to a boil. Carefully ladle the hot liquid over peaches, leaving ½-in. headspace. Remove air bubbles and adjust headspace, if necessary, by adding hot mixture. Wipe rims. Center lids on jars; screw on bands until fingertip tight.
3. Place jars into canner with simmering water, ensuring that they are completely covered with water. Bring to a boil; process for 15 minutes. Remove jars and cool.
4 pieces: 78 cal., 0 fat (0 sat. fat), 0 chol., 0 sod., 19g carb. (17g sugars, 2g fiber), 1g pro.

BLACKBERRY SHRUB

Making shrubs is a creative way to use up extra fruit all the way through Labor Day. They are as colorful and refreshing as summer drinks should be. I was inspired to create this blackberry version after sampling a few house-made shrubs at a marketplace in California.
—Gina Nistico, Denver, CO

- -

Prep: 10 min. • **Cook:** 20 min. + chilling
Makes: 2 cups

- 1½ cups fresh or frozen blackberries, crushed
- 1 cinnamon stick (about 3 in.)
- 1 cup cider vinegar
- 1½ cups sugar
- ½ cup water

SERVING SUGGESTION
Optional: Ice cubes, sparkling water and fresh blackberries

1. Place blackberries and cinnamon stick in a sterilized pint jar. Bring vinegar just to a boil; pour over fruit, leaving ¼-in. headspace. Center lid on jar; screw on the band until fingertip tight. Refrigerate for 1 week.
2. Strain vinegar mixture through a fine-mesh strainer into another sterilized pint jar. Press solids to extract juice; discard remaining fruit.
3. Bring sugar and water to a boil. Reduce heat; simmer until sugar is dissolved. Cool slightly. Stir into vinegar mixture; shake well. Store in the refrigerator up to 2 weeks.
4. To serve, add 1-2 Tbsp. to a glass of ice, top with sparkling water and garnish with fresh blackberries if desired.
2 Tbsp. blackberry shrub syrup: 83 cal., 0 fat (0 sat. fat), 0 chol., 1mg sod., 20g carb. (20g sugars, 1g fiber), 0 pro.

BLACKBERRY SHRUB

WATERMELON JELLY

With its beautiful color and intense watermelon flavor, this jelly preserves summer to enjoy long after the cool weather arrives.
—*Taste of Home* Test Kitchen

- -

Prep: 25 min. + standing • **Process:** 10 min.
Makes: 5 half-pints

- 6 cups seeded chopped watermelon
- 5 cups sugar
- ⅓ cup white wine vinegar or white balsamic vinegar
- ¼ cup lemon juice
- 2 to 3 drops red food coloring, optional
- 2 pouches (3 oz. each) liquid fruit pectin

1. Place watermelon in a food processor; cover and process until pureed. Line a strainer with 4 layers of cheesecloth and place over a bowl. Place pureed watermelon in prepared strainer; cover with edges of cheesecloth. Let stand 10 minutes or until liquid measures 2 cups.
2. Discard the watermelon pulp from cheesecloth; place liquid in a large saucepan. Stir in sugar, vinegar, lemon juice and, if desired, food coloring. Bring to a full rolling boil over high heat, stirring constantly. Stir in the pectin. Continue to boil 1 minute, stirring mixture constantly.
3. Remove from heat; skim off foam. Ladle hot mixture into 5 hot half-pint jars, leaving ¼-in. headspace. Wipe rims. Center lids on jars; screw on bands until fingertip tight.
4. Place jars into canner with simmering water, ensuring that they are completely covered with water. Bring to a boil; process for 10 minutes. Remove jars and cool.
Note: The processing time listed is for altitudes of 1,000 feet or less. Add 1 minute to the processing time for each 1,000 feet of additional altitude.
2 Tbsp.: 106 cal., 0 fat (0 sat. fat), 0 chol., 1mg sod., 27g carb. (27g sugars, 0 fiber), 0 pro.

COTTON CANDY CHAMPAGNE COCKTAILS

COTTON CANDY CHAMPAGNE COCKTAILS

You'll love these whimsical champagne cocktails. The cotton candy melts away, leaving behind its pretty pink color.
—*Taste of Home* Test Kitchen

- -

Takes: 5 min. • **Makes:** 6 servings

- 6 Tbsp. raspberry-flavored vodka
- 1 bottle (750 ml) champagne, chilled
- 1½ cups pink cotton candy

Add 1 Tbsp. vodka to each of 6 champagne flutes. Top with champagne; create a cotton candy garnish for each glass. To serve, stir in cotton candy.
1 cocktail: 125 cal., 0 fat (0 sat. fat), 0 chol., 0 sod., 4g carb. (2g sugars, 0 fiber), 0 pro.

STRAWBERRY POPPY SEED DRESSING

In the world of vinegars, strawberry is the new raspberry, giving you a fresh way to put those ruby red gems to good use.
—*Taste of Home* Test Kitchen

- -

Takes: 10 min. • **Makes:** 1 cup

- ⅓ cup confectioners' sugar
- ¼ cup raspberry vinegar
- 2 Tbsp. orange juice
- ½ tsp. onion powder
- ¼ tsp. salt
- ¼ tsp. ground ginger
- ⅓ cup canola oil
- ½ tsp. poppy seeds

In a blender, combine first 6 ingredients; cover and process until blended. While processing, gradually add oil in a steady stream. Stir in the poppy seeds. Chill dressing until serving.
2 Tbsp.: 108 cal., 9g fat (1g sat. fat), 0 chol., 74mg sod., 6g carb. (5g sugars, 0 fiber), 0 pro. **Diabetic exchanges:** 1½ fat, ½ starch.

WATERMELON
JELLY

HONEY-THYME BUTTER

Laced with honey and fresh thyme, this butter is perfect for either sweet or savory dishes. It's amazing on bread and rolls fresh out of the oven but it's just as good on a stack of blueberry pancakes.
—*Taste of Home* Test Kitchen

- -

Takes: 5 min. • **Makes:** 1¼ cups

- ½ cup butter, softened
- ⅓ cup honey
- 2 tsp. fresh thyme leaves

In a small bowl, beat the butter until light and fluffy. Add the honey and thyme; beat just until blended. Store in refrigerator.
1 Tbsp.: 58 cal., 5g fat (3g sat. fat), 12mg chol., 37mg sod., 5g carb. (5g sugars, 0 fiber), 0 pro.

SWEDISH ROSE SPRITZ

A spritz is a still or sparkling wine-based cocktail served with a small amount of liqueur and a splash of seltzer or soda.
—*Taste of Home* Test Kitchen

- -

Takes: 5 min. • **Makes:** 1 serving

- 3 oz. dry rosé wine
- 1 oz. elderflower liqueur
  Lemon seltzer water

Fill a wine glass or tumbler three-fourths full of ice. Add wine and elderflower liqueur. Top with a splash of lemon seltzer; stir gently.
1 serving: 189 cal., 0 fat (0 sat. fat), 0 chol., 7mg sod., 19g carb. (14g sugars, 0 fiber), 0 pro.

GINGER DRESSING

I love this flavorful dressing because it's super easy to make and uses pantry staples. It's a speedy recipe to serve with salad greens or veggies on a weeknight.
—Rashanda Cobbins, Food Editor

- -

Prep: 10 min. • **Makes:** 1½ cups

- ⅓ cup rice vinegar
- 3 Tbsp. finely chopped onion
- 2 Tbsp. minced fresh gingerroot
- 2 Tbsp. soy sauce
- 1 Tbsp. honey
- ¼ tsp. pepper
- ¾ cup olive or peanut oil

In a blender, combine first 6 ingredients; cover and process until blended. While processing, gradually add oil in a steady stream. Chill until serving.
2 Tbsp.: 137 cal., 14g fat (2g sat. fat), 0 chol., 260mg sod., 4g carb. (4g sugars, 0 fiber), 0 pro.

HONEY-THYME BUTTER

WATERMELON-LIME COOLER

When temps heat up, chill some glasses and cool down with a slushy blend of lime, ginger ale and watermelon. Make, slurp and repeat!
—*Taste of Home* Test Kitchen

- -

Takes: 10 min. • **Makes:** 12 servings

12 **cups cubed seedless watermelon, frozen, divided**
¾ **tsp. grated lime zest, divided**
6 **cups chilled ginger ale, divided**

Place 4 cups frozen watermelon, ¼ tsp. lime zest and 2 cups ginger ale in a blender; cover and process until slushy. Repeat twice. Serve immediately.
1 cup: 82 cal., 0 fat (0 sat. fat), 0 chol., 14mg sod., 24g carb. (23g sugars, 1g fiber), 1g pro.

SRIRACHA SALT

Add a hint of subtle spice when you sprinkle this kicked-up salt on foods like eggs, grilled chicken, roasted veggies or popcorn.
—James Schend, Deputy Editor, Culinary

- -

Prep: 5 min. + standing • **Makes:** ½ cup

½ **cup kosher salt**
5 **tsp. Sriracha chili sauce**
½ **tsp. lime juice**

Combine salt, chili sauce and lime juice; spread into a parchment-lined 15x10x1-in. baking pan. Let stand at least 8 hours or overnight. Store in an airtight container at room temperature.
¼ tsp.: 0 cal., 0 fat (0 sat. fat), 0 chol., 488mg sod., 0 carb. (0 sugars, 0 fiber), 0 pro.

TOASTED PECAN VINAIGRETTE

I can always mix together this tasty dressing, even when time is particularly short. The pecans make it perfect for autumn salads.
—Sarah Farmer, Executive Culinary Director

- -

Prep: 5 min. • **Makes:** 1 cup

¼ **cup red wine vinegar**
1 **shallot, finely chopped**
1 **tsp. Dijon mustard**
½ **tsp. salt**
¼ **tsp. coarsely ground pepper**
¾ **cup extra virgin olive oil**
⅓ **cup finely chopped pecans, toasted**

In a large bowl, whisk together the first 5 ingredients. Slowly add olive oil while whisking constantly. Stir in pecans just before serving.
2 Tbsp.: 215 cal., 24g fat (3g sat. fat), 0 chol., 164mg sod., 2g carb. (0 sugars, 0 fiber), 1g pro.

TEST KITCHEN TIP
To get the most flavor out of these simple ingredients, mix up the vinaigrette and let it stand at room temperature for 1-3 hours before serving. Refrigerate any leftovers; bring cold vinaigrette to room temperature before shaking to combine.

WATERMELON-LIME COOLER

PEPPERMINT MILKSHAKES

Rich ice cream and refreshing peppermint make these shakes a special treat, especially during the holidays. For a twist on this tasty classic, stir in chocolate syrup and top with chocolate shavings.
—*Taste of Home* Test Kitchen

Takes: 5 min. • **Makes:** 3 servings

- 1 cup 2% milk
- 2 cups vanilla ice cream
- ½ tsp. peppermint extract
- ½ cup crushed peppermint candies, divided
  Sweetened whipped cream

In a blender, combine milk, ice cream and extract; cover and process for 30 seconds or until smooth. Stir in ¼ cup peppermint candies. Pour into chilled glasses. Top with whipped cream and remaining peppermint candies; serve immediately.

1 cup: 284 cal., 11g fat (7g sat. fat), 45mg chol., 115mg sod., 39g carb. (32g sugars, 1g fiber), 6g pro.

BEST EVER MAC & CHEESE

For this amazing mac, I make a sauce loaded with three different cheeses to toss with the noodles. When baked, it's ooey-gooey and cheesy good. And don't get me started on the crunchy topping!
—Beth Jacobson, Milwaukee, WI

Prep: 40 min. • **Bake:** 10 min.
Makes: 12 servings

- 1 pkg. (16 oz.) uncooked elbow macaroni
- 4 slices hearty white bread (4 oz.), torn into large pieces
- 6 Tbsp. butter, cubed and divided
- ½ cup grated Parmesan cheese
- 1 tsp. salt, divided
- 1 tsp. pepper, divided
- ¼ cup finely chopped onion
- 1 tsp. ground mustard
- ¼ tsp. cayenne pepper
- ¼ cup all-purpose flour
- 3 cups whole milk
- 2 cups half-and-half cream
- 1 cup (4 oz.) cubed Velveeta
- 1 block (8 oz.) sharp cheddar cheese, shredded
- 1 block (8 oz.) Monterey Jack cheese, shredded
- 1 tsp. Worcestershire sauce

1. Preheat oven to 400°. In a stockpot or Dutch oven, cook pasta according to package directions for al dente; drain and return to pan. Pulse bread, 2 Tbsp. butter, Parmesan, ½ tsp. salt and ½ tsp. pepper in a food processor until coarsely ground.
2. Meanwhile, in a large skillet over medium heat, melt remaining butter. Add onions and cook until tender, about 3 minutes. Add ground mustard and cayenne; stir until blended. Stir in flour until smooth, about 3 minutes. Slowly whisk in milk and cream; bring to a boil. Reduce heat to medium-low; simmer, stirring constantly, until thickened, about 5 minutes. Remove from heat; stir in Velveeta. Slowly add remaining cheeses a handful at a time, stirring until cheese is melted. Add Worcestershire and remaining salt and pepper. Pour over the pasta; toss to coat.
3. Transfer to a greased 13x9-in baking dish. Sprinkle bread crumbs over top of casserole. Bake until topping is golden brown and sauce is bubbly, 10-12 minutes.

1 cup: 762 cal., 43g fat (25g sat. fat), 134mg chol., 1138mg sod., 61g carb. (10g sugars, 3g fiber), 32g pro.

ASK SARAH

WHAT TOPPINGS CAN I ADD TO MY MAC & CHEESE?

It's easy to twist up casseroles with different toppings. If you're tired of bread-crumb toppings, considering dressing up pasta bakes with coarsely crushed pork rinds, potato chips or butter-flavored crackers.

PEPPERMINT MILKSHAKES

BEST EVER
MAC & CHEESE

CANNED NECTARINES
IN HONEY SYRUP

CANNED NECTARINES IN HONEY SYRUP

Nectarines are in season for such a short time, you'll want to do whatever you can to extend the season. With this quick method for canning nectarines, you'll have delicious fruit all year long.
—*Taste of Home* Test Kitchen

Prep: 30 min. • **Process:** 20 min./batch
Makes: 8 pint jars

- 1 gallon water
- 1 tsp. ascorbic acid powder
- 5 lbs. nectarines, halved, pitted and sliced into 1-in. slices
- 2 cups water
- ⅔ cup sugar
- ½ cup honey

1. Combine water and ascorbic acid powder until dissolved; place nectarines in liquid immediately after cutting each one. In a Dutch oven, combine water, sugar and honey. Bring to a boil, stirring to dissolve sugar. Drain nectarines and add to the canning syrup; return just to a boil. Remove from heat.
2. Carefully ladle hot mixture into 8 hot wide-mouth 1-pint jars, leaving ½-in. headspace. Remove air bubbles and, if necessary, adjust headspace by adding hot cooking liquid. Wipe rims. Center lids on jars; screw on bands until fingertip tight.
3. Place jars into canner with simmering water, ensuring they are completely covered with water. Bring to a boil; process for 20 minutes. Remove jars and cool.
½ cup: 64 cal., 0 fat (0 sat. fat), 0 chol., 1mg sod., 17g carb. (17g sugars, 0 fiber), 0 pro.

RICH HOT CHOCOLATE

Each February my friends and I gather for an outdoor party called Mittenfest. We skip the Bloody Marys and fill our thermoses with this hot cocoa instead. It's great with or without the rum.
—Gina Nistico, Denver, CO

Takes: 15 min. • **Makes:** 2 servings

- ⅔ cup heavy whipping cream
- 1 cup 2% milk
- 4 oz. dark chocolate candy bar, chopped
- 3 Tbsp. sugar
  Vanilla rum, optional
  Sweetened heavy whipping cream, whipped

In a small saucepan, heat heavy whipping cream, milk, chocolate and sugar over medium heat just until mixture comes to a simmer, stirring constantly. Remove from heat; stir until smooth. If desired, add rum. Pour into 2 mugs; top with sweetened whipped cream.
1 cup: 653 cal., 49g fat (32g sat. fat), 107mg chol., 79mg sod., 60g carb. (56g sugars, 4g fiber), 9g pro.

TEST KITCHEN TIP
Try stirring a few tablespoons of this hot chocolate into to a piping hot cup of coffee. Yum!

RICH HOT CHOCOLATE

OVER-THE-TOP CHERRY JAM

We live in Door County, an area known for its wonderful tart cherries. This beautiful sweet jam makes lovely gifts.
—Karen Haen, Sturgeon Bay, WI

Prep: 35 min. • **Process:** 5 min.
Makes: 6 half-pints

- 2½ lbs. fresh tart cherries, pitted
- 1 pkg. (1¾ oz.) powdered fruit pectin
- ½ tsp. butter
- 4¾ cups sugar

1. In a food processor, cover and process cherries in batches until finely chopped. Transfer to a Dutch oven; stir in pectin and butter. Bring to a full rolling boil over high heat, stirring constantly. Stir in sugar; return to a full rolling boil. Boil and stir 1 minute.

2. Remove from heat; skim off foam. Ladle hot mixture into 6 hot sterilized half-pint jars, leaving ¼-in. headspace. Remove air bubbles and adjust headspace, if necessary, by adding hot mixture. Wipe rims. Center lids on jars; screw on bands until fingertip tight.

3. Place jars into canner with simmering water, ensuring that they are completely covered with water. Bring to a boil; process for 5 minutes. Remove jars and cool.

Note: The processing time is for altitudes of 1,000 feet or less. Add 1 minute to the processing time for each 1,000 feet of additional altitude.

2 Tbsp.: 89 cal., 0 fat (0 sat. fat), 0 chol., 1mg sod., 23g carb. (22g sugars, 0 fiber), 0 pro.

RUBY ROSE PALOMA

Rose water adds a delicate touch to citrusy grapefruit and lime. If rose water isn't available in your area, look for it online.
—Gina Nistico, Denver, CO

Takes: 10 min. • **Makes:** 2 servings

- 1 cup ruby red grapefruit juice
- 4 oz. mezcal or tequila
- 1 Tbsp. fresh lime juice
- 1½ tsp. rosewater
- 1 Tbsp. kosher salt
- 1 tsp. coarse sugar
- ½ cup grapefruit soda
  Grapefruit slices

1. In a small pitcher, combine the first 4 ingredients.

2. Mix salt and sugar on a plate. Moisten the rims of 2 cocktail glasses with water. Hold each glass upside down and dip the moistened rim into salt mixture. Discard the remaining salt mixture.

3. To serve, fill glasses with ice. Add half the grapefruit juice mixture to each; top with grapefruit soda and grapefruit slices.

1 serving: 214 cal., 0 fat (0 sat. fat), 0 chol., 324mg sod., 19g carb. (7g sugars, 0 fiber), 1g pro.

OVER-THE-TOP CHERRY JAM

PRESSURE-COOKER
HOMEMADE
CHICKEN BROTH

APPLE GRAVY

You might want to make a double batch of this rich apple gravy. Yep, it's sensational with beef, but you've gotta try it on mashed potatoes, chops, roasted veggies—pretty much anything goes.
—Kathryn Conrad, Milwaukee, WI

Prep: 20 min. • **Cook:** 25 min.
Makes: 1 cup

- 1 Tbsp. plus 2 tsp. butter, divided
- 1 large apple (Jonagold or Honeycrisp), peeled and chopped
- ¼ cup apple brandy
- 1 cup beef broth
- ⅛ tsp. salt
- ¼ tsp. coarsely ground pepper, optional

1. In a small saucepan, heat 1 Tbsp. butter over medium heat. Add apple; saute until dark brown, adding 1 tsp. butter to prevent scorching. Remove from heat; add brandy. Cook over medium-high heat, stirring to loosen browned bits from pan.
2. Add broth and salt. Reduce heat; simmer 15 minutes. Using a blender or an immersion blender, puree apple mixture. Return to saucepan; simmer until liquid is reduced to 1 cup. Remove from heat. Whisk in the remaining butter. If desired, add pepper.
2 Tbsp.: 36 cal., 2g fat (1g sat. fat), 5mg chol., 163mg sod., 3g carb. (2g sugars, 0 fiber), 0 pro.

PRESSURE-COOKER HOMEMADE CHICKEN BROTH

There's nothing better or more satisfying than making your own chicken broth. You can control the amount of seasoning and salt, so you can customize it for whatever recipes you're using it in.
—*Taste of Home* Test Kitchen

Prep: 10 min. • **Cook:** 45 minutes + chilling
Makes: about 6 cups

- 2½ lbs. bony chicken pieces (legs, wings, necks or back bones)
- 2 celery ribs with leaves, cut into chunks
- 2 medium carrots, cut into chunks
- 2 medium onions, quartered
- 2 bay leaves
- ½ tsp. dried rosemary, crushed
- ½ tsp. dried thyme
- 8 to 10 whole peppercorns
- 6 cups cold water

1. Place all ingredients in a 6-qt. electric pressure cooker. Lock lid; make sure vent is closed. Select manual setting; adjust pressure to high and set time for 45 minutes. When finished cooking, allow pressure to naturally release.
2. Remove the chicken; set aside until cool enough to handle. Remove the meat from the bones. Discard bones; save meat for another use. Strain the broth, discarding vegetables and seasonings. Refrigerate 8 hours or overnight. Skim fat from surface.
1 cup: 25 cal., 0 fat (0 sat. fat), 0 chol., 130mg sod., 2g carb. (0 sugars, 0 fiber), 4g pro.

TEST KITCHEN TIP
Homemade chicken broth can be kept in the refrigerator for 4 to 5 days, and it can be stored in the freezer for up to 3 months.

BANANA BARS WITH CREAM
CHEESE FROSTING, PAGE 203

Cookies, Brownies & Bars

The cookie jar at the *Taste of Home* Test Kitchen
is always loaded with sweet surprises, and
now we're sharing our tastiest treats with you.
Try the brownies, bars and other delights we
prepare in our own homes, take to bake sales
and contribute to church potlucks.

GRANDMA'S PECAN RUM BARS

My grandmother handed down the recipe for these gooey bars, which we all love. The candied cherries are a must.
—Deborah Pennington, Falkville, AL

- -

Prep: 20 min. • **Bake:** 1 hour + cooling
Makes: 2 dozen

- 4 cups chopped pecans, divided
- 1 cup butter, softened
- 2¼ cups packed brown sugar
- 4 large eggs, room temperature
- 2 Tbsp. vanilla extract
- 1 cup all-purpose flour
- 2¼ cups red candied cherries
- 1½ cups chopped candied pineapple
- ½ cup chopped candied citron
- ⅓ cup rum

1. Sprinkle 3 cups pecans over a greased 15x10x1-in. baking pan.
2. Preheat oven to 350°. Cream the butter and brown sugar until light and fluffy, 5-7 minutes. Add eggs, 1 at a time, beating well after each addition. Beat in vanilla. Gradually add flour to creamed mixture, beating well.
3. Spread batter into prepared pan. Combine candied fruit and remaining pecans. Spread the fruit and pecans evenly over creamed mixture; press gently to help the mixtures adhere. Bake until a toothpick inserted in center comes out clean, about 1 hour. Sprinkle rum over the top; cool completely in pan on a wire rack. Cut into bars. Store in an airtight container.
1 bar: 401 cal., 22g fat (6g sat. fat), 51mg chol., 123mg sod., 49g carb. (40g sugars, 2g fiber), 4g pro.

DATE-NUT PINWHEELS

Pinwheel cookies with dates and walnuts are a family treasure. Since there are a few steps for prepping, I sometimes freeze the dough and bake the cookies later.
—Frieda Whiteley, Lisbon, CT

- -

Prep: 30 min. + chilling • **Bake:** 10 min./batch
Makes: about 9 dozen

- 1 cup butter, softened
- 1 cup sugar
- 1 cup packed brown sugar
- 2 large eggs, room temperature
- 4 cups all-purpose flour
- ½ tsp. baking soda

FILLING
- 2 pkg. (8 oz. each) pitted dates
- 1 cup water
- ½ cup sugar
- ½ cup chopped walnuts

1. In a large bowl, cream butter and sugars until light and fluffy, 5-7 minutes. Beat in eggs. In another bowl, whisk flour and baking soda; gradually beat into creamed mixture. Divide dough into 3 portions; shape each into a disk. Cover and refrigerate 1 hour or until firm enough to roll.
2. For filling, place dates, water and sugar in a large saucepan. Bring to a boil. Reduce heat; simmer, uncovered, until dates are tender and liquid is almost evaporated. Stir in walnuts; cool completely.
3. Roll each dough portion between 2 sheets of waxed paper into a 12x10-in. rectangle. Refrigerate for 30 minutes. Remove waxed paper. Spread a third of the filling over each rectangle. Roll up tightly jelly-roll style, starting with a long side. Wrap securely. Refrigerate until firm.
4. Preheat oven to 350°. Unwrap and cut dough crosswise into ⅓-in. slices. Place 2 in. apart on greased baking sheets. Bake 10-12 minutes or until set. Remove from pans to wire racks to cool.
1 cookie: 67 cal., 2g fat (1g sat. fat), 8mg chol., 21mg sod., 12g carb. (7g sugars, 1g fiber), 1g pro.

DATE-NUT PINWHEELS

CINNAMON ROLL MACARONS

SALTED CARAMEL PRETZEL RICE KRISPIES TREATS

Craving a snack that's both salty and sweet? These salted caramel Rice Krispies treats can't be beat.
—*Taste of Home* Test Kitchen

Prep: 20 + standing • **Makes:** 2 dozen

- 1 pkg. (10 oz.) miniature marshmallows
- 3 Tbsp. canola oil
- 6 cups Rice Krispies
- 1 cup caramels, chopped and divided
- 1 cup miniature pretzels, chopped and divided
- 1 pkg. (11½ oz.) milk chocolate chips, melted
  Sea salt, optional

In a microwave or in a large saucepan over low heat, melt marshmallows in oil; stir until smooth. Remove from heat; stir in cereal, ⅔ cup each caramels and pretzels. Press mixture into a lightly greased 13x9-in. baking pan, using waxed paper or a lightly greased spatula. Cool to room temperature. Spread melted chocolate over top; sprinkle with remaining caramels and pretzels. If desired, sprinkle with sea salt. Cut into bars.

1 bar: 115 cal., 3g fat (0 sat. fat), 1mg chol., 93mg sod., 23g carb. (12g sugars, 0 fiber), 1g pro.

CINNAMON ROLL MACARONS

These macarons are a winter/fall staple for me—inspired by the classic cinnamon roll, they are a delicious treat for a cold or snowy day. These pair well with a mug of tea, and can be eaten as a dessert or just a snack. Other fillings would taste great , too. Try custard, mousse, ganache or another other buttercream flavor.
—Elizabeth Ding, El Cerrito, CA

Prep: 45 min. • **Bake:** 10 min./batch
Makes: 5 dozen

- 4 large egg whites
- 1½ cups almond flour
- 1¼ cups confectioners' sugar
- ½ tsp. ground cinnamon
- ¾ cup sugar

FILLING
- 4 oz. cream cheese, softened
- 3 Tbsp. butter, softened
- 1 tsp. vanilla extract
- 1½ cups confectioners' sugar
  Additional ground cinnamon

1. Place egg whites in a small bowl; let stand at room temperature for 30 minutes. Sift almond flour, 1¼ cups confectioners' sugar and cinnamon together twice.

2. Preheat oven to 325°. Beat egg whites on medium speed until soft peaks form. Gradually add sugar, 1 Tbsp. at a time, beating on high until stiff peaks form. Fold in almond flour mixture.

3. With a pastry bag, pipe 1-in.-diameter cookies 2 in. apart onto parchment-lined baking sheets. Bake until lightly browned and firm to the touch, 9-12 minutes. Keeping cookies on the parchment, transfer to wire racks; cool completely.

4. For filling, in a small bowl, beat cream cheese and butter until creamy. Beat in vanilla. Gradually beat in confectioners' sugar until fluffy. Refrigerate until mixture firms to a spreading consistency, about 10 minutes.

5. Spread about ¼ tsp. filling onto the bottom of each of half of the cookies; top with remaining cookies. Sprinkle with additional cinnamon. Store in airtight containers in the refrigerator.

1 sandwich cookie: 60 cal., 3g fat (1g sat. fat), 3mg chol., 15mg sod., 9g carb. (8g sugars, 0 fiber), 1g pro.

CARAMEL BROWNIES

I love to bake. My family can't possibly eat all the sweets I whip up, so my co-workers are more than happy to help, particularly when it comes to these rich, chewy brownies that are full of gooey caramel, chocolate chips and crunchy walnuts.
—Clara Bakke, Coon Rapids, MN

- -

Prep: 20 min. • **Bake:** 35 min. + cooling
Makes: 2 dozen

2	cups sugar
¾	cup baking cocoa
1	cup canola oil
4	large eggs, room temperature
¼	cup 2% milk
1½	cups all-purpose flour
1	tsp. salt
1	tsp. baking powder
1	cup semisweet chocolate chips
1	cup chopped walnuts, divided
1	pkg. (14 oz.) caramels
1	can (14 oz.) sweetened condensed milk

1. Preheat oven to 350°. In a large bowl, beat the sugar, cocoa, oil, eggs and milk. Combine flour, salt and baking powder; gradually add to egg mixture until well blended. Fold in chocolate chips and ½ cup walnuts.
2. Spoon two-thirds of the brownie batter into a greased 13x9-in. baking pan. Bake for 12 minutes.
3. Meanwhile, in a large saucepan, heat the caramels and condensed milk over low heat until caramels are melted. Carefully pour over baked brownie layer. Sprinkle with the remaining walnuts.
4. Drop remaining batter by teaspoonfuls over caramel layer; carefully swirl brownie batter with a knife.
5. Bake until a toothpick inserted in the center comes out with moist crumbs, 35-40 minutes (do not overbake). Cool on a wire rack.

1 brownie: 376 cal., 18g fat (5g sat. fat), 43mg chol., 189mg sod., 51g carb. (40g sugars, 2g fiber), 6g pro.

CARAMEL BROWNIES

HOMEMADE CHOCOLATE SHORTBREAD

This recipe has been in my files for a long time, probably since I first learned to bake. Any chocolate lover will like these—they melt in your mouth. I make them year-round with variations. They're even richer with a thin coat of icing or as a sandwich cookie with frosting in the middle.
—Sarah Bueckert, Austin, MB

- -

Prep: 10 min. • **Bake:** 20 min. + cooling
Makes: about 1 dozen

¼ cup butter, softened
¼ tsp. vanilla extract
½ cup all-purpose flour
¼ cup confectioners' sugar
1 to 2 Tbsp. baking cocoa

1. Preheat oven to 300°. In a small bowl, cream butter until light and fluffy. Beat in vanilla. Combine the flour, sugar and cocoa; add to creamed mixture. Beat until dough holds together, about 3 minutes.
2. Pat dough into a 9x4-in. rectangle. Cut into 2x1½-in. strips. Place 1 in. apart on ungreased baking sheets. Prick dough with a fork.
3. Bake until set, 20-25 minutes. Cool for 5 minutes before removing from pan to a wire rack to cool completely.
1 cookie: 64 cal., 4g fat (2g sat. fat), 10mg chol., 31mg sod., 7g carb. (2g sugars, 0 fiber), 1g pro. **Diabetic exchanges:** 1½ fat, 1 starch.

ICEBOX COOKIES

This cookie recipe from my grandmother was my grandfather's favorite. I always keep a batch of the dough in the freezer.
—Chris Paulsen, Glendale, AZ

- -

Prep: 20 min. + freezing • **Bake:** 10 min.
Makes: about 7 dozen

½ cup butter, softened
1 cup packed brown sugar
1 large egg, room temperature, beaten
½ tsp. vanilla extract
2 cups all-purpose flour
½ tsp. baking soda
½ tsp. cream of tartar
½ tsp. salt
1 cup chopped walnuts, optional

1. Preheat oven to 350°. In a bowl, cream the butter and brown sugar. Add egg and vanilla; beat well. Combine dry ingredients; add to creamed mixture. Stir in nuts if desired.
2. On a lightly floured surface, shape the dough into three 10x1-in. rolls. Tightly wrap each roll in waxed paper. Freeze for at least 12 hours.
3. Cut into ⅜-in. slices and place on greased baking sheets. Bake for 6-8 minutes. Remove to a wire rack to cool.
1 cookie: 31 cal., 1 fat (1 sat. fat), 5mg chol., 32mg sod., 5g carb. (3g sugars, 0 fiber), 0 pro.

ICEBOX COOKIES

GRANDMA'S SCOTTISH SHORTBREAD

My Scottish grandmother was renowned for her baked goods, and these thick shortbread bars are an example why.
—Jane Kelly, Wayland, MA

- -

Prep: 15 min. • **Bake:** 45 min. + cooling
Makes: 4 dozen

- 1   lb. butter, softened
- 8   oz. superfine sugar (about 1¼ cups)
- 1   lb. all-purpose flour (3⅔ cups)
- 8   oz. white rice flour (1⅓ cups)

1. Preheat oven to 300°. Cream the butter and sugar until light and fluffy, 5-7 minutes. Combine flours; gradually beat into creamed mixture. Press dough into an ungreased 13x9-in. baking pan. Prick with a fork.
2. Bake until light brown, 45-50 minutes. Cut into 48 bars or triangles while warm. Cool completely on a wire rack.
1 bar: 139 cal., 8g fat (5g sat. fat), 20mg chol., 61mg sod., 16g carb. (5g sugars, 0 fiber), 1g pro.

WHITE VELVET CUTOUTS

WHITE VELVET CUTOUTS

We make these cutouts every Christmas and give lots of them as gifts. Last year, we baked a batch a week all through December to be sure we'd have plenty for ourselves, too. These rich cookies melt in your mouth!
—Kim Hinkle, Wauseon, OH

- -

Prep: 25 min. + chilling
Bake: 10 min./batch + cooling
Makes: about 5½ dozen

- 2   cups butter, softened
- 1   pkg. (8 oz.) cream cheese, softened
- 2   cups sugar
- 2   large egg yolks, room temperature
- 1   tsp. vanilla extract
- 4½   cups all-purpose flour

FROSTING

- 3   Tbsp. butter, softened
- 1   Tbsp. shortening
- ½   tsp. vanilla extract
- 3½   cups confectioners' sugar
- 4   to 5 Tbsp. 2% milk
      Food coloring, optional

1. In a large bowl, cream butter, cream cheese and sugar until light and fluffy, 5-7 minutes. Beat in egg yolks and vanilla. Gradually beat flour into creamed mixture. Divide dough in half. Shape each into a disk; wrap and refrigerate until firm enough to roll, about 2 hours.
2. Preheat oven to 350°. On a lightly floured surface, roll each portion of dough to ¼-in. thickness. Cut with floured 3-in. cookie cutters. Place 1 in. apart on greased baking sheets. Bake until set (do not brown), 10-12 minutes. Cool on pans 5 minutes. Remove to wire racks to cool completely.
3. For the frosting, in a bowl, beat butter, shortening and vanilla until blended. Beat in confectioners' sugar and enough milk to reach spreading consistency; beat until light and fluffy, about 3 minutes. If desired, beat in food coloring. Frost cookies. (Keep the frosting covered with a damp towel to prevent it from drying out.)
1 cookie: 149 cal., 8g fat (5g sat. fat), 26mg chol., 62mg sod., 19g carb. (13g sugars, 0 fiber), 1g pro.

FROSTED FUDGE BROWNIES

A neighbor brought over a pan of these rich brownies when I came home from the hospital with our baby daughter. I asked her how to make brownies like that, and I've made them ever since for family occasions, potlucks and parties at work. They're great!
—Sue Soderlund, Elgin, IL

- -

Prep: 10 min. + cooling
Bake: 25 min. + cooling • **Makes:** 2 dozen

- 1   cup plus 3 Tbsp. butter, cubed
- ¾   cup baking cocoa
- 4   large eggs, room temperature
- 2   cups sugar
- 1½ cups all-purpose flour
- 1   tsp. baking powder
- 1   tsp. salt
- 1   tsp. vanilla extract
- **FROSTING**
- 6   Tbsp. butter, softened
- 2⅔ cups confectioners' sugar
- ½   cup baking cocoa
- 1   tsp. vanilla extract
- ¼   to ⅓ cup 2% milk

1. In a saucepan, melt butter. Remove from the heat. Stir in cocoa; cool. In a large bowl, beat eggs and sugar until blended. Combine flour, baking powder and salt; gradually add to egg mixture. Stir in vanilla and the cooled chocolate mixture until well blended.
2. Spread into a greased 13x9-in. baking pan. Bake at 350° until a toothpick inserted in the center comes out clean, 25-28 minutes (do not overbake). Cool on a wire rack.
3. For the frosting, in a large bowl, cream butter and confectioners' sugar until light and fluffy, 5-7 minutes. Beat in cocoa and vanilla. Add enough milk for the frosting to achieve spreading consistency. Spread over brownies. Cut into bars.
1 brownie: 277 cal., 13g fat (8g sat. fat), 68mg chol., 248mg sod., 39g carb. (29g sugars, 1g fiber), 3g pro.

HONEY-PEANUT BUTTER COOKIES

It's not unusual for my husband to request these cookies by name. You'll love 'em.
—Lucile Proctor, Panguitch, UT

- -

Prep: 15 min. • **Bake:** 10 min./batch
Makes: 5 dozen

- ½   cup shortening
- 1   cup creamy peanut butter
- 1   cup honey
- 2   large eggs, room temperature, lightly beaten
- 3   cups all-purpose flour
- 1   cup sugar
- 1½ tsp. baking soda
- 1   tsp. baking powder
- ½   tsp. salt

1. Preheat oven to 350°. In a bowl, mix the shortening, peanut butter and honey. Add eggs; mix well. Combine flour, sugar, baking soda, baking powder and salt; add to peanut butter mixture and mix well.
2. Roll into 1- to 1½-in. balls and place on ungreased baking sheets. Flatten with a fork dipped in flour. Bake until set, 8-10 minutes. Remove to wire racks to cool.
1 cookie: 95 cal., 4g fat (1g sat. fat), 6mg chol., 80mg sod., 14g carb. (8g sugars, 0 fiber), 2g pro.

FROSTED FUDGE BROWNIES

BROADWAY BROWNIE BARS

I named these dessert bars for Broadway because they're a hit every time I serve them. I especially like to make these for the holidays, or for hostess gifts. They're always sure to please any sweet tooth!
—Anne Frederick, New Hartford, NY

Prep: 20 min. + chilling • **Bake:** 30 min.
Makes: 2½ dozen

FILLING
- 6 oz. cream cheese, softened
- ½ cup sugar
- ¼ cup butter, softened
- 2 Tbsp. all-purpose flour
- 1 large egg, room temperature, lightly beaten
- ½ tsp. vanilla extract

BROWNIE
- ½ cup butter, cubed
- 1 oz. unsweetened chocolate
- 2 large eggs, room temperature, lightly beaten
- 1 tsp. vanilla extract
- 1 cup sugar
- 1 cup all-purpose flour
- 1 tsp. baking powder
- 1 cup chopped walnuts

TOPPING
- 1 cup semisweet chocolate chips
- ¼ cup chopped walnuts
- 2 cups miniature marshmallows

FROSTING
- ¼ cup butter
- ¼ cup 2% milk
- 2 oz. cream cheese
- 1 oz. unsweetened chocolate
- 3 cups confectioners' sugar
- 1 tsp. vanilla extract

1. Preheat oven to 350°. In a small bowl, combine the first 6 ingredients until smooth; set aside.

2. In a large saucepan over medium heat, melt butter and chocolate. Remove from the heat and let cool. Stir in eggs and vanilla. Add sugar, flour, baking powder and nuts, stirring until blended.

3. Spread batter in a 13x9-in. baking pan coated with cooking spray. Gently spread filling over batter. For topping, in small bowl, combine chocolate chips and nuts; sprinkle over filling.

4. Bake until almost set, about 28 minutes. Sprinkle with the marshmallows; bake 2 minutes longer.

5. For frosting, in a large saucepan, heat butter, milk, cream cheese and chocolate until melted, stirring until smooth. Remove from heat; stir in the confectioners' sugar and vanilla extract. Immediately drizzle over marshmallows. Chill well; cut into bars.

1 brownie: 271 cal., 15g fat (7g sat. fat), 46mg chol., 108mg sod., 33g carb. (26g sugars, 1g fiber), 4g pro.

MAPLE & BACON BARS

This is the perfect treat when you're craving something that's both salty and sweet. The aroma will tantalize you while the bars bake in the oven.
—*Taste of Home* Test Kitchen

Prep: 15 min. • **Bake:** 20 min. + cooling
Makes: 9 servings

- ½ cup butter, softened
- ¾ cup packed brown sugar
- 2 large eggs, room temperature
- 1 Tbsp. 2% milk
- 1 tsp. vanilla extract
- ¾ cup all-purpose flour
- ¾ cup quick-cooking oats
- ½ tsp. baking powder
- ¼ tsp. salt
- 4 bacon strips, cooked and crumbled
- ⅓ cup chopped pecans, toasted

MAPLE GLAZE
- 1 cup confectioners' sugar
- 2 Tbsp. maple syrup
- ½ to 1 tsp. maple flavoring, optional

1. Preheat oven to 350°. In a large bowl, cream butter and brown sugar until light and fluffy, 5-7 minutes. Beat in eggs, milk and vanilla. Combine flour, oats, baking powder and salt; gradually add to creamed mixture. Fold in bacon and pecans.

2. Spread into a greased 9-in. square baking pan. Bake until a toothpick inserted in center comes out clean, 20-25 minutes. Cool on a wire rack. For glaze, in a small bowl, mix confectioners' sugar, syrup and, if desired, maple flavoring. Drizzle over bars; let stand until set.

1 bar: 351 cal., 16g fat (8g sat. fat), 72mg chol., 261mg sod., 48g carb. (34g sugars, 1g fiber), 5g pro.

BROADWAY BROWNIE BARS

MAPLE &
BACON BARS

CREAM CHEESE SWIRL BROWNIES

I'm a chocolate lover, and this treat has satisfied my cravings many times. No one guesses the brownies are light because their chewy texture and rich chocolate taste can't be beat. My family requests them often, and I'm happy to oblige.
—Heidi Johnson, Worland, WY

- -

Prep: 20 min. • **Bake:** 25 min.
Makes: 1 dozen

    3   large eggs, room temperature,
         divided use
    6   Tbsp. reduced-fat butter, softened
    1   cup sugar, divided
    3   tsp. vanilla extract
    ½   cup all-purpose flour
    ¼   cup baking cocoa
    1   pkg. (8 oz.) reduced-fat
         cream cheese

1. Preheat oven to 350°. Separate 2 eggs, putting each white in a separate bowl (discard yolks or save for another use); set aside. In a small bowl, beat butter and ¾ cup sugar until crumbly. Beat in the remaining whole egg, 1 egg white and vanilla until well combined. Combine flour and cocoa; gradually add to egg mixture until blended. Pour into a 9-in. square baking pan coated with cooking spray; set aside.
2. In a small bowl, beat cream cheese and remaining sugar until smooth. Beat in second egg white. Drop by rounded tablespoonfuls over the batter; cut through batter with a knife to swirl.
3. Bake 25-30 minutes or until set and edges pull away from the sides of pan. Cool on a wire rack.
1 brownie: 172 cal., 8g fat (5g sat. fat), 36mg chol., 145mg sod., 23g carb. (18g sugars, 0 fiber), 4g pro. **Diabetic exchanges:** 1½ starch, 1½ fat.

WHIPPED SHORTBREAD

This version of shortbread melts in your mouth. Mostly I make it for the holidays, but I'll also prepare it year-round for wedding showers and afternoon teas.
—Jane Ficiur, Bow Island, AB

- -

Prep: 50 min. • **Bake:** 20 min./batch
Makes: 8 dozen

    3   cups butter, softened
    1½   cups confectioners' sugar, sifted
    4½   cups all-purpose flour
    1½   cups cornstarch
         Nonpareils and/or halved
         candied cherries

1. In a large bowl, cream the butter and confectioners' sugar until light and fluffy, about 5 minutes. Gradually add flour and cornstarch, beating until well blended.
2. With hands lightly dusted with additional cornstarch, roll dough into 1-in. balls. Place 1 in. apart on ungreased baking sheets. Press lightly with a floured fork. Top with the nonpareils or cherry halves.
3. Bake at 300° until bottoms are lightly browned, 20-22 minutes. Cool for 5 minutes before removing from pans to wire racks.
1 cookie: 87 cal., 6g fat (4g sat. fat), 15mg chol., 46mg sod., 8g carb. (2g sugars, 0 fiber), 1g pro.

**CREAM CHEESE
SWIRL BROWNIES**

BAKI'S OLD-WORLD
COOKIES

CHOCOLATE CHIP BLONDIES

Folks who love chocolate chip cookies will enjoy that same great flavor in these golden bars. They can be mixed up in a jiffy, taste wonderful, and are perfect for occasions when company drops by unexpectedly or you need a treat in a hurry.
—Rhonda Knight, Hecker, IL

- -

Prep: 10 min. • **Bake:** 20 min. + cooling
Makes: 3 dozen

- 1½ cups packed brown sugar
- ½ cup butter, melted
- 2 large eggs, lightly beaten,
  room temperature
- 1 tsp. vanilla extract
- 1½ cups all-purpose flour
- ½ tsp. baking powder
- ½ tsp. salt
- 1 cup semisweet chocolate chips

1. In a large bowl, combine the brown sugar, butter, eggs and vanilla just until blended. Combine the flour, baking powder and salt; add to the brown sugar mixture. Stir in the chocolate chips.
2. Spread into a greased 13x9-in. baking pan. Bake at 350° until a toothpick inserted in the center comes out clean, 18-20 minutes. Cool on a wire rack. Cut into bars.
1 blondie: 102 cal., 4g fat (2g sat. fat), 19mg chol., 72mg sod., 16g carb. (12g sugars, 0 fiber), 1g pro.

BAKI'S OLD-WORLD COOKIES

My uncles have always called these cupcake cookies because of the unique and pretty way they're baked. My grandmother mixed up many a batch.
—Marilyn Louise Riggenbach, Ravenna, OH

- -

Prep: 25 min. + chilling • **Bake:** 20 min./batch
Makes: 3 dozen

- 1 cup butter, softened
- 1 cup sugar
- 2 large eggs, room temperature
- 1 cup ground walnuts
- 1½ cups all-purpose flour
- 1½ tsp. ground cinnamon
- 1 tsp. ground cloves
- 2 tsp. vanilla extract
  Confectioners' sugar

1. Preheat oven to 350°. Cream butter and sugar until light and fluffy, 5-7 minutes. Add eggs, 1 at a time, beating well after each addition. Add nuts. In another bowl, sift together flour, cinnamon and cloves; add with vanilla to creamed mixture. Refrigerate, covered, for 1 hour.

2. Fill 36 generously greased muffin cups or individual 3-in. tins one-third to half full. Press dough around the sides, leaving a depression in center. (If dough is too soft, add flour.)
3. Bake until light brown, about 18 minutes. Cool 2 minutes; tap tins to remove cookies. Dust with confectioners' sugar.
1 cookie: 105 cal., 7g fat (3g sat. fat), 24mg chol., 45mg sod., 10g carb. (6g sugars, 0 fiber), 1g pro.

ASK SARAH

CAN I REPLACE BUTTER WITH MARGARINE?

With its extra water content, margarine isn't an equal substitute for butter. In baking, use what the recipe calls for.

LAYERED CHOCOLATE MARSHMALLOW PEANUT BUTTER BROWNIES

After a friend gave me this recipe, I added my own touch—chunky peanut butter! When I take these to a group gathering, I always get requests for the recipe. The secret's in the peanut butter, if you ask me.
—Judy Sims, Weatherford, TX

- -

Prep: 30 min. • **Bake:** 20 min. + chilling
Makes: 4 dozen

1½ cups butter, divided
¾ cup baking cocoa, divided
4 large eggs, room temperature
2 cups sugar
1 tsp. vanilla extract
1½ cups all-purpose flour
½ tsp. salt
1 jar (16.3 oz.) chunky peanut butter
⅓ cup 2% milk
10 large marshmallows
2 cups confectioners' sugar

1. Preheat oven to 350°. In a small saucepan, melt 1 cup butter; stir in ½ cup cocoa until smooth. Remove from heat. In a large bowl, beat eggs, sugar and vanilla until blended. Combine flour and salt; gradually add to egg mixture. Beat in cocoa mixture.

2. Transfer to a greased 15x10x1-in. baking pan. Bake until a toothpick inserted in the center comes out clean, 18-22 minutes. Cool on a wire rack for 3-4 minutes.

3. Meanwhile, in a microwave, heat peanut butter, uncovered, on high until softened, about 30 seconds. Stir and spread over warm brownies. Refrigerate until peanut butter is set, about 45 minutes.

4. In a heavy saucepan, combine milk, marshmallows, remaining cocoa and remaining butter. Cook and stir over medium-low heat until the butter and marshmallows are melted and mixture is smooth. Remove from heat. Gradually stir in the confectioners' sugar until smooth. Spread over peanut butter layer. Refrigerate at least 30 minutes. Cut into squares.

1 brownie: 189 cal., 11g fat (5g sat. fat), 31mg chol., 125mg sod., 21g carb. (15g sugars, 1g fiber), 4g pro.

OAT-RAGEOUS CHOCOLATE CHIP COOKIES

My aunt gave me this recipe, and my family thinks these cookies are delicious. We enjoy all different kinds of cookies, and this recipe combines three of our favorites—oatmeal, peanut butter and chocolate chip—in one!
—Jaymie Noble, Kalamazoo, MI

- -

Prep: 25 min. • **Bake:** 10 min./batch
Makes: about 3 dozen

½ cup butter, softened
½ cup creamy peanut butter
½ cup sugar
⅓ cup packed brown sugar
1 large egg, room temperature
½ tsp. vanilla extract
1 cup all-purpose flour
½ cup quick-cooking oats
1 tsp. baking soda
¼ tsp. salt
1 cup semisweet chocolate chips

In a bowl, cream butter, peanut butter and sugars; beat in egg and vanilla. Combine flour, oats, baking soda and salt. Add to the creamed mixture and mix well. Stir in the chocolate chips. Drop by rounded tablespoonfuls onto ungreased baking sheets. Bake at 350° for 10-12 minutes or until lightly browned.

1 cookie: 104 cal., 6g fat (3g sat. fat), 12mg chol., 90mg sod., 12g carb. (8g sugars, 1g fiber), 2g pro.

LAYERED CHOCOLATE MARSHMALLOW PEANUT BUTTER BROWNIES

ALMOND BISCOTTI

I've learned to bake a double batch of these crisp dunking cookies, because one batch goes too fast!
—H. Michaelsen, St. Charles, IL

- -

Prep: 15 min. • **Bake:** 35 min. + cooling
Makes: 3 dozen

- ½ cup butter, softened
- 1¼ cups sugar, divided
- 3 large eggs, room temperature
- 1 tsp. anise extract
- 2 cups all-purpose flour
- 2 tsp. baking powder
  Dash salt
- ½ cup chopped almonds
- 2 tsp. 2% milk

1. In a large bowl, cream butter and 1 cup sugar until light and fluffy, 5-7 minutes. Add eggs, 1 at a time, beating well after each addition. Beat in anise extract. Combine the dry ingredients; gradually add to creamed mixture and mix well. Stir in almonds.

2. Line a baking sheet with foil and grease the foil. Divide dough in half; on the foil, shape each portion into a 12x3-in. rectangle. Brush with milk; sprinkle with remaining sugar.

3. Bake at 375° until golden brown and firm to the touch, 15-20 minutes. Gently lift foil with the rectangles onto a wire rack; cool for 15 minutes. Reduce heat to 300°.

4. Transfer rectangles to a cutting board; cut diagonally with a serrated knife into ½-in. slices. Place cut side down on ungreased baking sheets.

5. Bake for 10 minutes. Turn and bake until firm, 10 minutes longer. Remove to wire racks to cool. Store in an airtight container.

1 cookie: 207 cal., 9g fat (4g sat. fat), 50mg chol., 129mg sod., 29g carb. (16g sugars, 1g fiber), 4g pro.

ALMOND BISCOTTI

JAMMY
DODGERS

JAMMY DODGERS

On my first trip to Great Britain, I stumbled upon these cookies (or biscuits, as cookies are called in the U.K.). These iconic treats, sold as Jammie Dodgers, can be found everywhere over there. I couldn't find them in the States, though, so I had to make my own version.

—James Schend, Deputy Editor, Culinary

Prep: 20 min. + chilling
Bake: 15 min. + cooling
Makes: about 1 dozen

- 2 cups all-purpose flour
- ½ cup sugar
  Dash salt
- 1 cup cold butter, cubed
- 1 large egg yolk, room temperature
- 1 Tbsp. cold water
- 1 tsp. vanilla extract
- ½ cup seedless strawberry jam
  Confectioners' sugar, for dusting

1. In a large bowl, combine the flour, sugar and salt; cut in cold butter until the mixture resembles coarse crumbs. Stir in egg yolk, water and extract until mixture forms a ball.
2. On a lightly floured sheet of parchment, roll out dough to ⅛-in. thickness. Transfer dough and paper to a baking sheet and refrigerate until firm, about 10 minutes. Cut with a lightly floured 2½-in. round cookie cutter. Using a floured 1-in. round cookie cutter, cut out the centers of half of the cookies. Place solid and window cookies 1 in. apart on ungreased baking sheets. Cover and refrigerate for 30 minutes.
3. Bake at 325° until the edges are lightly browned, 15-20 minutes. Cool for 2 minutes before removing to wire racks to cool completely. Dust window cookies with confectioners' sugar. Spread 2 tsp. jam on the bottoms of the solid cookies; top with the window cookies.
1 cookie: 283 cal., 16g fat (10g sat. fat), 56mg chol., 135mg sod., 33g carb. (17g sugars, 1g fiber), 3g pro.

FUDGY LAYERED IRISH MOCHA BROWNIES

FUDGY LAYERED IRISH MOCHA BROWNIES

My husband and I are big fans of Irish cream, so I wanted to incorporate it into a brownie. I started with my mom's brownie recipe, then added frosting and ganache. This decadent recipe is the result, and we are really enjoying them!

—Sue Gronholz, Beaver Dam, WI

Prep: 35 min. • **Bake:** 25 min. + chilling
Makes: 16 servings

- ⅔ cup all-purpose flour
- ½ tsp. baking powder
- ¼ tsp. salt
- ⅓ cup butter
- 6 Tbsp. baking cocoa
- 2 Tbsp. canola oil
- ½ tsp. instant coffee granules
- 1 cup sugar
- 2 large eggs, room temperature, beaten
- 1 tsp. vanilla extract

FROSTING
- 2 cups confectioners' sugar
- ¼ cup butter, softened
- 3 Tbsp. Irish cream liqueur

GANACHE TOPPING
- 1 cup semisweet chocolate chips
- 3 Tbsp. Irish cream liqueur
- 2 Tbsp. heavy whipping cream
- ½ tsp. instant coffee granules

1. Preheat oven to 350°. Sift together flour, baking powder and salt; set aside. In a small saucepan over low heat, melt the butter. Remove from heat; stir in cocoa, oil and instant coffee granules. Cool slightly; stir in sugar and beaten eggs. Gradually add flour mixture and vanilla; mix well. Spread batter into a greased 8-in. square pan; bake until the center is set (do not overbake), about 25 minutes. Cool in pan on wire rack.
2. For the frosting, whisk confectioners' sugar and butter (mixture will be lumpy). Gradually whisk in the Irish cream liqueur; beat until smooth. Spread over slightly warm brownies. Refrigerate until frosting is set, about 1 hour.
3. Meanwhile, prepare ganache: Combine all ingredients and microwave on high for 1 minute; stir. Microwave 30 seconds longer; stir until smooth. Cool slightly until ganache reaches a spreading consistency. Spread over the frosting. Refrigerate until set, 45-60 minutes.
1 brownie: 295 cal., 14g fat (7g sat. fat), 43mg chol., 116mg sod., 41g carb. (34g sugars, 1g fiber), 2g pro.

COFFEE & CREAM BROWNIES

A friend gave me the recipe for these rich cakelike brownies topped with a creamy coffee-enhanced filling and a chocolate glaze. I like to garnish each square with a chocolate-covered coffee bean.
—Michelle Tiemstra, Lacombe, AB

Prep: 35 min. • **Bake:** 25 min. + standing
Makes: 16 servings

- ½ cup butter, cubed
- 3 oz. unsweetened chocolate, chopped
- 2 large eggs, room temperature
- 1 cup sugar
- 1 tsp. vanilla extract
- ⅔ cup all-purpose flour
- ¼ tsp. baking soda

FILLING
- 1 tsp. instant coffee granules
- 3 Tbsp. heavy whipping cream
- 1 cup confectioners' sugar
- 2 Tbsp. butter, softened

GLAZE
- 1 cup semisweet chocolate chips
- ⅓ cup heavy whipping cream

1. Preheat oven to 350°. In a microwave, melt butter and chocolate; stir until smooth. Cool slightly. In a small bowl, beat the eggs, sugar and vanilla; stir in chocolate mixture. Combine flour and baking soda; stir into chocolate mixture.

2. Spread into a greased 8-in. square baking pan. Bake 25-30 minutes or until a toothpick inserted in center comes out clean (do not overbake). Cool on a wire rack.

3. For filling, dissolve coffee granules in cream. Add the confectioners' sugar and butter; beat just until light and fluffy (do not overbeat). Spread over the brownies. Refrigerate until set.

4. In a small saucepan, combine chips and cream. Cook and stir over low heat until chips are melted. Cool slightly. Carefully spread over filling. Let stand for 30 minutes or until glaze is set. Cut into squares. Store in refrigerator.

1 brownie: 282 cal., 17g fat (10g sat. fat), 51mg chol., 91mg sod., 33g carb. (26g sugars, 2g fiber), 3g pro.

CHOCOLATE
MERINGUE STARS

CHOCOLATE MERINGUE STARS

These light, delicate, chewy cookies sure make for merry munching. With their big chocolate flavor, it's difficult to keep the kids away from them long enough to get any on the cookie tray!
—Edna Lee, Greeley, CO

Prep: 25 min. • **Bake:** 30 min./batch + cooling
Makes: about 4 dozen

- 3 large egg whites
- ¾ tsp. vanilla extract
- ¾ cup sugar
- ¼ cup baking cocoa

GLAZE
- 3 oz. semisweet chocolate, chopped
- 1 Tbsp. shortening

1. Place egg whites in a large bowl; let stand at room temperature for 30 minutes. Add vanilla; beat on medium speed until soft peaks form. Gradually add sugar, about 2 Tbsp. at a time, beating until stiff peaks form and sugar is dissolved. Gently fold in cocoa.

2. Line baking sheets with parchment. Insert a large open star tip into a pastry bag; fill half full with meringue. Pipe stars (about 1¼-in. diameter) onto prepared sheets, or drop them by rounded teaspoonfuls.

3. Bake at 300° until lightly browned, 30-35 minutes. Remove meringues from paper; cool on wire racks.

4. In a microwave, melt chocolate and shortening; stir until smooth. Dip cookies halfway into glaze; allow excess to drip off. Place on waxed paper; let stand until set.

1 meringue: 27 cal., 1g fat (0 sat. fat), 0 chol., 3mg sod., 4g carb. (3g sugars, 0 fiber), 0 pro.

"I made these without the glaze, and they were still really good. I haven't quite gotten meringues down yet, but this recipe helps!"

—ARIELLE ANTTONEN, DESIGNER

BANANA BARS WITH CREAM CHEESE FROSTING

I make these moist bars whenever I have ripe bananas on hand, then store them in the freezer to share later at a potluck. With creamy frosting and big banana flavor, this treat is a real crowd-pleaser.
—Debbie Knight, Marion, IA

- -

Prep: 15 min. • **Bake:** 20 min. + cooling
Makes: 4 dozen

- ½ cup butter, softened
- 1½ cups sugar
- 2 large eggs, room temperature
- 1 cup sour cream
- 1 tsp. vanilla extract
- 2 cups all-purpose flour
- 1 tsp. baking soda
- ¼ tsp. salt
- 2 medium ripe bananas, mashed (about 1 cup)

FROSTING

- 1 pkg. (8 oz.) cream cheese, softened
- ½ cup butter, softened
- 2 tsp. vanilla extract
- 3¾ to 4 cups confectioners' sugar

1. Preheat oven to 350°. Cream butter and sugar until light and fluffy, 5-7 minutes. Add eggs, sour cream and vanilla. Combine flour, baking soda and salt; gradually add to the creamed mixture. Stir in bananas.
2. Spread into a greased 15x10x1-in. baking pan. Bake until a toothpick inserted in the center comes out clean (do not overbake), 20-25 minutes. Cool.
3. For frosting, in a large bowl, beat the cream cheese, butter and vanilla until fluffy. Gradually beat in enough confectioners' sugar to achieve desired consistency. Frost bars. Store in the refrigerator.
1 bar: 148 cal., 7g fat (4g sat. fat), 28mg chol., 96mg sod., 21g carb. (16g sugars, 0 fiber), 1g pro.

CHOCOLATE MALTED COOKIES

Like the flavor of good old-fashioned malted milk? Here's the next best thing! Malted milk powder, chocolate syrup, and chocolate chips and chunks make these the yummiest cookies I've ever tasted...and with six kids, I've made a lot of them over the years!
—Teri Rasey, Cadillac, MI

- -

Takes: 30 min. • **Makes:** about 1½ dozen

- 1 cup butter-flavored shortening
- 1¼ cups packed brown sugar
- ½ cup malted milk powder
- 2 Tbsp. chocolate syrup
- 1 Tbsp. vanilla extract
- 1 large egg, room temperature
- 2 cups all-purpose flour
- 1 tsp. baking soda
- ½ tsp. salt
- 1½ cups semisweet chocolate chunks
- 1 cup milk chocolate chips

1. Preheat oven to 375°. In a large bowl, beat the shortening, brown sugar, malted milk powder, chocolate syrup and vanilla for 2 minutes. Add egg.
2. Combine the flour, baking soda and salt; gradually add to creamed mixture, mixing well after each addition. Stir in chocolate chunks and chips.
3. Shape into 2-in. balls; place 3 in. apart on ungreased baking sheets. Bake 12-14 minutes or until golden brown. Cool for 2 minutes before removing to a wire rack.
1 cookie: 363 cal., 18g fat (7g sat. fat), 14mg chol., 172mg sod., 47g carb. (33g sugars, 2g fiber), 4g pro.

BANANA BARS WITH CREAM CHEESE FROSTING

CHOCOLATE LEBKUCHEN CHERRY BALLS

Here's my twist on the traditional German holiday lebkuchen—with a surprise inside. Maraschino cherries add a sweet and unexpected punch of flavor to the holiday spice of gingersnaps.
—Arlene Erlbach, Morton Grove, IL

Prep: 45 min. + chilling • **Makes:** 5 dozen

- 40 gingersnap cookies
- 1 pkg. (8 oz.) cream cheese, softened
- 1½ cups semisweet chocolate chips, divided
- 1¼ cups sliced almonds, divided
- 2 Tbsp. chopped candied orange peel
- 1 tsp. almond extract
- 60 maraschino cherries, stems removed

1. Place gingersnaps, cream cheese, ½ cup chocolate chips, ½ cup almonds, orange peel and almond extract in a food processor; process until combined. Refrigerate until firm enough to form into balls. Pat cherries dry with paper towels. Wrap each cherry with a rounded tablespoonful of cream cheese mixture; shape into a ball. Freeze until firm, about 20 minutes.

2. Chop remaining sliced almonds; set aside. In a double boiler, melt remaining chocolate chips; stir until smooth. Dip cherry balls in chocolate; allow excess to drip off. Sprinkle balls with almonds. Place on waxed paper. Refrigerate until set, about 1 hour.

1 ball: 76 cal., 4g fat (2g sat. fat), 4mg chol., 37mg sod., 10g carb. (7g sugars, 1g fiber), 1g pro.

TEST KITCHEN TIP
These make great gifts during the holidays. Instead of topping them with almonds, consider toasted coconut, red and green sprinkes, or even colored sugar.

CHOCOLATE LEBKUCHEN
CHERRY BALLS

GINGER CRINKLES

I came up with these cookies by combining ingredients from two other recipes. It's the perfect ginger cookie—crispy outside and chewy in the middle. I often send batches of these to my son, and he shares them with his employees. Whenever I ask what kind of cookies to send, these are always at the very top of the list.

—Judy Wilson, Sun City West, AZ

Prep: 25 min. + chilling • **Bake:** 10 min./batch
Makes: about 2½ dozen

- ¾ cup butter-flavored shortening
- 1½ cups sugar, divided
- 1 large egg, room temperature
- ¼ cup molasses
- 2 cups all-purpose flour
- 2 tsp. baking soda
- 1½ tsp. ground ginger
- 1 tsp. ground cinnamon
- ½ tsp. salt
- ½ tsp. ground cloves

1. In a large bowl, cream shortening and 1 cup sugar until light and fluffy, 5-7 minutes. Beat in egg and molasses. In another bowl, whisk flour, baking soda, ginger, cinnamon, salt and cloves; gradually beat into creamed mixture. Refrigerate, covered, until firm, about 1 hour.
2. Preheat oven to 350°. Place the remaining ½ cup sugar in a shallow bowl. Shape dough into 1-in. balls; roll in sugar. Place 2 in. apart on parchment-lined baking sheets.
3. Bake until cookies are set and tops are cracked, 10-12 minutes. Cool on pans for 2 minutes. Remove to wire racks to cool.
1 cookie: 118 cal., 5g fat (1g sat. fat), 6mg chol., 127mg sod., 17g carb. (10g sugars, 0 fiber), 1g pro.

CHOCOLATE MONSTER COOKIES

My four grandsons started attending "Grandma's cooking school" when they were as young as 4. These easy monster cookies are a favorite of the youngest. He has fun making them and is always delighted with the results, as is the rest of the family.
—Helen Hilbert, Liverpool, NY

Prep: 20 min. + chilling • **Bake:** 15 min.
Makes: 7½ dozen

- 2 cups butter, softened
- 2 cups sugar
- 2 cups packed brown sugar
- 4 large eggs, room temperature
- 2 tsp. vanilla extract
- 4 cups all-purpose flour
- 3 tsp. baking powder
- 2 tsp. baking soda
- 1 tsp. salt
- 2 cups cornflakes
- 2 cups rolled oats
- 1 pkg. (8 oz.) sweetened shredded coconut
- 1 pkg. (12 oz.) semisweet chocolate chips
- 1 cup chopped walnuts

1. In a large bowl, cream butter and sugars. Beat in eggs and vanilla. Combine the flour, baking powder, baking soda and salt; gradually add to creamed mixture and mix well. Stir in the cornflakes, oats and coconut. (It may be necessary to transfer to a larger bowl to stir in the cornflakes, oats and coconut.) Stir in chocolate chips and nuts.
2. Shape dough into 1½-in. balls and place in an airtight container, separating layers with waxed paper or parchment; refrigerate, covered, overnight.
3. To bake, place dough portions 3 in. apart on ungreased baking sheets; let stand at room temperature 30 minutes before baking. Bake at 350° until the edges are browned, 13-15 minutes. Remove to wire racks to cool.
1 cookie: 143 cal., 7g fat (4g sat. fat), 20mg chol., 125mg sod., 19g carb. (12g sugars, 1g fiber), 2g pro.

CHOCOLATE MONSTER COOKIES

WHITE CHOCOLATE CRANBERRY-ORANGE BARS

Our family is scattered across the country now. Making a recipe inspired by my mom reminds me of home.
—Erin Powell, Amarillo, TX

Prep: 10 min. • **Bake:** 30 min. + cooling
Makes: 2 dozen

- 1½ cups all-purpose flour
- ½ cup packed brown sugar
- ½ cup cold butter, cubed
FILLING
- 1 large egg
- 1 can (14 oz.) sweetened condensed milk
- 1 tsp. grated orange zest
- 1 tsp. orange extract
- 1½ cups white baking chips
- 1 cup dried cranberries

1. Preheat oven to 350°. Line a 13x9-in. pan with foil, letting ends extend up sides; grease foil. In a bowl, mix flour and brown sugar; cut in butter until crumbly. Press onto bottom of prepared pan. Bake until light golden brown, 10-12 minutes. Cool on a wire rack.
2. For filling, whisk egg, milk, orange zest and extract until blended; stir in baking chips and cranberries. Spread evenly over crust. Bake until top is golden brown, 20-25 minutes longer. Cool 15 minutes in pan on a wire rack. Lifting with foil, remove bars from pan. Cut into bars. Refrigerate leftovers.
Freeze option: Freeze cooled bars in freezer containers, separating layers with waxed paper. To use, thaw before serving.
1 bar: 214 cal., 9g fat (5g sat. fat), 26mg chol., 66mg sod., 31g carb. (25g sugars, 1g fiber), 3g pro.

ANDES MINT CHIP COOKIES

Transform your favorite candy into a baked treat! These Andes mint cookies are better than any after-dinner mint.
—*Taste of Home* Test Kitchen

Prep: 15 min. • **Bake:** 10 min./batch
Makes: 3 dozen

- ¾ cup butter, softened
- 1 cup packed brown sugar
- ½ cup sugar
- 1 tsp. vanilla extract
- 2 large eggs, room temperature
- 2⅓ cups all-purpose flour
- ½ tsp. baking powder
- ½ tsp. baking soda
- ½ tsp. salt
- 1 pkg. (10 oz.) Andes creme de menthe baking chips

1. Preheat oven to 350°. In a large bowl, cream butter, sugars and vanilla until light and fluffy, 5-7 minutes. Beat in eggs. In another bowl, whisk flour, baking powder, baking soda and salt; gradually beat into creamed mixture. Stir in baking chips.
2. Drop dough by rounded tablespoonfuls 3 in. apart onto greased baking sheets. Bake 10-12 minutes or until light brown. Remove from pans to wire racks to cool.
1 cookie: 155 cal., 8g fat (6g sat. fat), 24mg chol., 107mg sod., 20g carb. (13g sugars, 0 fiber), 2g pro.

WHITE CHOCOLATE
CRANBERRY-ORANGE BARS

ALMOND
RASPBERRY
STARS

OATMEAL CHOCOLATE CHIP PEANUT BUTTER BARS

Oatmeal, peanut butter and chocolate chips make these bars a big hit with kids of all ages. Since I always have these basic ingredients on hand, it's easy to whip up a batch any time I'd like.
—Patricia Staudt, Marble Rock, IA

- -

Prep: 15 min. • **Bake:** 20 min. + cooling
Makes: 4 dozen

- ½ cup butter, softened
- ½ cup sugar
- ½ cup packed brown sugar
- ½ cup creamy peanut butter
- 1 large egg, room temperature
- 1 tsp. vanilla extract
- 1 cup all-purpose flour
- ½ cup quick-cooking oats
- 1 tsp. baking soda
- ¼ tsp. salt
- 1 cup semisweet chocolate chips

ICING
- ½ cup confectioners' sugar
- 2 Tbsp. creamy peanut butter
- 2 Tbsp. milk

1. In a large bowl, cream the butter, sugars and peanut butter until light and fluffy, 5-7 minutes. Beat in egg and vanilla. Combine flour, oats, baking soda and salt; gradually beat into creamed mixture and mix well. Spread into a greased 13x9-in. baking pan. Sprinkle with chocolate chips.
2. Bake at 350° for 20-25 minutes or until lightly browned. Cool on a wire rack for 10 minutes.
3. Combine icing ingredients; drizzle over the top. Cool completely. Cut into bars.
1 bar: 90 cal., 5g fat (2g sat. fat), 9mg chol., 71mg sod., 11g carb. (8g sugars, 1g fiber), 1g pro.

ALMOND RASPBERRY STARS

The first Christmas that I baked these, I ended up quickly making a second batch! The whole family enjoyed them.
—Darlene Weaver, Lebanon, PA

- -

Prep: 35 min. + chilling
Bake: 10 min./batch + cooling
Makes: about 1½ dozen

- ¾ cup butter, softened
- ½ cup confectioners' sugar
- 1 tsp. vanilla extract
- ½ tsp. almond extract
- 1¾ cups plus 2 Tbsp. all-purpose flour
- 1 Tbsp. finely chopped almonds
- 1 Tbsp. sugar
- ½ tsp. ground cinnamon
- 1 large egg white, beaten
- ⅓ cup raspberry jam

1. Cream butter and confectioners' sugar until light and fluffy, 5-7 minutes. Beat in extracts. Gradually beat flour into creamed mixture. Shape into a ball; refrigerate, covered, for 15 minutes.

2. Preheat oven to 350°. On a lightly floured surface, roll dough to ¼-in. thickness. With floured cookie cutters, cut the dough into equal numbers of 2½-in. and 1½-in. stars. Combine almonds, sugar and cinnamon. Brush the small stars with egg white; immediately sprinkle with almond mixture. Leave large stars plain.
3. Place all stars 1 in. apart on ungreased baking sheets, using separate sheets for the small and the large stars. Bake just until the tips begin to brown, about 10 minutes for small stars and 12 minutes for large. Cool completely on wire racks.
4. To assemble, spread enough jam over large stars to cover centers. Top with small stars; press lightly (jam should show around edge of small stars). Let jam set before storing cookies in an airtight container.
1 sandwich cookie: 150 cal., 8g fat (5g sat. fat), 20mg chol., 64mg sod., 18g carb. (8g sugars, 0 fiber), 2g pro.

BLUEBARB PIE
PAGE 229

Cakes & Pies

Our Test Kitchen is bustling with excitement whenever cakes and pies are on the day's schedule. These popular treats put smiles on everyone's faces, particularly when they're the thumbs-up winners found here.

MAMA'S COCONUT PIE

My mama showed me how to make this buttermilk coconut pie about 40 years ago, and her mama showed her how to make it. I was 6 when Mawmaw passed away, but I still remember her cooking in the kitchen in her beautiful cotton dresses dusted with flour. I am honored to teach my daughter how to make this pie.
—Lisa Allen, Joppa, AL

Prep: 20 min. • **Bake:** 50 min.
Makes: 8 servings

    Dough for single-crust pie
1   cup sugar
3   large eggs
½   cup buttermilk
½   cup unsalted butter,
    melted and cooled
2   Tbsp. all-purpose flour
1½ tsp. vanilla extract
    Dash salt
1½ cups sweetened shredded coconut

1. Preheat oven to 325°. On a lightly floured surface, roll dough to a ⅛-in.-thick circle; transfer to a 9-in. pie plate. Trim to ½ in. beyond rim of plate; flute edge. Place pie plate on a rimmed baking sheet.
2. In a large bowl, beat the sugar, eggs, buttermilk, melted butter, flour, vanilla and salt until blended. Stir in coconut. Pour into crust. Bake until top is light golden brown and center is almost set, 50-60 minutes. Cool on a wire rack; serve or refrigerate within 2 hours.
Dough for single-crust pie: Combine 1¼ cups all-purpose flour and ¼ tsp. salt; cut in ½ cup cold butter until crumbly. Gradually add 3-5 Tbsp. ice water, tossing with a fork until dough holds together when pressed. Shape into a disk; wrap and refrigerate 1 hour.
1 piece: 550 cal., 35g fat (23g sat. fat), 142mg chol., 318mg sod., 54g carb. (34g sugars, 1g fiber), 6g pro.

CARROT SHEET CAKE

We sold pieces of this to-die-for carrot cake at an art show. Before long, we sold out of all the 10 cakes we had made!
—Dottie Cosgrove, South El Monte, CA

Prep: 20 min. • **Bake:** 35 min. + cooling
Makes: 30 servings

4   large eggs, room temperature
1   cup canola oil
2   cups sugar
2   cups all-purpose flour
2   tsp. baking soda
¼   tsp. baking powder
2   tsp. ground cinnamon
½   tsp. salt
3   cups shredded carrots
⅔   cup chopped walnuts
FROSTING
1   pkg. (8 oz.) cream cheese, softened
½   cup butter, softened
1   tsp. vanilla extract
4   cups confectioners' sugar
⅔   cup chopped walnuts

1. Preheat oven to 350°. In a bowl, beat eggs, oil and sugar until smooth. Combine flour, baking soda, baking powder, cinnamon and salt; add to egg mixture and [b]... carrots and ... 15x10x1-in. b... inserted in th... about 35 min...
2. For frosting... and vanilla in... sugar. Spread... Decorate as desired.
1 piece: 311 cal., 17g fat (5g sat... chol., 193mg sod., 38g carb. (29g sugars, 1g fiber), 4g pro.

MAMA'S
COCONUT PIE

OLD-FASHIONED RHUBARB CAKE

My great-aunt gave me this recipe. It's especially delicious when rhubarb is in season, and tastes even better with the old-fashioned milk topping. But you'll love it even made with frozen rhubarb and modern-day whipped topping.
—Marilyn Homola, Hazel, SD

Prep: 20 min. • **Bake:** 35 min.
Makes: 12 servings

- ½ cup butter, softened
- 1¼ cups sugar, divided
- 1 large egg, room temperature
- 1 cup buttermilk
- 1 tsp. vanilla extract
- 2 cups all-purpose flour
- 1 tsp. baking soda
- ½ tsp. salt
- 2 cups chopped rhubarb
- ½ tsp. ground cinnamon

MILK TOPPING
- 1½ cups whole milk
- ⅓ cup sugar
- 1 tsp. vanilla extract

1. Preheat oven to 350°. In a bowl, cream butter and 1 cup sugar. Add egg; beat well. Combine buttermilk and vanilla; set aside.
2. Combine flour, baking soda and salt; add alternately with buttermilk and vanilla to the creamed mixture. Stir in rhubarb. Spread in a greased 13x9-in. baking pan.
3. Combine remaining sugar with cinnamon; sprinkle over batter. Bake until a toothpick inserted in center comes out clean, about 35 minutes.
4. For topping, combine all ingredients; pour over individual squares.

1 piece: 286 cal., 9g fat (6g sat. fat), 40mg chol., 323mg sod., 46g carb. (29g sugars, 1g fiber), 5g pro.

OLD-FASHIONED
RHUBARB CAKE

PICNIC BERRY SHORTCAKES

You can make this berry sauce ahead of time and chill it. Then assemble these summery shortcakes a couple of hours before the picnic or party.
—*Taste of Home* Test Kitchen

Prep: 20 min. + chilling • **Makes:** 4 servings

- 2   Tbsp. sugar
- ½   tsp. cornstarch
- 2   Tbsp. water
- 2   cups sliced fresh strawberries, divided
- ½   tsp. grated lime zest
- 2   individual round sponge cakes
- 2   cups fresh blueberries
     Whipped topping, optional

1. In a small saucepan, mix sugar and cornstarch. Stir in water. Add 1 cup strawberries; mash mixture. Bring to a boil; cook and stir until thickened, 1-2 minutes. Remove from heat; stir in the lime zest. Transfer to a small bowl; refrigerate, covered, until chilled.
2. Cut sponge cakes crosswise in half; trim the cakes to fit in the bottoms of 4 wide-mouth half-pint canning jars. In a small bowl, mix blueberries and remaining strawberries; spoon over cakes. Top with sauce. If desired, serve with whipped topping.
1 serving: 124 cal., 1g fat (0 sat. fat), 10mg chol., 67mg sod., 29g carb. (21g sugars, 3g fiber), 2g pro. **Diabetic exchanges:** 1 starch, 1 fruit.

PUMPKIN PIE TARTLETS WITH MAPLE PECAN CRUST

I came up with this recipe after discovering multiple food sensitivities were affecting my health. It was important to me to continue participating in family holidays and events where food was being served, so I began developing dishes that would be safe for me, but that others would enjoy, too. These mini pumpkin pie tarts are so delicious, you would never suspect they're free of gluten, egg and dairy!
—Chantale Michaud, Guelph, ON

Prep: 45 min. + cooling
Bake: 35 min+ cooling • **Makes:** 1½ dozen

PUMPKIN PIE TARTLETS WITH MAPLE PECAN CRUST

- 2   cups old-fashioned oats
- 4   cups chopped pecans
- ½   cup maple syrup
- 2   tsp. ground cinnamon
- 1   tsp. sea salt
- 1   tsp. vanilla extract
- ¼   tsp. ground cloves

FILLING
- ½   cup maple syrup
- 3   Tbsp. cornstarch
- 2¼ cups canned pumpkin or homemade pumpkin puree
- ¼   cup cream of coconut, warmed
- 2   tsp. vanilla extract
- 2   tsp. ground cinnamon
- ½   tsp. sea salt
- ½   tsp. ground nutmeg
- ¼   tsp. ground ginger
- ¼   tsp. ground cloves

TOPPING
- ½   cup chopped pecans
- 2   tsp. maple syrup
     Dash sea salt

1. Preheat oven to 350°. Process oats in a food processor until a fine powder forms. Add pecans; pulse until nuts are chopped. Add next 5 ingredients; pulse until mixture is moistened. Remove from processor.

2. Fill 18 greased muffin cups with ⅓ cup oat mixture each. Using a wet 1 Tbsp. measure, press mixture onto bottom and up sides of muffin cups. Bake until lightly browned, about 10 minutes. Cool on a wire rack.
3. For the filling, whisk together the maple syrup and cornstarch. In another bowl, mix the remaining filling ingredients, then add maple syrup mixture. Spoon about 3 Tbsp. into each crust.
4. Combine topping ingredients; spoon about 1 tsp. onto each tartlet. Bake until dark golden and set, 35-40 minutes. Cool 10 minutes before removing tartlets to a wire rack; cool 1 hour. If desired, refrigerate before serving.
1 tartlet: 302 cal., 21g fat (2g sat. fat), 0 chol., 173mg sod., 28g carb. (16g sugars, 5g fiber), 4g pro.

> "These are a fun twist on a traditional Thanksgiving dessert. They're hand-held and have a nice thick crust, which I like, and they're dairy-free."
>
> —JAMES SCHEND, DEPUTY EDITOR, CULINARY

EASY PINK LEMONADE PIE

I love bringing something sweet to a potluck, but I don't like spending all day in the kitchen. This saltine crust is amazing with a no-bake, tart-sweet strawberry lemonade filling.
—Gina Nistico, Denver, CO

- -

Prep: 30 min. + chilling
Bake: 15 min. + cooling • **Makes:** 8 servings

- 2¾ cups coarsely crushed saltines (about 60 crackers)
- 1 cup sugar, divided
- ½ cup butter, melted
- 2 cups sliced fresh or frozen sliced strawberries, thawed
- 1 tsp. lemon juice
- 1 tsp. grated lemon zest
- ¼ cup cold water
- 1 envelope unflavored gelatin
- 2 pkg. (8 oz. each) cream cheese, softened
- ½ cup heavy whipping cream
  Lemon slices, optional

1. Preheat oven to 350°. Combine crushed crackers and ¼ cup sugar with melted butter. Using the bottom of a glass, press cracker mixture onto bottom and up the sides of a greased 9-in. deep-dish pie plate. Bake until set, 15-18 minutes. Cool completely on a wire rack.

2. Combine strawberries, ½ cup sugar, lemon juice and zest; let stand 10 minutes. Meanwhile, sprinkle gelatin over cold water; let stand 5 minutes. Transfer strawberry mixture to a food processor or blender; pulse until smooth. Microwave gelatin on high until melted, about 10 seconds; stir into strawberry mixture.

3. Beat cream cheese and remaining sugar until smooth. Gradually beat in cream and strawberry mixture. Transfer filling to the crust. Refrigerate, covered, until set, about 2 hours. If desired, top with lemon slices.

1 piece: 566 cal., 39g fat (23g sat. fat), 105mg chol., 502mg sod., 50g carb. (30g sugars, 2g fiber), 7g pro.

GOOEY BUTTER CAKE

A friend gave me a quick version of this recipe using a cake mix, but I prefer baking from scratch, so I made my own version. My family can't get enough! The middle will sink just a little; this is normal. This dessert is delicious served warm or cold.
—Cheri Foster, Vail, AZ

- -

Prep: 20 min. • **Bake:** 40 min. + cooling
Makes: 16 servings

- 2½ cups all-purpose flour
- 1¾ cups sugar
- 2½ tsp. baking powder
- ½ tsp. salt
- 1 cup butter, melted
- 1 large egg, room temperature
- 1½ tsp. vanilla extract

TOPPING

- 1 pkg. (8 oz.) cream cheese, softened
- 2 large eggs, beaten, room temperature
- 2 cups confectioners' sugar

1. Preheat oven to 325°. In a large bowl, combine flour, sugar, baking powder and salt. In another bowl, whisk together melted butter, egg and vanilla; add to flour mixture and stir to combine. Press onto bottom of a greased 13x9-in. baking dish.

2. For topping, in a large bowl, beat cream cheese and eggs until smooth. Add the confectioners' sugar and stir to combine. Pour over crust. Bake until center is almost set and edges start to brown, 40-45 minutes. Cool 1 hour on a wire rack. Sprinkle with additional confectioners' sugar if desired.

1 piece: 381 cal., 17g fat (10g sat. fat), 80mg chol., 299mg sod., 53g carb. (37g sugars, 1g fiber), 4g pro.

EASY PINK LEMONADE PIE

KEY LIME CREAM PIE

I am very proud of this luscious no-bake beauty. It's so cool and refreshing—perfect for any summer get-together. No matter where I take this pie, it disappears quickly.
—Shirley Rickis, The Villages, FL

- -

Prep: 40 min. + chilling • **Makes:** 12 servings

- 1 pkg. (11.3 oz.) pecan shortbread cookies, crushed (about 2 cups)
- ⅓ cup butter, melted
- 4 cups heavy whipping cream
- ¼ cup confectioners' sugar
- 1 tsp. coconut extract
- 1 pkg. (8 oz.) cream cheese, softened
- 1 can (14 oz.) sweetened condensed milk
- ½ cup Key lime juice
- ¼ cup sweetened shredded coconut, toasted

Optional: Maraschino cherries with stems and sliced Key limes

1. In a small bowl, mix crushed cookies and butter. Press onto bottom and up sides of a greased 9-in. deep-dish pie plate. In a large bowl, beat cream until it begins to thicken. Add confectioners' sugar and extract; beat until stiff peaks form. In another large bowl, beat cream cheese, condensed milk and lime juice until blended. Fold in 2 cups whipped cream. Spoon into prepared crust.

2. Top with the remaining whipped cream; sprinkle with toasted coconut. Refrigerate until serving, at least 4 hours. If desired, garnish with cherries and limes.

1 piece: 646 cal., 52g fat (30g sat. fat), 143mg chol., 252mg sod., 41g carb. (29g sugars, 0 fiber), 8g pro.

YUMMY CHOCOLATE CAKE

When you're trying to eat better but still crave sweets, this incredibly chocolaty cake is the solution!
—LaDonna Reed, Ponca City, OK

- -

Prep: 20 min. • **Bake:** 15 min. + cooling
Makes: 16 servings

- 1 pkg. chocolate cake mix (regular size)
- 1 pkg. (2.1 oz.) sugar-free instant chocolate pudding mix
- 1¾ cups water
- 3 large egg whites, room temperature

FROSTING

- 1¼ cups cold fat-free milk
- ¼ tsp. almond extract
- 1 pkg. (1.4 oz.) sugar-free instant chocolate pudding mix
- 1 carton (8 oz.) frozen reduced-fat whipped topping, thawed
   Chocolate curls, optional

1. Preheat oven to 350°. In a large bowl, combine cake mix, pudding mix, water and egg whites. Beat on low speed for 1 minute; beat on medium for 2 minutes. Pour into a greased 15x10x1-in. baking pan. Bake until a toothpick inserted in center comes out clean, 12-18 minutes. Cool on a wire rack.

2. For frosting, place milk and extract in a large bowl. Sprinkle with a third of the pudding mix; let stand for 1 minute. Whisk pudding mix into milk. Repeat twice with remaining pudding mix. Whisk the pudding 2 minutes longer. Let stand for 15 minutes. Fold in the whipped topping. Frost cake. If desired, garnish with chocolate curls.

1 piece: 184 cal., 3g fat (2g sat. fat), 0 chol., 465mg sod., 34g carb. (17g sugars, 1g fiber), 3g pro. **Diabetic exchanges:** 2 starch, ½ fat.

TEST KITCHEN TIP
If you're a fan of vanilla, it's easy to give this recipe a tasty twist. Simply swap out the chocolate cake and pudding mixes for vanilla. It's still yummy!

KEY LIME CREAM PIE

YUMMY CHOCOLATE
CAKE

FIREBALL PUMPKIN PIE

This pumpkin pie recipe takes the traditional fall dessert to a whole new level. Try adding a bit of whipped cream or cinnamon on top for some added sweetness.
—*Taste of Home* Test Kitchen

Prep: 25 min. • **Bake:** 1 hour + chilling
Makes: 8 servings

       Dough for single-crust pie
   2   **large eggs, room temperature**
   1   **can (15 oz.) pumpkin**
   1   **cup half-and-half cream**
   ¾   **cup sugar**
   ¼   **cup packed brown sugar**
   3   **Tbsp. Fireball cinnamon whiskey**
   ½   **tsp. pumpkin pie spice**
   ¼   **tsp. salt**
       Optional: Sweetened whipped cream and cinnamon

1. Preheat oven to 425° On a lightly floured surface, roll dough to a ⅛-in.-thick circle; transfer to a 9-in. pie plate. Trim crust to ½ in. beyond rim of plate; flute edge. In a large bowl, combine eggs, pumpkin, cream, sugars, whiskey, pumpkin pie spice and salt; beat until smooth. Add filling to crust.
2. Bake 15 minutes. Reduce heat to 350°. Bake until the crust is golden brown and top of pie is set, 45-50 minutes longer. Cover edges loosely with foil during last 15 minutes if needed to prevent overbrowning. Remove the foil. Cool pie on a wire rack for 1 hour. Refrigerate overnight or until set.
3. If desired, serve with whipped cream and sprinkle with cinnamon.

Dough for single-crust pie: Combine 1¼ cups all-purpose flour and ¼ tsp. salt; cut in ½ cup cold butter until crumbly. Gradually add 3-5 Tbsp. ice water, tossing with a fork until dough holds together when pressed. Shape into a disk; wrap and refrigerate 1 hour.
1 piece: 461 cal., 27g fat (17g sat. fat), 126mg chol., 274mg sod., 47g carb. (30g sugars, 2g fiber), 6g pro.

COCONUT-RUM CAKE POPS

We think these coconut-coated cake pops taste like paradise on a stick.
—*Taste of Home* Test Kitchen

Prep: 1½ hours + chilling • **Makes:** 4 dozen

   1   **pkg. (16 oz.) angel food cake mix**
   ¾   **cup canned vanilla frosting**
   1   **cup sweetened shredded coconut**
   1   **tsp. coconut extract**
   ½   **tsp. rum extract**
   48   **lollipop sticks**
   2½   **lbs. white candy coating, melted**
        Lightly toasted sweetened shredded coconut

1. Prepare and bake cake mix according to package directions. Cool completely on a wire rack.
2. In a large bowl, mix frosting, coconut and extracts. Tear cake into pieces. In batches, pulse cake in a food processor until crumbs form. Stir crumbs into frosting mixture. Shape into 1-in. balls; place on baking sheets. Insert sticks. Freeze for at least 2 hours or refrigerate for at least 3 hours, until firm.
3. Dip cake pops in melted candy coating, allowing excess to drip off. Roll in toasted coconut. Insert cake pops in a Styrofoam block; let stand until set.
1 cake pop: 188 cal., 8g fat (7g sat. fat), 0 chol., 92mg sod., 29g carb. (25g sugars, 0 fiber), 1g pro.

FIREBALL PUMPKIN PIE

ORANGE CHOCOLATE
MOUSSE MIRROR CAKE

ORANGE CHOCOLATE MOUSSE MIRROR CAKE

A shiny, mirrorlike orange glaze covers a chocolate mousse cake to create a delicious showstopping dessert your guests will be talking about for weeks to come.
—Matthew Hass, Ellison Bay, WI

- -

Prep: 45 min. + freezing • **Makes:** 16 servings

- 2 cups crushed Oreo cookies (about 20 cookies)
- 1 tsp. grated orange zest
- ¼ cup butter, melted

FILLING
- 1 envelope unflavored gelatin
- 6 Tbsp. orange juice
- 8 oz. semisweet chocolate, chopped
- 2½ cups heavy whipping cream, divided
- 3 pkg. (8 oz. each) cream cheese, softened
- ¾ cup sugar
- ¼ cup dark baking cocoa
- 1 Tbsp. grated orange zest

GLAZE
- 1 envelope unflavored gelatin
- ½ cup plus 1 tsp. water, divided
- ¾ cup sugar
- ⅓ cup sweetened condensed milk
- 1 cup white baking chips
  Orange paste food coloring

1. Mix the crushed cookies, orange zest and butter; press onto bottom of a greased 9-in. springform pan. Set aside.

2. In a small saucepan, sprinkle gelatin over orange juice; let stand 1 minute. Stir over low heat until gelatin is dissolved. Set aside.
3. For filling, melt chocolate with ½ cup cream in microwave; stir until smooth. Cool slightly; stir in dissolved gelatin. In a large bowl, beat cream cheese, sugar and cocoa until smooth. Gradually add the chocolate mixture and orange zest; mix well. In another bowl, beat remaining cream until stiff peaks form. Gently fold into cream cheese mixture. Spoon over the crust. Refrigerate, covered, until set, about 4 hours. Freeze dessert, covered, overnight.
4. For glaze, sprinkle gelatin over ¼ cup water in a small bowl; set aside (mixture will solidify). Meanwhile, in a small saucepan, combine sugar, milk and remaining water. Bring to a simmer over medium heat, stirring occasionally. Remove from heat. Stir in the gelatin mixture until dissolved. Add baking chips; stir with a whisk until melted. Stir in food coloring; mix well. Cool glaze, stirring occasionally, until it reaches 90°, about 40 minutes.
5. Place cake on an inverted 9-in. pie plate in a foil-lined 15x10x1-in. pan. Remove the sides of the springform. Pour cooled glaze over frozen cake, allowing excess to drip off. Let glaze set 15 minutes before removing drips from bottom edge of cake. Refrigerate 2 hours before serving.
1 piece: 610 cal., 43g fat (25g sat. fat), 97mg chol., 244mg sod., 47g carb. (40g sugars, 1g fiber), 7g pro.

CLASSIC PINEAPPLE UPSIDE-DOWN CAKE

A classic recipe like this never goes out of style! It's delicious with the traditional pineapple, but try it with peaches or a combination of cranberries and orange.
—Bernardine Melton, Paola, KS

- -

Prep: 20 min. • **Bake:** 30 min. + standing
Makes: 9 servings

- ⅓ cup butter, melted
- ⅔ cup packed brown sugar
- 1 can (20 oz.) sliced pineapple
- ½ cup chopped pecans
- 3 large eggs, separated, room temperature
- 1 cup sugar
- 1 tsp. vanilla extract
- 1 cup all-purpose flour
- 1 tsp. baking powder
- ¼ tsp. salt
- 9 maraschino cherries
  Whipped topping, optional

1. Preheat oven to 375°. In an ungreased 9-in. square baking pan, combine butter and brown sugar. Drain pineapple, reserving ⅓ cup juice. Arrange 9 pineapple slices in a single layer over sugar (refrigerate any remaining slices for another use). Sprinkle pecans over pineapple; set aside.
2. In a large bowl, beat egg yolks until thick and lemon-colored. Gradually add sugar, beating well. Blend in vanilla and reserved pineapple juice. Combine flour, baking powder and salt; add to batter, beating well.
3. In a small bowl with clean beaters, beat egg whites on high speed until stiff peaks form; fold into batter. Spoon into pan.
4. Bake 30-35 minutes or until a toothpick inserted in center comes out clean. Let stand 10 minutes before inverting onto serving plate. Place a cherry in the center of each pineapple slice. If desired, serve cake with whipped topping.
1 piece: 361 cal., 13g fat (5g sat. fat), 88mg chol., 193mg sod., 58g carb. (46g sugars, 2g fiber), 4g pro.

WALNUT PUMPKIN CAKE ROLL

This is one of my family's favorite dessert recipes, especially for holiday gatherings.
—Mary Gecha, Center Rutland, VT

Prep: 20 min. + chilling
Bake: 15 min. + cooling • **Makes:** 12 servings

- 3 large eggs, room temperature
- 1 cup sugar
- ⅔ cup canned pumpkin
- 1 tsp. lemon juice
- ¾ cup all-purpose flour
- 2 tsp. ground cinnamon
- 1 tsp. baking powder
- 1 tsp. ground ginger
- ½ tsp. salt
- ½ tsp. ground nutmeg
- 1 cup finely chopped walnuts
  Confectioners' sugar

FILLING

- 6 oz. cream cheese, softened
- 1 cup confectioners' sugar
- ¼ cup butter, softened
- ½ tsp. vanilla extract

1. Line a greased 15x10x1-in. baking pan with waxed paper. Grease the paper; set aside. In a bowl, beat eggs for 3 minutes. Gradually add sugar; beat for 2 minutes or until the mixture becomes thick and lemon-colored. Stir in pumpkin and lemon juice. Combine flour, cinnamon, baking powder, ginger, salt and nutmeg; fold into pumpkin mixture. Spread batter evenly in prepared pan. Sprinkle with walnuts.

2. Bake at 375° for 12-14 minutes or until cake springs back when lightly touched in center. Cool for 5 minutes. Turn cake out of pan onto a kitchen towel dusted with confectioners' sugar. Gently peel off waxed paper. Roll up cake in towel jelly-roll style, starting with a long side. Cool completely on a wire rack.

3. In a bowl, combine filling ingredients; beat until smooth. Unroll cake; spread evenly with filling to within ½ in. of edges. Roll up again without towel. Cover and refrigerate for 1 hour before cutting. Refrigerate leftovers.

1 piece: 312 cal., 17g fat (7g sat. fat), 81mg chol., 247mg sod., 36g carb. (26g sugars, 2g fiber), 6g pro.

WALNUT PUMPKIN CAKE ROLL

MINI BLUEBERRY TARTS

I served this dessert to my family while we were on vacation and they were all amazed! The best part: I didn't spend tons of time on it thanks to refrigerated pie crust. Watch your mini tarts around the 13-minute mark to make sure they don't brown too quickly. If you like, sprinkle the tops with coarse sugar for a beautiful finishing touch.
—Allison Bell, Hillsdale, NJ

Prep: 25 min. • **Bake:** 15 min. + cooling
Makes: 6 mini tarts

- 2 cups fresh blueberries
- ⅓ cup sugar
- 4 tsp. cornstarch
- 2 sheets refrigerated pie crust
- 1 large egg yolk, lightly beaten

1. Preheat oven to 425°. Crush half the blueberries. Sift together sugar and cornstarch. Add whole and crushed blueberries; toss until berries are well coated. Set aside.
2. On a lightly floured surface, unroll crusts. Cut out six 4½-in. circles; press circles onto bottoms and up sides of the greased muffin cups. Evenly spoon in blueberry mixture. Cut out six 2-in. circles from the remaining crust; place over filling. Brush with yolk.
3. Bake until the crust is golden and filling bubbles, 13-17 minutes. Cool in pans for 10 minutes; run a knife around the sides of the muffin cups and remove tarts to a serving plate.
1 mini tart: 383 cal., 18g fat (8g sat. fat), 43mg chol., 249mg sod., 52g carb. (18g sugars, 1g fiber), 3g pro.

HOMEMADE PEAR PIE

I entered this pie in a local baking contest and ended up winning! Bartlett pears always hold up well when baked, adding a nice layer of texture.
—Darlene Jacobson, Waterford, WI

Prep: 40 min. + chilling
Bake: 45 min. + cooling • **Makes:** 8 servings

- 2 cups all-purpose flour
- 1 tsp. salt
- ¾ cup shortening
- 6 Tbsp. cold water

FILLING
- 5 cups sliced peeled fresh pears
- 1 Tbsp. lemon juice
- ⅓ cup all-purpose flour
- ½ cup plus 1 Tbsp. sugar, divided
- 1 tsp. ground cinnamon
- 2 Tbsp. butter

1. In a large bowl, mix flour and salt; cut in shortening until crumbly. Gradually add water, tossing with a fork until dough holds together when pressed. Shape into a disk; wrap and refrigerate 1 hour or overnight.
2. Preheat oven to 425°. In a large bowl, toss pears with lemon juice. In a small bowl, mix flour, ½ cup sugar and cinnamon; add to pear mixture and toss to coat.
3. On a lightly floured surface, roll half the dough into a ⅛-in.-thick circle; transfer to a 9-in. pie plate. Trim crust even with rim. Add filling; dot with butter.
4. Roll the remaining dough to a ⅛-in.-thick circle. Place over the filling. Trim, seal and flute edges. Cut slits in top. Sprinkle with remaining sugar. Bake until crust is golden brown and filling is bubbly, 45-50 minutes. Cover edges loosely with foil during the last 20 minutes if needed to prevent overbrowning. Remove the foil. Cool on a wire rack.
1 piece: 438 cal., 21g fat (6g sat. fat), 8mg chol., 317mg sod., 58g carb. (25g sugars, 4g fiber), 4g pro.

HOMEMADE PEAR PIE

YELLOW CUPCAKES

We truly believe that on any given day, someone needs a homemade cupcake. This buttery, yellow cake base works with any frosting and decorates beautifully.
—*Taste of Home* Test Kitchen

Prep: 20 min. • **Bake:** 15 min. + cooling
Makes: 2 dozen

- ⅔ cup butter, softened
- 1¾ cups sugar
- 2 large eggs, room temperature
- 1½ tsp. vanilla extract
- 2½ cups all-purpose flour
- 2½ tsp. baking powder
- ½ tsp. salt
- 1¼ cups 2% milk
- Frosting of your choice

1. Preheat oven to 350°. Line 24 muffin cups with paper liners.
2. In a large bowl, cream butter and sugar until light and fluffy, 5-7 minutes. Add eggs, 1 at a time, beating well after each addition. Beat in the vanilla. In another bowl, whisk the flour, baking powder and salt; add to creamed mixture alternately with milk, beating well after each addition.
3. Fill prepared cups three-fourths full. Bake 15-20 minutes or until a toothpick inserted in center comes out clean. Cool in pans 10 minutes before removing to wire racks to cool completely. Spread with frosting.
1 cupcake: 163 cal., 6g fat (4g sat. fat), 32mg chol., 138mg sod., 25g carb. (15g sugars, 0 fiber), 2g pro.

CHERRY HAND PIES

CHERRY HAND PIES

There's nothing better than a sweet, from-scratch delight like traditional cherry pie. These precious little hand pies always go fast when I sell them at my pie bakery!
—Allison Cebulla, Milwaukee, WI

Prep: 45 min. • **Bake:** 25 min. + cooling
Makes: 8 servings

- 6 Tbsp. water, divided
- 2 Tbsp. sugar
- 2 Tbsp. cherry brandy
- 4½ tsp. cornstarch
- 1½ tsp. lemon juice
- 1 tsp. quick-cooking tapioca
- ¼ tsp. grated lemon zest
- Dash salt
- 2 cups fresh or frozen pitted tart cherries, thawed and halved
- 1 cup fresh or frozen pitted dark sweet cherries, thawed and halved
- Dough for double-crust pie
- 1 large egg

ICING
- 2⅔ cups confectioners' sugar
- 3 to 4 Tbsp. hot water
- 2 Tbsp. butter, melted
- ½ tsp. almond extract
- ¼ tsp. vanilla extract
- Dash salt
- Freeze-dried strawberries, crushed, optional

1. In a large saucepan, whisk 4 Tbsp. water, sugar, brandy, cornstarch, lemon juice, tapioca, lemon zest and salt until combined. Add cherries. Bring to a boil; cook and stir until thickened, 3-5 minutes. Remove from heat. Set aside to cool.
2. Preheat the oven to 400°. On a lightly floured surface, roll half the dough to a 14x9-in. rectangle. Cut out eight 3½ x 4½-in. rectangles. Repeat with remaining dough.
3. Transfer 8 rectangles to parchment-lined baking sheets; spoon about 3 Tbsp. cherry mixture in center of each. Whisk egg and remaining 2 Tbsp. water. Brush edges of crust with egg wash. Top with remaining 8 rectangles; press edges with a fork to seal. Brush tops with egg wash; cut slits in tops.
4. Bake until crust is golden brown and slightly puffed, 25-30 minutes. Remove from pans to wire racks to cool. Combine confectioners' sugar, hot water, melted butter, extracts and salt; drizzle over pies. Garnish with freeze-dried strawberries if desired. Let stand until set.
Dough for double-crust pie: Combine 1¼ cups all-purpose flour and ¼ tsp. salt; cut in ½ cup cold butter until crumbly. Gradually add 3-5 Tbsp. ice water, tossing with a fork until dough holds together when pressed. Wrap and refrigerate 1 hour.
1 pie: 589 cal., 27g fat (16g sat. fat), 91mg chol., 380mg sod., 83g carb. (49g sugars, 2g fiber), 6g pro.

SANDY'S CHOCOLATE CAKE

Years ago, I drove more than four hours to a cake contest, holding my entry on my lap the whole way. But it paid off. Just one bite and you'll see why this velvety beauty was named the best chocolate cake recipe and won first prize.
—Sandy Johnson, Tioga, PA

- -

Prep: 30 min. • **Bake:** 30 min. + cooling
Makes: 16 servings

- 1 cup butter, softened
- 3 cups packed brown sugar
- 4 large eggs, room temperature
- 2 tsp. vanilla extract
- 2⅔ cups all-purpose flour
- ¾ cup baking cocoa
- 3 tsp. baking soda
- ½ tsp. salt
- 1⅓ cups sour cream
- 1⅓ cups boiling water

FROSTING

- ½ cup butter, cubed
- 3 oz. unsweetened chocolate, chopped
- 3 oz. semisweet chocolate, chopped
- 5 cups confectioners' sugar

- 1 cup sour cream
- 2 tsp. vanilla extract

1. Preheat oven to 350°. Grease and flour three 9-in. round baking pans.
2. In a large bowl, cream butter and brown sugar until light and fluffy, 5-7 minutes. Add eggs, 1 at a time, beating well after each addition. Beat in vanilla. In another bowl, whisk flour, cocoa, baking soda and salt; add to creamed mixture alternately with sour cream, beating well after each addition. Stir in water until blended.
3. Transfer to prepared pans. Bake until a toothpick comes out clean, 30-35 minutes. Cool in pans 10 minutes; remove to wire racks to cool completely.
4. For the frosting, in a metal bowl over simmering water, melt the butter and chocolates; stir until smooth. Cool slightly.
5. In a large bowl, combine confectioners' sugar, sour cream and vanilla. Add chocolate mixture; beat until smooth. Spread frosting between layers and over top and sides of cake. Refrigerate leftovers.
1 piece: 685 cal., 29g fat (18g sat. fat), 115mg chol., 505mg sod., 102g carb. (81g sugars, 3g fiber), 7g pro.

EASY CREAM PIE

Fresh berries and cream pie—it's a simple, classic combination just like Grandma used to make. My version gets you out of the kitchen and into your patio lounge chair quickly. Enjoy!
—Gina Nistico, Denver, CO

- -

Prep: 10 min. • **Bake:** 15 min. + chilling
Makes: 8 servings

- 2¾ cups graham cracker crumbs
- ¾ cup sugar, divided
- ½ cup butter, melted
- 1 envelope unflavored gelatin
- ¼ cup cold water
- 2 pkg. (8 oz. each) cream cheese, softened
- 2 cups heavy whipping cream
- 2 tsp. vanilla extract
  Mixed fresh berries, optional

1. Preheat oven to 350°. Combine cracker crumbs and ¼ cup sugar with melted butter. Using the bottom of a glass, press cracker mixture onto bottom and up the sides of a greased 9-in. deep-dish pie plate. Bake until set, about 12-15 minutes. Cool completely on a wire rack.
2. Meanwhile, sprinkle the gelatin over cold water; let stand 5 minutes. Beat the cream cheese and remaining sugar until smooth. Slowly beat in cream and vanilla. Microwave gelatin on high until melted, about 10 seconds; beat into cream cheese mixture. Transfer filling to crust. Refrigerate, covered, until set, about 3 hours.
3. If desired, top with mixed fresh berries.
1 piece: 731 cal., 56g fat (33g sat. fat), 156mg chol., 445mg sod., 51g carb. (31g sugars, 1g fiber), 8g pro.

SANDY'S
CHOCOLATE CAKE

BEST LIME
TART

BEST LIME TART

This treat is the perfect balance between tart and sweet, and the almonds in the crust are just wonderful. It's one of my husband's favorite desserts, and I'm sure your family will love it, too!
—Charis O'Connell, Mohnton, PA

Prep: 35 min. • **Bake:** 15 min. + chilling
Makes: 12 servings

- 1¼ cups graham cracker crumbs
- 5 Tbsp. butter, melted
- ¼ cup ground almonds
- 3 Tbsp. sugar

FILLING

- 4 large egg yolks
- 1 can (14 oz.) sweetened condensed milk
- ½ cup lime juice
- 2 tsp. grated lime zest

TOPPING

- ½ cup heavy whipping cream
- 1 Tbsp. sugar
- ½ cup sour cream
- 1 tsp. grated lime zest
   Fresh raspberries and lime wedges

1. Preheat oven to 325°. In a small bowl, combine cracker crumbs, butter, almonds and sugar. Press onto the bottom and up the sides of a greased 9-in. tart pan. Bake until edges are lightly browned, 15-18 minutes.
2. In a large bowl, whisk egg yolks, milk, lime juice and zest. Pour over crust. Bake until center is almost set, 12-14 minutes. Cool on a wire rack. Refrigerate at least 2 hours.
3. In a large bowl, beat cream until it begins to thicken. Add sugar; beat until stiff peaks form. Fold in sour cream and grated lime zest. Spread over tart. Garnish with fresh raspberries and lime wedges.
1 piece: 288 cal., 16g fat (9g sat. fat), 112mg chol., 138mg sod., 31g carb. (26g sugars, 1g fiber), 5g pro.

YELLOW CAKE WITH BUTTERCREAM FROSTING

YELLOW CAKE WITH BUTTERCREAM FROSTING

This is a classic scratch cake. The homemade buttery frosting and crisp, sugared edges really make it stand out.
—Aria Thornton, Milwaukee, WI

Prep: 20 min. • **Bake:** 40 min. + cooling
Makes: 15 servings

- ⅔ cup butter, softened
- 1¾ cups sugar
- 1 Tbsp. vanilla extract
- 2 large eggs, room temperature
- 2½ cups all-purpose flour
- 2½ tsp. baking powder
- ½ tsp. salt
- 1¼ cups 2% milk

FROSTING

- 1 cup butter, softened
- 3 cups confectioners' sugar
- 4 tsp. vanilla extract
- 3 to 4 Tbsp. heavy whipping cream

1. Preheat oven to 350°. Grease a 13x9-in. baking pan.
2. Cream butter and sugar until light and fluffy, 5-7 minutes. Add vanilla and 1 egg at a time, beating well after each addition. In another bowl, whisk together the flour, baking powder and salt; beat into creamed mixture alternately with milk. Transfer to prepared pan.
3. Bake until a toothpick inserted in center comes out clean, 40-45 minutes. Place on a wire rack; cool completely.
4. For frosting, beat butter until creamy; gradually beat in the confectioners' sugar until smooth and light in color, about 3 minutes. Beat in vanilla and 3 Tbsp. cream until light and fluffy, about 2 minutes; thin with additional cream if desired. Spread frosting over cake.
1 piece: 477 cal., 23g fat (14g sat. fat), 84mg chol., 342mg sod., 65g carb. (48g sugars, 1g fiber), 4g pro.

PEAR CAKE WITH SOUR CREAM TOPPING

This is a great way to combine cake and fruit for an all-in-one breakfast treat. The cake is very tasty, and the change-of-pace topping is simply delicious.
—Norma Bluma, Emporia, KS

- -

Prep: 20 min. • **Bake:** 30 min.
Makes: 16 servings

- ½ cup butter, softened
- ½ cup sugar
- 3 large eggs, lightly beaten, room temperature
- 1 tsp. grated lemon zest
- 1¾ cups all-purpose flour
- 2 tsp. baking powder
- 1 tsp. salt
- ½ cup 2% milk
- 1 can (29 oz.) pear halves, drained

TOPPING
- 1 cup sour cream
- 2 Tbsp. brown sugar
- 1 Tbsp. grated lemon zest

1. Preheat oven to 350°. Cream butter and sugar until fluffy. Add eggs and lemon zest; mix well. In another bowl, combine flour, baking powder and salt; add to creamed mixture alternately with milk, beating well after each addition.
2. Spread batter into a greased 13x9-in. or 3-qt. baking dish. Slice pear halves; arrange slices in rows on top of batter. Mix topping ingredients until smooth; spread over pears. Bake until a toothpick inserted in center comes out clean, 30-35 minutes.
1 piece: 218 cal., 10g fat (6g sat. fat), 66mg chol., 282mg sod., 29g carb. (17g sugars, 1g fiber), 4g pro.

MICHIGAN CHERRY PIE

This tart Michigan cherry pie is delicious with the streusel topping but even better with a scoop of vanilla ice cream on top.
—Diane Selich, Vassar, MI

- -

Prep: 20 min. + chilling • **Bake:** 45 minutes
Makes: 8 servings

- Dough for single-crust pie (9 in.)
- 5 cups frozen pitted tart cherries, thawed and drained, or fresh tart cherries, pitted
- 1¼ cups dried cherries
- 1 Tbsp. lemon juice
- ½ tsp. grated lemon zest
- ½ tsp. almond extract
- 1 cup sugar
- ¼ cup cornstarch

TOPPING
- ¾ cup old-fashioned oats
- ½ cup all-purpose flour
- ½ cup packed brown sugar
- ⅓ cup butter, melted
- ¼ tsp. salt
- Vanilla ice cream, optional

1. On a lightly floured surface, roll pie dough to a ⅛-in.-thick circle; transfer to a 9-in. pie plate. Trim crust to ½ in. beyond rim of plate; flute edge. Refrigerate 30 minutes.
2. Meanwhile, preheat oven to 375°. In a large bowl, toss tart and dried cherries with lemon juice, lemon zest and almond extract. In a small bowl, mix sugar and cornstarch; add to cherry mixture and toss to coat. In a small bowl, mix topping ingredients until crumbly. Transfer cherry filling to crust; sprinkle topping over filling.
3. Bake on a lower oven rack 45-55 minutes or until crust is golden brown and filling is bubbly. Cool on a wire rack. If desired, serve with ice cream.

Dough for single-crust pie: Combine 1¼ cups all-purpose flour and ¼ tsp. salt; cut in ½ cup cold butter until crumbly. Gradually add 3-5 Tbsp. ice water, tossing with a fork until dough holds together when pressed. Wrap and refrigerate 1 hour.

1 piece: 590 cal., 20g fat (12g sat. fat), 50mg chol., 298mg sod., 99g carb. (65g sugars, 4g fiber), 5g pro.

MICHIGAN CHERRY PIE

CHAI
CUPCAKES

GINGER PLUM TART

Sweet cravings, begone: This free-form plum tart is done in only 35 minutes. It's extra awesome when served warm.
—*Taste of Home* Test Kitchen

Prep: 15 min. • **Bake:** 20 min. + cooling
Makes: 8 servings

- 1   sheet refrigerated pie crust
- 3½ cups sliced fresh plums (about 10 medium)
- 3   Tbsp. plus 1 tsp. coarse sugar, divided
- 1   Tbsp. cornstarch
- 2   tsp. finely chopped crystallized ginger
- 1   large egg white
- 1   Tbsp. water

1. Preheat oven to 400°. On a work surface, unroll crust. Roll to a 12-in. circle. Transfer to a parchment-lined baking sheet.
2. In a large bowl, toss plums with 3 Tbsp. sugar and cornstarch. Arrange plums on crust to within 2 in. of edges; sprinkle with ginger. Fold crust edge over plums, pleating as you go.
3. In a small bowl, whisk egg white and water; brush over folded crust. Sprinkle with the remaining sugar.
4. Bake until the crust is golden brown, 20-25 minutes. Cool in pan on a wire rack. Serve warm or at room temperature.

1 piece: 190 cal., 7g fat (3g sat. fat), 5mg chol., 108mg sod., 30g carb. (14g sugars, 1g fiber), 2g pro. **Diabetic exchanges:** 1½ starch, 1 fat, ½ fruit.

CHAI CUPCAKES

You'll get a double dose of the spicy blend that's frequently used to flavor tea in these tender single-size cakes. Both the cupcake and frosting use the sweet blend of spices.
—*Taste of Home* Test Kitchen

Prep: 25 min. • **Bake:** 25 min. + cooling
Makes: 1 dozen

- ½   tsp. each ground ginger, cinnamon, cardamom and cloves
- ⅛   tsp. pepper
- ½   cup butter, softened
- 1   cup sugar
- 1   large egg, room temperature
- ½   tsp. vanilla extract
- 1½ cups cake flour
- 1½ tsp. baking powder
- ¼   tsp. salt
- ⅔   cup 2% milk

FROSTING
- 6   Tbsp. butter, softened
- 3   cups confectioners' sugar
- ¾   tsp. vanilla extract
- 3   to 4 Tbsp. 2% milk

1. In a small bowl, combine the ginger, cinnamon, cardamom, cloves and pepper; set aside.
2. In a large bowl, cream butter and sugar until light and fluffy, 5-7 minutes. Beat in egg and vanilla. Combine the flour, baking powder, salt and 1½ tsp. spice mixture. Gradually add to the creamed mixture alternately with milk, beating well after each addition.
3. Fill 12 paper-lined muffin cups two-thirds full. Bake at 350° until a toothpick inserted in the center comes out clean, 24-28 minutes. Cool for 10 minutes before removing from pans to wire racks to cool completely.
4. In a large bowl, beat butter until fluffy; beat in the confectioners' sugar, vanilla and remaining spice mixture until smooth. Add enough milk to reach desired consistency. Pipe frosting over cupcakes.

1 cupcake: 377 cal., 14g fat (9g sat. fat), 54mg chol., 209mg sod., 61g carb. (46g sugars, 0 fiber), 3g pro.

ASK SARAH

DO I HAVE TO FROST THESE CUPCAKES?

We love the buttery vanilla frosting in this recipe but when you're tight on time, top these spice cakes with a sprinkling of confectioners' sugar.

SWEET POTATO-GINGERBREAD MERINGUE PIE

This delicious pie showcases gingerbread flavor in the meringue instead of the crust. Baking it on the bottom rack gets the crust nice and crisp without parbaking it.
—Shannon Norris, Senior Food Stylist

- -

Prep: 1 hour + chilling
Bake: 40 min. + broiling • **Makes:** 10 servings

1¼ cups all-purpose flour
4½ tsp. sugar
    Dash salt
6 Tbsp. cold butter, cubed
1 large egg yolk, room temperature
4 to 6 Tbsp. ice water

FILLING
3 lbs. medium sweet potatoes
1⅓ cups sugar
⅔ cup butter, softened
½ tsp. pumpkin pie spice
    Dash salt
4 large eggs, room temperature, lightly beaten
2 tsp. vanilla extract

MERINGUE
1 cup sugar
⅓ cup water
1 Tbsp. molasses
    Dash salt
5 large egg whites, room temperature
¾ tsp. cream of tartar
¾ tsp. pumpkin pie spice
½ tsp. ground ginger

1. Pulse the flour, sugar and salt in a food processor until blended. Add butter; pulse until butter is the size of peas. Combine the egg yolk and 2 Tbsp. ice water; slowly add to processor until the dough holds together, adding the remaining ice water, if needed, 1 Tbsp. at a time. Shape dough into a disk; wrap and refrigerate 1 hour or overnight.
2. Preheat oven to 400°. Scrub sweet potatoes; pierce several times with a fork. Bake until tender, 45-50 minutes. Cool potatoes slightly; peel and mash to yield about 4 cups. Reduce oven setting to 350°.
3. On a lightly floured surface, roll dough to a ⅛-in.-thick circle; transfer to a 9-in. deep-dish pie plate. Trim to ½ in. beyond rim of plate; flute edge. Refrigerate 30 minutes.

4. For filling, beat sugar, butter, pie spice and salt until blended. Add eggs and vanilla; beat in cooled sweet potatoes until smooth. Add filling to chilled crust. Bake on bottom rack until a knife inserted in center comes out clean, 40-45 minutes. Keep warm.
5. Meanwhile, for meringue, combine sugar, water, molasses and salt in a small saucepan over medium-high heat; using a pastry brush dipped in water, wash down sides of the pan to eliminate sugar crystals. When mixture comes to a boil, stop brushing. Cook without stirring until a thermometer reads 240° (soft-ball stage).
6. As molasses mixture cooks, preheat broiler. Beat egg whites, cream of tartar and spices on medium speed until soft peaks form. While beating, gradually drizzle hot molasses mixture over egg whites; continue beating until stiff glossy peaks form. Spread meringue over warm pie; broil 4-6 in. from heat until slightly browned, 1-2 minutes. Cool on a wire rack.
1 piece: 609 cal., 22g fat (13g sat. fat), 144mg chol., 663mg sod., 96g carb. (64g sugars, 5g fiber), 9g pro.

EASY KEY LIME PIE

You need only five ingredients to create this refreshing pie. It's easy enough to make for a weeknight dessert, but special enough to take to weekend potlucks.
—*Taste of Home* Test Kitchen

- -

Prep: 20 min. + chilling • **Makes:** 8 servings

1 pkg. (8 oz.) cream cheese, softened
1 can (14 oz.) sweetened condensed milk
½ cup Key lime juice or lime juice
1 graham cracker crust (9 in.)
2 cups whipped topping
    Lime slices, optional

In a large bowl, beat cream cheese until smooth. Beat in milk and lime juice until blended. Transfer to crust. Refrigerate, covered, at least 4 hours. Just before serving, garnish pie with whipped topping and, if desired, lime slices.
1 piece: 417 cal., 22g fat (13g sat. fat), 46mg chol., 274mg sod., 48g carb. (42g sugars, 0 fiber), 7g pro.

SWEET POTATO-GINGERBREAD MERINGUE PIE

STRAWBERRY LEMON CUPCAKES

My granddaughter Sydney has acquired a love of baking. While I was visiting her in Tampa, we whipped up these light, fluffy cupcakes. She's a natural—they turned out absolutely fantastic!
—Lonnie Hartstack, Clarinda, IA

- -

Prep: 15 min. • **Bake:** 20 min. + cooling
Makes: 2 dozen

- 1 pkg. white cake mix (regular size)
- 3 large eggs, room temperature
- ½ cup 2% milk
- ⅓ cup canola oil
- 2 Tbsp. grated lemon zest
- 3 Tbsp. lemon juice

FROSTING
- 4 cups confectioners' sugar
- 1 cup butter, softened
- ¼ cup crushed fresh strawberries
  Additional fresh strawberries

1. Preheat oven to 350°. Line 24 muffin cups with paper liners.

2. In a large bowl, combine the first 6 ingredients; beat on low 30 seconds. Beat on medium 2 minutes. Fill prepared cups half full. Bake until a toothpick inserted in center comes out clean, 18-20 minutes. Cool in pans 10 minutes before removing to wire racks to cool completely.

3. For frosting, in a large bowl, combine all ingredients, except additional strawberries; beat until smooth. Frost cupcakes. Garnish with additional strawberries. Store cupcakes in the refrigerator.

1 cupcake: 253 cal., 12g fat (6g sat. fat), 44mg chol., 198mg sod., 35g carb. (27g sugars, 1g fiber), 2g pro.

STRAWBERRY
LEMON CUPCAKES

CREAMY HAZELNUT PIE

I've always been a huge fan of peanut butter. Then I tried Nutella—I was hooked! I even changed this favorite pie recipe by adding that ingredient.
—Lisa Varner, El Paso, TX

- -

Prep: 10 min. + chilling • **Makes:** 8 servings

    1   pkg. (8 oz.) cream cheese, softened
    1   cup confectioners' sugar
  1¼   cups Nutella, divided
    1   carton (8 oz.) frozen
        whipped topping, thawed
    1   chocolate crumb crust (9 in.)

1. In a large bowl, beat the cream cheese, confectioners' sugar and 1 cup Nutella until smooth. Fold in whipped topping. Spread evenly into crust.
2. Warm remaining Nutella in microwave for 15-20 seconds; drizzle over pie. Refrigerate at least 4 hours or overnight.
1 piece: 567 cal., 33g fat (13g sat. fat), 32mg chol., 224mg sod., 65g carb. (51g sugars, 2g fiber), 6g pro.

HUMMINGBIRD CAKE

This impressive cake is my dad's favorite, so I always make it for his birthday. The beautiful, old-fashioned layered delight makes a memorable celebration dessert any time of year.
—Nancy Zimmerman,
Cape May Court House, NJ

- -

Prep: 40 min. • **Bake:** 25 min. + cooling
Makes: 14 servings

    2   cups mashed ripe bananas
  1½   cups canola oil
    3   large eggs, room temperature
    1   can (8 oz.) unsweetened
        crushed pineapple, undrained
  1½   tsp. vanilla extract
    3   cups all-purpose flour
    2   cups sugar
    1   tsp. salt
    1   tsp. baking soda
    1   tsp. ground cinnamon
    1   cup chopped walnuts
PINEAPPLE FROSTING
    ¼   cup shortening
    2   Tbsp. butter, softened
    1   tsp. grated lemon zest
    ¼   tsp. salt
    6   cups confectioners' sugar
    ½   cup unsweetened pineapple juice
    2   tsp. half-and-half cream
        Chopped walnuts, optional

1. In a large bowl, beat the bananas, oil, eggs, pineapple and vanilla until well blended. In another bowl, combine the flour, sugar, salt, baking soda and cinnamon; gradually beat into banana mixture until blended. Stir in the walnuts.
2. Pour into 3 greased and floured 9-in. round baking pans. Bake at 350° until a toothpick inserted in the center comes out clean, 25-30 minutes. Cool for 10 minutes before removing from pans to wire racks to cool completely.
3. For frosting, in a large bowl, beat the shortening, butter, lemon zest and salt until fluffy. Add confectioners' sugar alternately with pineapple juice. Beat in cream. Spread between layers and over top and sides of cake. If desired, sprinkle with walnuts.
1 piece: 777 cal., 35g fat (6g sat. fat), 50mg chol., 333mg sod., 113g carb. (85g sugars, 2g fiber), 7g pro.

HUMMINGBIRD CAKE

BLUEBARB
PIE

BLUEBERRY PAN-CAKE WITH MAPLE FROSTING

Here's your excuse to have cake for breakfast. The batter is made easily with pancake mix.
—Matthew Hass, Ellison Bay, WI

- -

Prep: 10 min. • **Bake:** 15 min. + cooling
Makes: 12 servings

- 3 cups complete buttermilk pancake mix
- 1¾ cups water
- 1 cup fresh blueberries
- 2 tsp. all-purpose flour
- FROSTING
- 2 cups confectioners' sugar
- ⅓ cup maple syrup
- ¼ cup butter, softened

1. Preheat oven to 350°. Stir pancake mix and water just until moistened. In another bowl, toss blueberries with flour. Fold into the batter.
2. Transfer to a greased 13x9-in. baking pan. Bake until a toothpick inserted in center comes out clean, 15-18 minutes. Cool completely in pan on a wire rack.
3. Beat frosting ingredients until smooth; spread over cooled cake.
1 piece: 257 cal., 5g fat (2g sat. fat), 10mg chol., 449mg sod., 51g carb. (30g sugars, 1g fiber), 3g pro.

BLUEBARB PIE

Blueberries provide a sweet counterpoint to tart rhubarb in this fabulous summertime treat topped with a flaky homemade crust.
—Steve Gyuro, Franklin, WI

- -

Prep: 50 min. + chilling
Bake: 40 min. + cooling • **Makes:** 8 servings

- 2 cups all-purpose flour
- 1 tsp. salt
- ⅔ cup shortening
- 6 to 8 Tbsp. ice water
- FILLING
- 1½ cups sugar
- 3 Tbsp. quick-cooking tapioca
- ¼ tsp. salt
- 4 cups sliced fresh or frozen rhubarb, thawed
- 2 cups fresh or frozen blueberries, thawed
- 1 Tbsp. butter
- 1 tsp. 2% milk
  Coarse sugar or sugar, optional

1. In a small bowl, combine flour and salt; cut in the shortening until crumbly. Gradually add water, tossing with a fork until dough forms a ball. Divide the dough in half, with 1 portion slightly larger than the other; wrap separately and refrigerate for 4 hours or until easy to handle.
2. On a lightly floured surface, roll out larger portion of dough to fit a 9-in. deep-dish pie plate or cast-iron skillet. Transfer pastry to pie plate. Trim pastry even with edge.
3. For filling, in a large bowl, combine the sugar, tapioca and salt. Add rhubarb and blueberries; toss to coat. Let stand 15 minutes. Transfer to crust. Dot with butter.
4. Roll out remaining pastry to fit top of pie. Place over filling. Trim, seal and flute edges. Cut slits in pastry. If desired, make additional dough and use to create small cutouts to decorate top of pie. Brush with milk; sprinkle with coarse sugar if desired.
5. Bake at 400° until crust is golden brown and filling is bubbly, 40-45 minutes. Cover edges with foil during the last 15 minutes to prevent overbrowning if necessary. Cool on a wire rack.
1 piece: 471 cal., 18g fat (5g sat. fat), 4mg chol., 383mg sod., 74g carb. (43g sugars, 3g fiber), 4g pro.

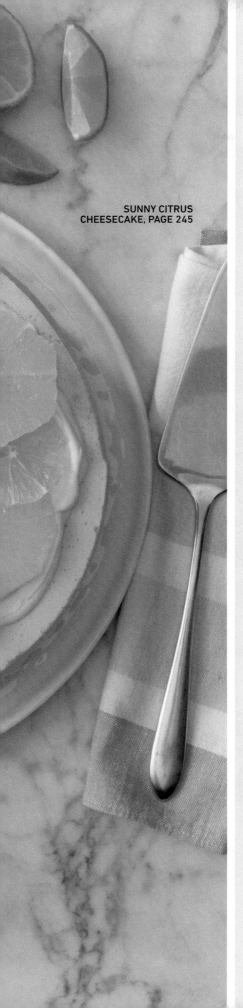

SUNNY CITRUS
CHEESECAKE, PAGE 245

FAVORITE

Desserts

There's always room for dessert, so our food experts make sure there are plenty of sweets to review in the Test Kitchen. See which tantalizing specialties they deem best of the best with this popular chapter.

SLOW-COOKER FLAN IN A JAR

Spoil yourself or the people you love with these delightful portable custards. They're a cute and fun take on the Mexican dessert classic. Tuck a jar into your lunchbox for a sweet treat.
—Megumi Garcia, Milwaukee, WI

Prep: 25 min. • **Cook:** 2 hours + chilling
Makes: 6 servings

- ½ cup sugar
- 1 Tbsp. plus 3 cups hot water (110°-115°)
- 1 cup coconut or whole milk
- ⅓ cup whole milk
- ⅓ cup sweetened condensed milk
- 2 large eggs plus 1 large egg yolk, room temperature, lightly beaten Pinch salt
- 1 tsp. vanilla extract
- 1 tsp. dark rum, optional

1. In a small heavy saucepan, spread sugar; cook, without stirring, over medium-low heat until it begins to melt. Gently drag the melted sugar to the center of the pan so sugar melts evenly. Cook, stirring constantly, until melted sugar turns a deep amber color, about 2 minutes. Immediately remove the saucepan from the heat and carefully stir in 1 Tbsp. hot water. Quickly ladle hot mixture into 6 hot 4-oz. jars.

2. In a small saucepan, heat coconut milk and whole milk until bubbles form around sides of pan; remove from heat. In a large bowl, whisk condensed milk, eggs, egg yolk and salt until blended but not foamy. Slowly stir in hot milk; stir in vanilla and, if desired, rum. Strain through a fine sieve. Pour egg mixture into prepared jars. Center lids on jars; screw on bands until fingertip tight.

3. Add remaining hot water to a 6-qt. slow cooker; place jars in slow cooker. Cook, covered, on high 2 hours or until centers are set. Cool 10 minutes on a wire rack. Remove jars to a 13x9-in. baking pan filled halfway with ice water; cool 10 minutes. Refrigerate until cold, about 1 hour. Run a knife around sides of jars; invert flans onto dessert plates.

⅓ cup: 224 cal., 10g fat (8g sat. fat), 100mg chol., 87mg sod., 28g carb. (27g sugars, 0 fiber), 5g pro.

BERRY BLISS COBBLER

A little bit sweet, a little bit tart, topped off with golden sugar-kissed biscuits, this cobbler is summer perfection.
—*Taste of Home* Test Kitchen

Prep: 10 min. + standing • **Bake:** 20 min.
Makes: 6 servings

- 3 cups fresh strawberries, halved
- 1½ cups fresh raspberries
- 1½ cups fresh blueberries
- ⅔ cup plus 1 Tbsp. sugar, divided
- 3 Tbsp. quick-cooking tapioca
- 1 cup all-purpose flour
- 2 tsp. baking powder
- ¼ tsp. salt
- ¼ cup cold butter, cubed
- 1 large egg, room temperature
- ¼ cup plus 2 Tbsp. 2% milk
  Coarse sugar

1. Preheat oven to 400°. Toss strawberries, raspberries and blueberries with ⅔ cup sugar and tapioca. Transfer to a greased 10-in. cast-iron or other ovenproof skillet; let stand 20 minutes.

2. Meanwhile, whisk flour, remaining 1 Tbsp. sugar, baking powder and salt. Cut in butter until mixture resembles coarse crumbs. In another bowl, whisk together egg and milk; stir into crumb mixture just until moistened. Drop by tablespoonfuls onto fruit. Sprinkle with coarse sugar.

3. Bake, uncovered, until filling is bubbly and topping is golden brown, 20-25 minutes. Serve warm.

1 serving: 335 cal., 9g fat (5g sat. fat), 52mg chol., 298mg sod., 60g carb. (34g sugars, 5g fiber), 5g pro.

SLOW-COOKER FLAN IN A JAR

KEY LIME TRIFLE

When I saw a recipe for banana cream pie trifle I was inspired to invent a version than spun off my favorite pie, Key lime. My family loved it! Some friends got to try it, too, and they enjoyed it immensely as well.
—Rebecah Lytle, Ocala, FL

Prep: 30 min. • **Bake:** 10 min. + chilling
Makes: 16 servings

- 2 cups graham cracker crumbs
- 1 cup chopped pecans
- ½ cup packed brown sugar
- 1 cup butter, melted

FILLING
- 2 pkg. (8 oz. each) cream cheese, softened
- 2 cans (14 oz. each) sweetened condensed milk
- 1½ cups Key lime juice

WHIPPED CREAM
- 3 cups heavy whipping cream
- ⅓ cup confectioners' sugar
- 3 tsp. vanilla extract

TOPPING
- ½ cup chopped pecans, toasted
- ¼ cup flaked coconut, toasted

1. Preheat oven to 400°. Mix the cracker crumbs, pecans and brown sugar; stir in butter. Press onto bottom of a 15x10-in. pan. Bake 10-12 minutes. Stir to break up crumbs; cool on a wire rack.

2. For filling, in another bowl, beat cream cheese and condensed milk until blended. Stir in lime juice. In another bowl, beat heavy whipping cream until it begins to thicken. Add confectioners' sugar and vanilla; beat until stiff peaks form.

3. In a 4-qt. glass bowl, layer half of each of the following: crumb mixture, filling and whipped cream. Repeat layers. Sprinkle with pecans and coconut. Refrigerate, covered, at least 2 hours or overnight.

1 cup: 689 cal., 51g fat (27g sat.fat), 127mg chol., 319mg sod., 53g carb. (43g sugars, 2g fiber), 9g pro.

KEY LIME TRIFLE

STRAWBERRY GELATO

You'll love this smooth and creamy gelato with bright strawberry flavor and just a hint of sea salt and honey.

—Shelly Bevington, Hermiston, OR

Prep: 10 min. + chilling • **Process:** 25 min.
Makes: 12 servings (1½ qt.)

2	cups whole milk
2	Tbsp. light corn syrup
1	Tbsp. honey
¾	cup sugar
½	tsp. sea salt
2½	cups fresh strawberries (about 12 oz.), halved
½	cup heavy whipping cream
1	tsp. lemon juice

1. Place first 6 ingredients in a blender; cover and process until blended. While processing, gradually add cream, processing just until combined. Remove to a bowl; stir in lemon juice. Refrigerate, covered, until cold, about 4 hours.

2. Fill cylinder of ice cream maker no more than two-thirds full; freeze according to manufacturer's directions. (Refrigerate any remaining mixture until ready to freeze.)

3. Transfer ice cream to freezer containers, allowing headspace for expansion. Freeze until firm, 3-4 hours.

½ cup: 160 cal., 6g fat (4g sat. fat), 18mg chol., 124mg sod., 26g carb. (25g sugars, 1g fiber), 2g pro.

PRESSURE-COOKER VERY VANILLA CHEESECAKE

Cinnamon and vanilla give this cheesecake so much flavor, and making it in the electric pressure cooker creates a silky, smooth texture that's hard to resist.

—Krista Lanphier, Milwaukee, WI

Prep: 20 min. • **Cook:** 65 min. + cooling
Makes: 6 servings

1	cup water
¾	cup graham cracker crumbs
1	Tbsp. plus ⅔ cup sugar, divided
¼	tsp. ground cinnamon
2½	Tbsp. butter, melted
2	pkg. (8 oz. each) cream cheese, softened
2	to 3 tsp. vanilla extract
2	large eggs, lightly beaten

TOPPING (OPTIONAL)

4	oz. white baking chocolate, chopped
3	Tbsp. heavy whipping cream
	Sliced fresh strawberries or raspberries, optional

1. Grease a 6-in. springform pan; pour water into a 6-qt. electric pressure cooker.

2. Mix cracker crumbs, 1 Tbsp. sugar and cinnamon; stir in butter. Press onto bottom and about 1 in. up sides of prepared pan.

3. In another bowl, beat cream cheese and remaining sugar until smooth. Beat in vanilla. Add the eggs; beat on low speed just until combined. Pour over crust.

4. Cover cheesecake tightly with foil. Place springform pan on a trivet with handles; lower into cooker. Lock lid; make sure vent is closed. Select manual setting; adjust pressure to low, and set time for 1 hour and 5 minutes. When finished cooking, quick-release the pressure. The cheesecake should be jiggly but set in center.

5. Remove springform pan from pressure cooker; remove foil. Cool cheesecake on a wire rack 1 hour. Loosen sides from pan with a knife. Refrigerate overnight, covering when completely cooled.

6. For topping, melt chocolate and cream in a microwave; stir until smooth. Cool slightly. Remove rim from springform pan. Pour chocolate mixture over cheesecake. If desired, sprinkle with berries to serve.

1 piece: 484 cal., 34g fat (19g sat. fat), 151mg chol., 357mg sod., 39g carb. (31g sugars, 0 fiber), 8g pro.

CHOCOLATE CHIP COOKIE DELIGHT

This is a simple chocolate delight recipe for any type of potluck occasion, and the pan always comes home empty.
—Diane Windley, Grace, ID

- -

Prep: 35 min. + chilling • **Makes:** 15 servings

- 1   tube (16½ oz.) refrigerated chocolate chip cookie dough
- 1   pkg. (8 oz.) cream cheese, softened
- 1   cup confectioners' sugar
- 1   carton (12 oz.) frozen whipped topping, thawed, divided
- 3   cups cold 2% milk
- 1   pkg. (3.9 oz.) instant chocolate pudding mix
- 1   pkg. (3.4 oz.) instant vanilla pudding mix
  Optional: Chopped nuts, chocolate curls and miniature semisweet chocolate chips

1. Let the cookie dough stand at room temperature for 5-10 minutes to soften. Press dough into an ungreased 13x9-in. baking pan. Bake at 350° until golden brown, 14-16 minutes. Cool on a wire rack.

2. In a large bowl, beat cream cheese and confectioners' sugar until smooth. Fold in 1¾ cups whipped topping. Spread over the crust.

3. In a large bowl, whisk milk and pudding mixes for 2 minutes. Spread over cream cheese layer. Top with remaining whipped topping. Sprinkle with nuts and chocolate curls if desired.

4. Cover and refrigerate until firm, 8 hours or overnight.

1 piece: 365 cal., 17g fat (10g sat. fat), 29mg chol., 329mg sod., 47g carb. (22g sugars, 1g fiber), 4g pro.

BANANAS FOSTER SAUCE

This sweet treat is very appealing and versatile! It's an impressive ending to everyday meals as a dessert, or with waffles for brunch.
—*Taste of Home* Test Kitchen

- -

Takes: 15 min. • **Makes:** 4 servings

- ¼   cup butter, cubed
- ¾   cup packed brown sugar
- ¼   tsp. ground cinnamon
- ⅛   tsp. ground nutmeg
  Dash ground cloves
- ¼   cup heavy whipping cream
- 3   medium firm bananas, halved lengthwise and cut into thirds
- ¼   tsp. rum extract
  Optional: Waffles, pancakes or vanilla ice cream

In a large skillet, melt butter. Stir in the brown sugar, cinnamon, nutmeg and cloves. Cook and stir until sugar is dissolved, about 2 minutes. Stir in cream. Add bananas and extract. Serve warm, with waffles, pancakes or vanilla ice cream if desired.

½ cup: 589 cal., 28g fat (17g sat. fat), 95mg chol., 218mg sod., 85g carb. (74g sugars, 2g fiber), 5g pro.

CHOCOLATE CHIP COOKIE DELIGHT

BUTTERSCOTCH PECAN DESSERT

Light and creamy, this terrific treat never lasts long when I serve it. The fluffy cream cheese layer topped with cool butterscotch pudding is a lip-smacking combination.
—Becky Harrison, Albion, IL

- -

Prep: 15 min. + chilling
Bake: 20 min. + cooling • **Makes:** 20 servings

½ cup cold butter, cubed
1 cup all-purpose flour
¾ cup chopped pecans, divided
1 pkg. (8 oz.) cream cheese, softened
1 cup confectioners' sugar
1 carton (8 oz.) frozen whipped topping, thawed, divided
3½ cups cold 2% milk
2 pkg. (3.4 or 3.5 oz. each) instant butterscotch or vanilla pudding mix

1. Preheat oven to 350°. In a small bowl, cut butter into flour until crumbly; stir in ½ cup pecans. Press into an ungreased 13x9-in. baking dish. Bake until lightly browned, about 20 minutes. Cool.
2. In a small bowl, beat cream cheese and sugar until fluffy. Fold in 1 cup whipped topping; spread over crust.
3. In a large bowl, whisk milk and pudding mix for 2 minutes. Let stand for 2 minutes or until soft-set; pour over cream cheese layer. Refrigerate until set, 15-20 minutes. Top with remaining whipped topping and pecans. Refrigerate for 1-2 hours.
1 piece: 242 cal., 14g fat (8g sat. fat), 27mg chol., 247mg sod., 23g carb. (18g sugars, 1g fiber), 3g pro.

RAINBOW SHERBET ANGEL FOOD CAKE

Talk about a dessert that pops off the plate! Sometimes I make this cake even more eye-catching by coloring the whipped cream, too. Use whatever sherbet flavor combination you like.
—Bonnie Hawkins, Elkhorn, WI

- -

Prep: 25 min. + freezing • **Makes:** 12 servings

1 prepared angel food cake (8 to 10 oz.)
3 cups rainbow sherbet, softened if necessary
WHIPPED CREAM
2 cups heavy whipping cream
⅓ cup confectioners' sugar
1 tsp. vanilla extract

1. Using a long serrated knife, cut the cake horizontally into 4 layers. Place bottom layer on a freezer-safe serving plate; spread with 1 cup sherbet. Repeat twice with the middle cake layers and remaining sherbet. Top with remaining cake layer. Freeze, covered, until sherbet is firm, about 1 hour.
2. In a large bowl, beat cream until it begins to thicken. Add confectioners' sugar and vanilla; beat until soft peaks form. Frost top and sides of cake. Freeze until firm.
3. Thaw in refrigerator 30 minutes before serving. Cut cake with a serrated knife.
1 piece: 253 cal., 16g fat (10g sat. fat), 54mg chol., 174mg sod., 27g carb. (12g sugars, 2g fiber), 2g pro.

BUTTERSCOTCH PECAN DESSERT

WHITE CHOCOLATE-RASPBERRY MOUSSE CHEESECAKE

Here's a dessert perfect for the holidays. These flavors are a match made in heaven.
—Crystal Morris, Alliance, OH

Prep: 50 min. • **Bake:** 50 min. + chilling
Makes: 16 servings

- 2 cups graham cracker crumbs
- ½ cup butter, melted
- ⅓ cup sugar

FILLING
- 2 cups white baking chips, divided
- 3 pkg. (8 oz. each) cream cheese, softened
- ¾ cup sugar
- ⅓ cup sour cream
- 1 Tbsp. all-purpose flour
- 1 tsp. vanilla extract
- 3 large eggs, lightly beaten

MOUSSE
- 1 envelope unflavored gelatin
- 3 Tbsp. cold water
- 1 Tbsp. lemon juice
- 1 pkg. (12 oz.) frozen unsweetened raspberries, thawed
- ½ cup sugar
- 1 large egg plus 1 large egg yolk, beaten
- ¼ cup raspberry liqueur
- 1½ cups heavy whipping cream, whipped
   Optional: Fresh raspberries, white chocolate curls and mint leaves

1. Place a greased 10-in. springform pan on a double thickness of heavy-duty foil (about 18 in. square). Securely wrap foil around pan.
2. In a small bowl, combine cracker crumbs, butter and sugar. Press onto the bottom of prepared pan.
3. In a microwave, melt 1 cup white chips; stir until smooth. Set aside to cool. In a large bowl, beat cream cheese and sugar until smooth. Beat in the sour cream, flour and vanilla. Beat in melted chips. Add eggs; beat on low speed just until combined. Fold in the remaining chips. Pour into crust.
4. Place springform pan in a large baking pan; add 1 in. of hot water to larger pan. Bake at 325° until center is just set and top appears dull, 50-60 minutes. Remove springform pan from water bath. Cool on a wire rack for 10 minutes. Carefully run a knife around edge of pan to loosen; cool 1 hour longer.

5. Meanwhile, in a small bowl, sprinkle gelatin over cold water and lemon juice; let stand for 1 minute. Place raspberries in a food processor. Cover and process until smooth. Strain; discard seeds.
6. In a small heavy saucepan, heat sugar and ½ cup raspberry puree until bubbles form around sides of pan. Whisk a small amount of hot mixture into egg mixture. Return all to the pan, whisking constantly. Cook and stir over low heat until mixture reaches 160°. Remove from the heat.
7. Whisk a small amount of hot liquid into gelatin mixture; stir until gelatin is completely dissolved. Stir in liqueur and the remaining hot raspberry mixture. Stir in remaining raspberry puree. Cover and refrigerate for 30 minutes. Fold in whipped cream. Spread over cheesecake.
8. Refrigerate overnight. Remove sides of pan. Garnish with raspberries, white chocolate curls and mint leaves if desired.
Note: Heavy whipping cream contains 36%-40% butterfat and doubles in volume when whipped. It may also be sold as heavy cream or whipping cream.
1 piece: 569 cal., 39g fat (23g sat. fat), 164mg chol., 278mg sod., 46g carb. (38g sugars, 1g fiber), 8g pro.

> "Want to feel like a dessert superhero? Give this recipe a try! Every time I make this layered cheesecake, folks stop in their tracks. The textures, the flavors, the beautiful appearance (especially when garnished) make this one sensational sweet that's perfect for special occasions!"
>
> —SARAH FARMER, EXECUTIVE CULINARY DIRECTOR

PUMPKIN PIE CUSTARD

Instead of pumpkin pie, try my light dessert with only 120 calories. My husband's aunt shared the recipe after she brought this treat to a family party.
—Nancy Zimmerman, Cape May Court House, NJ

Prep: 20 min. • **Bake:** 35 min. + chilling
Makes: 10 servings

- 1 can (15 oz.) canned pumpkin
- 1 can (12 oz.) fat-free evaporated milk
- 8 large egg whites
- ½ cup fat-free milk
- ¾ cup sugar
- ¼ tsp. salt
- 1 tsp. ground cinnamon
- ½ tsp. ground ginger
- ¼ tsp. ground cloves
- ¼ tsp. ground nutmeg
   Optional: Sweetened whipped cream and additional cinnamon

1. Preheat oven to 350°. Place ten 6-oz. ramekins or custard cups coated with cooking spray in a 15x10x1-in. baking pan.
2. In a large bowl, beat first 4 ingredients until smooth. Add sugar, salt and spices; mix well. Divide among ramekins.
3. Bake until a knife inserted in the center comes out clean, 40-45 minutes. Cool on a wire rack; serve or refrigerate within 2 hours. If desired, top with whipped cream and sprinkle with cinnamon.
1 serving: 120 cal., 0 fat (0 sat. fat), 2mg chol., 151mg sod., 24g carb. (21g sugars, 2g fiber), 7g pro. **Diabetic exchanges:** 1½ starch.

**CANTALOUPE
A LA MODE**

HOLIDAY PISTACHIO DESSERT

For my best festive menu, I make this dessert, which my children gobble up immediately. It's a hit at every gathering!
—Edie DeSpain, Logan, UT

Prep: 30 min. + chilling • **Makes:** 15 servings

- 1¼ cups biscuit/baking mix
- ½ cup chopped walnuts
- 1 Tbsp. brown sugar
- 6 Tbsp. cold butter
- 1 pkg. (8 oz.) cream cheese, softened
- 1 cup plus 1 Tbsp. confectioners' sugar, divided
- 1 cup heavy whipping cream, whipped, divided
- 2½ cups cold 2% milk
- 2 pkg. (3.4 oz. each) instant pistachio pudding mix
  Chocolate curls, optional

1. In a small bowl, combine the biscuit mix, walnuts and brown sugar. Cut in butter until mixture resembles coarse crumbs.
2. Press into an ungreased 13x9-in. baking pan. Bake at 375° until lightly browned, 10-12 minutes. Cool on a wire rack.
3. In a small bowl, beat cream cheese and 1 cup confectioners' sugar until fluffy. Fold in half of the whipped cream; spread over crust. Stir remaining confectioners' sugar into remaining whipped cream; refrigerate until serving.
4. In another bowl, whisk milk and pudding mixes for 2 minutes. Let stand until soft-set, about 2 minutes. Spread over cream cheese layer. Cover;refrigerate for at least 4 hours before serving.
5. Garnish with sweetened whipped cream and, if desired, chocolate curls.
1 piece: 279 cal., 16g fat (8g sat. fat), 38mg chol., 392mg sod., 30g carb. (20g sugars, 0 fiber), 4g pro.

CANTALOUPE A LA MODE

This special dessert is a refreshing finale to a warm-weather meal.
—Nancy Walker, Granite City, IL

Takes: 15 min.
Makes: 4 servings (1 cup sauce)

- ½ cup water
- ½ cup sugar
- 2 Tbsp. lemon juice
- 1 Tbsp. cornstarch
- 1 tsp. grated lemon zest
- 1 cup fresh or frozen blueberries
- 2 small cantaloupes, halved and seeded
- 2 cups vanilla ice cream
  Fresh mint, optional

In a saucepan, combine first 5 ingredients; bring to a boil over medium heat. Boil and stir until thickened, about 2 minutes. Add blueberries; cook until heated through. Fill each cantaloupe half with ice cream; top with sauce. Garnish with mint if desired.
1 serving: 337 cal., 8g fat (5g sat. fat), 29mg chol., 74mg sod., 67g carb. (56g sugars, 3g fiber), 5g pro.

ASK SARAH

WHAT ELSE CAN I DO WITH THIS BLUEBERRY SAUCE?

This lovely sauce is great over pancakes and waffles. You can also chill it and use it a dressing for fresh fruit salads.

HOLIDAY PISTACHIO
DESSERT

CHOCOLATE ECLAIR DELIGHT

It's amazing how the layers of this eclair torte soften overnight to a cakelike texture. Just before serving this dessert, I dust the top with cocoa.
—Agnes Ward, Stratford, ON

- -

Prep: 15 min. • **Cook:** 15 min. + chilling
Makes: 9 servings

- ½   cup sugar
- ⅓   cup baking cocoa
- 2   Tbsp. plus 1 tsp. cornstarch
- ⅛   tsp. salt
- ⅛   tsp. ground cinnamon
- 1   can (12 oz.) fat-free evaporated milk
- 1   cup fat-free milk
- ½   cup egg substitute
- 1   tsp. vanilla extract

TOPPING
- 2   cups reduced-fat whipped topping
- 1   Tbsp. plus ½ tsp. baking cocoa, divided
- 9   whole graham crackers, halved

1. In a large heavy saucepan, combine first 5 ingredients. Gradually whisk in the milks until smooth. Cook and stir over medium heat until mixture comes to a boil. Reduce heat; cook and stir until thickened, about 2 minutes longer.

2. Remove from the heat. Stir a small amount of hot filling into egg substitute; return all to pan, stirring constantly. Bring to a gentle boil; cook and stir 2 minutes longer. Remove from the heat. Gently stir in vanilla. Press plastic wrap onto surface of filling; cover and refrigerate until cooled.

3. Meanwhile, in a small bowl, combine whipped topping and 1 Tbsp. cocoa; set aside. Arrange half the graham crackers in a 9-in. square pan coated with cooking spray. Layer half of the filling and topping over crackers. Repeat layers. Cover; refrigerate overnight. Just before serving, sprinkle with remaining cocoa.

1 piece: 209 cal., 4g fat (2g sat. fat), 2mg chol., 213mg sod., 37g carb. (22g sugars, 1g fiber), 7g pro.

EASY NUTELLA CHEESECAKE

EASY NUTELLA CHEESECAKE

Creamy chocolate-hazelnut spread tops a crust made of crushed Oreo cookies to make this irresistible baked cheesecake.
—Nick Iverson, Denver, CO

- -

Prep: 35 min. • **Bake:** 1¼ hours + chilling
Makes: 16 servings

- 2½   cups lightly crushed Oreo cookies (about 24 cookies)
- ¼   cup sugar
- ¼   cup butter, melted

FILLING
- 4   pkg. (8 oz. each) cream cheese, softened
- ½   cup sugar
- 2   jars (26½ oz. each) Nutella
- 1   cup heavy whipping cream
- 1   tsp. salt
- 4   large eggs, room temperature, lightly beaten
- ½   cup chopped hazelnuts, toasted

1. Preheat oven to 325°. Pulse cookies and sugar in a food processor until fine crumbs form. Continue processing while gradually adding butter in a steady stream. Press mixture onto bottom of a greased 10x3-in. springform pan. Securely wrap the bottom and sides of pan in a double thickness of heavy-duty foil (about 18 in. square).

2. For filling, beat cream cheese and sugar until smooth. Beat in Nutella, cream and salt. Add the eggs; beat on low speed just until blended. Pour over crust.

3. Bake until a thermometer inserted in center reads 160°, about 1¼ hours. Cool for 1¼ hours on a wire rack. Refrigerate overnight, covering when completely cooled.

4. Gently loosen sides from the pan with a knife; remove rim. Top cheesecake with chopped hazelnuts.

1 slice: 900 cal., 62g fat (22g sat. fat), 129mg chol., 478mg sod., 84g carb. (71g sugars, 4g fiber), 12g pro.

PEANUT BUTTER PUDDING DESSERT

Here's a fun layered dessert that will appeal to all ages. If you want it even nuttier, you can use chunky peanut butter. If you're not a fan of cashews, substitute your favorite nut.
—Barbara Schindler, Napoleon, OH

Prep: 25 min. • **Bake:** 25 min. + chilling
Makes: 16 servings

- 1 cup all-purpose flour
- ½ cup cold butter, cubed
- 1½ cups chopped cashews, divided
- 1 pkg. (8 oz.) cream cheese, softened
- ⅓ cup creamy peanut butter
- 1 cup confectioners' sugar
- 1 carton (12 oz.) frozen whipped topping, thawed, divided
- 2⅔ cups cold 2% milk
- 1 pkg. (3.9 oz.) instant chocolate pudding mix
- 1 pkg. (3.4 oz.) instant vanilla pudding mix
- 1 milk chocolate candy bar (1.55 oz.), coarsely chopped

1. Preheat oven to 350°. Place flour and butter in a food processor; cover and process until mixture resembles coarse crumbs. Add 1 cup cashews; pulse a few times until combined.
2. Press into a greased 13x9-in. baking dish. Bake until golden brown, 25-28 minutes. Cool completely on a wire rack.
3. In a small bowl, beat the cream cheese, peanut butter and confectioners' sugar until smooth. Fold in 1 cup whipped topping. Spoon over crust.
4. In another bowl, whisk milk and both pudding mixes for 2 minutes. Let stand until soft-set, about 2 minutes. Spread over the cream cheese layer. Top with remaining whipped topping. Sprinkle with chopped candy bar and remaining cashews. Cover and refrigerate for at least 1 hour before serving.
1 piece: 406 cal., 25g fat (13g sat. fat), 33mg chol., 288mg sod., 40g carb. (25g sugars, 1g fiber), 7g pro.

SIMPLE LEMON MOUSSE

This classic, simple mousse is the refreshing dessert you need. Serve it with fresh fruit or enjoy it on its own.
—*Taste of Home* Test Kitchen

Prep: 20 min. • **Cook:** 10 min. + chilling
Makes: 6 servings

- ⅔ cup sugar
- 2 Tbsp. cornstarch
  Dash salt
- 3 large egg yolks
- ⅔ cup whole milk
- ½ cup lemon juice
- 2 tsp. grated lemon zest
- 1 cup heavy whipping cream
  Lemon slices, optional

1. In a small saucepan, mix sugar, cornstarch and salt; whisk in egg yolks and milk until smooth. Whisk in lemon juice until blended; bring to a boil over medium heat, stirring constantly. Cook and stir until thickened slightly, 2 minutes longer. Stir in lemon zest.
2. Transfer mixture to a bowl. Cover surface with plastic wrap; refrigerate until cold.
3. To serve, in a small bowl, beat cream on high speed until soft peaks form. Fold into lemon mixture. Spoon into serving dishes. If desired, top mousse with additional whipped cream and lemon slices.
½ cup: 282 cal., 18g fat (11g sat. fat), 140mg chol., 52mg sod., 29g carb. (25g sugars, 0 fiber), 3g pro.

PEANUT BUTTER PUDDING DESSERT

FROZEN GREEK VANILLA YOGURT

It's so simple and easy to make your own frozen Greek yogurt, you might even want to get the kids in on the fun.
—*Taste of Home* Test Kitchen

- -

Prep: 15 min+ chilling
Process: 15 min+ freezing • **Makes:** 2½ cups

3	cups reduced-fat plain Greek yogurt
¾	cup sugar
1½	tsp. vanilla extract
1	Tbsp. cold water
1	Tbsp. lemon juice
1	tsp. unflavored gelatin

1. Line a strainer or colander with 4 layers of cheesecloth or 1 coffee filter; place over a bowl. Place yogurt in prepared strainer; cover yogurt with sides of cheesecloth. Refrigerate 2-4 hours.

2. Remove yogurt from cheesecloth to a bowl; discard strained liquid. Add sugar and vanilla extract to the yogurt, stirring until sugar is dissolved.

3. In a small microwave-safe bowl, combine cold water and lemon juice; sprinkle with gelatin and let stand 1 minute. Microwave on high for 30 seconds. Stir and let mixture stand 1 minute or until gelatin is completely dissolved; cool slightly. Stir gelatin mixture into yogurt. Cover and refrigerate until cold, about 40 minutes.

4. Pour yogurt mixture into cylinder of ice cream freezer; freeze according to the manufacturer's directions.

5. Transfer frozen yogurt to a freezer container. Freeze 2-4 hours or until firm enough to scoop.

½ cup: 225 cal., 3g fat (2g sat. fat), 8mg chol., 57mg sod., 36g carb. (36g sugars, 0 fiber), 14g pro.

FROZEN GREEK VANILLA YOGURT

OLD-FASHIONED RICE PUDDING

This dessert is a wonderful way to end any meal. As a girl, I always waited eagerly for the first heavenly bite. Today, my husband likes to top his with a scoop of ice cream.
—Sandra Melnychenko, Grandview, MB

- -

Prep: 10 min. • **Bake:** 1 hour
Makes: 6 servings

3½	cups 2% milk
½	cup uncooked long grain rice
⅓	cup sugar
½	tsp. salt
½	cup raisins
1	tsp. vanilla extract
	Ground cinnamon, optional

1. Preheat oven to 325°. Place the first 4 ingredients in a large saucepan; bring to a boil over medium heat, stirring constantly. Transfer to a greased 1½-qt. baking dish.

2. Bake, covered, 45 minutes, stirring every 15 minutes. Stir in raisins and vanilla; bake, covered, until the rice is tender, about 15 minutes. If desired, sprinkle with cinnamon. Serve warm or refrigerate and serve cold.

¾ cup: 214 cal., 3g fat (2g sat. fat), 11mg chol., 266mg sod., 41g carb. (25g sugars, 1g fiber), 6g pro.

AIR-FRYER PECAN STRAWBERRY RHUBARB COBBLER

Chock-full of berries and rhubarb, this pretty cobbler is the perfect finale for a dinner for two. The pecans in the topping and the delicious dessert sauce make it something truly special.
—Lily Julow, Lawrenceville, GA

Prep: 20 min. + standing • **Cook:** 25 min.
Makes: 2 servings

- 1 cup sliced fresh or frozen rhubarb
- 1 cup sliced fresh strawberries
- ¼ cup sugar
- 1 Tbsp. quick-cooking tapioca
- 1 tsp. lemon juice
  Dash salt

TOPPING
- ⅓ cup all-purpose flour
- ¼ cup chopped pecans
- 3 Tbsp. sugar
- ⅛ tsp. baking powder
  Dash salt
- 2 Tbsp. cold butter
- 1 large egg

SAUCE
- ½ cup vanilla ice cream
- 2¼ tsp. Marsala wine

1. Preheat air fryer to 375°. Combine the first 6 ingredients; divide between 2 greased 8-oz. ramekins or custard cups. Let stand for 15 minutes.

2. In a small bowl, combine the flour, pecans, sugar, baking powder and salt; cut in butter until mixture resembles coarse crumbs. Stir in egg. Drop by spoonfuls over fruit mixture; spread evenly.

3. Place the ramekins on tray in air-fryer basket. Cook until filling is bubbly and a toothpick inserted in topping comes out clean, 25-30 minutes.

4. In a microwave-safe bowl, combine the ice cream and wine. Cook, uncovered, at 50% power for 1-2 minutes or until heated through; stir until blended. Serve with the warm cobbler.

1 cobbler: 615 cal., 28g fat (11g sat. fat), 138mg chol., 335mg sod., 85g carb. (57g sugars, 5g fiber), 9g pro.

AIR-FRYER PECAN STRAWBERRY
RHUBARB COBBLER

SUNNY CITRUS
CHEESECAKE

SUNNY CITRUS CHEESECAKE

I love to create new cheesecake recipes! This one not only looks gorgeous, but tastes great. I like to test my new recipes on family and friends, and this one resulted in rave reviews from everyone who tried it. The beautiful layered cheesecake takes a bit longer to make, but the end result is so worth it! To save some time, I've made this cheesecake a week in advance and frozen it without the sour cream topping. I thaw it in the refrigerator overnight and spread with the topping before serving.
—Sue Gronholz, Beaver Dam, WI

- -

Prep: 35 min. + cooling
Bake: 1 hour 25 min. + chilling
Makes: 16 servings

```
1   cup all-purpose flour
⅓   cup sugar
1   tsp. grated lemon zest
⅓   cup cold butter, cubed
FILLING
4   pkg. (8 oz. each) cream
    cheese, softened
1⅓  cups sugar
2   Tbsp. all-purpose flour
1   tsp. vanilla extract
4   large eggs, room temperature,
    lightly beaten
¼   cup lime juice
1   Tbsp. grated lime zest
3   drops green food coloring
¼   cup lemon juice
1   Tbsp. grated lemon zest
6   drops yellow food coloring, divided
¼   cup orange juice
1   Tbsp. grated orange zest
2   drops red food coloring
TOPPING
¾   cup sour cream
1   Tbsp. sugar
¼   tsp. lemon extract
    Optional: Orange slices, lime slices
    and lemon slices
```

1. Preheat oven to 325°. Place a greased 9-in. springform pan on a double thickness of heavy-duty foil (about 18 in. square). Wrap foil securely around the pan. Place on a baking sheet.
2. In a small bowl, mix flour, sugar and zest; cut in butter until crumbly. Press onto the bottom of prepared pan. Bake until edges are lightly browned, 25-30 minutes. Cool on a wire rack.
3. In a large bowl, beat the cream cheese and sugar until smooth. Beat in flour and vanilla. Add eggs; beat on low speed just until blended. Divide batter into thirds. To 1 portion, add lime juice, lime zest and green food coloring. Pour batter over crust.
4. Place springform pan in a larger baking pan; add 1 in. of hot water to larger pan. Bake until center is just set and top appears dull, about 25 minutes.
5. Meanwhile, to another portion of batter, add lemon juice, lemon zest and 3 drops yellow food coloring. Carefully remove pan from oven. Gently spoon over the lime layer. Return to oven; bake until center is just set and top appears dull, about 25 minutes.
6. To remaining batter, add orange juice, orange zest, red food coloring and the remaining 3 drops yellow food coloring. Carefully remove pan from oven. Gently spoon over lemon layer.
7. Return to oven; bake until center is just set and top appears dull, 30-35 minutes. Carefully remove pan from oven.
8. In a small bowl, whisk topping ingredients. Gently spoon over cheesecake in small dollops; spread carefully. Return to oven; bake 5 minutes.
9. Remove springform pan from water bath. Cool cheesecake on a wire rack 10 minutes. Loosen sides from pan with a knife; remove the foil. Cool 1 hour longer. Refrigerate overnight, covering when completely cooled. Remove rim from the pan. If desired, top with the orange, lime and lemon slices. Refrigerate leftovers.
1 piece: 394 cal., 27g fat (16g sat. fat), 117mg chol., 231mg sod., 33g carb. (25g sugars, 0 fiber), 6g pro.

SLOW-COOKER CHOCOLATE POTS DE CREME

Lunch on the go just got a whole lot sweeter. Tuck jars of this rich custard into lunch bags for a midday treat. These desserts in a jar are fun for picnics, too.
—Nick Iverson, Denver, CO

- -

Prep: 20 min. • **Cook:** 4 hours + chilling
Makes: 8 servings

```
2   cups heavy whipping cream
8   oz. bittersweet chocolate,
    finely chopped
1   Tbsp. instant espresso powder
4   large egg yolks, room temperature
¼   cup sugar
¼   tsp. salt
1   Tbsp. vanilla extract
3   cups hot water
    Optional: Whipped cream, grated
    chocolate and fresh raspberries
```

1. Place cream, chocolate and espresso in a microwave-safe bowl; microwave on high until chocolate is melted and cream is hot, about 4 minutes. Whisk to combine.
2. In a large bowl, whisk egg yolks, sugar and salt until blended but not foamy. Slowly whisk in cream mixture; stir in extract.
3. Ladle egg mixture into eight 4-oz. jars. Center lids on jars and screw on bands until fingertip tight. Add hot water to a 7-qt. slow cooker; place jars in slow cooker. Cook, covered, on low for 4 hours or until set. Remove jars from slow cooker; cool on counter for 30 minutes. Refrigerate until cold, about 2 hours.
4. If desired, top servings with whipped cream, grated chocolate and raspberries.
1 serving: 424 cal., 34g fat (21g sat. fat), 160mg chol., 94mg sod., 13g carb. (11g sugars, 1g fiber), 5g pro.

RASPBERRY-BANANA SOFT SERVE

When I make this ice cream, I mix and match bananas for their ripeness. Very ripe ones add more banana flavor. Less ripe ones have a fluffier texture.
—Melissa Hansen, Ellison Bay, WI

- -

Prep: 10 min. + freezing • **Makes:** 2½ cups

- 4   medium ripe bananas
- ½   cup fat-free plain yogurt
- 1   to 2 Tbsp. maple syrup
- ½   cup frozen unsweetened raspberries
     Fresh raspberries, optional

1. Thinly slice bananas. Arrange in single layer on baking sheet. Freeze overnight.
2. Pulse the bananas in a food processor until finely chopped. Add yogurt, maple syrup and raspberries. Process just until smooth, scraping sides as needed. Serve immediately, adding fresh berries if desired.

½ cup: 104 cal., 0 fat (0 sat. fat), 1mg chol., 15mg sod., 26g carb. (15g sugars, 2g fiber), 2g pro. **Diabetic exchanges:** 1 fruit, ½ starch.

CHERRY FUDGE TRUFFLE COCONUT CHEESECAKE

Cherries and chocolate come together in this dazzling coconut cheesecake. It's a holiday showstopper!
—Jeanne Holt, St. Paul, MN

- -

Prep: 40 min. • **Bake:** 1 hour 20 min. + chilling
Makes: 16 servings

- 1⅔ cups crushed Oreo cookies (about 17 cookies)
- ⅔   cup sweetened shredded coconut, toasted
- ¼   cup butter, melted

FILLING
- 4   pkg. (8 oz. each) cream cheese, softened, divided
- 1   cup sugar
- ¾   cup cream of coconut
- 1   tsp. coconut extract
- 3   large eggs, room temperature, lightly beaten
- ¼   cup chopped maraschino cherries
- 1   cup 60% cacao bittersweet chocolate baking chips, melted and cooled

CHERRY FUDGE TRUFFLE COCONUT CHEESECAKE

- ⅓   cup cherry preserves, finely chopped

TOPPING
- ½   cup 60% cacao bittersweet chocolate baking chips, melted and cooled
- 1   cup sweetened whipped cream
- ⅓   cup sweetened shredded coconut, toasted
- 16 maraschino cherries with stems, patted dry

1. Preheat oven to 375°. Place a greased 10-in. springform pan on a double thickness of heavy-duty foil (about 18 in. square). Wrap foil securely around pan. Place on a baking sheet.
2. In a small bowl, mix crushed cookies and coconut; stir in butter. Press onto bottom and ½ in. up sides of prepared pan. Bake 10 minutes. Cool on a wire rack. Reduce oven setting to 325°.
3. In a large bowl, beat 3 packages of cream cheese and sugar until smooth. Beat in the cream of coconut and extract. Add eggs; beat on low speed just until blended. Stir in chopped cherries. Pour 3 cups batter into crust. In another bowl, beat remaining 8 oz. cream cheese until smooth. Beat in cooled chocolate and cherry preserves. Drop by tablespoonfuls over coconut batter.

Carefully spoon remaining coconut batter over top. Place springform pan in a larger baking pan; add 1 in. hot water to larger pan.
4. Bake until center is just set and top appears dull, 80-85 minutes. Remove springform pan from water bath. Cool cheesecake on a wire rack 10 minutes. Loosen sides from pan with a knife; remove foil. Cool for 1 hour longer. Refrigerate overnight, covering when completely cooled.
5. Remove rim from pan. Top cheesecake with melted chocolate, whipped cream, toasted coconut and cherries.

1 piece: 545 cal., 37g fat (22g sat. fat), 108mg chol., 290mg sod., 52g carb. (44g sugars, 2g fiber), 6g pro.

> "I like this innovation of using shredded coconut in addition to the cream of coconut in the filling. The cherries and the chocolate cookies in the crust are all the right balance. It's just really over the top!"
> —RASHANDA COBBINS, FOOD EDITOR

TRIPLE CHOCOLATE RICOTTA ICE CREAM

You're going to fall in love with this thick, rich ice cream made from ricotta cheese. It has a creamy texture that can't be beat.
—Colleen Delawder, Herndon, VA

- -

Prep: 20 min. • **Process:** 20 min. + freezing
Makes: 1½ qt.

- 1   carton (15 oz.) whole-milk ricotta cheese
- 1¼ cups whole milk
- 1   cup sugar
- 4   oz. cream cheese, softened
- ½   cup baking cocoa
- ½   tsp. instant espresso powder
- ¼   tsp. salt
- 1   cup heavy whipping cream
- 3½ oz. milk chocolate, melted and cooled
- 3½ oz. dark chocolate candy bar, chopped

1. Place the first 7 ingredients in a blender; cover and process until combined, about 1 minute. Add cream and cooled melted chocolate; cover and process until slightly thickened, 30 seconds.

2. Fill cylinder of ice cream maker no more than two-thirds full; freeze according to manufacturer's directions, adding dark chocolate during the last 5 minutes of processing in proportion to the amount of the mixture in the cylinder. Refrigerate any remaining mixture until ready to freeze.

3. Transfer ice cream to freezer containers, allowing headspace for expansion. Freeze until firm, 2-4 hours.

½ cup: 321 cal., 20g fat (12g sat. fat), 53mg chol., 141mg sod., 33g carb. (30g sugars, 2g fiber), 8g pro.

APPLE CORNBREAD CRISP

With its hearty ingredients and quick prep time, this warm apple crisp makes a smart dessert for any fall night. It reminds me of the recipe my grandmother would serve after our big family seafood dinners. It's absolutely wonderful.
—Julie Peterson, Crofton, MD

- -

Prep: 10 min. • **Bake:** 30 min.
Makes: 6 servings

- 4   cups peeled sliced tart apples (about 4-5 medium)
- ¾   cup packed brown sugar, divided
- 1   pkg. (8½ oz.) cornbread/muffin mix
- ½   cup quick-cooking oats
- 1   tsp. ground cinnamon (or to taste)
- 5   Tbsp. cold butter, cubed

1. Preheat oven to 350°. Stir together apples and ¼ cup brown sugar. In another bowl, combine cornbread mix, oats, cinnamon and remaining brown sugar. Cut in the butter until crumbly.

2. Add ½ cup cornbread mixture to apples. Transfer to a greased 8-in. square baking dish. Sprinkle remaining cornbread mixture over top. Bake until filling is bubbly and topping golden brown, 30-35 minutes. Serve warm.

1 serving: 421 cal., 15g fat (7g sat. fat), 26mg chol., 413mg sod., 70g carb. (43g sugars, 5g fiber), 4g pro.

TRIPLE CHOCOLATE RICOTTA ICE CREAM

LEMON RASPBERRY BUCKLE

I've given a fresh summery twist to the classic blueberry buckle everyone loves by swapping out blueberries for raspberries and adding sweet and tart lemon curd.
—Jenna Fleming, Lowville, NY

- -

Prep: 30 min. • **Bake:** 45 min.
Makes: 15 servings

- ½ cup butter, softened
- 1 cup sugar
- 2 large eggs plus 1 large egg yolk, room temperature
- 1 tsp. vanilla extract
- 1½ cups all-purpose flour
- 1½ tsp. baking powder
- ¼ tsp. salt
- ⅔ cup buttermilk
- 4 cups fresh raspberries
- ¼ cup sugar
- 1 jar (10 oz.) lemon curd

TOPPING

- ½ cup sugar
- ½ cup all-purpose flour
- ¼ cup butter, melted
- ½ tsp. ground cinnamon
  Whipped cream, optional

1. Preheat oven to 350°. In a large bowl, cream butter and sugar until light and fluffy, 5-7 minutes. Add eggs and egg yolk, 1 at a time, beating well after each addition. Beat in the vanilla. In another bowl, whisk flour, baking powder and salt; add to creamed mixture alternately with the buttermilk, beating well after each addition. Transfer to a greased 13x9-in. baking dish.
2. In a bowl, combine raspberries and sugar; sprinkle over batter. Drop lemon curd by tablespoonfuls over raspberries. Combine the topping ingredients; sprinkle over batter. Bake until the fruit is bubbly and a toothpick inserted into the cake comes out clean, 45-50 minutes. Let stand 20 minutes before serving. If desired, serve with whipped cream and more fresh raspberries.
Note: To substitute for each cup of buttermilk, use 1 Tbsp. white vinegar or lemon juice plus enough milk to measure 1 cup. Stir, then let stand 5 minutes. Or, use 1 cup plain yogurt, or 1¾ tsp. cream of tartar plus 1 cup milk.
1 piece: 335 cal., 12g fat (7g sat. fat), 76mg chol., 206mg sod., 54g carb. (38g sugars, 3g fiber), 4g pro.

LEMON RASPBERRY BUCKLE

ICE CREAM COOKIE DESSERT

Our family loves dessert, and this chocolaty, layered treat is one of my mother's most requested recipes. It's so easy to prepare.
—Kimberly Laabs, Hartford, WI

- -

Prep: 15 min. + freezing • **Makes:** 12 servings

- 1 pkg. (15½ oz.) Oreo cookies, crushed, divided
- ¼ cup butter, melted
- ½ gallon vanilla ice cream, softened
- 1 jar (16 oz.) hot fudge ice cream topping, warmed
- 1 carton (8 oz.) frozen whipped topping, thawed

1. In a large bowl, combine 3¾ cups cookie crumbs and butter. Press into a greased 13x9-in. dish. Spread with ice cream; cover and freeze until set.

2. Drizzle fudge topping over ice cream; cover and freeze until set. Spread with whipped topping; sprinkle with remaining cookie crumbs. Cover and freeze 2 hours or until firm. Remove from the freezer 10 minutes before serving.

1 piece: 573 cal., 27g fat (14g sat. fat), 49mg chol., 353mg sod., 76g carb. (46g sugars, 2g fiber), 6g pro.

LUSCIOUS ALMOND CHEESECAKE

Almonds and almond extract lend a tasty twist to traditional sour cream-topped cheesecake with this tasty treat.
—Brenda Clifford, Overland Park, KS

- -

Prep: 15 min. • **Bake:** 55 min. + chilling
Makes: 16 servings

- 1¼ cups crushed vanilla wafers (about 40 wafers)
- ¾ cup finely chopped almonds
- ¼ cup sugar
- ⅓ cup butter, melted

FILLING

- 4 pkg. (8 oz. each) cream cheese, softened
- 1¼ cups sugar
- 4 large eggs, room temperature, lightly beaten
- 1½ tsp. almond extract
- 1 tsp. vanilla extract

TOPPING

- 2 cups sour cream
- ¼ cup sugar
- 1 tsp. vanilla extract
- ⅛ cup toasted sliced almonds

1. In a bowl, combine the wafer crumbs, almonds and sugar; stir in the butter and mix well. Press into the bottom of a greased 10-in. springform pan; set aside.

2. In a large bowl, beat cream cheese and sugar until smooth. Add eggs; beat on low speed just until combined. Stir in extracts. Pour into crust. Place on a baking sheet.

3. Bake at 350° for 50-55 minutes or until center is almost set. Remove from the oven; let stand for 5 minutes (leave oven on). Combine the sour cream, sugar and vanilla. Spoon around edge of cheesecake; carefully spread over filling. Bake 5 minutes longer. Cool on a wire rack for 10 minutes. Carefully run a knife around edge of pan to loosen; cool 1 hour longer. Refrigerate overnight.

4. Just before serving, sprinkle with the almonds and remove sides of the pan. Refrigerate leftovers.

1 piece: 329 cal., 20g fat (10g sat. fat), 100mg chol., 140mg sod., 32g carb. (26g sugars, 1g fiber), 5g pro.

LUSCIOUS ALMOND CHEESECAKE

BUTTER PECAN PUMPKIN PIE

Whenever I serve this pie, everyone thinks I worked all day to make it, but it's actually easy to assemble. It's handy to have in the freezer when unexpected company stops in for coffee and dessert.
—Arletta Slocum, Venice, FL

- -

Prep: 30 min. + freezing • **Makes:** 8 servings

- 1   sheet refrigerated pie crust
- 1   qt. butter pecan ice cream, softened
- 1   cup canned pumpkin
- ½   cup sugar
- ¼   tsp. each ground cinnamon, ginger and nutmeg
- 1   cup heavy whipping cream, whipped
  Optional: Hot caramel ice cream topping and chocolate ice cream topping

1. Unroll crust into a 9-in. pie plate; flute edge. Refrigerate 30 minutes. Preheat oven to 400°.
2. Line crust with a double thickness of foil. Fill with pie weights, dried beans or uncooked rice. Bake on a lower oven rack until edges are golden brown, 15-20 minutes. Remove foil and weights; bake until bottom is golden brown, 3-6 minutes longer. Cool on a wire rack.
3. Spread the ice cream into crust; freeze until firm, about 2 hours.
4. In a small bowl, combine pumpkin, sugar, cinnamon, ginger and nutmeg; fold in the whipped cream. Spread over ice cream. Cover and freeze until firm, about 2 hours. (Pie may be frozen for up to 2 months.)
5. Remove pie from freezer 15 minutes before slicing. If desired, drizzle with the ice cream toppings and dollop with additional whipped cream.
1 piece: 412 cal., 24g fat (12g sat. fat), 49mg chol., 210mg sod., 46g carb. (27g sugars, 2g fiber), 4g pro.

RASPBERRY MOUSSE

This creamy, smooth raspberry mousse is guaranteed to be a refreshing finale to any summer meal.
—*Taste of Home* Test Kitchen

- -

Prep: 25 min. + chilling • **Makes:** 8 servings

- 2   cups fresh raspberries
- ½   cup sugar
- 1   Tbsp. lemon juice
- 1½   tsp. unflavored gelatin
- ¼   cup cold water
- 1   cup heavy whipping cream

1. Place the raspberries in a food processor; cover and puree. Strain and discard seeds. Transfer puree to a large bowl. Stir in sugar and lemon juice; set aside.
2. In a small saucepan, sprinkle gelatin over cold water; let stand for 1 minute. Stir over low heat until gelatin is completely dissolved. Stir into raspberry mixture. Refrigerate until slightly thickened, about 1 hour.
3. Transfer gelatin mixture to a large bowl. Beat on high speed until foamy. Gradually add cream; beat until thickened, about 2 minutes. Spoon into dessert dishes. Cover and refrigerate until set, 1-2 hours.
½ cup: 169 cal., 11g fat (7g sat. fat), 34mg chol., 9mg sod., 17g carb. (15g sugars, 2g fiber), 2g pro.

BUTTER PECAN PUMPKIN PIE

STRAWBERRY LEMON TRIFLE

QUICK ICEBOX SANDWICHES

My mother liked making these cool, creamy treats when I was growing up in the States because she could make them so quickly. Now my three kids enjoy them!
—Sandy Armijo, Naples, Italy

Prep: 20 min. + freezing • **Makes:** 2 dozen

- 1 pkg. (3.4 oz.) instant vanilla pudding mix
- 2 cups cold 2% milk
- 2 cups whipped topping
- 1 cup miniature semisweet chocolate chips
- 24 whole graham crackers, halved

1. Mix the pudding and milk according to package directions; refrigerate until set. Fold in whipped topping and chocolate chips.
2. Place 24 graham cracker halves on a baking sheet; top each with about 3 Tbsp. filling. Place another graham cracker half on top. Wrap individually in plastic; freeze until firm, about 1 hour. Serve sandwiches frozen.
1 sandwich: 142 cal., 5g fat (3g sat. fat), 2mg chol., 131mg sod., 23g carb. (13g sugars, 1g fiber), 2g pro.

STRAWBERRY LEMON TRIFLE

This refreshingly fruity dessert is one of our favorites. It looks so beautiful layered in a glass bowl that people will think it took lots of time to make. The secret is starting with a purchased angel food cake.
—Lynn Marie Frucci, LaCenter, WA

Prep: 20 min. + chilling • **Makes:** 14 servings

- 4 oz. fat-free cream cheese, softened
- 1 cup fat-free vanilla yogurt
- 2 cups fat-free milk
- 1 pkg. (3.4 oz.) instant lemon pudding mix
- 2 tsp. grated lemon zest
- 2½ cups sliced fresh strawberries, divided
- 1 Tbsp. white grape juice or water
- 1 prepared angel food cake (12 oz.)
  Optional: Whipped topping and additional strawberries

1. In a large bowl, beat cream cheese and yogurt. Add the milk, dry pudding mix and lemon zest; beat until smooth. In a blender, process ½ cup strawberries and grape juice until blended.
2. Tear cake into 1-in. cubes; place a third in a trifle bowl or 3-qt. serving bowl. Top with a third of the pudding mixture and half of the remaining strawberries. Drizzle with half of the strawberry sauce. Repeat all layers. Top with remaining cake and pudding mixture. Garnish with the whipped topping and additional strawberries, if desired. Cover and refrigerate for at least 2 hours.
½ cup: 108 cal., 0 fat (0 sat. fat), 2mg chol., 279mg sod., 21g carb. (10g sugars, 1g fiber), 4g pro. **Diabetic exchanges:** 1½ starch.

TEST KITCHEN TIP

Mix things up by swapping out the strawberries in this trifle and replacing them with blueberries or raspberries.

Recipe Index

Equivalents & Substitutions

EQUIVALENT MEASURES

3 teaspoons = 1 tablespoon	**16 tablespoons** = 1 cup
4 tablespoons = ¼ cup	**2 cups** = 1 pint
5⅓ tablespoons = ⅓ cup	**4 cups** = 1 quart
8 tablespoons = ½ cup	**4 quarts** = 1 gallon

FOOD EQUIVALENTS

Macaroni	1 cup (3½ ounces) uncooked = 2½ cups cooked
Noodles Medium	3 cups (4 ounces) uncooked = 4 cups cooked
Popcorn	⅓-½ cup unpopped = 8 cups popped
Rice Long Grain	1 cup uncooked = 3 cups cooked
Rice Quick-Cooking	1 cup uncooked = 2 cups cooked
Spaghetti	8 ounces uncooked = 4 cups cooked

Bread	1 slice = ¾ cup soft crumbs or ¼ cup fine dry crumbs
Graham Crackers	7 squares = ½ cup finely crushed
Buttery Round Crackers	12 crackers = ½ cup finely crushed
Saltine Crackers	14 crackers = ½ cup finely crushed

Bananas	1 medium = ⅓ cup mashed
Lemons	1 medium = 3 tablespoons juice + 2 teaspoons grated zest
Limes	1 medium = 2 tablespoons juice + 1½ teaspoons grated zest
Oranges	1 medium = ¼-⅓ cup juice + 4 teaspoons grated zest

Cabbage	1 head = 5 cups shredded	**Green Pepper**	1 large = 1 cup chopped
Carrots	1 pound = 3 cups shredded	**Mushrooms**	½ pound = 3 cups sliced
Celery	1 rib = ½ cup chopped	**Onions**	1 medium = ½ cup chopped
Corn	1 ear fresh = ⅔ cup kernels	**Potatoes**	3 medium = 2 cups cubed

Almonds	1 pound = 3 cups chopped	**Pecan Halves**	1 pound = 4½ cups chopped
Ground Nuts	3¾ ounces = 1 cup	**Walnuts**	1 pound = 3¾ cups chopped

EASY SUBSTITUTIONS

WHEN YOU NEED...		USE...
Baking Powder	1 teaspoon	½ teaspoon cream of tartar + ¼ teaspoon baking soda
Buttermilk	1 cup	1 tablespoon lemon juice or vinegar + enough milk to measure 1 cup (let stand 5 minutes before using)
Cornstarch	1 tablespoon	2 tablespoons all-purpose flour
Honey	1 cup	1¼ cups sugar + ¼ cup water
Half-and-Half Cream	1 cup	1 tablespoon melted butter + enough whole milk to measure 1 cup
Onion	1 small chopped (⅓ cup)	1 teaspoon onion powder or 1 tablespoon dried minced onion
Tomato Juice	1 cup	½ cup tomato sauce + ½ cup water
Tomato Sauce	2 cups	¾ cup tomato paste + 1 cup water
Unsweetened Chocolate	1 square (1 ounce)	3 tablespoons baking cocoa + 1 tablespoon shortening or oil
Whole Milk	1 cup	½ cup evaporated milk + ½ cup water

HONEY: BW FOLSOM/SHUTTERSTOCK

Cutting Techniques

MINCING AND CHOPPING

Holding the handle of a chef's knife with one hand, rest the fingers of your other hand on the top of the blade near the tip. Using the handle to guide and apply pressure, move knife in an arc across the food with a rocking motion until pieces of food are the desired size. Mincing results in pieces no larger than ⅛ in. and chopping produces ¼- to ½-in. pieces.

DICING AND CUBING

Using a utility knife, trim each side of the frui, vegetable or other food, squaring it off. Cut lengthwise into evenly spaced strips. The narrower the strips, the smaller the pieces will be. Stack the strips and cut lengthwise into uniformly sized strips. Arrange the square-shaped strips into a pile and cut widthwise into uniform pieces.

MAKING BIAS OR DIAGONAL CUTS

Holding a chef's knife at an angle to the length of the food slice as thick or thin as desired. This technique is often used in stir-fry recipes.

MAKING JULIENNE STRIPS

Using a utility knife, cut a thin strip from one side of vegetable. Turn so flat side is down. Cut into 2-in. lengths, then cut each piece lengthwise into thin strips. Stack the strips and cut lengthwise into thinner strips.

CUTTING WEDGES

Using a chef's knife or serrated knife cut the produce in half from stem end to blossom end. Lay halves cut side down on a cutting board. Set knife at the center of one the halves and cut in half vertically, then cut each quarter in half vertically. Repeat with other half.

ZESTING

Pull a citrus zester across limes, lemons or oranges being careful not to remove the bitter white pith. The small holes in the zester will yield thin, narrow strips of zest. Use full strips to garnish or, if recipe instructs, chop into fine pieces and use as directed.

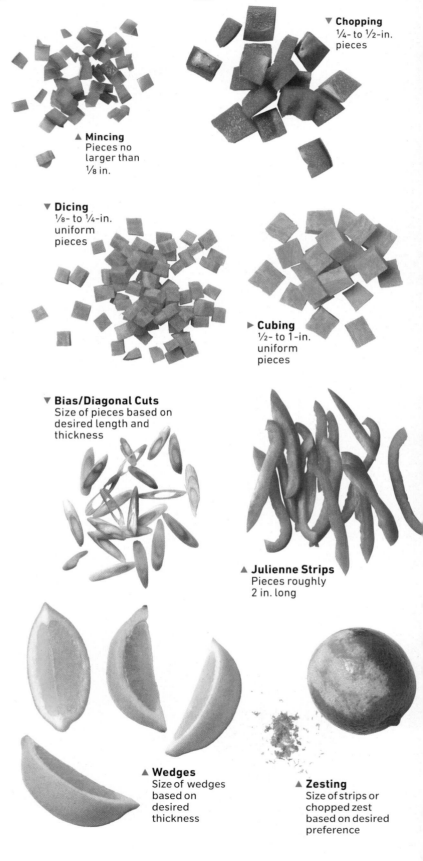

▲ **Mincing**
Pieces no larger than ⅛ in.

▼ **Chopping**
¼- to ½-in. pieces

▼ **Dicing**
⅛- to ¼-in. uniform pieces

▶ **Cubing**
½- to 1-in. uniform pieces

▼ **Bias/Diagonal Cuts**
Size of pieces based on desired length and thickness

▲ **Julienne Strips**
Pieces roughly 2 in. long

▲ **Wedges**
Size of wedges based on desired thickness

▲ **Zesting**
Size of strips or chopped zest based on desired preference